An Introduction
to the Economics
of Education

Mark Blaug

Allen Lane The Penguin Press

First published 1970
Copyright © Mark Blaug, 1970

Allen Lane The Penguin Press
Vigo Street, London W1

ISBN   0 7139 0150 0

Made and printed in Great Britain by
Cox & Wyman Ltd, London, Reading and Fakenham
Set in Monotype Times

To Rachel

Contents

Editorial Foreword

Professor Blaug has written a very important book. It is a textbook in as much as it brings together on a systematic basis all the many different economic considerations which bear (or should bear) upon educational policy. It will be used as a textbook both by educationalists and by economists. Not only students of the economics of education but students of development economics, labour economics and agricultural economics will find in it fresh analytical insights and a discussion of numerous policy considerations which bear upon economic growth and upon the efficient allocation and use of man power. All students of 'welfare economics' will find their understanding of both issues and methodology deepened by this work.

In calling this book a textbook, however, Professor Blaug may run the risk that only those engaged on a course of formal education will read it. This would be a great misfortune, especially for educational policy. Some educationalists have reacted strongly to the suggestion that their activities should be assessed according to economists' criteria, but most now recognize that such assessment is proper. Indeed many educationalists have rested their case for the expansion of education, or for a particular system and structure of educational provision, on the relationship between education and economic factors such as growth rates and adaptability to technological change. Professor Blaug's concern is with such relationships, and especially with the problems of economic planning. The tenets of the 'conventional wisdom' of educational policy makers are examined critically and some are shown to be unsubstantiated, insecure or plain wrong.

One of Professor Blaug's strengths is that his focus on the economic does not blind him to the importance of the history, sociology and psychology of education, nor to the extent to which personal and social value judgements must influence decisions. Whereas most of the inputs of the educational system which can be influenced by the policy makers and administrators are capable of economic analysis, and a substantial part of the output of the educational system is also economic in character, educational policy has to be concerned with more than the balance struck between these economic inputs and outputs. While Professor Blaug helps us to consider this balance of input and output from several fresh angles, he does not overlook the wider issues.

Of particular interest is the discussion of the relationship between the structure of educational provision and the responsiveness of labour supply to changes in the pattern of demand for labour. The comparison drawn between U.S.A. and U.K. education and economies is illuminating and the discussion of these related problems has a very direct bearing upon certain major issues of educational policy currently under discussion. This is merely one illustration of the wealth of practical example that is used to illuminate the analysis which is the core of the book. With detailed discussion of the educational problems of India, Africa, U.S.A. and U.K. and much pointed criticism of policies being applied or recommended, the reader is not only given information on the economics of education but a valuable treatment of comparative educational policies.

Professor Blaug modestly distinguishes his textbook from research. To refute that view would require a brief exploration of alternative definitions of research for which this is not the place. In case any reader is misled, however, let it be stated quite clearly that this is a book of real scholarship and much originality. Throughout the treatment is lively, fresh and stimulating. It has been written to influence educational policy and it is quite certain that the ideas of its readers will be clarified, changed and enlarged.

K. J. W. Alexander

Preface

Shaw's maxim: 'He who can, does. He who cannot, teaches' was long ago altered to 'He who can, does. He who cannot, teaches. He who cannot teach, takes up research.' It seems that it must now be revised once again to 'He who can, does. He who cannot, teaches. He who cannot teach, takes up research. And he who fails at all of these, writes textbooks.' Writing this textbook on the economics of education, 'that repulsive hybrid' as Tawney once called it, has given me a certain masochistic pleasure and the most that I can hope for is that it will do as much for the reader, whoever he is.

It is only fair to say, however, that I had a particular reader in mind. This book assumes no prior knowledge of economics except that of elementary economics: anything beyond that is explained as we go along. Occasionally, statistical concepts are invoked but little is lost if these are passed over. In short, the book is addressed to undergraduates, and even sixth formers who are well advanced in A-level economics will find nothing here that they cannot grasp. Postgraduates too may find some of it useful, but only if their education in economics has been neglected – which of course it frequently has. Indeed, the surprising thing about the economics of education is the extent to which the subject invariably draws upon the most basic concepts of economics – substitution at the margin, opportunity costs, the distinction between stocks and flows, discounting, maximization subject to constraints, etc. We do not need to know a great deal of economics to apply it to education, but the little we do know we must have in our bones

A number of articles and excerpts from books to which reference is made in the text are reproduced in inexpensive paperback form in *Economics of Education* (two volumes), edited by myself, in the Penguin Modern Economics Readings series. These sources are picked out in the text by an asterisk *, and cross-reference to the Penguin series is made in the list of references on page 333.

I want to thank Richard Layard and Maureen Woodhall, both of whom read through the entire manuscript and gave me many valuable suggestions. I also want to express my gratitude to my wife, Ruth, who thought that she could improve this book – which turned out to be true. Finally, I wish to thank Christine Buchta for her efficient typing of the manuscript.

M.B.

Introduction

The economics of education is a branch of economics. This is worth saying because the subject is sometimes thought to be confined to such problems as the costing and financing of school places. These indeed constitute aspects of the subject. But there is more to the economics of education: it deals fundamentally with the impact of education on such phenomena as the occupational structure of the labour force, the recruitment and promotion practices of employers, the migration of labour between regions within a country and between different countries, the patterns of international trade, the size distribution of personal income, the propensity to save out of current income and, most general of all, the prospects of economic growth. Frequently, its main purpose is to describe and explain. Sometimes, however, it seeks to prescribe and recommend: educational systems are almost everywhere largely owned and operated by the State and the question naturally arises whether economists can provide something like investment criteria for education, in the same way that they pronounce on the appropriate scale and composition of the rest of the public sector. This is the area of educational planning, a field of activity where economists have been almost as thick on the ground in the last ten years as they have been in general economic planning.

Definitions of new subjects go out of date as soon as they are written. 'Economics is what economists do' and I will make no attempt here to define the economics of education as a separate field of inquiry. It is easy to see that at various points it shades off imperceptibly into labour economics, public sector economics, welfare economics, growth theory and development economics, only coming into its own whenever education in one form or the other appears as a significant variable in an argument otherwise like ordinary economic analysis. What draws it all together is the basic idea that the acquisition of education in a modern economy provides opportunities for individuals to invest in themselves; unlike defence expenditure, public educational expenditure is to some extent the outcome of individual choices registered at times other than election times and these private decisions are profoundly influenced by expected economic returns. This opens the door both to an economic analysis of the private demand for education and the formulation of economic criteria for the collective provision of educational facilities. It is this insight that has inspired the subject from the outset and that still continues to motivate present research in the area. What one writer has called 'the human investment revolution in economic thought', a phenomenon of the late 1950s, constitutes to this day the *raison d'être* of the economics of education.

Education is, of course, only one type of investment in human beings. People can invest in themselves by spending on medical care, by migrating to more prosperous regions, by purchasing information about job opportunities and career prospects and by choosing jobs with relatively high training content. To that extent, the economics of education partakes of a much wider subject that has come to be labelled, somewhat grandiosely, 'the economics of human resources'. Inevitably, this book touches on these wider issues. Still, it was thought better in an introduction like this to restrict the range of topics to the smaller but better defined area of education. The scope of our discussion, however, does extend beyond formal education provided in schools: out-of-school education in the form of labour training, adult education and agricultural extension are too important to be left out of account entirely.

Quite apart from the investment aspects of education, however, the peculiarities of the educational system considered as an industry (is it really possible to call it an 'industry'?) would in itself justify special economic treatment. First of all, it pursues multiple objectives, none of which include maximization of profits or any proxy for profits. Secondly, it is burdened with an unusually long production cycle, which renders it necessary to build most of its facilities ahead of demand. Thirdly, it operates with a fairly rigid handicraft technology, in large part self-imposed by custom and tradition. And, fourthly, it purchases most of its inputs at administered rather than market-determined prices and feeds back an extraordinarily large part of its own output as subsequent inputs. All of these features reduce to (a) an inflexible production structure impervious, at least to some extent, to relative factor scarcities and (b) sharp discontinuities in the flow of output. This is a combination almost guaranteed to produce a state of chronic disequilibrium in the relevant factor and product markets, as witnessed by the repeated concern in most countries with so-called 'man-power shortages' and 'man-power surpluses'. Clearly, here is a fertile field for systematic forward planning, operations research, cost–effectiveness analysis and all the other tools that have been developed in the last decade or two to improve the management of non-marketable activities. Here too are troublesome problems perfectly designed to upset the economist's apple cart: if the industry producing skilled manpower for the rest of the economy is almost certainly conducted inefficiently, what becomes of the optimizing effects of competitive pricing systems much lauded in textbooks of economics?

The economics of education is an 'infant industry' and many of the questions raised in the preceding paragraphs have even now only begun to be tackled. The precise content and even the substantive core of the subject still remain in dispute. This is to say that no two experts in the field would wholly agree on the relative significance of the various findings to date, or even on the appropriate sequence of ideas in an introductory treatment such as this. The focus of this book is on the problems of educational planning and not everyone will concur that the policy aspects constitute the be all and end all of the economics of education. Nevertheless, there is wide agreement among educational policy makers these days that educational decisions should take account of the economic value of education and the contribution of education to economic growth. The question is: take account how? This is what the book is all about.

To investigate the economic value of education is not, however, to claim priority for economic ends or to approve the vocational aims of education; rather it is to accept things as they are. For better or for worse, students and parents take a keen interest in the employment opportunities opened up by successive educational qualifications, and educational authorities the world over are persuaded that economic growth can be accelerated by encouraging education. Not that the purely educational, social and political objectives of education stand in danger of being neglected. On the contrary, the real danger is that economic arguments will only receive a hearing when they are in harmony with all the other good reasons for educating more and better. The refusal on the part of both students and teachers in current debates on 'student power' to pay the slightest attention to the sources and patterns of finance for higher education is a sufficient reminder that economists frequently speak too softly rather than too loudly on the theme of education.

No country has ever operated an educational system merely to secure economic objectives, and I know of no economist who has ever advocated the pursuit of such a single-minded policy. But even if there was such an economist, his recommendations would have no more weight than those of any other citizen. Economists do, alas, make value judgements, but they have no right to them – to evaluate educational systems in terms of the effectiveness with which they secure vocational or other aims, yes; to express a preference for vocational aims, no. The discourses of 'is' and 'ought' are like East and West that never meet. Values or norms cannot be logically derived from facts; they may be vindicated by rational arguments but they are not susceptible to interpersonal demonstration in the way that statements of facts are. Some philosophers of science argue that all normative disputes, when reduced to their ultimate components, resolve into disputes about positive effects, and even that all empirical assertions of descriptive facts are only validated in terms of particular standards of scientific rigour, which in turn are nothing but value judgements. Be that as it may, value-free economics is possible at least in principle, although in practice economists still err by commission as much as by omission. And in saying that value-free economics is possible, I mean only that economists can distinguish their own value judgements from those of the economic agents they study or the decision makers they advise. The following pages will provide ample evidence that an argument can be appraised in the light of any declared value judgement, whether one personally agrees with it or not.

The economics of education is only part of the story of any educational issue. For the rest of it, we must draw on the psychology and sociology of education. Even the history of education is extremely relevant. It is not a question of one discipline being right and the others wrong, nor even of some being more important than others. The fundamental methodological rule of 'live and let live' among the different social sciences is nowhere better exemplified than in a field like education. And one cannot go far in the economics of education without in fact learning a good deal about those neighbouring disciplines that have been concerned in their own way with the multiple consequences of schooling.

Chapter 1
The Formation of
Human Capital

Human Capital: Metaphor or Analogy?

In all economies of which we have knowledge, people with more education earn on average higher incomes than people with less education, at least if the people being compared are of the same age. In other words, additional education pays off in the form of higher lifetime incomes. We will verify this fact in the next chapter, but for the time being we may accept it as established. Thus, in this very simple sense, the costs incurred by individuals in acquiring more education constitute an investment in their own future earning capacity.

But surely this is not the principal reason that students stay on in school after the legal school leaving age? Were any of us aware of lifetime earnings prospects when we decided to acquire O-levels or A-levels?[1] Probably not. What we did was to take the advice of our parents that 'it would be a good thing', or simply imitated our friends who were no doubt being advised by their parents along similar lines. And why did our parents consider it 'a good thing'? Because everyone knows that 'you need more education nowadays to get a good job'. And translated into the language of economists: 'because education nowadays is a profitable private investment'. We do not have to assume fully conscious motivation or perfect knowledge of the distribution of earnings by age and educational qualifications. Nor do we need to ignore all other motives for staying on in school. All that is required is the idea that the higher earnings of educated people is a significant element in the demand for education.

Even if additional education did not raise lifetime earnings, education might still be an investment from the social point of view. If a growing economy requires an increasing supply of highly educated

1. Readers who are mystified by British educational terms should consult the glossary on p. 327.

man power, the State might encourage students to stay on as a way of investing in the future productive capacity of the population. Here no question of motives is involved since by definition individuals do not now share in the fruits of increased productive capacity, at least in proportion to the amount of education they have personally acquired. Nevertheless, education remains a type of investment, not for the individual but for society as a whole.

All this is obvious enough and yet its implications for economic behaviour were not really understood until quite recently. This is the more surprising since the basic idea – that an educated man is a sort of expensive machine – was stated 200 years ago in the *fons et origo* of economics, *The Wealth of Nations*. As Adam Smith put it:

When any expensive machine is erected, the extraordinary work to be performed by it before it is worn out, it must be expected, will replace the capital laid out upon it, with at least the ordinary profits. A man educated at the expense of much labour and time to any of those employments which require extraordinary dexterity and skill, may be compared to one of those expensive machines. The work which he learns to perform, it must be expected, over and above the usual wages of common labour, will replace to him the whole expense of his education, with at least the ordinary profits of an equally valuable capital. It must do this too in a reasonable time, regard being had to the very uncertain duration of human life, in the same manner as the more certain duration of the machine. The difference between the wages of skilled labour and those of common labour is founded upon this principle (Smith, 1776, bk 1, ch. 10, pt 1).

After so promising a start, why was it that the investment aspects of education were, in fact, almost completely neglected by economists throughout the nineteenth and the first half of the twentieth century? The standard answer to this question in histories of economic thought is that Alfred Marshall's *Principles of Economics* (1890) killed off such interest in the problem as had gradually developed outside the main stream of orthodox economics; Marshall rejected the notion of 'human capital' as unrealistic and his magisterial authority is said to have been responsible for its demise. As a matter of fact, however, what Marshall rejected was the idea of including the acquired skills of a population in the *measurement* of the 'wealth' or 'capital' of an economy, but he accepted Adam Smith's suggestion that an educated man may be usefully likened to an expensive machine.

As all readers of Cambridge economists know, nothing is worth saying in economics that has not been said by Marshall. And, indeed, Marshall is particularly fascinating to read on this topic. Writing more than a century after *The Wealth of Nations*, he was, of course, much less certain than Adam Smith that market forces do indeed secure equality between the yields of all types of investment in both physical and human capital. A succession of legislative enactments in the nineteenth century had accustomed him to the idea of State subsidies to education, and he was convinced that:

The wisdom of expending public and private funds on education is not to be measured by its direct fruits alone. It will be profitable as a mere investment, to give the masses of the people much greater opportunities than they can generally avail themselves of. For by this means many, who would have died unknown, are able to get the start needed for bringing out their latent abilities.... All that is spent during many years in opening the means of higher education to the masses would be well paid for if it called out one more Newton or Darwin, Shakespeare or Beethoven (Marshall, 1890, bk 4, ch. 6, § 7).[2]

In short, so long as the financial means to acquire education are unequally distributed, there is bound to be underinvestment in education in some sense. 'There are few practical problems', Marshall went on to say, 'in which the economist has a more direct interest than those relating to the principles on which the expense of the education of children should be divided between the State and the parents.' But instead of stating those principles – in which case the discipline now known as 'the economics of education' might have been born in 1890 instead of 1960 or thereabouts – he turned abruptly to other themes.

Twenty-five chapters later, he came back to the subject in a discussion of the forces that lead to cumulative disadvantages in the bargaining position of workers in labour markets. His comments deserve to be reproduced at some length for they illustrate a further development in the Smithian doctrine that an investment motive makes itself felt in the demand for education.

The first point to which we have to direct our attention is the fact that human agents of production are not bought and sold as machinery and other material agents of production are. The worker sells his work, but he himself remains his own property: those who bear the expenses of rearing and

2. The examples are badly chosen: Shakespeare and Beethoven did not enjoy the advantages of higher education.

educating him receive but very little of the price that is paid for his services in later years.... The action of competition ... tend[s] in the long run to put the building of factories and steam-engines into the hands of those who will be ready and able to incur every expense which will add more than it costs to their value as productive agents. But the investment of capital in the rearing and early training of the workers of England is limited by the resources of parents in the various grades of society, by their power of forecasting the future and by their willingness to sacrifice themselves for the sake of their children.

The evil is indeed of comparatively small importance with regard to the higher industrial grades. For in those grades most people distinctly realize the future and 'discount it at a low rate of interest'. They exert themselves much to select the best careers for their sons and the best trainings for those careers; and they are generally willing and able to incur a considerable expense for the purpose. The professional classes especially, while generally eager to save some capital *for* their children, are even more on the alert for opportunities of investing it *in* them. And whenever there occurs in the upper grades of industry a new opening for which an extra and special education is required, the future gains need not be very high relative to the present outlay, in order to secure a keen competition for the post.

But in the lower ranks of society the evil is great. For the slender means and education of the parents, and the comparative weakness of their power of distinctly realizing the future, prevent them from investing capital in the education and training of their children with the same free and bold enterprise with which capital is applied to improving the machinery of any well-managed factory.... But the point on which we have specially to insist now is that this evil is cumulative (Marshall, 1890, bk 6, ch. 4, § 2).

In other words, it may be true that the cost of an individual's education constitutes, as it were, an investment in future earning capacity. Therefore, as Adam Smith rightly observed, it is no accident that educated people tend to earn more than those who lack education: without the promise of some monetary return from education roughly comparable to 'the ordinary profits of an equally valuable capital', the supply of educated people would soon dry up. Nevertheless, the fact that individuals cannot capitalize their earning capacity suggests that the decision to acquire education may involve considerations extraneous to a deliberate balancing of returns over costs.

In a non-slave society, the individual is his own property and this property is inalienable: he cannot give a lien on his services or make an enforceable contract to deliver his services for any considerable time in the future. Thus, non-slave societies lack capital markets in which rights to future earning power can be traded or in which the promise of earning power can be used as collateral for purposes of borrowing educational finance. In principle, of course, there is nothing to prevent anyone in these societies from going through the motions of capitalizing inalienable rights and borrowing accordingly; in the absence of transactions, however, measurement of values becomes arbitrary and hence lenders are reluctant to commit themselves. In practice, therefore, the individual is effectively restricted by the means of his parents or the uncertain benevolence of charitable institutions; in this way, the inequalities of income among the members of one generation are perpetuated and even aggravated among the members of the next.

Marshall was perfectly familiar with Irving Fisher's definition of 'capital' as simply any stock existing at a given instant that yields a stream of services over time, all flows of 'income' therefore being the product of some item of 'capital' whose value is calculated by capitalizing the income flow at an appropriate discount rate. He conceded that 'the writings of Professor Fisher contain a masterly argument, rich in fertile suggestion, in favour of a comprehensive use of the term [capital]'. Nevertheless, he concluded that Fisher 'seems to take too little account of the necessity for keeping realistic discussions in touch with the language of the market-place' (Marshall, 1890, app. E, § 2). In the final analysis, Marshall preferred the more conventional definition of his day which did not count the skills of the population as forming part of the capital stock or 'wealth' of an economy. But this definitional caveat did not stop him from making use of the analogy of capital accumulation in analysing the causes and effects of improving the quality of labour by means of education. In one of the last chapters of his book, summarizing his 'general view of distribution', he referred once again to the investment analogy:

Wages and other earnings of effort have much in common with interest on capital. For there is a general correspondence between the causes that govern the supply price of material and of personal capital: the motives which induce a man to accumulate personal capital *in* his son's education are similar to those which control his accumulation of material capital *for* his son. There is a continuous transition from the father who works and waits in order that he may bequeath to his son a rich and firmly-established manufacturing or trading business, to one who works and waits in order to support his son while he is slowly acquiring a thorough medical education, and ultimately to buy for him a lucrative practice. Again, there is the same continuous transition from him to one who works and waits in order that his son may stay at school; and may afterwards work for some time almost without pay while learning a skilled trade, instead of being forced to support himself early in an occupation, such as that of an errand-boy, which offers comparatively high wages to young lads, because it does not lead the way to a future advance.

It is indeed true that the only persons who, as society is now constituted, are very likely to invest much in developing the personal capital of a youth's abilities are his parents: and that many first-rate abilities go for ever uncultivated because no one, who can develop them, has had any special interest in doing so. This fact is very important practically, for its effects are cumulative. But it does not give rise to a fundamental difference between the material and human agents of production ... on the whole the *money* cost of any kind of labour to the employers corresponds in the long run fairly well to the *real* cost of producing that labour (Marshall, 1890, bk 6, ch. 11, § 1).

The fact that the decision to invest in education is made by parents on behalf of their children rather than by the children themselves 'does *not* give rise to a fundamental difference between the material and human agents of production'. Clearly, this is as strong an endorsement of the concept of human capital formation as we are ever likely to find. Everything depends, of course, on what we mean by 'fundamental difference' but it is difficult to see how most commentators on Marshall (Kiker, 1966, p. 481; Shaffer, 1961, p. 47*) have perversely interpreted him to mean that educational expenditures should not be submitted to the same techniques of investment appraisal that we normally apply to expenditures on producers' durable equipment.[3]

It is not my purpose here to redress the rights and wrongs of the history of economic thought, nor to play the game of lending prestige to economic theories by displaying their ancient intellectual pedigree; the mystery of the neglect of the concept of human capital up to Marshall and beyond is left unsolved for others to fathom. Instead, my aim is to show that the Smithian doctrine that education and training can be regarded as a type of investment in 'human capital' constitutes a programme for research, rather than a pronouncement of an indisputable insight, as much in 1890 as in 1970.

It is perfectly true that modern economies lack 'capital markets for

3. For a vigorous dissent from the interpretation of Marshall, see Blandy (1967); also Kiker (1968).

labour' and that the abolition of slavery necessarily implies that human beings are not produced means of production in the full sense that capital goods are. After all, capital markets are simply markets which convert income into capital and capital into income, that is, convert the promise of a flow of future payments into a single advance payment and vice versa. Because a non-slave society prohibits people from contracting to deliver their future services, 'free' people must keep their human wealth tied up in the form of labour services and cannot hedge against unforeseen changes in the future demand for their services. But even 'free' people sometimes manage to sell rights to their future labour services: classic examples of such disguised sales are professional athletes who receive 'bonuses' for signing with a football or baseball club to play exclusively for the club, and popular entertainers who make exclusive contracts to work for a specified number of years in exchange for the payment of a capital sum. Furthermore, mortgage agreements typically reflect the borrower's earning capacity: invididuals with relatively high earnings in secure occupations usually find it easier to borrow money to buy a house. Similarly, when people insure themselves against loss of future income from death or disability, the amount of insurance that they buy tends to be roughly equal to the present capital value of their expected earnings for the rest of their lives. And, despite the fact that education in free societies has up to now been typically financed by gifts to students either from charities, the State or their families, the recent appearance of student loans schemes in a number of developed and under-developed countries suggests that something like a human capital market can be created by deliberate acts of policy. All of these considerations show that the absence of a capital market for labour is more a difference of degree between physical and human capital than a difference of kind.

The absence of a capital market for labour only suggests that human capital formation need not be carried to the point where the discounted value of the prospective returns equals its costs (this kind of jargon will be explained later), but it does not necessarily refute the idea that a broad tendency towards such an equilibrium at the margin nevertheless makes itself felt. That is to say, it *may* be fruitful to look at the demand for education and training as an investment demand geared to prospective lifetime earnings; it *might* be illuminating to view improvements in the quality of labour through education and training in terms of a pecuniary calculus of costs and returns. The proof of such 'as-if' hypotheses lies in the eating, not in the recipe. It is only by posing particular questions about education and training that we can assess the validity of the human capital approach.

The Economics of Slavery

It will sharpen our thinking to spend a moment considering the case in which the concept of human capital is more than just analogous with the concept of physical capital: the slave economy. This exercise involves some mental gymnastics that will pay handsome dividends at later stages of the book. But first a few words on the concept of machine rentals.

In any industrial economy, a producer has the option in principle of buying a machine and enjoying the flow of services that it renders to his enterprise at the cost of maintaining it until it is worn out, or of renting the machine from its owner and thereby avoiding the trouble, although not, of course, the cost of maintenance.[4] It is impossible for a producer to exercise this option unless he can borrow capital funds in anticipation of the future returns from a machine. Furthermore, even if he is for some reason prevented from borrowing the purchase price of the machine, the machine producer who is hiring out machines must normally obtain credit somewhere to finance himself while waiting for the receipt of machine rentals. In either case, the fact that the cost of making machines is incurred in the present, while the returns from machines accrue in the future, gives rise to a demand for investment loans. The function of the capital market is to meet these demands for investable funds out of current savings on the part of households and business enterprises, supplemented by bank credit and the issue of currency. If the capital market functions smoothly and is subject to perfect arbitrage, our producer will in fact be indifferent as to whether he buys a machine or rents it.

An example will show what we mean by 'perfect arbitrage'. At an interest rate of 10 per cent, arbitrageurs who are not themselves producers would snap up any machine with an infinite life (perpetual streams are easier to think about but the argument is the same for

---

4. In practice, however, this option is rarely available; computers in advanced economies provide a good modern example of the option.

finite lives) that rents for £10 per year but costs less than £100 to buy outright. The reason is that the arbitrageur can now borrow, say, £90 to purchase the machine, paying £9 a year interest on the loan, in order to rent it at £10 to a producer. The result is an insatiable demand for machines at £90, causing machine prices to rise until the profits of arbitrage are wiped out. Similarly, a machine price of more than £100 would cause arbitrageurs and producers to sell any machines they owned until machine prices had fallen back to £100. At the same time, machines must generate a gross return in production each year of at least £10 if producers are to have an incentive to hire machines at an annual rental of £10. And if £10 is indeed the annual expected return from the machine, the producer is no worse off if he borrows £100 to buy the machine – which is precisely why the price of the machine tends to settle at £100.

The problem is complicated in practice by the fact that machines depreciate in use and that their operation frequently involves maintenance and repair charges. Specialized machine producers may be more efficient in servicing machines, in which case there may be a real economic advantage in renting complicated equipment rather than owning it outright. The general principle, however, is that the annual *gross* rentals of machines tends to be brought into equality via the workings of the capital market with the annual interest charges on the required amount of borrowed capital *plus* the minimum annual running expenses, maintenance and depreciation charges, leaving individual producers indifferent between buying the machine and maintaining it themselves, or renting it and letting the machine owner service it.

We are now ready to think about the economics of slavery. In a slave economy, with a well-organized market for slaves, the relationship between the price of slaves and the going rentals per slave year is governed by the same mechanism as the one just outlined for machines: the price of a slave will tend to equality with the capitalized value of the entire stream of gross annual rental payments for the future services of a slave. Suppose, for example, that it costs £10 a year to rent a slave from an owner and that a particular slave is expected to be able to work with undiminished energy for another thirty years. In that case, when the interest rate in the slave economy is 10 per cent, the price of this slave will be £94 6s. For the fact that the rate of interest is 10 per cent means that £94 6s. today is equivalent to the right to receive £10 each year for the next thirty years (when the payments are made at the end of the year). That is to say, £94 6s. growing at 10 per cent a year will just be sufficient over thirty years to pay out £10 at the end of each year.[5]

All this assumes that slaves are always maintained by their owners. Thus individuals who prefer to rent slaves, without being responsible for their upkeep, can do so by paying the owner the cost of feeding and clothing them. Once again, competitive bidding on the slave market will eliminate any advantage between buying slaves and renting their services. Net rentals will of course differ from gross rentals by the amount 'required' to maintain slaves at full biological working efficiency.

But what is the amount 'required'? What determines the net rental of slaves? A moment's reflection will show that when slaves produce more than is necessary to provide for them, someone will realize that there is a profit to be made in breeding slaves. In consequence, so many slaves will be produced that their price will eventually fall down to the present value of the expected costs of maintaining them during their working lives plus the cost of rearing a sufficient number of children to replace them after death. Similarly, their *gross* annual rentals will eventually fall to the annual expense of maintaining them – to a 'subsistence wage' in fact – while the corresponding *net* rentals will fall to zero. At that point, the number of slaves stops growing and the stock of slaves is maintained at a constant level by the continuous threat to step up the production of slaves the moment it appears profitable to do so.

The reference to 'subsistence wages' suggests the familiar world of English classical political economy, for this is precisely how Malthus and Ricardo imagined that a 'subsistence wage' would be established in a capitalist society: the slightest reduction in wages below minimum-existence levels would cause wage earners to have fewer children; in a generation or two, the reduced supply of labour would drive wages up again; the same mechanism would also act to keep wages down to the subsistence level. This never was a very good theory because the

5. This answer can be looked up in any book of mathematical tables giving the present value of an 'annuity' received at the end of *n* years, where an 'annuity' denotes a series of fixed annual payments for a specified number of years. A review of the principles underlying such tables for those who have forgotten the mathematics of discounting appears on p. 54. For the moment, the niceties can be ignored.

subsistence level itself, far from being a biological datum, depended on the standard of living to which workers 'hoped to become accustomed', that is, on their own voluntary decisions about family size. And, unfortunately, the nature of these decisions was never fully explored by the classical economists.

Similarly, in a slave society it would be difficult to discover the minimum amount of food, clothing and shelter 'required' to maintain slaves at full working efficiency. The minimum would necessarily be influenced by the generosity of some slave owners while at the same time every hard task-master would have a myopic incentive to reduce it to the barest essentials, whatever the consequence for the quality of slaves in the next generation. Without protective legislation designed to force every slave owner to pay for the social costs of an under-nourished slave-labour force, such a system would soon be riddled with inefficient maintenance of the stock of human beings. That is to say, the price of slaves in such a system would be determined not by the facts of biology, but rather by the degree of humanity or more probably inhumanity of slave owners. This is indeed one of the great disadvantages of a slave economy: when employers buy workers themselves rather than the services of workers, the upkeep of workers is likely to be neglected and their utilization contaminated by non-productive considerations.[6]

Nevertheless, the economics of this slave state would be simplicity itself, compared with the economics of free societies, particularly if slave breeding had been carried to the point of depressing its profitability to zero. The capital value of a man who was an unskilled slave would be the present value of his lifetime subsistence income, just sufficient to maintain and replace him intact for ever. No one would train or educate a slave unless the costs of doing so would be recouped by his enhanced output or services over a lifetime. The gross and net rentals of educated slaves would, therefore, exceed that of uneducated slaves and the price of educated slaves would contain an element of human capital representing the value of the education embodied in

6. Furthermore, although a perfectly competitive slave economy would equalize the advantages at the margin of the use of slaves in households for domestic service and their use in mines and plantations to produce saleable output, the temptation to indulge in 'conspicuous consumption' of household slaves to advertise personal wealth would no doubt prove irresistible and thus produce further anomalies in the relation between the prices and rentals of slaves.

them. In such an economy, it might be said without any ambiguity that 'capital' was any stock that yielded a flow of services over time – sometimes taking the form of machines, buildings, raw materials and natural resources and sometimes the form of skilled and unskilled human beings – whereas 'income' was simply the surplus of these services above the amounts necessary to maintain and replace the stock of wealth. In the slave economy, 'interest' would be the only distributive income, payments to labour being merely the interest payments on the stock of human as distinct from non-human capital, and 'capital' in different forms would constitute the only factor of production.

The point is that the economics of capitalism is complicated by the fact that machinery is rarely, whereas labour is invariably, hired on a contractual basis for fixed periods of time: machines are typically bought and sold and their rentals per period of time must be imputed, while labour services are always rented and it is the price at which a stock of these services might have been bought and sold that has to be imputed.[7] These well-known features of capitalist societies account for what is a logical asymmetry in the standard presentation of economic theory. Thus, generations of students have been confused by the so-called 'marginal productivity theory of distribution', according to which the wage rate is said to be equated under conditions of perfect competition to the marginal value product of labour and the interest rate to the marginal value product of capital. On the face of it, this proposition is pure nonsense because the marginal value product of a factor is an absolute amount of money per unit of time; it is therefore in the same dimensions as the money wages of a man hour but in different dimensions from the interest rate. The rate of interest is obtained by dividing a flow of income (for example, pounds sterling per year) by a stock of capital (in pounds sterling) and hence is measured in a unit that is the inverse of a unit of time ('per year' in this case). Obviously, the marginal value product of capital (so many pounds sterling) cannot be equal to the interest rate (so many pounds

7. Karl Marx made a great fuss about his discovery that it is 'labour power' rather than 'labour' that becomes a 'commodity' under capitalism, a distinction which, he argued, held the key to the creation of surplus value: capitalists buy labour power but obtain something more than that, namely, the product of labour itself. All he had really discovered was the distinction between the services of labour and the stock of labour resources, and it is perfectly true that this distinction is peculiar to a non-slave society. Whether it proves anything about the nature of profits or surplus value is another question.

sterling per pound sterling per year). Rather, it is the money rental of an hour or a year of machine services that is equated to the marginal value product of capital in a 'free' economy, in a manner perfectly analogous to the determination of the money wages of a man hour or man year. Where the rate of interest comes in is to determine the price of a machine from a knowledge of machine rentals and vice versa (in the simple case of machines that last forever, the price is simply the annual rental divided by the interest rate). Since machines can be sold as well as rented, competition will ensure that the price of machines is equated via the interest rate to the expected stream of machine rentals.

Similarly, when human beings can be sold as well as rented, slave rentals – interest on the capital sunk in slaves – will be equated to the marginal product of human capital and the rate of interest will then determine the corresponding price of slaves as the present value of their expected future rentals. The same logical argument will now suffice both for slave prices and for machine prices. The rate of interest is only needed to go from payments for a flow of services over a given period of time to payments for a stock that is capable of yielding a flow of services until it is worn out. In this sense, the economics of slavery is actually simpler to grasp than the economics of capitalism.

Social accounting is also simpler in a slave society. The national income of a slave economy would be measured quite simply as the consumption expenditure of free men out of the interest they have earned on their capital. With the upkeep of slaves tending towards subsistence levels, and the costs of educating them just recouped by the extra product of educated slaves, consistent social accounting would demand that we deduct from gross national product to arrive at net national product or national income, not only depreciation of physical capital but also all payments necessary 'to keep human capital intact': maintenance charges in the form of subsistence 'wages' of slaves, and depreciation and replacement allowances in the form of expenditures on the training of adult slaves and the rearing and training of young slaves. Here, too, we are back in the world of classical economics: Ricardo and the physiocrats before him were perfectly consistent in deducting the whole of wages paid out from final output to arrive at a measure of the net returns to economic activity in a capitalist society; consumption out of subsistence wages necessarily represents 'intermediate products', not 'final goods and services'.

All this is not quite as far-fetched as it sounds. It is true, of course, that pure slave societies are a historical rarity and that slaves in most slave societies of the past were to be found working alongside other kinds of indentured, dependent and even free labour. It is also true that very few slave societies denied the individual slave control over his own reproduction, depriving him, that is to say, of the right to have a family of his own. Nevertheless, in the ante-bellum American South, although three-quarters of the free population had no connexion whatever with slavery either through direct ownership or the hire of slave labour, there was systematic breeding of slaves for profit: slaves were bred in depleted soil areas and exported to the high-yielding land areas for work on the cotton plantations. Indeed, there is no doubt that slavery in the American states was 'profitable', in the strict accounting sense of the term: the purchase of a slave brought expected returns at least equal to that attainable from other outlets to which slave capital might have been put (Conrad and Myer, 1964, p. 66; Genovese, 1965, pp. 275–87). There is, by the way, no evidence whatever to support the widely held view that the productivity of Negro slaves in the South was markedly inferior to that of free white labour. Furthermore, it appears that the life expectancy of Southern Negroes was greater in 1850 under slavery than in 1900 under capitalism, suggesting that perhaps slavery does provide adequate incentives to keep slaves fit and healthy. However, in some respects Southern slavery was as far removed from pure slavery as the slave states of the ancient world. For example, although the slaves of ancient Greece and Rome were frequently trained for and regularly employed in highly skilled occupations, most Southern slaves were kept unskilled and uneducated.[8]

So much and no more for the history of slavery. The upshot of the exercise in the economics of a pure slave economy is to show that the

8. In other respects, too, the slavery of the American South was unrepresentative. To the extent that slavery is profitable in the economic sense, there are strong forces making for manumission by self-purchase, if necessary on the basis of instalment payments. But an efficient slave system which, like the Roman, permits manumission may destroy itself in the absence of external sources of supply. Southern laws to restrict the freedom to manumit slaves, once the external sources of supply dried up, undoubtedly had much to do with the racial component in Southern slavery which accounts for so many of its other peculiar features.

abolition of slavery inevitably entails the co-existence of two factors of production, labour and capital, which really are different in kind. The classical economists used to talk of 'land, labour and capital', but modern economics has long since assimilated land to capital. To go one step further, however, and collapse labour into capital meets with the basic objection that children in free societies are not produced merely as 'capital goods' for the sake of a future return, but also as 'consumer goods' for the sake of psychic satisfaction in the present and in the future. Thus, the long-run supply of labour is not governed by the same economic considerations that determine the long-run supply of capital, and the phrase 'the capital value of a man', counting the full value of all the costs incurred from the cradle to the grave, conveys little even to insurance companies. What is true of procreation and the capital value of a man is almost as true of training and education and the corresponding stock of capital embodied in people: in one sense, these are merely investments that human beings make in themselves to improve their quality, but in another sense, they are motivated by considerations that enter only incidentally into expenditure on the improvement of buildings and equipment. And this is not to mention the conventions and taboos that enter into the hiring, remuneration and utilization of human effort, conventions and taboos that are far more pervasive and tenacious than those which interfere with the ruthless scrapping of obsolete machines or the proper maintenance of ancient equipment. Once again, the difference is one of degree: the same theory that may be helpful in explaining the demand for training and education may not throw much light on the 'demand for children'.

Granted then that the term 'human capital', not to mention 'the capital value of a man', has no direct counterpart in non-slave societies, the hypothesis that a capitalist society at least improves labour in essentially the same way as a slave society may well be revealing of insights. No doubt, abstract models of economic behaviour that ignore the context of institutions and values within which economic transactions take place can be misleading. At the same time, however, a scrupulous regard for time and place can be blinding as well as illuminating: it frequently contributes to the neglect of basic principles that relate apparently diverse phenomena. It is hard to believe that factory legislation and 'equal pay' for men and women has anything to do with the decline of the birth rate; that going to school or taking an apprenticeship is analogous to buying an annuity; that looking for work is like going for a medical check-up; that the decision to migrate is similar to that of accepting a low-paid job in which one acquires experience; that a state subsidy to education is equivalent to a reduction in death duties; that military conscription amounts to a progressive income tax in kind, and so on – and yet all of these paradoxical propositions are tied together by the human investment revolution in economic thought, and this despite the fact that 'human capital' is never bought or sold in a capitalist society.

Education as Consumption and Investment

Consumption and investment are concepts so familiar in modern economics that their meaning is usually taken to be self-evident. Their role in the Keynesian theory of income determination, as the expenditures of two different sectors of the economy, households and business enterprises, corresponds exactly to the way they are measured in national income accounting. This has contributed to the popular view that consumption and investment are mutually exclusive categories, and that in most cases there is no difficulty in deciding to which category an item belongs. But in the analysis of economic growth, expenditures that are measured by national income accountants as 'consumption' nevertheless appear to influence growth in the same way as other items labelled 'investment'. This gives rise to endless debates as to whether something really is consumption or investment, in the course of which the substance of the distinction gets lost.

'Consumption', as Adam Smith used to say, 'is the sole end and purpose of all production.' If the sole end were production, there would be no point in including goods 'consumed in the very instant of production' in national income; all outputs would be treated as inputs, consumption being merely the inputs into the household sector, and the proper measure of aggregate economic activity would be the gross sales of all producing units in the economy, including households as producers of labour services. On the other hand, if it is consumption that is the object of all economic activity, it is difficult to see why investment is counted at all in final output. As a matter of fact, Irving Fisher proposed to confine national income to expenditures on consumer goods, arguing that national income should represent a flow of final goods and services and that investment is, after all, fed back into the productive system; investment eventually yields additional consumer goods and these goods will be counted in national income when they are consumed in the future; but to count investment now as part of income is to count the same thing twice over, first when the increment to the capital stock is incurred and again later when its yield is consumed (Fisher, 1906, ch. 8). The essence of Fisher's argument is that it is inconsistent to add the *capitalized* value of future income, in the form of an increment to the capital stock, to *uncapitalized* present income that reflects past investment. Either add consumption to consumption or investment to investment, but not one to the other. In short, 'income' is not 'consumption plus net investment', as in the now familiar Keynesian identity, but simply 'consumption'.

The dominant tradition, however, best represented by the writings of Marshall and Pigou, has been to include additions to the stock of physical capital, as well as the production of consumption goods, in the definition of the total output of an economy. The chief justification for this peculiar use of terms is that the concept of national income is concerned with causation rather than with measurement: we are interested in all activities that have the effect of yielding satisfaction now or in the future, and net investment is taken into account as representing present economic activities that have known, expected consequences in the future.[9] Keynes adopted the Marshall–Pigou view of national output and linked it firmly to the behaviour of households and enterprises as distinct economic agents with distinct motivations for their actions. The precise nature of the goods purchased by the two economic agents was irrelevant to his purpose, thus confirming the now widely accepted view that the contrast between consumption and investment depends on who it is that makes the decision to purchase, rather than on the type of good that is being purchased.

In the Keynesian theory, therefore, there can be no problem as to whether education is consumption or investment: since expenditures on education are made by households or by the government acting on behalf of households out of taxes collected from them, formal education is clearly consumption. On-the-job training, on the other hand, is clearly investment because it is an expenditure incurred by

9. See the citations from Pigou and the general discussion in Bonner and Lees (1963). The puzzled reader may want to consult a more detailed review of the various measures of the concept of 'income' in economic theory by Kaldor (1955, ch. 1).

business enterprises. Thus, national income accounting, which is an outgrowth of Keynesian macroeconomics, treats educational expenditures as final consumption, without making any allowance for the fact that the education acquired by the labour force depreciates over time and gradually becomes obsolete in much the same way as machines with which the labour force is equipped. That is to say, we inconsistently include in the *net* national product or national income the *net* additions to the stock of physical capital but the *gross* additions to the stock of human capital, although both types of capital are used up in the process of contributing to output.

Unfortunately, the Keynesian view of education as consumption logically inhibits any consideration of the contribution of education to economic growth. Such a question is, of course, irrelevant to the Keynesian theory of income determination which is not concerned with growth. Unfortunately, in accepting the Keynesian definition of consumption and investment as dependent on the behaviour of expenditure units, rather than on the nature of the goods which are being purchased, most economists have tacitly identified it with the older classical meaning of the terms in which 'investment' denotes those uses of current output which generate higher levels of output in the future, and 'consumption' denotes those uses that are exhausted in the present calendar year. In classical economics, growth is maximized by 'investment' and minimized by 'consumption'. Thus, if the Keynesian institutional definitions of consumption and investment identify education as consumption, it is a contradiction in terms to talk of education contributing to economic growth. No one can say how much this terminological confusion contributed to the neglect, until very recently, of the human factor in economic development and the overemphasis on physical capital as the mainspring of economic growth. Even now all too many students of economics find it difficult to grasp the idea that whether something is consumption or investment in the classical sense of the terms is an empirical question, not to be determined by the now established accounting convention adopted as a self-evident identity in the Keynesian theory of income determination.

In modern income accounting, investment is simply that part of current output which is not used up during the period of one year: whatever is not consumption is investment (or saving). But in the classical system, what is now regarded in rich countries as quite obviously 'consumption', such as food and clothing, is in poor countries as much 'investment' as 'consumption', in that more food and clothing for the working population is capable of raising future productive capacity. As soon as this is true, the standard accounting identity between 'investment' and 'increments to the stock of physical capital', and between 'investment' and 'saving' measured *ex post*, which is of questionable value even in rich countries, becomes positively misleading: the important kind of investment going on in poor countries may be just what cannot be characterized as net additions to the stock of durable equipment.

Similar considerations pertain with respect to education. As the following chapters will show, a good case can now be made for the view that educational expenditure does partake to a surprising degree of the nature of investment in enhanced future output. To that extent, the consequences of education in the sense of skills embodied in people may be viewed as human capital, which is not to say that people themselves are being treated as capital. In other words, the maintenance and improvement of skills may be seen as investment in human beings, but the resources devoted to maintaining and increasing the stock of human beings remain consumption by virtue of the abolition of slavery. We do not go so far as Ricardo and treat food for the labour force in the same way as fuel for machines: human capital is the present value of past investments in the skills of people, not the value of people themselves.

Nothing we have said implies that all education everywhere and in any amounts constitutes 'investment'. On the contrary, education is almost always both investment and consumption, not only in the sense that education of one type in one country may act to increase future output while another type of education in the same country does not, but that the very same quantum of education, say, a year's schooling for someone, invariably shares both consumption and investment aspects. For example, a 'household' decides to acquire an additional year of schooling for one of its younger members. This is 'consumption' in the Keynesian world. But it turns out that the additional schooling renders the member of the household more productive once he enters the labour force. This makes it 'investment' according to the classical definition. Unfortunately, both the student and his parents are unaware that additional education acts to increase the future productivity and hence the lifetime earnings expectations of the student. This makes it 'consumption' again, at least if our definition emphasizes the personal motive for an expenditure; from a social point of view, however, it remains in part 'investment'. Thus, the definition of consumption and investment changes as the angle of vision does. Notice, however, that from every angle the definition involves knowledge of facts: facts about the behaviour of decision makers or facts about the economic consequences of decisions.

It is useful to think of a threefold category rather than a twofold one: education may be acquired by individuals as if it were (a) a non-durable consumer good, (b) a durable consumer good and (c) a capital good. From the viewpoint of individual choice, the essential distinction that is being made is between present and future satisfactions, that is, between the enjoyment of education for its own sake and the anticipated enjoyment of a higher monetary or psychic income in the future. A large part of what is usually thought of as the consumption component of education is in fact forward-looking, involving the anticipated consumption of the services of a durable consumer good; motivated as it is by utilities that accrue in the future, it is more akin to investment than to consumption.[10] Since this sort of consumption benefit of education is almost certainly positive – very few people enjoy life less for being educated – higher lifetime earnings are not the only motives that impel individuals to acquire more education. But the same thing is not necessarily true of the current consumption of education which, for all we know, may actually carry negative utility for the average student.

The more we begin to think about it, the more we realize how arbitrary are most of the assertions that are made every day about the consumption benefits of education, whether reaped in the present or in the future. Since tastes are directly affected by schooling, such assertions involve intertemporal comparisons of utility with a yard-stick that is itself constantly changing: the value that a sixteen year old places on the future enjoyment of a university education is surely different from his appraisal after graduation? It is perfectly true that there is an extraordinary consensus in most societies on the positive

10. In fact, even working with strictly Keynesian categories, consumer durables should be regarded as additional 'saving' at the time of purchase, 'consumption' in a year being confined to the annual depreciation of the durable asset in that year. Only lack of appropriate statistical data forces the national income accountant to assume that consumer durables are completely written off in the year of purchase.

psychic benefits of education but, of course, it is a consensus of educated people whose taste for learning has been affected by the learning process itself. It is not so much that the belief that education makes for a richer life is a value judgement that lies outside the domain of empirical knowledge, but that it is *ex post facto* and hence of a different kind from the *ex ante* value judgement that governs the choice to acquire more education (Peacock and Wiseman, 1968, pp. 348–9). John Stuart Mill used to say that 'the uncultivated cannot be competent judges of cultivation' – a proposition about consumer ignorance fundamental to his views about government policy in education – but he did not realize that the converse is just as true. Is it meaningful to ask someone with a Ph.D. to debate the motion that ignorance is bliss?

It could be argued that the decision to stay at school beyond the legal school-leaving age is frequently made by parents, while the choice of the kind of further or higher education to follow is left to the student. Hence, the decision to choose more or less education is indeed made by someone who places an ambiguously positive value on both the present and the future consumption benefits of education. Again, this is a question of fact about household choices with respect to education: who makes them and for what reason?

As soon as we tackle questions of social policy, however, the question of the actual magnitude of the consumption benefits of education changes character. If the electorate is persuaded that more education is desirable in its own right, and votes for a government to tax them accordingly, the value of education as a consumer good must be added to its value as an investment good in any appraisal of educational efforts. It would be more accurate to say that the value of education as consumption in this case takes precedence over its value as investment. Whether we ought somehow to add the two together clearly depends on whether the electorate is in fact trying to pursue two objectives rather than one, that is, education for its own sake and education as a contributor to future output. Since these two objectives are frequently in conflict with another, we can get no further without evidence on how much taxpayers are willing to pay to provide education as a pure luxury. Just as we cannot measure the private consumption benefits of education without more knowledge of household behaviour, so we cannot measure the social consumption benefits of education without more knowledge of collective behaviour. It follows that there can be no magic formula, the discovery of which will suddenly permit us to quantify the consumption components of education. It is true to say, however, that we would come much nearer to the final answer if only we could accurately measure the investment components. It is to this question that we now turn. How confidently can we assert the proposition that, whether education is consumption or not, it certainly is investment from both the private and the social point of view?

Chapter 2
Education as Private and Social Investment

Age–Earnings Profiles

We begin by demonstrating that the amount of education that an individual possesses is, in all modern economies of which we have knowledge, positively correlated with personal earnings. This is not true for each and every individual – the correlation is far from perfect – but it is true for the average person and indeed for most. Age, sex, race, native ability, social class background, place of residence, branch of employment, occupation and on-the-job training are other important determinants of personal earnings. But apart from age, none of them are as powerful in their influence on earnings as the numbers of years of schooling completed. In short, additional education can be more or less confidently expected to raise lifetime earnings and, in this sense, the acquisition of education is of the nature of a private investment decision geared to future returns.

The evidence to substantiate this proposition should ideally take the form of time series of the earnings and educational attainments of cohorts of individuals, 'longitudinal cohort studies' as they are sometimes called. Unfortunately, such evidence is rarely available, although some longitudinal investigations of particular cohorts of children now under way (e.g. Douglas, 1964, 1968) will eventually furnish true life-cycle data, at least for one or two advanced economies. In the meanwhile, we must make do with cross-sectional evidence of the relationship between earnings and education. There are drawbacks to the use of cross-section data, but there are also advantages: unlike time series, cross-section data are free from the influence of the business cycle and implicitly provide estimates of earnings in money of constant purchasing power. Furthermore, they have the additional advantage of reflecting the way in which private educational choices are actually made: the average student forms his expectation of the

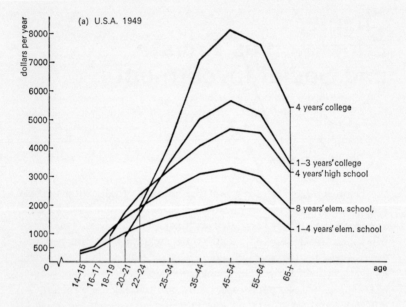

(a) U.S.A. 1949

dollars per year

4 years' college

1–3 years' college
4 years' high school

8 years' elem. school,

1–4 years' elem. school

age

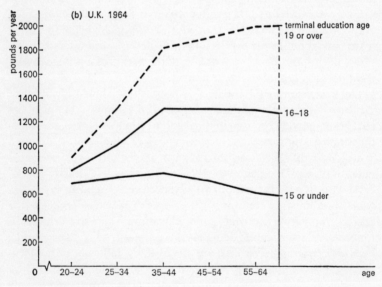

(b) U.K. 1964

pounds per year

terminal education age
19 or over

16–18

15 or under

age

Note: the sample sizes for each age cohort for the TEA group 19 or over are too small
to provide reliable results

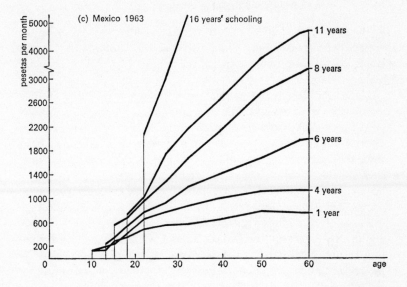

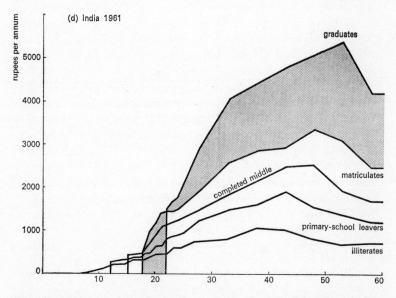

Figure 1　Age–earnings profiles in four countries. *Sources:* (a) W. Lee Hansen (1963, table 1)*; (b) Henderson-Stewart (1965); (c) Carnoy (1967b); (d) Blaug, Layard and Woodhall (1969)

financial benefits of additional years of schooling by comparing the *present* earnings of adults with various amounts of education, that is, by cross-section comparisons of the relationship between earnings and education.

The crucial element that enables the individual to deduce his lifetime earnings from a cross-section observation of the earnings of educated people is the factor of age. What we are after is evidence on earnings by education by age, in other words, a cross-tabulation of the labour force by sex, age, earnings and educational attainments (and, whenever possible, by race, region of employment, sector of activity and occupation). From such a cross-tabulation, we can construct what we will call *age–earnings profiles* by levels of education. To date, firm evidence of this kind is available for only a dozen or more countries, and in only two cases (the United States and Canada) is the information regularly collected in the decennial census of population.[1] We have selected four sample countries, two rich and two poor, to illustrate the typical characteristics of age–earnings profiles (see Figure 1).

In each case, we have tried to confine the comparison to the earnings of male members of the labour force, that is, to standardize for sex and for labour-force participation rates. In the case of the U.S.A. and the U.K., however, the figures are for incomes, not earnings, thus including unearned property income which is itself positively associated with age and education. In the case of India, the figures refer to employed males only, which is troublesome because Indian unemployment is not uniformly distributed among educational categories. With the exception of the U.S. statistics, all the country studies omit the incomes of people past the age of retirement, owing to the difficulty of separating the current earnings of older people from pension income attributable to past employment. The U.S. data come from the *1950 Census of Population*. The U.K. data derive from a random sample of male heads of households which classified educational attainments by 'terminal education age', without distinction between full-time and part-time education. The Mexican data stem from a special sample survey of urban wage earners. The Indian figures derive from a

1. The earliest work relating education to age-specific earnings differentials dates back to the work of Soviet economists in the 1920s, although they in turn drew on still earlier work in Tsarist Russia in the 1890s (Kahan, 1965a). For indications of American work in the 1920s along similar lines, see Clark (1963, pp. 17–20).

national sample survey of urban males. Although all the four studies report mean incomes of educational cohorts at various ages, none of them use precisely the same age breakdowns. All of which is to say that the four charts are not really strictly comparable. Nevertheless, they suffice to show what age–earnings profiles look like; we might have presented data from Canada, New Zealand, the Soviet Union, the Netherlands, Sweden, Denmark, Greece, Israel, Nigeria, Kenya, Uganda, Zambia, the Philippines, Puerto Rico, Japan, Venezuela, Chile and Colombia – the remaining countries for which this sort of evidence is now available (see below Chapter 7, p. 230) – all of which would have conveyed more or less the same picture.

The profiles reveal three striking characteristics:

1. All profiles, irrespective of the years of schooling or level of education attained, increase with age up to a maximum point somewhere after the age of forty and then level off, or in some cases even decline.

2. The higher the educational attainment, the steeper the rise in earnings throughout the early phases of working life and usually, although not invariably, the higher the starting salary.

3. The higher the educational attainment, the later the year at which maximum earnings are reached and the higher retirement earnings.

In short, within a few years after leaving school, if not immediately, better educated people earn more than less educated ones; their advantage continues to widen with age and although they lose some of the gain after reaching their peak, the favourable differential persists until retirement. Another way of expressing the same idea is to say that age–earnings profiles either do not intersect at all or intersect only once in the first few years of employment. It is worth noting, however, that this generalization may break down if we look at profiles, not simply of *amounts* but also of different *kinds* of education that represent alternative rather than successive routes through the educational system. For example, one British sample survey of about 3000 monthly paid male workers employed in one large car firm and in four electrical engineering firms produced the following results:

In general, students wishing to pursue education after the statutory school-leaving age in Britain have two alternatives: either to remain at school full-time and to obtain academic qualifications, such as GCE O- and A-levels (educational levels 2 and 3 in Figure 2) which

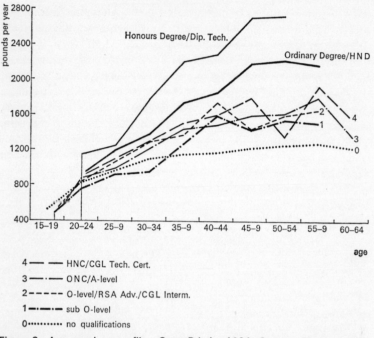

4 ——— HNC/CGL Tech. Cert.
3 ——·— ONC/A-level
2 ————— O-level/RSA Adv./CGL Interm.
1 —·—·— sub O-level
0 ············ no qualifications

Figure 2   Age–earnings profiles, Great Britain, 1964. *Source*: Blaug, Peston and Ziderman (1967, chart 1). *Note*: age groups 15–19 and 20–24 for some educational levels are omitted owing to insufficient numbers of observations. For further explanations of the educational levels, see Glossary of British Educational Terms, p. 327

qualify for entrance into higher education, or take a job and to attend a part-time course at a technical college leading to a professional qualification, such as those of the Royal Society of Arts (RSA) or the City and Guilds of London Institute (CGL) by means of 'day release' or evening study (educational levels 1, 2, 3 and 4 in Figure 2). Judged by what they pay, British employers seem to treat O-levels as equivalent to RSA Advanced Certificate and CGL Intermediate Certificate, and A-levels as equivalent to ONC (Ordinary National Certificate) and OND (Ordinary National Diploma). However, many school leavers stay on in schools to obtain some O-levels and then leave the world of full-time schooling at sixteen or seventeen to continue their education by part-time routes. It is difficult, therefore, to construct truly successive educational equivalences in Britain for the group with terminal education ages fifteen to eighteen. This goes a long way towards explaining the interlocking of the profiles relating to educational levels 1, 2, 3 and 4.

We return to the three striking characteristics of what we might call 'well-behaved' profiles: (a) they rise with age up to a peak regardless of the amount of schooling received; (b) they rise faster, the higher the amount of schooling received, intersecting once, if at all; and (c) they reach a peak that comes later, the longer the amount of schooling received. Of all these, the first is the easiest to explain: age acts as a proxy variable for amount of work experience acquired and 'learning by doing' tends to raise all earnings, although with diminishing effectiveness as time passes (Sen, 1966, pp. 161–5*).

However, the decline in age–earnings profiles in the last decade or so of working life may well be an illusion created by the cross-sectional character of the evidence. Age–earnings profiles based on longitudinal data differ from those based on cross-section data in a number of respects, the most important of which is the secular growth in earnings per head which almost all economies enjoy as a result of capital accumulation, technical progress, and the like. What this implies is that the future earnings at the age of fifty of a 1970 university graduate are not correctly indicated by the earnings of a fifty-year-old graduate observed in 1970: today's twenty-one-year-old graduate will be living in a richer economy when he reaches the age of fifty in 1999. We can adjust for this growth factor, however, by adding to each profile the expected annual rate of increase in earnings per head based on an extrapolation of past experience. When this treatment is applied to American cross-sectional age–earnings profiles (Becker, 1964, pp. 139–42), the result is to remove the decline at older ages: the profiles continue to rise through age sixty-five, the last age covered by the data. This is not surprising because the growth-adjustment is cumulative and indeed equivalent to the compounding effect of interest, interest on earned interest, and so on. We must take a sceptical attitude, therefore, to the cross-section finding that earnings peak well before retirement. The fact remains, however, that earnings rise with age at a decreasing rate, producing life-cycle profiles that are convex from below. Clearly, the most convincing explanation for this shape is the idea that 'learning by doing' is subject to diminishing returns, supplemented perhaps by the tendency of formal education itself to be subject to obsolescence after the passage of two or three decades.

None of this, however, helps to explain the fact that the earnings of more educated people rise faster with age than those of less educated people, and that the profiles of the better educated lie above those of the less educated for almost the whole of their working lives. To explain these characteristics of age–earnings profiles is in effect to explain the economic returns to education. It is obvious, however, that so far we have explained nothing more than the effect of work experience: taken at face value, age–earning profiles prove nothing about the economic values of education.

It may be that the better educated so frequently start at higher salaries because of social conventions in hiring policies, 'conspicuous consumption of the highly educated' some writers have called it (after Veblen). University graduates may have steeper profiles than school leavers[2] simply because they are now more able or better equipped to make use of what native ability they have by virtue of favourable home background, in consequence of which they rise faster in the occupational hierarchy. Similarly, they may reach their peak earnings at a later age than school leavers and suffer less decline of earnings in the last years of their working life, if indeed they suffer any decline at all, because they shift into executive positions where they are relatively immune from performance rating and hard to budge even after their efficiency has begun to wane. Again, a university degree or a secondary school diploma may function more as a certificate of diligence and perseverance than as evidence of the possession of particular verbal and mathematical skills. Employers may regard a paper qualification as a reliable indication of personal ability, achievement drive and perhaps docility, reasoning that, say, a graduate must make a better salesman than a man who has never met the challenge of higher education; the graduate gets the job and the better pay, not because higher education has improved his skills, but simply because the degree identifies him as the better man.[3]

2. Throughout this book, terms like 'university graduate', 'high school graduate', 'school leaver', etc. refer to individuals in terms of the highest educational qualification they have obtained or, in the case of 'school leaver', to someone who left at the legal school leaving age without any qualification.

3. As one economist has expressed it: 'To be sure, economic growth is *associated with* higher education, but which is cause and which effect? Who is to say that Enoch Powell is wrong? – higher education might be simply a consumption good for which rich communities develop a taste much as rich individuals like foreign travel. The so-called economic yield on higher education might be due to little

From one point of view, this last argument is not as damaging as it sounds: investment in a certificate of persistence and drive, particularly if the information is reliable and would have to be acquired anyway, is no less formation of human capital than investment in Virgil and calculus. Still, aptitude tests administered at the time of hiring, or probationary periods of employment for everyone, might be a cheaper way of separating the bright and energetic from the stupid and dull. Putting the same case more circumspectly, suppose that among all applicants otherwise the same, graduates would make better workers than non-graduates six times out of ten; an employer lacking other information and unwilling to incur screening costs or a high rate of labour turnover would nevertheless hire the graduate ten times out of ten; as a result, the non-graduate would experience longer periods of unemployment and would tend to earn less while working.

Negative explanations such as these can never be decisively refuted even by well-behaved age–earnings profiles, however carefully collected and extensive in coverage. On the other hand, confidence in these *ad hoc* interpretations is considerably weakened by the steady accumulation of age–education–earnings profiles in both rich and poor countries, all of which tend to reveal the three dominant characteristics of age–earnings profiles mentioned above. The simplest explanation of the universal association between education and earnings across sectors, industries and occupational categories around the world is that the better educated are generally more flexible and more motivated, adapt themselves more easily to changing circumstances, benefit more from work experience and training, act with greater initiative in problem-solving situations, assume supervisory responsibility more quickly and, in short, are more productive than the less educated even when their education has taught them no specific skills. Whether the process of formal education has actually fostered and encouraged these aptitudes, or whether it has merely acted as a handy screening

---

more than this: clever people usually get more money than stupid people, but they will also compete for degrees and pre-empt university places once a prejudice in favour of degrees has been established. And such a prejudice might be initially due to nothing more than the convenience to employers of a free external testing system; the universities, already existing in adequate numbers, happen to be able to certify, at an absurdly great cost, which *are* the clever ones. So employers demand degrees, and from there on the whole expansion might be a vicious circle' (Wiles, 1969, p. 195).

device selecting those with such inborn aptitudes for promotion and discarding the rest, is a different question – all those who are inclined to accept the latter interpretation should ask themselves whether they can conceive of an equally effective and less costly screening mechanism (Danière, 1964, p. 42).

This is not to deny that certification is clearly the prime economic (and sociological) function of upper secondary and higher education. This is borne out by the fact that no colleges or universities anywhere in the world refrain from ranking and grading their students: there are diploma mills in some countries which provide virtually no instruction but there are no institutions of higher education which offer instruction but no diplomas (Jencks and Riesman, 1968, pp. 61–4).[4] But the notion that the sheep could be separated from the goats without incurring the staggering costs of higher education presupposes that personal ability and achievement drive are simply inherited fixed capacities that require no development, only discovery. The essence of higher education as a selection device is precisely that it represents a *protracted* aptitude test for measuring certain aspects of character and intelligence. It is by no means obvious that the same function could be carried out as efficiently by observing a man at work even for periods as long as a year or two.

In whatever way the trick is accomplished, the certified products of the educational system are somehow more productive than the drop-outs. For this reason, they take first place in the employment line, earn more at almost every age and suffer less from obsolescence of knowledge. This is the simplest explanation of their higher lifetime earnings. It must be conceded, however, that truth is not always on the side of simplicity.

How Much is Due to Education?

The distribution of earnings from employment, not to mention the distribution of income from all sources, is the outcome of an extremely

4. This certification or selective function does not depend on the fact that higher education is almost everywhere limited to the few: even if all eighteen to twenty-two year olds went to colleges or universities, employers would still be anxious to discover which students were more competent and which less so; grades or rankings would then serve the same function that is now served by the possession of degrees. The recent demand from some student militants to abolish examinations blandly ignores the functional role of the certification process in the pretence that society can be changed by changing universities.

complicated interaction of such differentiating factors as sex, race, natural ability, family circumstance, community environment, length of schooling, quality of schooling and, thereafter, the sector, size of firm and occupation of employment. Any one of these is itself the complex product of a variety of elements. Natural ability, for example, is more than endowed intelligence as measured by I.Q. tests; there are whole batteries of tests that measure other inherited abilities and there may even be two fundamentally different kinds of intelligence characterized by 'convergent' and 'divergent' styles of thinking (Hudson, 1968). Family circumstance is a matter of size and spacing of children but, in addition, there is the education of the parents, the occupation and income of the father, and those of the mother if she is working, adding up to a working-class or middle-class attitude to the rearing and training of children. Community environment is a function of the urban or rural character of the neighbourhood, the region of the country in which the household is located, the average level of income of friends and relatives, and so on. Amount of schooling is, of course, influenced by the availability of educational facilities in the area, and quality of schooling, too, is a robe of many colours. Another factor is whether one finds employment in the public or in the private sector, in manufacturing or in commerce and trade, in a large multiplant firm or in a small office, in one category of jobs or in another. Furthermore there is the distribution of medical care, the provision of labour training in industry, the incidence of inter-regional and interoccupational mobility, the control over wages and salaries by trade unions and professional associations, and even the level of aggregate demand – all of which have some influence on the size distribution of earnings in an economy.

What is worse, however, is the degree to which all of these factors are intercorrelated, so that the effort to measure one of them frequently picks up the effects of some of the others. For example, one famous psychological study subjected six groups of children to I.Q. tests, the groups consisting of identical twins reared together, identical twins reared apart, fraternal twins reared together, siblings reared together and reared apart, and unrelated children reared together; the striking discovery was that the correlation coefficient between the two age-specific I.Q. scores declines steadily as we go down the list from twins with identical genetic constitutions to unrelated children reared together (Burt, 1955).[5] Clearly, therefore, the intelligence that is measured by I.Q. tests has a strong hereditary component; indeed, the standard view of psychologists is that about 50 per cent of observed intelligence at age seventeen is predictable at the age of four and that perhaps as much as 90 per cent of the variance in individual intelligence at the age of four is due to inherited factors. The now fashionable sociological view that intelligence is largely an acquired characteristic is in fact a downright misrepresentation of the available evidence (Jensen, 1969; S. Wiseman, 1964, p. 36). However, even at five, the age of entry into primary schools, the mean I.Q.s of working-class children are below those of middle-class children, where social class is measured by the occupation of the father. Furthermore, between the ages of eight and eleven, 'middle-class children improve their attainment scores and working-class children deteriorate at each level of ability' (Douglas, 1964, p. 46; but see Horobin, Oldman and Bytheway, 1967). Thus, when we measure I.Q. at eleven, we necessarily confuse native ability with acquired ability as conditioned by home background. This is even more true if we look at attainment tests rather than intelligence quotients: it is well known that home environment has a greater influence on attainment tests than on I.Q. scores (S. Wiseman, 1964, pp. 54–5, 155).

On the other hand, if we reduce the entire question to one of social class origins, as measured, say, by the occupation and education of the father, we confuse the effects of home background with those of native ability, community environment and local provision of schools. The crucial question about the influence of social class is: what is the source of the disadvantages of working-class children? Is it simply that stupid children leave school early to take up unskilled occupations, bequeathing their poor genetic endowments to their children who in turn are doomed to be uneducable? No, it is clearly not that simple: there is a world of difference between inborn intelligence and the capacities required to perform well at school. Is it perhaps that working-class families are larger and that, as has been demonstrated again and again, children from larger families do not perform as well at school as children from smaller families? Is this due to the material circumstances of such homes, or to the inability of parents of large

5. S. Wiseman (1964, ch. 4) and Lyall (1968, pp. 71–88) provide convenient summaries of this and related studies; see also the brilliant review of the literature by Jensen (1969).

families to take an active interest in their children's educational performance, a factor which has been shown to have a significant effect on educability in primary schools (*Plowden Report*, 1967, pp. 33–4)? Or is it that working-class parents somehow do not bring up their children with a strong inner drive to achieve, an attitude which McClelland has succeeded in measuring with a special 'need-achievement' test (McClelland, 1961, ch. 2)? Is it perhaps something deeper still, such as the 'restricted code' of language used in working-class homes (Bernstein, 1958)? If either Plowden, McClelland or Bernstein is right, the variable 'social class origins' reflects a good deal of what we might elsewhere investigate under the heading of 'measured ability'.

We might go on to suggest that family background, the quantity and quality of local secondary schools, and the entire ethos of the community interact with the availability of information about employment opportunities, the willingness to migrate to areas where jobs are plentiful, and finally the choice of ultimate career, but the main point is by now surely established? If we attempt to isolate the effect of education on earnings by means of multiple regression analysis,[6] standardizing for all the other factors that have an influence on earnings, we may, unless we are careful, succeed in virtually eliminating the relationship that we are investigating. For example, if we standardize for occupation and for geographic mobility we may in effect remove some of the indirect effects of education on earnings: people with more education have access to a wider range of occupations and are more inclined to migrate in search of higher pay; these are not factors additional to but rather the consequence of their education. This is, of course, not true of the factors that operate before schooling is completed, such as native ability and home background. But even here there is great danger of counting twice: if we standardize for father's occupation, mother's education, size of family, rental value of home, average income in the community, educational expenditure per pupil in the area, I.Q. and examination results, we may

6. Multiple regression analysis is a statistical technique for estimating the *causal* effect of a number of independent variables on a linearly related dependent variable, on the assumption that the combined effect of all the independent variables is simply the sum of their separate effects. This is not as restrictive as it sounds because many relationships which are not in a suitable linear form can be transformed so that they become linear. Walters (1968, ch. 5) is a good reference to begin with.

have removed acquired ability three or four times over and grossly minimized the effect of education as such.

What we face here is not just the standard econometric problem of intercorrelation among the explanatory variables. Not only can some of the variables affect others without themselves being affected by those others (social class background affecting educational attainment but not vice versa) so that the explanatory variables are linked up in a temporal series, but some of the variables (such as social class) perhaps never make themselves felt except *through* other variables (such as length of education). It is almost as if educational attainment were acting as a proxy for social class and measured ability. I say 'as if', because to assert that education is indeed a proxy for family background and ability is to make nonsense of all talk about 'equalizing educational opportunities'. So long as we assert that there are 'reserves of talent' that go unexploited because educational facilities are not equally available to all, we appeal in effect to the belief that there are children from poor families who have the natural capacity to benefit from more schooling than they now receive. In other words, we appeal to the notion that native intelligence, family background and measured achievement are *not* one and the same thing travelling in various guises. Thus, much educational policy around the world designed to equalize educational opportunities hinges in fact on unravelling the intercorrelations that prevail among the factors that determine personal earnings.

The standard way of dealing with intercorrelation is to take larger samples: with a big enough sample we can always cross-classify it by the relevant variables and so, for example, regress earnings on the amount of education of working-class adults of given ability. We shall review a few examples of this way of cutting through the Gordian knot, but such examples are still few and far between in the literature. In the meanwhile, we need constantly to remind ourselves that there is no absolutely correct statistical solution to the 'multicollinearity problem' in the effect of education on earnings.

We begin with an American study which posed but did not solve the problem entirely successfully. It applied the full power of multivariate analysis[7] to a well-designed national sample survey to test a variety of hypotheses about the determinants of family income. Taking separate

7. Multivariate analysis is a particular type of multiple regression analysis which converts all or some of the variables into 'dummy' variables, which take

account of such factors as sex, race, physical condition, occupation, city size, urban–rural migration, supervisory responsibility, need-achievement score, rank and progress in school and intelligence (as indicated by interviewers' assessment of ability to communicate), it concluded that even 'the net effect [of length of education] proves to be so powerful that it reinforces the popular notion that better education is the one sure path to achievement' (Morgan, David, Cohen and Brazer, 1962, p. 6).

The old problem of intercorrelation among the independent variables is present once again. For example, the most important factor determining the amount of education achieved by the head of an American household is not his intelligence or ability measured in various ways, nor the income of his parents, but rather the educational attainment of his father (Morgan *et al.*, 1962, pp. 359–94, 391–2, 401–2). In drawing conclusions about the effects of education on earnings, this inter-generation problem is eliminated by assuming that a variable like father's education influences the earnings of the head of the household directly without affecting his terminal education age. This suggests that the pure effect of this generation's education on this generation's earnings has been overestimated. On the other hand, when we have on the right-hand side of the regression equation such variables as length of education, occupation, geographical mobility and supervisory responsibility, the interaction between these factors reduces the effect of education alone. On the whole, the authors incline to the view that they adjusted too much and, therefore, underestimated the pure effect of education. In this sense, their basic finding that length of education is the most powerful single determinant of family income is even more impressive than it seems at first glance.

A special analysis of the same data which focused on the earnings of high-school and college graduates of white male non-farm households in the labour force showed that age and education alone accounted for 60 per cent of the gross earnings differentials in the age group eighteen to thirty-four and for as much as 88 per cent in the age group thirty-five to seventy-four. 'Objections to the use of simple average earnings of different age and education groups', the authors

---

the values of one if an individual belongs to a particular subclass and as zero if he does not; for a general discussion, see J. Johnston (1963, pp. 221–8), and for striking examples in the economics of education, see Carnoy (1967a), D. C. Rogers (1969) and Thias and Carnoy (1969).

sum up, 'are correct but quantitatively not terribly important' (Morgan and David, 1963, pp. 436–7). Nevertheless, the fact that the entire analysis 'explains' only 35 per cent of the variance in gross earnings (Morgan *et al.*, 1962, p. 60) must leave us feeling unconvinced: either some variables are mis-specified (for example, no pre-school measures of intelligence were used) or else there is some significant interaction between variables that has been left out of account.[8]

We turn now to specially selected samples, focusing for a moment on the earnings differential of American high-school and college graduates. The average I.Q. or quotient of mental age to actual age of American high-school graduates is 107 and that of college graduates 120·5; high-school graduates who do not go to college rank, on average, in the forty-fourth percentile of a high-school graduating class, whereas those who do go and successfully complete college rank in the sixty-eighth percentile of the same class (cited in Becker, 1964, p. 80). Thus, there can be no doubt that the 'measured ability' of college graduates exceeds that of high-school graduates. Moreover, 22 per cent of high-school graduates have fathers in 'professional, semi-professional or managerial' occupations, whereas the corresponding figure for college graduates is 45 per cent (cited in Becker, 1964, p. 80). Again, there is no doubt that college graduates tend to come from homes with fathers in top occupations more than do high-school graduates. Nevertheless, the effect of these considerations on earnings is much less than might be expected. Wolfle and Smith obtained annual salaries some fifteen to twenty years later of a sample of about 3000 males that had graduated from high schools in three American states in the 1930s.

The sample is confined to the top sixtieth percentile of all high-school graduates, that is, to the kinds of high-school graduates that tend to go to college in the United States. It is clear from a glance at all the rows in the table that going to college raises earnings even when we hold measured ability constant, and this is true whether we measure ability by class rank (combining the effects of natural ability, interest in schooling and perseverance) or by I.Q. scores (an unsatisfactory measure of one kind of natural ability). It is worth noting, however,

8. Another multivariate analysis of a sample survey in 1957 for the St Louis City-County area, which standardized earnings for a long list of factors but not for native ability or motivation, similarly failed to 'explain' 60 per cent of the income variation of heads of households (Hirsch and Segelhorst, 1965).

Table 1

Median Salaries in 1950 and 1955 of American High-School and College Graduates of Standard Ages by Class Rank and I.Q. Scores

Ability Measure	Education		
	High School	Some College	One College Degree or More
	$	$	$
Percentile rank in high-school class			
91–100	4880	5600	7100
81–90	4780	5400	6300
71–80	4720	5300	6500
61–70	4810	5700	5700
41–60	4655	5300	5700
Percentile rank in I.Q. Scores			
81–100	4000	5300	6300
45–80	4500	5200	6100
1–44	4300	4100	5200
I.Q.			
Over 120	5500	6100	7600
Under 120	5000	5700	7400

Source: Wolfle and Smith (1956, tables 2, 4 and 5), cited in Becker (1964, p. 83).

that the effect is weaker for those who rank low in their high-school class and low on intelligence tests. Looking down the columns, it appears that the earnings of high-school graduates are not much affected by either rank in class or rank in I.Q. scores. The pay-off from college, however, is greater for those with higher ranks and superior I.Q.s: the best college graduates earn about 15 per cent more than the worst, but all of them, we must emphasize again, earn from 20 to 50 per cent more than even the best high-school graduates. The same study also supplied information on the relationship between father's occupation, education and earnings. Again, high-school graduates with fathers in professional or managerial occupations earned only about 5 per cent more than those with fathers in unskilled or skilled occupations, whereas college graduates with fathers in top occupations earned about 15 per cent more than other college graduates. The central implication of the findings is now clear: high-school graduates with favourable home backgrounds and superior measured ability seem to require college education to translate their advantages into significantly higher earnings.

Unfortunately, the Wolfle–Smith study takes I.Q. scores at the high-school level, at which point the tests are themselves influenced to some extent by previous educational performance. However, one Swedish follow-up survey of a random sample of 1500 individuals provides data on earnings at age thirty-five by years of schooling completed, school grades, teachers' rating, family background and *I.Q. taken at the age of ten* (Husèn, 1968). It shows that earnings rise with additional education even when I.Q. at the age of ten is held constant (see Table 2). Further analysis of the data demonstrated that I.Q. does indeed 'explain' an additional 30 per cent of the variance in earnings; education alone, however, 'explains' about 60 per cent and the coefficient on years of schooling in the regression of earnings on

Table 2

Mean Incomes in Kroner before Tax of Males at Age Thirty-Five by Years of Schooling and I.Q. at Age Ten, City of Malmo, Sweden, 1964

I.Q.	Years of Schooling			
	Under 8	8–10	11–14	14 or more
−85	14,548	14,929	17,750	35,533
	(4041)	(4611)	(4763)	(6182)
86–92	17,744	17,462	20,500	—
	(10,306)	(5955)	(7527)	
93–107	15,266	18,176	21,735	31,400
	(5270)	(8118)	(7477)	(26,567)
108–114	16,625	19,538	19,429	41,000
	(5165)	(7793)	(12,893)	(18,267)
115+	17,450	21,943	33,750	43,158
	(4260)	(7363)	(35,238)	(19,219)

Source: Husèn (1968, table 16).
Note: The figures in brackets are the standard deviations of incomes.

education is virtually unaffected when I.Q. scores are added as an additional independent variable (Griliches, 1970, p. 34; D. C. Rogers, 1969).

Another table from the Swedish study depicts the effect of education on earnings when social-class origins rather than I.Q. are held constant. The first thing we notice is that earnings still rise with additional education, for each and every social class (see Table 3). The second

Table 3

**Mean Incomes in Kroner before Tax of Males at
Age Thirty-Five by Years of Schooling and Social Class,
City of Malmo, Sweden, 1964**

Father's Occupation	*Years of Schooling*			
	Under 8	*8–10*	*11–14*	*14 or more*
Unskilled workers	15,580	17,614	17,909	29,667
	(5554)	(3943)	(1986)	(9391)
Skilled workers	16,297	18,571	21,778	28,000
	(7083)	(7212)	(8038)	(4082)
Subprofessional	14,897	18,022	24,393	34,500
middle class	(4630)	(6820)	(7811)	(11,056)
Professional,	15,000	23,071	35,458	45,384
managerial group	(2000)	(10,782)	(40,713)	(18,470)

Source: Husèn (1968, table 15).
Note: The figures in brackets are the standard deviations of incomes.

thing is that the range of earnings associated with education widens as we move up the educational ladder: the full effect of favourable home background does not materialize unless more education is acquired. Lastly, and by way of summarizing Table 3, educated working-class males receive roughly double the income at age thirty-five of working-class males who left school at age fourteen or fifteen; the same effect for males from the top social class is to triple incomes. Thus, speaking crudely, social class appears to be responsible for one-third of the earnings differentials between university-educated upper-class boys and working-class school leavers.

A unique American study, much earlier than any of these so far considered, examined a selective sample of 200 boys, all of whom had brothers within the same sample, educated and gainfully employed in the state of Indiana in the year 1927 in an attempt, as the author put it, 'to separate the effect that schooling has upon income from the combined effects that schooling, inheritance, health, good luck, bad luck and other factors have upon income' (Gorseline, 1932). By limiting himself to blood brothers, the author succeeded in holding constant many of the determinants of 'measured ability'; not all, of course, because order of birth has an influence on educability. He showed that brothers with more schooling earned in 1927 significantly more than brothers with less schooling at each and every age above twenty-five (see data cited in Becker, 1964, pp. 132–3). After analysing the sample for differences in age, length of education, grades attained in school, scores on standardized test, occupational rank, place of residence, size of family, windfall income and medical expenses, he concluded that approximately half of the mean income differentials between the least and the most educated brothers in an average year were attributable to education.

Our last piece of evidence comes from Mexico and is, in fact, the only example to date of the attempt to isolate the net effect of education on earnings in underdeveloped countries. The study in question is based on a non-random sample of male wage earners taken in three Mexican cities in 1963. Evidence was obtained on salary, age, number of years of schooling completed, father's occupation, own occupation, industry and city employed and subject studied in post-secondary education where relevant. The technique of analysis was once again multivariate analysis and the central finding was that variables other than age and schooling added little to the 'explanation' of income variation between Mexican urban workers. Particularly striking is the small effect of correcting for father's occupation, which the author interpreted to mean that 'the effect of having environmental training in the form of more educated (and wealthier) parents is to increase an individual's drive and ability to take more schooling, but does not enhance his earning power over his less "fortunate" colleagues who completed the same level of schooling' (Carnoy, 1967a, p. 419).

It is worth noting that this study is only indirectly related to the question we have been examining, namely, the interaction between educational attainments and the slippery concepts of ability and intelligence. To be sure, father's occupation is partly a proxy for a variable such as informal education in the home, but father's occupation is highly correlated with parental income, and high parental income enables the student in most countries to buy additional schooling, or at any rate better quality schooling. Since the earnings that will have to be forgone to qualify for entry into higher education discriminate against poorer students, it is hardly surprising that the better educated tend to be the sons of fathers with top occupations. This has itself nothing to do with the superior home training that constitutes an aspect of the greater measured ability of privileged children. We are again reminded that there is no real substitute for objective test scores, preferably at early ages.

Let us take the argument a little further. If we are trying to *explain* or measure the contribution of education to earnings differentials, we certainly go wrong if we ignore the dimension of 'ability'. It is not at all clear that we do so if instead we are interested in *predicting* the effect on earnings differentials of extending education to more students. There was a time in Great Britain when the metaphor of a 'pool of ability' was constantly employed to justify the restricted scale of British higher education: 'More Means Worse' was the cry. But the *Robbins Report* effectively destroyed the notion that educational expansion in British circumstances would mean the drawing down of a limited stock of relevant abilities (*Robbins Report*, 1963, pp. 49–54; app. 1, pp. 77–89; evidence, pt 2, pp. 170–77). Similarly, there is little evidence even in America that the steady diffusion of education has started to scrape the bottom of the barrel of talent. On the contrary, for both countries there is an overwhelming body of data pointing to the failure of lower-class children to share in the provision of education in accordance with their natural abilities. For purposes of practical policy, therefore, we may safely ignore the intercorrelation between measured ability and schooling: it exists but it will continue to exist in much the same way over any likely planning horizon. In short, we may make good predictions even without being able to discover the separate influence of all the explanatory variables that impinge on earnings differentials, provided they continue to vary together in the future as they have in the past.[9]

9. The point is a general one about the statistical difference between 'explanation' and 'prediction'. A special case of it is the well-known fact that ordinary least squares is 'biased' and 'inconsistent' in estimating the structural parameters of a regression equation but 'unbiased' and 'efficient' in predicting the values of endogenous variables; see Walters (1968, pp. 188–90) or any other standard text in econometrics.

Similar remarks pertain to some of the variables which are frequently used as proxies for measured ability. Both here and in America, the distribution of university and college students by social class, as measured by father's occupation, has not changed significantly in the last thirty years (Griliches, 1970, pp. 39–40; Westergaard and Little, 1967). Thus, if we merely want to know how much earnings differentials would change if higher education were expanded, we can safely neglect the factor of social-class origins. It is perfectly obvious, of course, that this line of reasoning breaks down if we are thinking of a dramatic non-marginal change in the scale of higher education, or a radical reform in the financing of either upper-secondary or higher education. The significance of the intercorrelations between ability, family background and educational attainment varies with the policy we are contemplating. The problem is much more serious when we are explaining rather than forecasting and, in the case of the latter, it is the more serious the more revolutionary the policy proposal in question.

We must now sum up the main drift of the discussion. It is perfectly obvious that age–earnings profiles as such overestimate the effect of education on earnings. In any society where progress through upper-secondary into higher education depends on the outcome of a selection process – and if that applies to American society where access to higher education is relatively easy, how much more does it apply to Britain – the better educated must inevitably be more 'able', in some sense, than the rest of their age cohort. None of the evidence we have reviewed denies the fact that favourable home background determines to some extent who it is that obtains additional education; nevertheless, it does not *explain* why the better educated receive higher lifetime incomes. That is to say, it is perfectly true that better educated people tend to have better-educated parents, to come from smaller families, to obtain financial help more easily, to live in cities, to be more highly motivated, to achieve higher scores on intelligence and aptitude tests, to attain better academic grade records, to gain more from self-education, and generally to suffer less unemployment, to live longer and to be healthier. But this is not at all equivalent to saying that, in the words of two destructive critics, 'expenditure on education is highly correlated to income and wealth of parents, to ability and motivation, to educational opportunities such as urban residence and proximity to educational centres, to access to well-paid jobs through family and other connexions, *any of which could either by itself or in conjunction with any of the others account for superior earnings'* (Balogh and Streeten, 1963, p. 102,* my italics). The italicized remark is unsubstantiated, nay, positively refuted by such evidence as we have.

Of course, social-class origins, native intelligence and community environment are so intimately intertwined with educational attainment that the task of disentangling them can easily be made to look hopeless. But to throw up our hands at the task is to make a mockery of the goal of equality of educational opportunity. If the superior earnings of better-educated people are simply a matter of privileged birth, then apparently schools merely select people for innate ability, putting them through finer and finer selection sieves but adding nothing whatever along the way. Why then advocate more schooling for the underprivileged? It is simply inconsistent to assert, on the one hand, that nature and nurture are so mixed up that their separate effects cannot be unravelled and, on the other hand, to advocate egalitarian redistribution of schooling based on assertions which are only true if most of the determining factors have been unravelled.

Admittedly, the evidence about the pure effect of education is still far from completely convincing, and it is always possible that what is true in America and Sweden is not true elsewhere. In the meanwhile, casual empiricism occasionally feeds the belief that education is *not* an important element in higher earnings. So long as abilities to learn, opportunities to learn and quality of schools differ, some individuals with less education will earn more than their better-educated contemporaries; we will remember these cases when we meet them precisely because they are exceptional. That is to say, the positive association between earnings and education is a statement about the mean earnings of different educational cohorts, around which there is, of course, considerable variance (Becker, 1964, pp. 104–13; Lassiter, 1966, pp. 7–13; Miller, 1960). Indeed, if there were no variance about the mean, it would be tantamount to the assertion that earnings are determined by education and by nothing else, a patently false proposition.

To reject the notion that the higher lifetime earnings of the better educated is simply the consequence of class origins and family connexions is not, however, to prove that the better educated are better rewarded because they are more productive. It is still conceivable that the labour market somehow finds it more convenient to use a proxy variable like educational qualification in place of a battery of psychological tests designed to discover the native ability of job applicants. It is interesting to ask oneself, however, what costs would be imposed on employers if the educational system issued no certificates of competence whatever.

Net Earnings Streams

What we have been discussing is the contribution that education makes to the earnings differentials between people with different amounts of education, and not to the absolute level nor to the percentage distribution of these earnings. If we were interested in explaining the demand for graduates, the fact that this is a function of the relative price of graduates – relative, that is, to the wages and rentals of other kinds of inputs – would have impelled us to emphasize the *ratio* of the earnings of college graduates to those of high-school graduates rather than the absolute differences between them. However, from the point of view of education as a private or social investment, what is relevant is in fact the absolute differentials between more and less educated people. Clearly, the high-school graduate who is contemplating the pecuniary sacrifice that is involved in attendance at college cares about how much more he will earn, not whether he will earn a certain percentage more than if he went to work immediately. Likewise, a government, evaluating a given expenditure on education for the sake of a future increase in national income, must compare like with like: the fact that an increase in the supply of highly educated people may reduce their relative advantage over the less educated is neither here nor there.

It is clear from simple arithmetic that a narrowing of relative earnings differentials through time may be perfectly compatible with constant or even increasing absolute earnings differentials: take the case where secondary-school graduates earn £1000 and university graduates earn £2000, and where the former raise their earnings by 10 per cent and the latter by 6 per cent; relative differentials have narrowed but absolute differentials have risen from £1000 to £1020. As a matter of fact, wage data for the United States going back to 1900 show a marked decline in the relative spread of the occupational wage structure and an equally marked increase in the absolute differences between the wage rates of different occupations (Becker, 1964, p. 54).

To emphasize the importance of absolute earnings differentials in the formation of human capital by means of investment in education, let us go back to the age–earnings profiles in Figure 1. We want to show how to obtain *net returns streams* from data on the gross returns to education. By way of example, we select the Indian age–earnings profiles and reproduce them here for easy reference, but with a difference: the difference is that we now include the direct costs incurred at various levels of education (in the form of outlays on teachers, buildings and equipment) as negative earnings depicted below the horizontal axis (see Figure 3). Consider now the absolute earnings differentials between university graduates and matriculates (the Indian equivalent of a secondary leaving certificate); it is shown in (a) of Figure 3 in the form of the shaded area and then separately in the lower part (b), the value of the net absolute returns being negative when the shaded area lies below the matriculate stream and positive when it lies above it.

It is clear that the shaded area below the horizontal axis represents the direct costs of university education. But what is the crossed area and why should it now appear below the horizontal axis instead of above it? A moment's reflection will show that it is the earnings which Indian university students forgo while studying between the ages of seventeen and twenty-one. For them it represents an indirect cost of going to university. For the Indian economy, it is a measure of the output that is lost from a cohort of individuals that could have been working between the ages of seventeen and twenty-one, which is no less a social cost of university education than the resources used up in the form of teachers and buildings. Figure 3 depicts earnings before tax and takes account of the total resource costs of education, that is, the value of the time of teachers and administrative staff (as represented by their salaries), the value of equipment and materials (as represented by their prices), the imputed rent on educational buildings (imputed because educational buildings are rarely rented in practice) and, finally, the value of students' time (as measured by earnings forgone). Notice that we do not count scholarships, bursaries and other students' grants, because these merely represent transfers of purchasing power from all taxpayers to students and involve no using up of resources. If instead we had regard to private returns and private costs, we would take earnings after deducting income tax, since taxes paid out are not part of the returns from education to an individual, and we would ignore all costs not incurred by the individual. That is to say, we would

TEOE–C

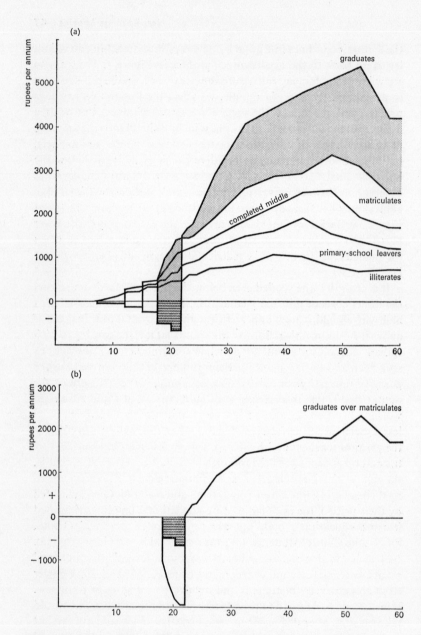

Figure 3 Age–earnings profiles and net returns stream to graduates over matriculates, India, 1961. *Source:* Blaug, Layard and Woodhall (1969)

count out-of-pocket costs such as tuition fees, books, uniforms, and travel expenses (but not living expenses because they are incurred anyway) *minus* scholarships and grants received if any *plus* earnings forgone.

It is no accident that the crossed area below the horizontal axis in (b) exceeds the shaded area: the indirect costs universally exceed the direct costs of education, irrespective of whether we look at social costs or at private costs. In the U.S.A., forgone earnings constitute over half of the total resource costs of high school and college and about 75 per cent of the private costs borne by students (Schultz, 1963, pp. 5–6, 27–32); in Britain, they represent 42 per cent of the total costs of higher education (*Robbins Report*, 1963, vol. 2 (B), pp. 216–23; vol. 4, pp. 109, 148, 153) and nearly 100 per cent of private costs, given the fact that British student grants include an allowance for fees, books and travel. British grants for maintenance even cover about 40 per cent of the earnings forgone by students but they still leave the average university student paying indirectly for about 25 per cent of the total costs of higher education. In consequence, even so-called 'free' university education is far from completely free.

In India, children who have never been to school or have completed only a year or two of schooling can find employment at the age of eight or nine. We can, therefore, record earnings forgone in India even for those who have only completed primary education. In the advanced countries, however, legal restraints eliminate the alternative of employment below the age of fourteen or fifteen, and, as there is no choice, no meaning can be given to the private sacrifice involved in elementary schooling. But from the point of view of society, 100 per cent enrolment of the age group six to fourteen or five to fifteen does involve a real cost in terms of alternative output forgone. In upper secondary and higher education, on the other hand, earnings forgone represent both a private and a social cost. The fact that at these levels education is typically twice as costly as households and public budgets indicate is of central significance to prevailing thinking about education.

Firstly, it helps to explain why the drop-out rate after the school-leaving age is everywhere inversely related to the income of households: families with low incomes cannot easily afford to forgo the earnings of their children. Also, it puts a rather different complexion on the common passion of educators for a rise in the school-leaving age: the bulk of the costs of such a change would fall on parents with children of school leaving ages and it would obviously hurt working-class parents more than middle-class parents. Secondly, the tendency to treat about half of the real costs of education after fifteen as if they were 'free' is a potent source of irrational planning and accounts in good part for the failure of educational systems to economize on the time of students as a participating input in the learning process. Thirdly, and perhaps most important of all, it contributes to a massive understatement of investment in education in national income accounts.

Notice that earnings forgone do not have to be approximated: they enter automatically in the net returns streams, calculated as they are by deducting one age–earnings profile from the one immediately above it. But even if they did have to be crudely estimated, that would be no reason for leaving them out in a calculation of costs rather than budgetary expenditures. The notion that imputed charges and indirect costs are somehow less 'real' than direct financial outlays has a certain intuitive appeal but it is none the less an elementary economic fallacy.[10] Although the time of teachers and the use of buildings and equipment are measured directly by 'what is put in', while the time of students is measured indirectly by 'what is done without', the distinction is one of statistical expediency, not of theoretical principle; after all, the actual money outlays on teachers, plant and equipment are themselves only estimates of the goods and services forgone for other purposes (Bowman, 1966). Admittedly, all these estimates, including

10. According to Vaizey (1962, p. 43), 'the inclusion of income forgone in the costs of education opens the gate to a flood of approximations which would take the concept of national income away from its origin as an estimation of the measurable flows of the economy'; furthermore, 'if income forgone is added to educational costs, it must also be added to other sectors of the economy (notably housewives, mothers, unpaid sitters-in, voluntary work of all sort)'; also 'it would be necessary to adjust the costs by some notional estimate of the benefits incurred while being educated, and these are usually considerable'. Upon close inspection, it appears that this paragraph consists of a misunderstanding of the purposes of national income accounting, followed by two *non sequiturs*. To measure the net flow of goods and services in the economy is one thing; to measure the real cost of a particular activity is another. The fallacy of identifying the two is made apparent by substituting 'unemployment' for 'education' in Vaizey's leading sentence. The equivalent argument then reads: it would be wrong to include incomes forgone in a calculation of the cost of unemployment because measured national income does not include the goods and services the unemployed would have produced if they had been working.

that of earnings forgone, are only reliable indicators of opportunity costs for *marginal* changes. For example, for a major shift in resource allocation, such as raising the school leaving age by a year, the use of cross-sectional data on earnings to estimate the value of students' time minimizes the consequent loss in output. Similarly, since there is evidence that the personal incidence of unemployment is correlated with the amount of education received, estimates of earnings forgone in a less than fully employed economy will tend to understate the loss in output from additional investment in education. This tendency can of course be allowed for in any specific instance.

The memorandum submitted by H.M. Treasury to the Robbins Committee tries to take account of the fact that students would consume more if they were working rather than studying by deducting from earnings forgone by students the difference between the consumption of students and the consumption of young workers (*Robbins Report*, 1963, evidence, vol. 1, pp. 1973–5). But this appears to be a mistake: the fact that an individual consumes less if he is a student does not reduce the social loss of output involved in keeping him at school. What it does is to raise the real income of the rest of the community at the expense of the student. Unless we argue that the welfare of students counts for less than the welfare of the employed population, there are no grounds for treating the asceticism of students as a reduction in the resource costs of education. Even from the point of view of the private calculus, reduced consumption is one of the sacrifices of alternatives which ought to be included in an estimate of what the student forgoes to stay at school; it is included automatically if we count earnings forgone at full value. Only if we believed the old adage that 'a university teaches you to despise the money which it prevents you from earning' would we be justified in deducting anything from earnings forgone.

We come back now to the question of attributing the earnings differentials that we observe to be associated with different amounts of education to the effect of education as such. After examining the evidence of the Wolfle–Smith survey (see Table 1, p. 39), Denison concluded that about 66 per cent of the gross earnings differentials between college and high school graduates can be statistically attributed to education alone, in the sense that on average about a third of the earnings differentials disappear when one standardizes for differences in father's occupation, rank in high-school class, and I.Q.

scores (Denison, 1964, pp. 78–9),[11] a result which has been confirmed by Becker (1964, pp. 80–88) and by Weisbrod and Karpoff (1968). This fraction (two-thirds), Denison applied in turn to each net earnings stream, although he had no independent evidence about the net effect of education on differentials at levels below high school. Denison's one-third adjustment is a generous one and it has been argued that it overestimates the impact of ability and family environment on earnings (Griliches, 1968, pp. 42–3). In point of fact, Denison arrived at the one-third adjustment by attributing about 3 per cent of the observed differentials in the Wolfle–Smith survey to I.Q., another 6 per cent to rank in high school class, a further 7 per cent to father's occupation and a final 17 per cent to the difference between earnings in the sample in question and earnings in the United States as a whole (Denison, 1964, pp. 95–7). It is not difficult to see that if his adjustment is wrong, it errs on the side of underestimating the pure effect of education. Perhaps this is all to the good. The point to be emphasized, however, is that any judgement as to whether he has gone too far depends entirely on the purpose to which his estimates are put. The charge that he has not done justice to the impact of education on earnings gathers strength if we are merely predicting the short-term effects of a steady expansion of educational provision.

On the whole, we shall not go far wrong in analysing American data if we simply multiply the gross earnings differentials between college and high-school graduates by what we will call an *alpha coefficient* of 0·66 (alpha as a mnemonic for 'ability'), leaving education substantially unaffected as a generator of higher future earnings. But what of the earnings differentials between high-school graduates and high-school drop-outs? We should probably apply a *lower* alpha coefficient to this differential on the grounds that acquired ability and family circumstance have more influence on the decision to complete high school than on that of going on to college. But in the absence of relevant evidence, we might follow Denison in applying 0·66 again as a rough-and-ready principle. After all, any results we obtain will be more convincing if in every doubtful case we opt for the adjustment that minimizes the pure effect of education.

So much then for the ability adjustment in the United States. But

11. Earlier, in his book, *The Sources of Economic Growth in the United States and the Alternatives Before Us*, Denison had assumed arbitrarily that the correct figure was 67·7 per cent, which proved to be a happy guess.

what use is all this in analysing the returns to education in other countries, where almost no evidence exists to separate the effects of ability and education? For example, would it be reasonable to assume that the alpha coefficient in a country like Britain is about the same as in America? On the one hand, people with secondary and higher education appear to be scarcer in Britain than in the U.S.A., in the sense that they constitute a much smaller fraction of the labour force. This argues for a premium on education in this country and hence a higher value for alpha, that is, less allowance for the effects of measured ability. However, we can make no *a priori* assumptions about the relative scarcity of educated people solely from a knowledge of their supply: the demand for them is also likely to be different in different countries. On the other hand, the tripartite character of British secondary education and the restricted character of the entry into universities suggests that the selective effects of social-class determinants operate with much greater force here than in the U.S.A. This argues for a lower alpha value, that is, more play for the ability factor.

On balance, it would seem that an alpha coefficient of 0·66 is somewhat on the high side for secondary-school leavers, given the finding that 'early leaving' is highly correlated with social class (*Robbins Report*, 1963, vol. 1, pp. 38–84). But, likewise, the true alpha coefficient for British university graduates is probably much in excess of 0·66. Once students have entered sixth forms, the divisive influence of social-class membership, with all that it implies in differential home background, has largely ceased to operate; the evidence shows that it has very little effect in deciding whether a student in the sixth form applies to a university, none at all in determining whether he or she is accepted or not, and very little in governing performance in university courses (Furneaux, 1961, p. 71; *Robbins Report*, vol. 1, pp. 52–3; vol. 2 (A), pp. 135–6, 155–6). Social-class origin is of course only one of the components of the alpha coefficient; nevertheless, it is not to be doubted that students in British higher education are more homogeneous with respect to measured ability than secondary-school students. Thus, one approach in analysing educational investment in Britain is to apply an alpha coefficient of 0·66 to the profiles of secondary-school graduates and a range of coefficients from 0·66 to 1·0 to the profiles of university graduates. What we are doing in the latter case is, in effect, to test the sensitivity of the results to a variety of assumptions about the interaction between ability, family background, and education (see below Chapter 8, p. 241). This is crude but it is much better than assuming that all the earnings differentials associated with different amounts of education are entirely attributable to education.

In the rest of this book, whenever we speak of age–earnings profiles adjusted for ability differences, we will mean by it the application of a Denison-type alpha coefficient to the gross earnings differentials between levels of education.

How to Calculate Rates of Return

Having come this far, we may as well spend a few more moments on problems of technique. We have seen that education is one way that people invest in themselves. By accepting some costs in the present, they can generate equivalent or greater returns in the future. Similarly, entire communities acting in concert can in this way convert present into future income. But if the phrase 'education is investment' is to be more than a metaphor, it ought to be possible to calculate rates of return on transforming present into future income via educational investment. This is not a simple matter of looking up answers in compound interest or present value tables, because these are invariably calculated for uniform cash-flows; but, as we have seen, the net earnings streams associated with or attributable to education vary with age.

Nevertheless, the calculation, while sometimes arduous, is simplicity itself and involves nothing more erudite than the laws of arithmetic. By way of example, let us suppose that an individual expects to earn £1100 next year. Let us further suppose that he could invest his money, if he so desired, at the rate of 10 per cent per year. The 'present value' of the £1100 is therefore the amount which he would have to invest now so that in one year's time it would appreciate to £1100. Let us call this amount V_1. Clearly, then, it must be the case that

$$V_1(1+0\cdot10) = £1100.$$

Therefore $\quad V_1 = \dfrac{£1100}{(1\cdot10)} = £1000.$

Likewise, if the individual expected to earn nothing next year but

£1210 two years from now, the present value of this amount can be found from the expression:

$$V_2 = \frac{£1210}{(1\cdot10)} = £1000,$$

which is simply to say that £1000 would grow into £1210 in two years' time if it earned interest at 10 per cent (at the end of each year), the interest being ploughed back itself to earn interest.

In general, if we designate expected earnings t years hence as E_t, we may calculate the present value of E_t by the formula

$$V_t = \frac{E_t}{(1+r)^t}$$

where r is the going rate of interest. Similarly, if the individual expected to earn £1100 in the first year following the current year and £1210 in the second year, the present value of this *stream* of earnings is simply the sum of the individual V_t s:

$$V = V_1 + V_2 = \frac{E_1}{(1+r)} + \frac{E_2}{(1+r)^2},$$

or in general

$$V = \sum_{t=1}^{n} \frac{E_t}{(1+r)^t}$$

where $n =$ the length of working life. In the example before us, $V = £2000$. Since any calculation of the present value of a future stream is simply the reverse of calculating the stream that results from earning compound-interest, the answer can be checked by going through the compound-interest argument: £2000 invested for one year at 10 per cent would yield £2200 of interest plus principal in the first year; half of this could be withdrawn to cover expected earnings in year 1; the rest will be reinvested and would suffice to yield £1210 to cover expected earnings in year 2; $V = £2000$ is the correct answer.[12]

12. The reader who finds all this puzzling may want to consult a more careful exposition of the inverse relationship between discounting and compounding in Alchian and Allen (1967, ch. 13).

Knowing E_t and r, as in the previous examples, we can always deduce V_t. On the other hand, knowing V_t and E_t, we can similarly deduce *the internal rate of return* on the investment project, that is, the rate at which V would accumulate to E_t in t years. Suppose for example that all the costs of education were incurred in the current year, then, writing C for the known costs of education and i for the unknown internal rate of return, the formula

$$V = C = \sum_{t=1}^{n} \frac{E_t}{(1+i)^t}$$

would permit calculation of i. Unfortunately, the costs of education are themselves incurred over a number of years. What we really have is

$$V = \sum_{t=1}^{n} \frac{E_t}{(1+i)^t} - \sum_{t=1}^{n} \frac{C_t}{(1+i)^t}, \tag{1}$$

that is, four variables of which two, V and i, are unknown. But what are we trying to do? We want to find the rate at which the costs of education grow into the earnings from education, when the costs themselves grow at this rate for a few years. In other words, we are looking for that i which makes the present value of the earnings stream equal to the present value of the cost stream: that i which sets $V = 0$. Now as soon as we set $V = 0$, the problem is solved. We now have three knowns which together determine i, the one unknown.

The final solving equation is

$$V = \sum_{t=15}^{60} \frac{(E_t - C_t)}{(1+i)^t} = 0, \tag{2}$$

where $t = 15$ is the legal school leaving age and $t = 60$ the retirement age. $\sum(E_t - C_t)$ is, of course, our old friend the net returns stream: the stream is negative during the years of schooling and positive during years of employment.

This still does not tell us how we actually calculate i. The answer is: by trial-and-error, which can be made, however, to converge fairly quickly on the answer. Let us go back to the net returns stream for Indian graduates in Figure 3 (p. 48), ignoring the fact that they are not ability-adjusted. If we had the figures before us, they would read:

Age	t	Net returns (rupees)	
18	1	−995	
19	2	−1498	
20	3	−1866	C_t
21	4	−2095	
22	5	+27	
23	6	+235	
—	—	—	E_t
—	—	—	
60	43	+1722	

Writing out equation **1**, we have

$$V = \frac{-995}{(1+i)} + \frac{-1498}{(1+i)^2} + \frac{-1866}{(1+i)^3} + \cdots + \frac{1722}{(1+i)^{43}}.$$

We start with any i, say 5 per cent, and compute the sum just indicated – presumably with a desk calculator or else with a computer if we are well endowed with research facilities – recording the answer as a point in a Cartesian plane that maps various is into corresponding present values. We now repeat the entire operation

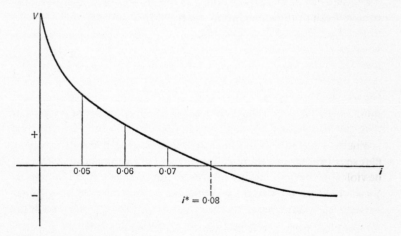

Figure 4   Present value curve

with a lower i, and once again record the answer; as we continue to take larger and larger is, we discover that the locus of the recorded Vs falls monotonically as i increases.

This is hardly surprising: a glance at the last equation for V shows that as we take higher and higher values of i, we divide the successive net returns by larger and larger denominators; obviously, V varies inversely with i. Moreover, since the denominators in the successive terms are raised to higher and higher powers, the effect of taking larger and larger is is equivalent to giving less weight to later ages and more and more to earlier ones ('increasing time preference' this is sometimes called); since the earlier ones are actually negative, one would expect the curve of present values to intersect the horizontal axis at some relatively high i and to become negative thereafter. That i which makes the present value V_t of the net returns stream $\sum (E_t - C_i)$ equal to zero ($i^* = 0.08$ in Figure 4), is the internal rate of return on investment in Indian higher education, for it equates the present value of the costs of an Indian degree to the present value of the financial returns from first degrees. The calculation is, as we said, somewhat tedious, but can it be denied that it is elementary?

It is worth noting that this method only works if (a) the absolute sum of the undiscounted gross returns actually exceeds the absolute sum of the undiscounted costs, and if (b) the undiscounted gross returns stream cuts the horizontal age axis once and once only, or to put it another way, if there is only one change of signs in the age–earnings profile. Both of these conditions are fulfilled by all age–earnings profiles so far collected, and it is difficult to imagine how they could ever be violated – an entire educational cohort would have to return to full-time education in adult life and once again suffer negative earnings. At any rate, when they are violated, we may obtain multiple present values for the same i; in short, equation 2 cannot be solved for a unique i and we would have to resort to other methods of evaluating investment projects.[13]

Figure 4 has other convenient properties. Recall the British age–earnings profiles in Figure 2. When these are supplemented by cost data and converted into net returns streams, we can plot the present value of the net returns to, say, educational level 4 *over* level 3 against various discount rates, as we do in Figure 5. But we could also have

13. For an example where the internal-rate-of-return approach breaks down, see Wilkinson (1966, p. 557).

plotted the present value of the age–earnings profiles 3 and 4 themselves in which case we would have arrived at the same answer. When we plot the excess of level 4 over level 3, as we do in Figure 5, the horizontal axis in effect represents level 3. When we plot the actual

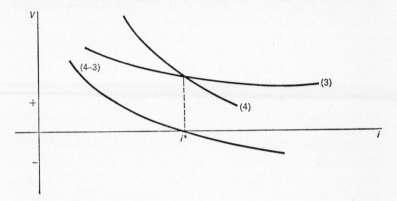

Figure 5   Present value curves

profiles corresponding to level 3 and to level 4, we are in effect using level zero as our base. For the purpose of comparing the two levels 3 and 4, we obtain exactly the same result whichever base we use: the choice of the base cannot affect the answer for i^*. Thus, in Figure 6, we compare educational levels 1, 2 and 3, using level 1 as a base in (a), and level 2 as a base in (b). The values of i_1^*, i_2^*, i_3^*, giving the internal rates of return between various pairs of levels, must be identical in both presentations, as must be the differentials in present values between any two levels at any i. The choice of one level or another as base, therefore, depends entirely on convenience and clarity of presentation.

Having shown how rates of return to educational investments are calculated, we shall postpone a discussion of their meaning until Chapter 7. At least we know now what is meant by saying education is a kind of investment in people for the sake of future earnings. Of course, we have not yet shown that these are always profitable investments. Since profitability is a relative concept, it can only be judged by comparing the internal rate of return on educational investments with the yields of alternative investment opportunities. Which alternative yields are relevant is left for now as an open question (see below Chapter 6, p. 173, and Chapter 7, p. 231).

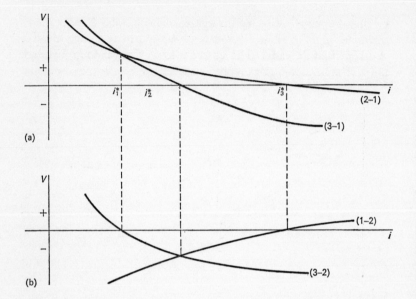

Figure 6　Present value curves

Chapter 3
The Contribution of Education
to Economic Growth

International Comparisons of Income, Literacy Rates and Student Enrolments

Economic growth is normally measured by the rates of increase of national income; national income is by definition the sum of all earned and unearned income in the economy; the extension of education tends to raise the earnings of those who have benefited from it; therefore, investment in education accelerates economic growth. Is there anything wrong with this argument?

The answer is: alas, yes. If only it were as simple as that. We have indeed demonstrated that additional education raises earning power but we have not demonstrated that it does so by making people more capable of producing goods and services. If business men simply pay graduates more because of the snob appeal of a university degree despite the fact that graduates are no more productive than secondary-school leavers – 'conspicuous consumption' of graduates we labelled it earlier – the effect is either to reduce profits, or, if profits are maintained, to reduce the earnings of non-graduates. In consequence, the higher earnings of graduates simply redistribute national income without augmenting it. It is exactly as if industry suddenly decided to pay blondes more than brunettes: dyeing one's hair would now produce positive returns in the form of greater lifetime earnings, but this would last only as long as there were brunettes to 'exploit'. National income would not increase as a result of it. As a matter of fact, it would soon fall, everything else being the same, because hair dyeing involves the using up of resources. But of course as much is true of the provision of education. If the association between education and earnings is simply due to the 'conspicuous consumption' of educated man power, the extension of education would decelerate economic growth as it is now measured, not accelerate it.

The conspicuous-consumption hypothesis might be tested by inter-firm comparisons: if we could discover cases in which some firms employing more highly educated personnel made less profits, or produced less output, or paid school leavers less than other firms in the same industry, the hypothesis would be confirmed. The technical difficulties of interfirm analysis are great. Besides, without much more precise knowledge than we now possess of the optimum 'densities' of education required by the activities of industrial firms, it would not be easy to identify firms employing excessive amounts of educated personnel, or to pronounce with any degree of confidence on the reasons that they did so.

We may derive some comfort from the fact that so-called 'conspicuous consumption' of educated man power, if it exists at all, must apply as much to secondary as to tertiary education: people with higher education everywhere earn more than people with secondary education, who in turn earn more than people with only primary education, and so on. Is it conceivable that business men the world over are always content to surrender profits for the sake of prestige, or that the less educated always allow themselves to be 'exploited' by the more educated? Surely, if it were merely the by-product of snobbery, some countries would by now have broken the chain?

This immediately suggests a wholly different way of looking at the relation between education and income, not cross-sectionally between individuals within countries, but either between countries at a given point in time or within countries over a period of time. What can we learn from international comparisons of national income, its rate of growth and various indicators of the extension of education? This is a rich field of investigation which has perhaps been more fully explored in the last decade than any other area of the economics of education. To convey the flavour of much of this work, we will begin by considering an outstanding contribution to the literature by Bowman and Anderson (1963).

They looked, first of all, at *literacy rates* (the percentages of adults who have achieved rudimentary literacy) in 1950 and GNP per head in 1955, measured in U.S. dollars in eighty-three countries. They found that the countries could be divided fairly neatly into three groups. (a) thirty-two poor countries with adult literacy rates below 40 per cent in which 1955 *per capita* incomes never exceeded $300 (except for oil-rich Sabah); (b) twenty-seven mixed countries in which literacy rates ranged from 30 to 70 per cent and in which income was virtually uncorrelated with literacy; and (c) twenty-four rich countries with literacy rates above 70 per cent, including twenty-one very rich countries with literacy rates over 90 per cent, where 1955 *per capita* incomes always exceeded $500. Despite reluctance to infer causation from correlations, the authors concluded that something like a 40 per cent literacy rate seems to be a pre-requisite for incomes per head to exceed $300, and similarly that 90 per cent literacy seems to be necessary to realize incomes over $500.

Now, the world mean literacy rate in 1950 (calculated from the available statistics of 136 countries) was 56 per cent, and the whole of Africa (except the Republic of South Africa), Asia, South-East Asia, the Middle East and large stretches of Latin and Central America (fifty-four countries in all) fell below this mean (Bhagwati, 1966, fig. 7). Similarly, the world mean *per capita* GNP in 1950 (calculated from the available statistics of ninety-six countries) was $200 and once again the whole of Africa, Asia and the Middle East, but not Latin America, fell below the world mean (Bhagwati, 1966, fig. 1). Thus, the implication of the Bowman–Anderson finding is that any attempt on the part of poor countries to exceed the world mean *per capita* GNP of $200 must be accompanied by efforts to raise the average literacy rate above 40 per cent. But even a *per capita* GNP of $300 still leaves a country relatively underdeveloped: incomes per head of about $300 were attained in 1950 by such countries as Rumania, British Guiana, Costa Rica and Malaya. Where incomes exceed $300 per head, Bowman and Anderson showed that literacy does not always cure poverty, although apparently affluence always eradicates illiteracy. In short, the popular notion that literacy is the sure way to attain development is a fallacy, but like all popular notions it contains a grain of truth.

The problem might be attacked in another way by asking whether we can learn anything from the history of the now developed countries. What was the literacy rate in England in 1800, when she had already achieved a standard of living that would be envied today throughout Africa and Asia? What was it in 1850, when she had passed through the Industrial Revolution and had become 'the workshop of the world'? The standard view of historians – generalizing from a variety of data around 1840 about the ability to sign the marriage register, subscriptions to working-class newspapers, sales of books, attendance rates at Sunday schools and evening institutes, and so forth – is that between 65 and 75 per cent of the British working class had by then achieved rudimentary literacy (Cipolla, 1969, pp. 77–80; West, 1965, pp. 128–35). There are no quantitative estimates for earlier years, but we are left with a general impression from knowledge of reading habits and newspaper circulation in eighteenth-century Britain that literacy rates of 65 to 75 per cent may have been more or less achieved as early as 1800.[1] This leaves us none the wiser, of course, with respect to causation. Did Britain's Industrial Revolution raise literacy standards or did increased literacy in earlier centuries promote industrialization? Still, it is a striking fact that apparently no major industrial power has ever achieved steady economic growth with a literacy rate of less than 40 per cent. Indeed, after a review of the historical evidence for the major developed countries like Britain, the United States, France and Tsarist Russia, Anderson concluded that a 40 per cent literacy rate may be regarded as a general threshold level for economic development (Anderson, 1965a; Kahan, 1965b). Therefore, if we believe that we can learn from history, we may tentatively conclude that a 40 per cent literacy rate is a necessary but of course not a sufficient condition for rapid economic advance. A closely related finding tells us that the same thing is true of a 10 per cent primary school enrolment rate: in the last 100 years, no country has ever achieved significant economic growth without first enrolling 10 per cent of the total population in primary schools (Peaslee, 1967).

Unfortunately, there are reasons for thinking that in this particular case history may be an unreliable guide. The present literacy threshold level in poor countries may be lower than 40 per cent due to the better technical facilities for oral communication that are available

1. Scotland achieved almost universal literacy, at least in the Lowlands, as early as 1760 (Smout, 1969, pp. 455, 466, 472). It is worth noting that Scotland was unique in the eighteenth century for its national system of education: a law of 1696 decreed that a school should be provided in every parish in the Kingdom and the salary of the teacher met by a tax on local landowners and tenants. Education was not compulsory or free but private and municipal charity provided the fees for some of the children of the poor. Nevertheless, by 1833, when England took the first feeble step towards a public educational system, more Scottish children attended fee-paying private schools than publicly financed and charity day schools and the proportion of the age group six to fourteen enrolled in all schools was virtually identical in Scotland and England (Smout, 1969, pp. 449–52).

in the modern world. On the other hand, it may be higher owing to the demands of the more complex technology of the twentieth century. It is difficult to sustain the view that these two opposite considerations exactly cancel out, leaving us where we were before we invoked the Muse of History. But we can still take refuge in the cross-sectional evidence that a 40 per cent literacy or a 10 per cent primary-school enrolment rate does mark a turning point in a country's development.

We need to keep in mind, however, the difference between rudimentary literacy as recorded by national census statistics and functional literacy, which is what really matters for economic activity (see below Chapter 8, p. 260). When it is realized that the cross-sectional data we have just considered includes some countries like India where the census schedule defines a person as literate when he replies affirmatively to the question 'Can you read and write?', and other countries like Ceylon where literacy is defined as the ability to write a short letter and to read the reply to it (UNESCO, 1961, ch. 3), all confidence in even the limited results that have so far been established tends to vanish.

Levels of adult literacy indicate the minimum educational accomplishments of a population. Enrolments of students in post-primary schooling as a percentage of the total population, on the other hand, measure adult educational levels only to the extent that they are correlated with similar enrolments of an earlier generation. Bowman and Anderson go on to show that literacy and post-primary enrolment rates are positively but not highly correlated around the world and that there are even striking exceptions to the positive correlation: Egypt, Jordan and India, for example. The correlation between post-primary enrolment rates in 1950 and GNP per head in 1955 was low and deteriorated when countries with literacy rates as high as 90 per cent or more were excluded. As a matter of fact, literacy alone proved a considerably better predictor of incomes per head, both in this range and for all countries (Bowman and Anderson, 1963, figs. 4–6).

The most striking of their results, however, emerged when they regressed 1955 GNP per head on the percentage of the population aged 5–14 who were in primary schools in 1930, and then reversed the argument by relating both 1930 and 1950 primary enrolments to 1938 and 1955 *per capita* incomes. The investment hypothesis that education causes income x years later was *not* upheld: 1938 incomes predict 1950 education of children remarkably well for all countries and even more remarkably when countries with better than 90 per cent literacy rates are excluded (Bowman and Anderson, 1963, table 3). Of course, incomes over time are serially correlated and it is true that 1938 income predicts 1950 income better than does any index of education. Nevertheless, changes in primary enrolments from 1930 to 1950 and changes in *per capita* incomes from 1938 to 1955 were not highly correlated, thus casting further doubt on the idea that the former produces the latter. Besides, 1950 enrolments cannot produce 1950 incomes. In short, the evidence seems to show that the causal chain runs from income to education and not vice versa.

When 1955 *per capita* GNP was replaced by 1950 *per capita* energy consumption and the tests re-run, the findings were unaffected, indicating that they do not depend sensitively on how economic growth is actually measured. When the relations were re-examined on a continental basis, it turned out, much as one might have expected, that both 1950 literacy rate and 1950 post-primary enrolments were barely associated with 1955 incomes in Europe, even when the U.S.A. and some of the richer Commonwealth countries were included; in Latin America, 1930 primary enrolments were the poorest predictors of incomes, while literacy rates predicted much better; in Africa, low literacy and low income were highly correlated but there was little association between primary or post-primary enrolments and income; and Asia was so heterogeneous that almost nothing can be said that is both general and brief.

It is perfectly evident from all this that the relationship between education and economic growth may be quite different in one time and place from another, and that the causal forces are not always in the same direction. Since Bowman and Anderson's pioneering paper, far more complicated correlations between education and GNP have been tested which have not, however, brought us very much further. Kaser (1966) has pooled both time series going back to 1850 and cross-section observations for a dozen industrialized countries of real GNP per head and five different educational indicators: (a) enrolment rates for three levels of education; (b) the ratio of students in secondary and higher education to primary school children; (c) the pupil/teacher ratio; (d) total money outlays per student in all three levels; and (e) teachers' salaries as a proportion of GNP per head at current prices. Taking explicit account of the time lag between the modal age of students and the average age of entry into the labour force, Kaser concludes that, at similar levels of GNP per head, the more children there are now at school, the higher the rate of growth of GNP during the following decade. Furthermore, neither outlays per student nor teachers' salaries are clearly associated with *levels* of GNP (Kaser, 1966, pp. 117, 123).

However, even these results are hedged about with considerable qualifications and are undermined by the fact that GNP is being compared between countries on the basis of official exchange rates instead of purchasing power parity ratios. Furthermore, changes in the age of distribution of the school population through time throw doubt on the use in this sort of comparison of *enrolment ratios* (the ratio of students to total population): the proportion of the relevant age group enrolled in schools (*enrolment rates*) would have been a preferable indicator of the quantity of education provided.[2] But much more significant than any of these technical objections is the argument that a conclusive test of the causal influences of education on GNP calls, not for figures on the amount of education currently provided to students, but for data on the stock of education embodied in the labour force and the rate of increase of this stock. The link between the enrolments of today and the educated workers of tomorrow is so remote and involves so many other intervening variables that striking conclusions can hardly be expected from even lagged correlations between student enrolments and GNP.

One difficulty with the international comparisons reviewed so far is that they treat education as if it were only distinguished by levels and never by types. However, Bennett (1967) has recently investigated the relationship between vocational and general secondary education in the development process. Drawing on 1955–6 data for secondary schools in sixty-nine countries (excluding the whole of Africa), and defining 'vocational education' as any course of study closely geared to particular occupations in which a large part of the curriculum is devoted to learning specific skills, and 'general education' as everything else, he found that economic variables were generally more highly correlated (rank-order correlations this time) with vocational than with academic schooling. The economic variables in question were GNP per head, calories per day per head and gross energy consump-

2. The reader is warned that this terminological distinction is not standard in the literature. We will, however, adhere to it throughout this book.

tion per head, all defined for 1960. Even more interesting was the finding that the correlation between economic indicators and secondary vocational education, when broken down by regions, was actually negative for the industrialized nations of North America and Europe; high positive correlations were found only for Asia, the Middle East and Latin America, that is, for the least developed nations.

When the *ratio* of vocational to general secondary education (VE/GE) is graphed against GNP per head, the observations fall around a curve that looks almost like a normal distribution, the 'mean' being a GNP per head of $500 (Bennett, 1967, fig. 1). In other words, the vocational–academic mix of secondary education is highly related to economic development, but in such a way that it increases up to a certain point in the development process (roughly indicated by a GNP per head of $500) and then declines again. This is cross-sectional evidence, but the finding is upheld for time series. For about half of the countries in his sample, Bennett found time series going back to 1940 which showed that nations with *per capita* GNPs of less than $500 in 1965 had consistently improved the proportion of vocational education in the secondary education mix over the sixteen-year period; similarly, in nations with GNPs per head of more than $500, VE/GE had either declined or remained roughly the same between 1940 and 1956 (Bennett, 1967, table 4).

The upshot of this study is to throw light on the low correlations that are usually obtained between secondary education and indicators of economic development.If Bennett's results are taken at face value, it is the heterogeneous character of secondary education that inhibits the emergence of meaningful relationships; when we distinguish between types of secondary education, we do obtain significant results. Clearly, there is a lesson here for practitioners of the international-comparisons approach: higher education is no less heterogeneous than secondary education and there too further disaggregation might reveal hitherto concealed patterns.

We have saved for the last the most famous of all these kinds of international comparisons – the Harbison–Myers Composite Index of Levels of Human Resource Development. In a sense, it deserves its fame for it embodies virtually every mistake that it is possible to make in international comparisons of income and education.

Harbison and Myers (1964, ch. 3*) begin by collecting data on primary, secondary and tertiary enrolment rates for seventy-five countries in 1960 or thereabouts. They then combine these into a single weighted enrolment rate which they misleadingly call the 'Composite Index of Human Resource Development'. The weights themselves are selected in an entirely arbitrary and intuitive way. The primary enrolment rate turned out to be poorly correlated with GNP per head, so it was discarded; asserting blandly that 'higher education should be weighted *more* heavily than second-level' (Harbison and Myers, 1964, p. 32*), the authors leap without any explanation whatever to the conclusion that 1 and 5 constitute suitable weights for secondary and tertiary education respectively. In other words, using mnemonic letters for the enrolment rates, the Composite Index of Human Resource Development $= 1S + 5T$. The ultimate justification for this procedure is the triumphant discovery that this particular index is highly correlated with GNP *per capita* ($r^2 = 0.789$).

Having ranked the seventy-five countries according to the Composite Index (ranging from 0.3 for Niger to 261.3 for the USA), the authors then divide the countries into four levels or stages of development, using once again entirely arbitrary cut-off points. Although they note that 'the distinction between countries is better described as a gradient or slope (than as a series of sharply defined steps)' (Harbison and Myers, 1964, p. 32*), they spend the rest of the book doling out blueprints for 'optimal man-power strategies' appropriate to each of the four levels, as if these corresponded to well-defined stages of educational development.

Now and then – twice in 223 pages as a matter of fact – there is a warning that correlation is not causation, but most of the time we read comments such as these:

A rough estimate for the average level I country which seeks in ten to twenty years to reach the average development of level II might be the following: According to table 2 in chapter 3 [a table of the arithmetic means of eight measures of 'human resource development', including the Composite Index], it would try to double its GNP *per capita*, to double its primary enrolment ratio, to increase its secondary enrolment ratio about four and a half times, and to increase its higher education enrolment ten times (Harbison and Myers, 1964, p. 72).

Clearly, the authors believe that a cross-section correlation between current educational efforts and current GNP establishes the causal influence of education on income, or, in other words, that children in school determine GNP (Bowman, 1966a*; Rado, 1966). The book contains some pertinent advice on man-power policies in poor countries but the advice is unrelated to the Composite Index of enrolments, which is simply a red herring calculated to mislead readers into thinking that there are definite stages of educational development much like Rostow's stages of economic growth.[3]

Amusingly enough, even the high correlation between the Composite Index and GNP per head turns out to be a spurious finding. If we go back to the Harbison–Myers weights for combining secondary and tertiary enrolments, namely, one and five, and ask what system of weights would maximize the correlation coefficient between the Composite Index and GNP per head, it turns out that weights of one and 5·9 in fact do so (Sen, 1966, p. 70*).[4] Harbison and Myers do not explain how they came to choose their particular weights. We are, therefore, free to infer that some such calculation as the one just mentioned influenced them in selecting weights one and five.

3. Adelman and Morris (1967, p. 124; also 1968, pp. 1195, 1208) have extended the Harbison–Myers Composite Index to seventy-four underdeveloped countries, interpreting it however as an index of 'the rate of improvement in human resources ... rather than an average of the related stocks of education'. They incorporate it uncritically into a 'factor analysis' of forty-one indicators of socio-political and economic development, but their conclusions about development policies hardly make reference to it.

4. To be precise, the regression (without a constant term of GNP per head (Y/P) on secondary (S) and tertiary (T) enrolment rates which maximizes r^2 is

$$Y/P = 8·41S + 49·19T \quad (R^2 = 0·771)$$
$$\quad\quad (4·6) \quad\quad (5·3)$$

which gives weights in the ratio 1:5·9. One slightly disturbing aspect of this result that Harbison and Myers appear to have done even better than this ($r^2 = 0·789$), possibly because of rounding errors or because of errors in calculating the Composite Index (see Nyasaland and Saudi Arabia in Harbison and Myers, 1964, table 5, p. 45*). If we include primary (P) enrolments in the calculation, the regression (still without a constant term) becomes

$$Y/P = -0·83P + 7·39S + 48·38T \quad (R^2 = 0·774)$$
$$\quad\quad (0·85) \quad\quad (3·4) \quad\quad (5·2)$$

which gives the weights in the ratio 1:9:60. Thus, the introduction of P changes the ratio between S and T. Still further changes, including a negative weight for secondary education, are created by calculating the regression separately for each of the four Harbison–Myers levels, but perhaps enough has now been said to cast some doubt on the Composite Index. (The calculations in this footnote were kindly prepared for me by J. Bibby of the Higher Education Research Unit at the London School of Economics.)

International Comparisons of Income and Education of the Labour Force

After all this, it comes as a great surprise to learn that there *is* a significant relationship between incomes per head in different countries and the proportion of highly educated people in the labour force. This is a much stronger test of the hypothesis that education is investment than that provided by correlations between income and enrolments, inasmuch as labour force participation rates differ significantly between countries. A strong cross-section correlation between income and the stock of educated man power is difficult to explain by the idea that education is consumption because income today can at best generate enrolments today which will not furnish educated man power until so many years later. It must be conceded, however, that even this difficulty is not fatal to the notion that education is demanded as a consumption good, since income is almost always positively 'serially correlated', that is, correlated with itself through time. Nevertheless, this sort of evidence does come closer to testing the hypothesis that education is at least in part investment.

What we are after is something like a one-variable 'production function', a regression of income per head on stocks of man power characterized by their educational attainment. But for reasons that will become apparent as we go along, most of the work in this area has started at the other end, estimating what are in effect naïve 'demand equations' for educated labour. The Netherlands Economic Institute, for example, ran the following regressions on 1957 data for different countries:

$$N^3 = \alpha_1 \, (Y)^{\beta_1} \left(\frac{Y}{P}\right)^2 + u$$

$$N^2 = \alpha_2 \, (Y)^{\beta_2} \left(\frac{Y}{P}\right)^2 + u$$

where $\quad N^3 =$ third-level educated man power in the labour force, that is, the economically active population who have completed higher education,

$\quad N^2 =$ second-level educated man power in the labour force, that is those who have completed secondary education,

Y = national income in millions of U.S. dollars in 1957 prices,

P = population,

u = residual and

α_1, α_2, β_1 and β_2 = constants to be estimated.

They found only twenty-three countries for which this kind of evidence is available, about half of which are poor countries. Be that as it may, the least-square regression produced the following estimates (Netherlands Economic Institute, 1966a, p. 61):[5]

$$N^3 = 5\cdot20\,Y^{1\cdot202} \left(\frac{Y}{P}\right)^{-0\cdot164} \quad (R^2 = 0\cdot845) \tag{1}$$

$$N^2 = 163\cdot67\,Y^{1\cdot314} \left(\frac{Y}{P}\right)^{-0\cdot655} \quad (R^2 = 0\cdot857) \tag{2}$$

Equation 1 can be rewritten as:

$$N^3 = 5\cdot20\,Y^{1\cdot202-0\cdot164}\,P^{0\cdot164}$$
$$= 5\cdot20\,Y^{1\cdot038}\,P^{0\cdot164}$$

and, similarly, for equation 2:

$$N^2 = 163\cdot67\;Y^{0\cdot659}\,P^{0\cdot655}.$$

If we treat cross-section estimates 1 and 2 *as if* they were time series, we can take logarithms of N, Y and P and differentiate these with respect to time.

Writing $\dot{X} = \dfrac{1}{X}\dfrac{dX}{dt}$

for the growth rate per unit of time of any variable X, we get

$$\dot{N}^3 = 1\cdot038\,\dot{Y} + 0\cdot164\dot{P} \tag{3}$$

$$\dot{N}^2 = 0\cdot659\,\dot{Y} + 0\cdot655\dot{P}. \tag{4}$$

5. Slightly different equations are estimated and reported in greater detail in an accompanying document (Netherlands Economic Institute, 1966b).

In other words, a 1 per cent increase in national income tends to be associated with a 1·038 per cent increase in third-level and a 0·659 per cent increase in second-level man-power stocks, while the corresponding population elasticities are 0·164 and 0·655 respectively.

Having produced these findings, the Netherlands Economic Institute moved without further ado to the conclusion that the number of university graduates in active employment, and other professional men whose work requires a college degree or its equivalent, 'should' grow at just about the same rate as national income, while likewise the numbers of secondary-school graduates 'should' grow at about two-thirds the rate of national income. This daring *non sequitur* has had an enormous influence on educational planning in many poor countries. Inspired by the example of the Institute, who employed regressions **1** and **2** to make forecasts of 'man-power requirements' for Africa, Asia and Latin America up to 1975, educational planners the world over have eagerly leaped from the established fact that $\dot{N}^3/\dot{Y} = 1·038$ and $\dot{N}^2/\dot{Y} = 0·659$ to the idea that such numbers provide firm guides to policy (see below Chapter 5, p. 150).

This extremely simple 'theory of educational planning' has a short but notorious history. One of the first educational plans for an under-developed country that was based on the man-power forecasting approach, namely the *Ashby Report* (1960) on Nigeria, employed an empirical rule-of-thumb invented by Harbison: N^3 should grow twice as fast and N^2 three times as fast as GNP. What the Harbison rule implies is that for the next decade or two the ratio of the absolute stock of educated man power to absolute national income does not matter: all that counts is their rates of growth. No rationale and certainly no international comparative evidence was ever published, either by Harbison or by anyone else, to justify the famous 2:1 and 3:1 ratios, and, as we have just seen, the best evidence is that the actual ratios in different countries are nearer 1:1 and $\frac{2}{3}$:1.[6]

The fundamental point, however, is that regressions **1** and **2** represent the outcome of the intersection of a series of demand and supply schedules and not the demand for N^3 or N^2 in the economist's sense of the term 'demand', nor even the stocks of educated man power 'required' in a purely technical sense to produce a given level or rate of growth of national income. In the jargon of econometrics, the

6. Even from a purely theoretical point of view, the Harbison rule-of-thumb makes little sense; see Rado and Jolly (1965, pp. 80–84)*.

demand for N is not 'identified' and the equations represent 'reduced forms' of a more general simultaneous system of demand and supply equations. Therefore, although we may interpret equations 1 and 2 as indicating *feasible* paths of growth of N^2 and N^3 for given rates of growth of national income, in the sense of having been attained by some countries, they are far from specifying *optimal* rates of growth, which is presumably what we are after in educational planning. They can tell the educational planner 'what is' or 'what has been' but they cannot by themselves tell him 'what should be'.

Caveats aside, the finding that the incremental labour–output ratio (ILOR) for tertiary educated turns out to be close to unity appears to be one of the more robust results in the area of international comparisons. It is true even of third-level educated teachers considered separately, as well as of qualified scientists and engineers (Netherlands Economic Institute, 1966b, pp. 29, 31). We will meet it again when we begin to cross-classify the labour force by sectors and occupations. Indeed, the importance of regressions 1 and 2 in educational planning justifies a special label: hereafter we will refer to these as *Tinbergen Regressions* after Tinbergen, the now retired Director of the Netherlands Economic Institute.

We turn now to international comparisons of education and income per head disaggregated to individual sectors of the economy and individual occupations within sectors. For practical reasons, these types of studies are just as likely to regress output on education as education on output: they may attempt to explain output per worker in a given industry by the education-cum-occupational composition of the work force in that industry, rather than the educational–occupational mix by the value added per worker employed.

We look first at a pioneering study that actually stopped short of translating occupation into education; nevertheless, it deserves mention for its careful collection of 1960 data for fifty-eight industries in twenty-six countries and for its characteristic approach to the task at hand (Horowitz, Zymelman and Herrnstadt, 1966). The aim of this study was to provide a reliable cross-section measure of the relationship between the average productivity of labour (output per man) in an industry and its occupational composition, for purposes of facilitating 'man-power projections' in underdeveloped countries. Thus, the authors estimated a linear regression of value added per worker in different industries on the proportions of workers in five occupational categories: (a) professional and technical workers, (b) administrators and managers, (c) clerical workers, (d) sales workers and (e) manual workers. They obtain values of R^2 (the coefficient of multiple determination) ranging from a minimum of 0·306 for electrical machinery to a maximum of 0·880 for lumber and wood products, and fail to produce a single industry in which all the regression coefficients are significant at the 95 per cent confidence level. In many cases, only two out of the five occupational groupings yielded significant coefficients and the others are simply dropped (Horowitz, Zymelman and Herrnstadt, 1966, vol. 1, tables 3, 4). Undismayed by these results, the authors conclude:

These tables show that variations in productivity can be explained by differences in occupational structures; that variations in the proportion of professional and technical workers are a major determinant of productivity in almost every industry [because the coefficient of this explanatory variable almost always has a higher value than of any other]; and that the importance of other groups vary from industry to industry.... The results of these correlations clearly indicate that the data of the tables ... can be used to project future man-power requirements (Horowitz, Zymelman and Herrnstadt, 1966, vol. 1, pp. 33, 38).

After this it may be truly said: the sins of the transgressor are as nothing next to the sins of the regressor! But even if their results had been statistically impeccable, there would be questions to raise about their central conclusion.

After an excellent criticism of official occupational classifications on the grounds that they group traditional job titles by products or processes rather than by skill levels or work content, they opt in the end for the very same census categories (Horowitz, Zymelman and Herrnstadt, 1966, pp. 12–19). But if the skills required by occupations remain undefined or are mis-specified, what sense is there in talking of the 'man-power requirements' of certain 'occupations'?

We are moving ahead of our story, however. We will take up the pitfalls in occupational classifications in a later chapter (see below Chapter 5, p. 153). Here we are concerned simply with the relationship between income or output and education, as mediated by the occupational composition of the labour force, with a view to testing the hypothesis that education contributes to economic growth.

We come now to an analysis by Layard and Saigal (1966) which postulates the dependence of the occupational composition of the labour force on the sectoral productivity of labour, almost the exact reverse of the Horowitz study just considered (not quite, because it looks at sectors rather than industries); furthermore, it takes explicit account of the amount of education associated with occupations. The argument is conducted in three stages, namely, (a) the occupational structure of economic sectors, (b) the structure of educational attainments of occupations and (c) the educational structure of economic sectors.

The corresponding equations that were fitted in log-linear form are:

$$\frac{L_{jk}}{L_j} = a_1 \left(\frac{X_j}{L_j}\right)^{b_1} \qquad\qquad 5$$

$$\frac{L_{ik}}{L_k} = a_2 \left(\frac{X}{L}\right)^{b_2} \qquad\qquad 6a$$

$$M_k = a_3 \left(\frac{X}{L}\right)^{b_3} \qquad\qquad 6b$$

$$\frac{L_{ij}}{L_j} = a_4 \left(\frac{X_j}{L_j}\right)^{b_4} \qquad\qquad 7a$$

$$M_j = a_5 \left(\frac{X_j}{L_j}\right)^{b_5} \qquad\qquad 7b$$

where X = net output in U.S. dollars in 1960 prices,

L = labour force,

M = mean (or median) years of education,

$i = 1 \ldots n$ refers to educational category,

$j = 1 \ldots m$ refers to economic sector,

$k = 1 \ldots t$ refers to occupation, and

s and bs = constants to be estimated.

What do these equations mean? Consider **6a**: it says that the percentage of workers in the kth occupation who have education to the ith level is determined by the average productivity of labour in the whole economy. Similarly, equation **7b** says that the average years of education embodied in the labour force of a particular sector is determined by the average productivity of labour in that sector. It is immediately obvious that these Layard–Saigal equations are disaggregated and extended versions of the Tinbergen Regressions considered earlier.

Layard and Saigal look separately at eight one-digit sectors, nine one-digit occupations as well as some two-digit occupational groups, and two different measures of educational attainment over thirty countries around the year 1960. Their purpose is once again to serve the needs of man-power planning by providing reliable estimates of the *b*-coefficients. As they put it:

> The most interesting statistic wanted by the man-power planner from a study of this kind is the coefficient *b* which indicates the proportionate change in L_i/L (or L_k/L) associated with a unit proportionate change in X/L (for small changes in X/L). Or, to use the language of growth rates, he wants to know the growth rate for each L_i/L if X/L is expected to grow by *y* per cent per year (Layard and Saigal, 1966, p. 240).

Their results can be summed up in the same order as the three stages of their argument.

Firstly, the relationship between occupational structure and output per worker *in the whole economy* is strongest for professional occupations ($r^2 = 0.83$) and weakest for sales workers ($r^2 = 0.25$), with administrative and managerial workers falling in between ($r^2 = 0.58$). The values of *b* are just over half for professional and clerical occupations, slightly higher for administrative occupations and never significantly exceed unity for any occupation. One might have expected stronger relationships within sectors than for the economy as a whole. But, on the contrary, the sectoral relationships yield much lower squared correlation coefficients than are obtained in the aggregate comparisons. In general, the results for regression **5** are as uneven as those obtained in the Horowitz study which, however, tested the inverse of the relationship in question on the industry level.

Passing over the sea of diverse sectoral elasticities or *b*-coefficients, we turn to the question of the educational structure of occupations, equations **6a** and **6b**. In general, there is a tendency for the educational levels of occupations to rise with output per worker. For most occupations the pattern is rather indistinct but for sales workers it is well defined at each educational level. Figure 7 conveys the Layard–Saigal

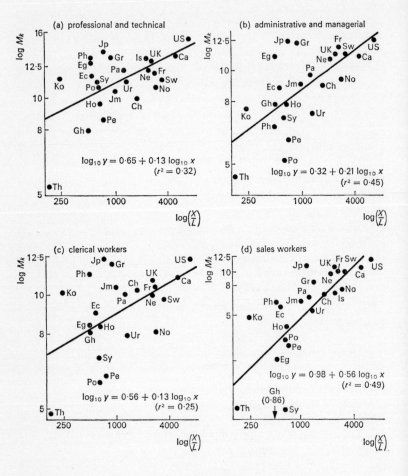

Figure 7   Mean years of schooling of specified occupation groups
Key to country abbreviations

Argentina	Ar	Korea (Republic of)	Ko
Canada	Ca	Mexico	Me
Chile	Ch	Netherlands	Ne
Costa Rica	Co	Norway	No
Ecuador	Ec	Panama	Pa
Egypt (U.A.R.)	Eg	Peru	Pe
Finland	Fi	Philippines	Ph
France	Fr	Portugal	Po

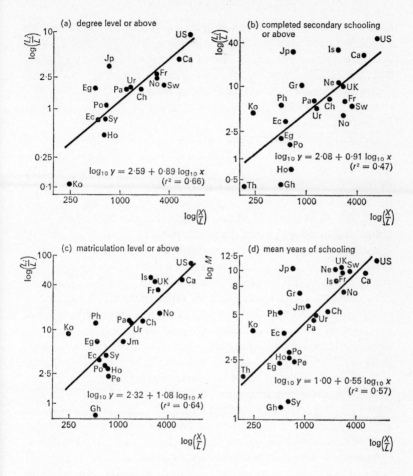

Figure 8 Educational levels; the whole economy
Key to country abbreviations

Ghana	Gh	Sweden	Sw
Greece	Gr	Syria	Sy
Honduras	Ho	Thailand	Th
India	In	Turkey	Tu
Israel	Is	United Kingdom	UK
Jamaica	Jm	United States	US
Japan	Jp	Uruguay	Ur

Note: The *y* and *x* in the reported regression equations refer to the corresponding ordinate and abscissa values

TEOE–D

results for mean years of schooling better than words can. It will be seen that the average schooling of administrative and clerical workers is in all countries lower than that of professional workers and, likewise, the average schooling of sales workers is in all cases lower than that of all other non-manual occupations. Notice also that the b-coefficient for sales workers (0·56) exceeds that for all other occupational groups.

Lastly, we have equations **7a** and **7b** – the educational structure of economic sectors. The results here are distinctly unimpressive: if the sectors are ranked according to the amount of variance 'explained', the first are commerce and agriculture followed by manufacturing – the same three as with the regressions for occupational structure. It will be noticed that the first three panels of Figure 8 refer to 'educational level or above', while the fourth panel refers to mean years of schooling. It is apparent from mere inspection that these two ways of measuring educational attainment do not give the same result. Indeed, one of the most interesting by-products of the Layard–Saigal study is to show that one always obtains different results, whether for occupations, sectors or the economy as a whole, when education is measured in terms of cumulative frequencies (people having more than stated levels of education) rather than in terms of mean or median years of schooling. For most purposes, the man-power planner needs to know the minimum stock of people that have completed each level, that is, the cumulative frequencies of workers with at least x years of schooling. But analyses involving cumulative frequencies throw no light on the question of substitution between workers with different levels of education, which is frequently the inspiration for international comparisons. Thus, Layard and Saigal carried out their analysis in terms of two measures: percentages of workers having attained more than particular levels of education and average years of schooling. The contrast in the results one obtains can be substantial: for an admittedly extreme example, Layard and Saigal obtain the following estimates for the educational structure of occupations in sales:

$$\frac{L_{ik}}{L_k} = 0·0015 \left(\frac{X}{L}\right)^{1·09} \quad (r^2 = 0·30),$$

using the cumulative frequency measure of completed secondary education or above, and

$$M_k = 0.105 \left(\frac{X}{L}\right)^{0.56} \quad (r^2 = 0.49),$$

using the measure of mean years of schooling of sales workers.

What are we to make of all this? It would appear that there is a great deal of unexplained variance in the output of educated workers within and between occupations and sectors across different countries, even when due allowance is made for the effect of scale by considering proportions of educated man power rather than absolute numbers. Layard and Saigal (1966, pp. 248–9) frankly concede the limited value of their results for educational planning, but even they can barely suppress their dismay at the bewildering array of r^2s and b-coefficients. They naturally attribute their failure to produce tidy answers to the vagaries of occupational categories, the lack of an internationally accepted method of classifying educational levels and the drawbacks of comparing sectoral outputs at official exchange rates. Clearly, they hoped to obtain more dramatic conclusions than in fact emerged from the analysis. But what indeed are the *a priori* grounds for expecting *any* unique pattern of skill requirements for a given output per worker throughout the world? Their own efforts to formulate a model that would rationalize the dependence of the skill mix of the labour force on a single variable like output per worker, calls for such strong assumptions – a 'putty–clay' theory of investment or fixed capital–labour ratios and a fixed occupational structure for given techniques of production;[7] all countries on the same production function; constant returns to scale; and natural resource endowments randomly distributed around the world – that we are surprised, not that they failed to produce definite answers, but rather that meaningful answers of some kind did in the end emerge.

It is high time that we probed the underlying rationale of these international comparisons. It is none other than the assumption that there are unique 'world man-power growth paths'; in other words,

7. A 'putty–clay' theory of investment conceives of capital as putty in choosing a particular technique of production, in the sense that it can be combined with labour in a wide variety of patterns depending on relative factor prices. Once a particular technique is chosen, however, the putty turns to clay in that capital now requires a fixed complement of labour skills to produce output. Why a short-run theory of investment such as the 'putty–clay' one should be deemed appropriate to an analysis geared to the needs of long-term man-power planning is indeed the question.

that all economies are on the same growth paths, stipulating definite patterns of the occupational and educational distribution of the labour force, though clearly at different stages on it, and hence that the richer country shows the poorer one where it will be so many years from now. As Hollister (1965) has argued, the conditions that have to be met to validate the existence of this concept are so stringent that it seems highly unlikely to be realized in practice. Even if we concede that there is no reason why a given level of national income in an economy should be associated with a particular distribution of output between sectors and industries, and so much seems to be admitted by those who study the problem at the sector or industry level, there is evidence to suggest that the productivity of labour and hence employment in a sector varies with the past rate of growth of output of a sector; even when the same sectors in different countries have the same *level* of output, employment will be lower in the rapidly growing ones.

Furthermore, the occupational distribution of the labour force in the sector will change in relation to the relative supplies of skills: an increase in the relative supply of a particular skill will tend to lower its relative price and thus bring about either (a) the substitution of the skill in question for other more expensive skills, or (b) the substitution of human skills of all kinds for capital equipment, or (c) a change in the product mix in the direction of goods using more of the cheaper skill, or, when all these changes are precluded, (d) an increase in the volume of output. What actually happens depends on the actual substitution possibilities and on the technical importance of the particular skill in the productive process. If skills are not easily substitutable for one another and if capital tends to combine with labour in fairly rigid proportions, the response is likely to fall entirely on output. Only if skill-substitution is easy will there be a change in the occupational distribution of the labour force. But even if we face the extreme case where the productive structure is rigidly determined by technical conditions independent of relative factor prices, the fact that consumers will be responsive to some extent both to the type of output produced and to its price means that output will either change or increase when one of the inputs has fallen in price. And while there may be few possibilities of substitution for one kind of output and at one level of output, it is going too far to deny substitutability at every kind and level of output. We may conclude, therefore, that the occupational or educational composition of the labour force in a country is always to some extent the outcome of both demand and supply forces. As a matter of fact, the tendency to upgrade the minimal hiring standards for particular jobs when the supply of labour becomes more favourable is one of the best-attested phenomena of the labour market and affords a typical instance of the interaction of supply and demand in creating a given skill mix.

What is true of occupation is true of education. Even if all countries had identical demand schedules for, say, university graduates in professional occupations in manufacturing, simple differences in the scales of different systems of higher education (as a result of differences in incomes per head, subsidies to higher education and variations in 'tastes' for higher education), combined with the pursuit of full employment policies on the part of some national governments, would guarantee differences in the educational structure of the labour force in manufacturing in different countries. And the same argument applies to every kind of educational attainment and to every occupation and sector in turn. There is, therefore, little reason to think that all countries move along the same man-power growth paths, that is, arrive at similar occupational distributions of the sectoral or industrial labour force for identical levels of output per worker.

And why output per *worker*? Business firms care about total-factor productivity: only by maximizing output per unit of *all* inputs can firms minimize cost per unit of output and thus maximize profits. Now it is true that output per worker or the average productivity of labour is easy to measure while total-factor productivity involves the difficult task of measuring capital. But there is nothing in economic theory to suggest that labour productivity is a good proxy for total-factor productivity. Any cross-section comparison would almost certainly reveal wide discrepancies between the two. But even time series, at least for the United States where the necessary statistics are available on the sector level, show that the changes in labour productivity and total-factor productivity in various sectors over time are by no means highly correlated and that, moreover, neither exhibits a simple regular pattern (Hollister, 1965, pp. 98–100). The results of the Horowitz and Layard studies, which did at least include some meaningful relationships between different countries, must therefore be regarded as nearly miraculous, unless of course we take the cynical view that all economic variables are so highly intercorrelated that the regression of any variable on any other always yields a pattern of some kind.

OECD has recently gone one better than Horowitz and Layard, not only by re-running its equations on a much larger body of data (eight one-digit economic sectors, ten two-digit occupations and four levels of education for fifty-three countries), but also by running many more types of equations, making use of additional measures such as energy consumption per worker, gross capital formation (the cumulative sum of gross investment over the last eight years) per worker and composite indicators of 'levels of living'. After an exhaustive, and indeed exhausting, analysis of all its evidence, the OECD writers conclude by contrasting the 'push' factors that originate from the expansion of educational systems with the 'pull' factors that reflect 'requirements' for qualified workers. 'In the vast majority of cases', it notes, 'the influence of the available supply (the "push" factors) strongly prevailed. This should not come as a surprise when it is remembered that no country has ever seriously subordinated the growth of its educational system to strictly economic needs' (OECD, 1970, p. 382, also pp. 248, 307, 310). Like Horowitz and Layard they reach highly uneven and even erratic results but, unlike some previous exponents of the international-comparisons approach, they concede frankly that 'the analyses carried out in this study – both with regard to occupational and educational percentages and to occupational and educational coefficients – strongly suggest that possibilities of partial substitution between different types of labour exist at given levels of economic and technological development. As has already been indicated several times in the course of the analysis, other reasons besides substitution possibilities may exist to explain our findings, but the least one can say is that they cast serious doubts on the complementarity hypotheses usually adopted in man-power forecasts' (OECD, 1970, p. 383, also pp. 150, 266–8, 332).

The question of substitution possibilities is so important that we would do well to reiterate the argument: almost infinite are the variations on the theme of substitution between factors in an economy. Even when different types of labour and capital have to be combined in absolutely rigid proportions at any level of output, the proportions themselves may well be different at different levels of output – the case of non-constant returns to scale. But even if returns to scale are constant in every industry, the so-called 'input coefficients' might differ in different industries; variations over time in the industrial distribution of total output, because of variations in the pattern of demand, will therefore produce substitution between factors across industries. Even if the industrial distribution of total output does not vary over time, however, the list of goods imported and exported might vary; we can still get factor substitution from this source of variation and for many economies this proves to be a significant source of changes in factor proportions for the economy as a whole. Putting it all together, it is not obvious that there is always much scope for substituting different factors for each other in each and every economy; it *is* obvious, however, that there is some scope for substitution in any economy (Bowles, 1969, ch. 3).

International Comparisons of Social and Political Indicators

Just to complicate matters still further, let us now consider some efforts by non-economists to quantify the social and economic impact of education by means of international comparisons. First in line is the attempt by McClelland to demonstrate that better-educated countries do 'grow' faster on average and that the prevalence of the 'achievement motive' in a country adds significantly to the impact of education on economic growth (McClelland, 1966).

McClelland's approach to the problem is highly idiosyncratic. First of all, he rejects national income as an index of economic growth and replaces it by electricity consumption (the two are of course highly but by no means perfectly correlated). Secondly, he rejects the use of percentage increases as a measure of growth, because percentage changes are often negatively correlated with starting levels, and instead defines growth in terms of a regression of the absolute increase in electricity consumption between 1952 and 1958 on the initial level of electricity consumption in 1952. Thus, if actual electricity consumption exceeds that indicated by the fitted regression equation, this is interpreted as a high rate of growth and vice versa. It is as if growth meant 'doing better than could have been expected from a country of that size'. A diagram may clarify this procedure. Defining the annual absolute gain in electricity consumption per head between 1952 and 1958 as $(e_t - e_o)$ and the *per capita* consumption of electricity in 1950 as e_o, he regresses the former on the latter and obtains: $(e_t - e_o)$ measured in kWh $= 147 + 1 \cdot 01 e_o$. Countries above this line have positive growth rates; countries below the line have negative growth rates. After this it comes as no surprise to learn that McClelland is a psychologist.

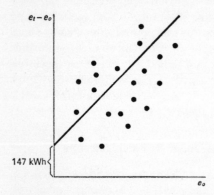

Figure 9

McClelland purports to show that economic (= electrical) growth over the years 1952 to 1958 was influenced by the amount of secondary education in the 1930s. He measures secondary education by a ratio: cumulating the total numbers enrolled between the sixth years of education and the year of entry into higher education for each year from 1930 to 1939, he divides the resulting sum by the total population in 1950. The notion is that the secondary education of the 1930s would have borne fruit by 1950. He now divides his list of twenty-eight countries into four groups in terms of 1950 levels of electricity production (having first eliminated a number of very small countries and all tropical countries because 'climate and the different diurnal distribution of light and dark might make the electricity measure less valid for such countries') and defines a country as more or less educated 'depending on whether it is above or below the median in years of secondary schooling per 1000 inhabitants *within a group of countries* roughly at the same economic level' (McClelland, 1966, p. 265). After this double piece of legerdemain, we are ready for anything, including the finding that the better-educated countries in 1950 grew faster in the next decade than the less-educated ones (McClelland, 1966, p. 266).

When it is realized that McClelland's method of measuring growth inhibits a comparison between the growth performance of England

and France, since these two do not belong to the same electricity group, while his measure of education attributes a greater relative stock of secondary-educated adults in 1950 to England than to the United States (McClelland, 1966, table 1), we shall lose no sleep pondering his results. Similar remarks pertain to the more interesting part of his work in which he attempts to show that while 'need achievement' (see above Chapter 2, p. 35), is not significantly related to secondary education, countries which are high in both 'need achievement' and stocks of educated man power nevertheless grow significantly faster in subsequent time periods than countries which are high in only one of the two factors. The statistical procedure is once again so indirect that his results simply cannot be interpreted: it remains measurement without theory. It is probably true that need achievement is a specific type of motivation involving a strong inner drive to excel (an important ingredient of what is otherwise known as the Protestant Ethic) and that McClelland and his associates have, in fact, succeeded in measuring it by means of thematic apperception tests. It is also probably true that the presence of this motivation in certain societies, fostered as it is by definite patterns of child rearing and family life, has much to do with the phenomenon of economic growth. But this is not to say that McClelland has established the case that societies with high levels of measured 'need achievement' grow faster (see Schatz, 1965, for a devastating critique), nor that 'need achievement' somehow increases the economic returns from education.

We turn now to a less bizarre interdisciplinary effort employing the simple correlation approach. Noting that some forms of education are more conducive to development than others, and that historically education has more frequently stunted rather than promoted the capacity for social change owing to its associations with the outlook of ruling élites, Curle (1964a) constructed a sample of fifty-seven countries for which he collected a variety of economic, educational and political data around the year 1958. Altogether he marshalled evidence on ten indicators: (a) domestic fixed capital formation as a percentage of GNP, (b) public expenditures on education as a percentage of national income, (c) the infant mortality rate, (d) rank orders of *per capita* GNP, (e) rank orders of the rate of growth of GNP 1954–9, (f) rank orders of the post-primary enrolment rate, (g) the nature of the 'political system', and (h), (i) and (j) as the rank orders of (a), (b) and (c).

Most of Curle's results are as expected: high rank order correlations between educational expenditures as a proportion of national income, on the one hand, and both *per capita* GNP and post-primary enrolments, on the other; likewise, high correlations between rank orders of domestic savings and post-primary enrolments, but no significant correlations even at the 5 per cent level between any of the two educational variables and economic growth in the previous five years. The results we want to emphasize, however, have to do with the connexions between 'political development' and the other economic and educational variables. Adopting the ratings by Almond and Coleman (1960) to discriminate between competitive, semi-competitive, and authoritarian political systems, Curle ran chi-square tests on the relationships between competitive systems and savings, infant mortality rates and expenditures on education. All of these, with the possible exception of the first, proved to be highly significant, suggesting that competitive forms of government are associated with greater degrees of development and with greater expenditures on education. Going one step further, Curle divided the independent countries of Africa, Asia and Latin America into two groups, egalitarian and non-egalitarian, depending on whether the country in question has a relatively open or a relatively selective system of secondary and higher education (the criteria are not explained and are presumably based on judgement)[8]. He found that egalitarian countries generally achieved higher *per capita* income and invariably both higher *per capita* expenditures on education and higher post-primary enrolment rates, concluding that commitment to egalitarian principles is a significant independent factor in a country's educational efforts (Curle, 1964a, pp. 232–3).

Lack of space prevents consideration of some of his other fascinating findings but the main implication of our précis is already self-evident: if we really want to use international comparisons to throw light on the relations between income and education, we cannot afford to ignore psychological and political variables which appear to have some explanatory power, and certainly not much less power than the output and income variables which figure so heavily in the writings of economists.

8. In Africa, for example, he grouped Egypt, Ghana, Guinea, Nigeria and Tunisia together as egalitarian and Angola, Ethiopia, Liberia, South Africa and Southern Rhodesia as non-egalitarian (Curle, 1964a, table 2).

Production Functions and the Quality of Labour

We bring our tour to a close with a study by Denison which was initially addressed to the problem of measuring the contribution of education to American economic growth in recent decades, and which only later came to be used for purposes of making international comparisons between the growth rates of various countries. Furthermore, it differs from all the other studies reviewed in this chapter in that it uses earnings differentials attributable to education as a measure of the economic value of education and in that sense fails to answer the question we posed at the outset of the chapter. Nevertheless, Denison's study is so famous in its own right – its results have been cited more frequently than any other mentioned in this book – that it deserves something like full-scale treatment; it is, after all, the only work in the literature that actually assigns a cardinal number to the contribution of education to national income.

Denison's *magnum opus*, *The Sources of Economic Growth in the United States and the Alternatives before Us*, consists essentially of (a) an *implicit* estimate of the aggregate production function of the American economy with the aid of data for the years 1910 to 1960, and (b) an attempt to resolve 'the residual' that always tends to emerge from statistically fitted aggregate production functions into its constituent elements. One, but only one, of these constituent elements is education and Denison concludes that the diffusion of education in the United States during the period 1930–60 accounted for as much as 23 per cent of the annual growth rate, more in fact than any other single source of growth, except the increase of the labour force itself. The basis of this magical number is step (a) rather than step (b) and we must, therefore, digress a moment on the question of production functions if we are to grasp how Denison actually arrived at his results.[9]

A *production function* defines a boundary in the input–output space, specifying the maximum *physical* output that can be obtained from every possible combination of *physical* inputs, given the existing level of technical knowledge. It assumes, as it were, the solution of an engineering problem before turning to the economic problem of

9. What follows is a very bald summary of some fairly advanced economic theory: for a more detailed explanation, in the historical context in which the ideas arose, see Blaug (1968a, pp. 446–87).

choosing the optimum combination of inputs in response to relative input prices. As relative input prices change, we move along the production function. On the other hand, technical change that raises the productivity of all input combinations is depicted by an upward shift of the function; if the function shifts without changing its basic shape, technical change is 'neutral'.

All economically meaningful production functions are homogeneous functions but homogeneous functions can be of any degree. Among all possible types of homogeneous production functions, economists have always favoured those of the first degree because of their convenient properties such as constant returns to scale. Similarly, among all possible types of first-degree homogeneous production functions, economists have long been fatally enamoured of the so-called Cobb–Douglas production function which not only possesses all the beautiful properties of linearly homogeneous functions but a few additional ones as a pleasant bonus.

A simple two-factor Cobb–Douglas production function takes the following form:

$$Q = AN^\alpha K^\beta$$

where Q = physical output,

N = inputs of labour measured in man hours,

K = inputs of capital measured in machine hours, and

A, α and β = constants to be estimated.

If we write this in logarithmic form, we end up with a log-linear equation:

$$\log Q = \log A + \alpha \log N + \beta \log K$$

which can be estimated from time series observations by ordinary least squares. If A = A(t), A becomes a shift-parameter representing 'technical progress' so-called. α and β, on the other hand, stand for the elasticities of output Q with reference to N and K respectively: they tell us, for every given A, the percentage increase of output that is associated with a 1 per cent increase in the amount of labour and a 1 per cent increase in the amount of capital applied. Surprisingly enough, α and β are more than this: they are also the relative shares of wages and profits in Q, at least if the two productive factors are rewarded in accordance with their marginal products. This means that, once having estimated α and β by the method of least squares, we can ask whether they do in fact add up to unity since relative shares of output must by definition do so. If they do, we have demonstrated that the production function in question is linearly homogeneous and that constant returns to scale prevail.

When α and β do not add up to unity, we can only conclude that factors are not being paid their respective marginal product; indeed, decreasing or increasing returns to scale imply disequilibrium in both product and factor markets and hence violation of the marginal productivity conditions.

If we are talking about an aggregate production function for the economy as a whole and *assume* competitive equilibrium and, there-fore, payments to factors in accordance with marginal productivity, we have already constrained the production function to be linearly homogeneous. In that case, we do not need to estimate α and β but can simply read them off from data on the factor shares of national income, data that are available for any advanced country. Not quite, however: the argument so far refers only to infinitely small changes in N and K along the production function. But the statistics on relative shares involve annual and hence rather large changes, confusing move-ments along the production function with shifts of the production function itself. In order to equate α and β to relative factor shares, we have to place constraints on the character of technical progress. A measure of how relative shares change as we move *along* the produc-tion function is provided by Hicks' 'elasticity of substitution', defined as the percentage change in the ratio of capital to labour employed to produce a given level of output that results from a 1 per cent change in the relative price of labour to capital. For a Cobb–Douglas pro-duction function, this measure is by definition equal to unity, meaning that the relative shares never change along the production function be-cause as the amount of capital increases relative to the amount of labour, its relative price (the rental per machine hour divided by the wage rate per man hour) declines at the same rate. If we now add the condition that technical progress is 'neutral', so that α and β are con-stants through time because the production function never changes shape as it shifts upwards, we can estimate a Cobb–Douglas pro-duction function effortlessly by consulting income accounting data on relative shares. This is the free bonus of which we spoke earlier.

Thus, if one can be persuaded to believe that the aggregate production function of an economy is linearly homogeneous and of the Cobb–Douglas form, and that technical progress is 'neutral', the calculation of the magnitude of technical progress is child's play: if

$$Q = AN^\alpha K^\beta \qquad (\alpha + \beta = 1).$$

Taking logs and differentiating with respect to time, the rate of growth of output is

$$\dot{Q} = \dot{A} + \alpha\dot{N} + \beta\dot{K}.$$

Since α and β are constants, we can interpret $\dot{A}$ as the rate of growth of total-factor productivity or 'technical progress', frequently called 'the residual', namely, that part of the rate of growth of total output that cannot be explained by the growth of labour and capital. For example, for the United States over the period 1929 to 1957,

$\dot{Q} = 2\cdot93$ per cent

$\dot{N} = 1\cdot09$ per cent

$\dot{K} = 0\cdot45$ per cent

$\alpha = 0\cdot73$

$\beta = 0\cdot27$

$\alpha\dot{N} + \beta\dot{K} = 0\cdot92$ per cent

so that $\dot{A} = 2\cdot01$ per cent.

In short, two-thirds of America's growth rate between 1929 and 1957 cannot be explained by a Cobb–Douglas production function.

We are now ready to consider Denison's approach to the 'sources' of economic growth. The unexplained 'residual' $\dot{A}$ is obviously a grab-bag of many dimensions. One of these dimensions is the improved quality of labour and capital: in the course of time, as we apply additional men and machines, the men and the machines somehow become better. One of the ways in which the men get better is that they have more education. Within the context of the Cobb–Douglas growth model, any improvement in the quality of labour is bound to have a much larger effect on national income than improvements in the quality of capital simply because the elasticity of output with respect to labour (α) is so much larger than the elasticity of output with respect to capital (β). In fact, α is roughly three times the value of β, that is, labour receives about three-quarters of national income while capital receives only one-quarter. No wonder then that Denison concludes that education is an important source of growth.

Denison achieves numerical precision in measuring the sources of growth by equating α with the relative share of labour, a procedure which implies a Cobb–Douglas production function and neutral technical progress. But Denison never mentions the concept of a production function in his book, much less the Cobb–Douglas production function and, in fact, attributes about 10 per cent of economic growth in the U.S.A. between 1929 and 1957 to 'economies of scale', thus denying the constant-returns-to-scale property of linearly homogeneous production functions. The truth of the matter is that he can only be said to have *implicitly* estimated an aggregate production function. What he actually did was to construct an index of national product per unit of composite inputs, or in National Bureau language, an index of total-factor productivity ($\dot{A}$). The problem in such an index is how to choose weights to combine the various inputs for purposes of dividing them into an index of output. Economic theory suggests that the appropriate weights are base-year factor prices. Unfortunately, relative factor prices are always changing and hence base-year weights give different answers from end-year weights. It is much easier to use base-year factor shares as weights, since these are fairly stable over relatively long periods of time. At this point, we can appeal to *a priori* reasoning to show that estimates of $\dot{A}$ where inputs are weighted by factor shares gives the same answer as an estimate which weights inputs by relative factor prices, provided the aggregate production function is linearly homogeneous and technical progress is neutral. We have come back full circle: Denison's results do depend on a particular form of the aggregate production function and on particular assumptions about the character of technical progress.

Denison starts with the mean incomes of American males twenty-five years of age or over, taken before tax and classified by age and years of schooling completed, as derived from the *1950 Census of Population*. Next he makes the assumption that three-fifths of the income differentials in column 1 of Table 4 are actually attributable to education (see above Chapter 2, p. 51), from which he derives a new set of differentials shown in column 2 of Table 4.

Table 4

Mean Income Differentials by Years of Schooling Completed, U.S.A., 1950

Years of School Completed		Income as Percentage of Mean Income of Eight Graders	3/5 (col. 1–100)+100
		1	2
None		50	70 (65)
Elementary school:	1–4 years	65	79 (78)
	5–7 years	80	88 (86)
	8 years	100	100 (100)
High school:	1–3 years	115	109 (110)
	4 years	140	124 (126)
College:	1–3 years	165	139 (142)
	4 years or more	235	181 (183)

Source: Denison (1962, table 8).

Note: The figures in brackets in column 2 represent new estimates based on later findings (Denison, 1964).

The new differentials are now applied to the distribution of males by years of schooling completed at various past dates so as to estimate the growth in income that was due solely to the lengthening of education since 1910. That is to say, Denison calculates what the average earnings of males over twenty-five would have been in past years if earnings at each educational level were a constant fraction of actual 1949 earnings of eight graders. Since there has been a rise in the number of school days per year over the last fifty years as well as a rise in the average number of school years completed, it was necessary to adjust the distribution of males by amounts of education completed. This he did by making the simplest assumption possible, namely, that a given percentage increase in the number of days of school attended during a year is equivalent to an equal percentage increase in the number of school years completed. In other words, going to school 220 days per year instead of 200 has exactly the same effect on output as staying in school eleven years instead of ten.

Table 5

Labour Earnings per Man Adjusted for Total Days of Education Received, U.S.A., 1950

Period	Percentage Change	Annual Percentage Rate of Change
1910–20	4·9	0·48
1920–30	6·9	0·67
1930–40	8·8	0·85
1940–50	10·4	1·00
1950–60	10·3	0·99
1910–30	12·1	0·57
1930–60	32·6	0·94
1910–60	48·6	0·79

Source: (Denison 1962, table 9).

The meaning of the results can be seen by considering the period 1930 to 1960. As Denison observes:

There are considerable advantages in using growth rates rather than percentage changes in the calculations, and this is what I have actually done. Thus, if the labor input increased at an average annual rate of 1 per cent over some period and labor earnings averaged 73 per cent of the national income in this period, the assumption is that the increase in labor inputs contributed 0·73 percentage points to the growth of total real national income.

Therefore, as earnings per man rose by 32·6 per cent at an annual rate of 0·94 per cent over the period 1930–60, and since labour's relative share over the same period averaged out to 73 per cent, longer education contributed 0·68 percentage points (being 73 per cent of 0·94) to the growth rate of national income. National income in this period was increasing at approximately 3 per cent per year. Thus, of the growth rate experienced from 1930–60, almost 23 per cent (since 0·68 is almost 23 per cent of 3·0) was due to the increased education of the labour force. The result is even more impressive on a *per capita* basis: education contributed 42 per cent of the 1·6 percentage point growth rate in output per man employed in the United States over the years 1929 to 1957 (Denison, 1962, p. 73).

Denison's complete list of 'sources of economic growth' includes (a) increases in the physical quantities of labour and capital, (b) improvements in the quality of labour, (c) improvements in the quality of capital, (d) removals of 'restrictions against optimum use of resources', (e) reductions of 'waste in agriculture', (f) interindustry shifts of resources, (g) the 'advance of knowledge', (h) the 'change in lag of application of knowledge' and (i) 'economies of scale'. Factor (b), improvements in the quality of labour, is in turn broken down to (i) more education, (ii) increased employment of women, (iii) changes in the age–sex composition of the labour force and (iv) reductions in the length of the work week and in the work year. The model he uses only permits precise calculations of the effects of (a), (b) and (c), where the growth in the size of the labour force and improvements in its education dominate all the other factors. The rest of the list is estimated on a more or less *ad hoc* basis. As any mistakes in estimating factors (d) to (i) leave the estimate of (c) unaffected, we may ignore the treatment of these other factors.

A few minor caveats are in order before attempting to evaluate Denison's general results. Denison's findings on the contribution of education are extremely sensitive to the alpha coefficient, namely, the assumption that 0·6 per cent of the earnings differentials associated with additional education are directly attributable to education (see above Chapter 2, p. 51). As Denison himself suggests (1962, pp. 73–4), the effects of alternative alpha coefficient can be approximated by multiplying the figures in Table 4 by the ratio of some desired alternative percentage to 60 per cent. Thus, if we assumed that alpha was 0·75 – native ability and social class background having a smaller influence than Denison actually assumed – we would credit 29 per cent instead of 23 per cent of the growth in income from 1930 to 1960 to education. Similarly, the substitution of alpha = 0·5 would reduce education's contribution to economic growth to 19 per cent. The evidence on the alpha-adjustment even for the United States is far from conclusive. And as we argued (see above Chapter 2, p. 43), for purposes of predicting education's contribution in the near future, there is little reason for making any alpha adjustment. It would appear, therefore, that even the most convinced advocate of Denison's method of assessing the economic contribution of education cannot be certain, in face of the available evidence, whether education in the past has contributed less than 20 or almost 30 per cent to America's growth rate.

Further doubt about Denison's numbers is created by reworking his estimates using data on hourly earnings of non-agricultural workers instead of the annual incomes of the total population. This has the surprising consequence of cutting in half his estimate of education's contribution to the growth rate (Schwartzman, 1968; but see Denison, 1969). Although it is probably better to use weekly or annual earnings rather than hourly earnings as a measure of the productivity of differently educated workers, Schwartzman's results do indicate the extraordinary sensitivity of Denison's numbers to the choice of the earnings index.

These and many other points one might make are little more than quibbles: if anything they demonstrate the advantages of Denison's approach in that disputes are now tied to the discipline of providing different estimates of the actual magnitudes of effects. What is really mysterious about Denison's work is the contrast between the pains-taking calculations of most of his numbers and the cavalier pre-sentation, without any attempt at justification, of his basic model involving a linear aggregate production function of the Cobb–Douglas type and neutrality of technical progress. To be sure, these are stan-dard assumptions in neo-classical growth theory, but it is one thing to make certain strong assumptions in order to display the pure logic of the growth process and quite another to use such assumptions to estimate the contributions of various components to growth in the real world. It is important to realize that, owing to the inherent limitations of his model and the way in which he tacks on special assumptions at various stages in the argument, his findings can be attacked at quite different levels. Some critics, particularly if they have imbibed econo-mics at Cambridge, reject his work *in toto* simply because he operates with the marginal productivity principle. Others, particularly mathe-matically inclined economists, reject his conclusions on the ground that aggregate production functions are meaningless without some rule for aggregating the production functions of individual industries; even if all industries operate with linearly homogeneous Cobb–Douglas production functions, the aggregate production function is only Cobb–Douglas under certain very restricted conditions. Yet another group of critics accepts the marginal productivity theory of factor rewards, as far as it goes, and even the concept of an aggregate production function without an explicit microeconomic foundation, but cannot swallow the notion of neutral technical progress. Lastly, there are critics who are willing to work with Denison's basic model but quarrel with the particular adjustments that he made in measuring the labour and capital inputs. Many of the criticisms of Denison that have appeared in the literature are spoiled by not revealing the level at which *The Sources of Economic Growth in the United States* is being attacked.[9]

Denison has given his critics new food for thought by applying the same basic framework to a comparison of the postwar growth rates of nine European countries. He compares educational efforts in terms of the number of years of schooling embodied in the labour force weighted by the U.S. earnings differentials attributable to different levels of schooling. This begs a number of questions, particularly that of the different qualities of full-time schooling in the nine countries. Taking this for granted, Denison (1967, p. 78) establishes unambiguously that education does *not* help to explain why growth rates in Europe since 1950 have been higher than in the United States but, on the contrary, adds to the difference that must be explained by the other sources. Furthermore, education has contributed more to growth in the United Kingdom than to growth anywhere else in Europe: 13 per cent of the annual growth rate of the U.K. since 1950 but only 1·4 per cent of the German growth rate and only 6 per cent of the French growth rate is due to education (Denison, 1967, p. 199). This is not to say, however, that Britain's slow growth relative to the rest of Western Europe can be explained by the 'human factor'. Intercountry differences in the quality of labour do not in fact explain much of the interEuropean differences in growth rates (Beckerman, 1965, pp. 24–5, concurs with Denison), and Denison in the end seems to favour national differences in the intensity of work (an element not incorporated in his model) as an explanation of Britain's economic stagnation (Denison, 1967, pp. 113–14).

Denison's model has now been independently applied to Canada (Bertram, 1966; Lithwick, Post and Rymes, 1967), to Greece (Bowles, 1969), to Mexico, Chile and India (Selowsky, 1967), to Hawaii

---

9. For a compendium of criticisms, see the OECD symposium on Denison's book (Vaizey, 1964). Perhaps the most balanced assessments are Abramovitz (1962) and Bowman (1964a).

(Psacharopoulos, 1969a), to the Philippines (Williamson, 1969) and to the U.S.S.R. (Bergson, 1968, pp. 25, 92), each time with provocative results. Of course, such estimates do not prove or disprove anything by themselves and to take them at face value would be hopelessly naïve. Nevertheless, they present us with rough indicators of the quantitative significance of different sources of growth and thus mark out the ground for a fruitful debate on short-term growth policies. Jorgensen and Griliches (1967, pp. 273–4) have taken Denison one step further by showing that virtually the whole of the growth of output can be explained by movements along a linearly homogeneous aggregate production fuction, once we eliminate errors in the measurement of inputs and adjust the capital variable for quality changes in the same way that Denison corrected the labour variable. Their *tour de force* reduces 'technical progress', or 'the residual' to a trivial 0·1 per cent per year and demotes the contribution of education to American economic growth to a relatively minor element compared to quantitative and qualitative changes in the capital stock. And so the debate continues.

The fundamental difficulty is not only that the empirical evidence for the linearity and homogeneity of aggregate production functions is still somewhat shaky[10] but that so far no one has succeeded in introducing education into production functions except as a pure labour-augmenting variable. What if improved education, better machines and greater allocative efficiency are all interdependent contributors to growth, or if at any rate education contributes just as much to speeding up the introduction of new technology as it does to multiplying the power of the labour input? The model that answers this question has yet to be constructed (Nelson, 1967, pp. 482–4; Welch, 1970).

Denison-type measurements of the contribution of education to economic growth depend on many of the same assumptions as rate-of-return calculations of educational investments, such as that the bulk of earnings differentials associated with differences in educational attainments are attributable to the effect of education, that earnings differentials reflect differences in the marginal productivity of individual workers, and so on. Nevertheless, there is no simple and obvious connexion between Denison's estimate of the fraction of growth that can be ascribed to education and the notion that investments in various

10. Walters (1968, pp. 327–39) provides an excellent review of the evidence.

amounts of education yield particular rates of return. It is perfectly possible to believe that earnings differentials are largely attributable to education, and also that education contributes a great deal to growth, without accepting the numbers that appear in Denison's book or even the idea that we can approximate these numbers by estimating an aggregate production function. 'What is the contribution of education to economic growth?' is simply a very ambitious question. We may be able to allocate resources in education more efficiently than we now do without knowing precisely how much more efficiently; investment criteria provide signals of direction, not quantitative estimates of amounts of growth secured. It is worth remembering, however, that the really disputable issue about economic growth is not so much whether education is one of the sources of growth but whether it is a more significant source than physical capital or than other types of social expenditures.

We have covered so much territory in this chapter that we have practically lost sight of the problem to which it was addressed. Can we infer from the higher earnings of the better educated that education renders people more productive? Or are educated people simply exploiting their less fortunate contemporaries? Despairing of finding the answers to these questions in interpersonal and intertemporal comparisons within countries, we turned to international comparisons. Are nations rich because they are better educated or are they better educated because they are rich? We have seen that this simple question has no simple answer. Indeed, the question is badly formulated because in one sense both are true, depending on time, place and circumstance. Even at the level of an occupation within a given industry, no universal relationships can be laid down between the education of workers and the output of the productive processes in which they participate. Countries progress along a variety of man-power growth paths and the range of alternatives is almost as wide as the range of their living standards. Differences in attitudes and in political systems, not to mention the costs and finance of educational systems, widen the range even further. In short, we learn from international comparisons, at least in this area, that we do not learn from international comparisons. The Mecca of the economics of education lies elsewhere.

Chapter 4
Educational Planning
for What?

The Case for Planning Education

The next few chapters will develop the techniques that are employed by economists to provide criteria for educational planning. 'Planning' is an emotive word which tends to be bandied about with honorific connotations. We must explain, therefore, what we are going to mean by 'educational planning'. Planning, it has been rightly observed, denotes nothing more than 'a process of preparing a set of decisions for action in the future' (Anderson and Bowman, 1967, p. 355*). The essential features of planning are conveyed by the words 'process', 'decisions' and 'future'. In short, educational planning necessarily involves making conscious decisions now that have further consequences for actions that will have to be taken in the future. The question that naturally arises is: why is it that educational authorities have to make such decisions? Why not abandon the educational system to the market mechanism, that is, to the uncoordinated decisions of students and parents? To be sure, State-owned educational systems must involve some central decisions by State authorities but even these might be designed to maximize the scope of individual choice. That would be to say that State ownership of schools and colleges is simply a product of history whose consequences must be endured, provided everything is done to minimize central direction and control over educational choices. But what if State ownership and public finance of education arose out of the inherent characteristics of the educational process? In other words, what if education is a case of 'market failure', so that appeals to the free play of market forces are irrelevant and immaterial? Is there an economic case for educational planning? This is clearly a question we must try to answer before moving on to techniques of educational planning. After all, *how* we plan is hardly independent of *why* we plan in the first place.

In a competitive market economy, the efforts of entrepreneurs to minimize costs and to maximize returns on capital invested result in a set of prices which reflect both the *opportunity costs* of different goods and services (the most valuable use to which the resources devoted to their production might otherwise have been put) and the sacrifices that consumers are prepared to make to obtain them. Provided certain conditions are met, the existence of such a price system guarantees an optimum allocation of resources, in the sense of a position from which it is impossible to improve anyone's welfare without impairing at least one other person's welfare. The phrase 'welfare' in the last sentence means simply 'a position that a person prefers according to his own standards', so that the proposition expressed involves only intrapersonal not interpersonal comparisons of preferences. Summing up, the proposition is that, provided certain conditions hold, perfect competition leads to efficient allocation of resources and every efficient allocation is a competitive equilibrium. This is the standard definition of Pareto optimality, or what has been more colourfully labelled the Invisible Hand Theorem. Notice that perfect competition is not the same thing as private ownership of the means of production and indeed Pareto optimality might be easier to achieve in a socialist society.

But what are the conditions that have to be met? First of all, the distribution of income is given at the outset of the argument. Pareto optimality can be achieved under perfect competition with any distribution of income. Thus, there is an infinite number of Pareto optima between which we can make no comparisons without introducing value judgements about the initial income distribution. This is not so much a condition that has to hold for the proposition to be true as an elaboration of what the proposition means. The real initial conditions that must be fulfilled are four: (a) informed consumers, (b) absence of internal economies of scale in production, (c) absence of externalities either in production or in consumption and (d) absence of public goods. *Market failure* refers to any one of these four causes of inefficient resource allocation under conditions of perfect competition. That is to say, starting with any distribution of income *you* like, and even granting the existence of profit-maximizing producers and utility-maximizing consumers, each endowed with perfect knowledge of all perfectly certain outcomes of the market process, the presence of either consumer ignorance, economies of scale, externalities or public goods results in a divergence between private and public costs and benefits, such that interference with the market mechanism by a government is capable of making at least some people better off without making anyone else worse off. This long breath-taking sentence is *the* economist's way of stating the case for State intervention.[1]

Does education violate any of the four conditions for competitive equilibrium? Let us first consider condition (b), absence of internal economies of scale, which is quickly dealt with. Why is it there at all among the four conditions? The concept of efficient resource allocation boils down in the end to the statement that all resources should be equally productive in every possible use. If there are increasing returns to scale in any industry, resources cannot be equally productive in all possible uses, because we could have more output from given resources by shifting them to the industry in question. Are there economies of scale in education, such that average costs per student in an educational institution would be lower if only there were more students?

Very little work has been done on this question. There are some American studies which purport to have discovered economies of scale in urban high schools up to 2000 students (Kiesling, 1968; Riew, 1966), and there is casual evidence that some British universities and some American private colleges are too small to reap the full advantages of scale. No doubt, there are still areas even in industrialized countries that are so sparsely settled that it would be more efficient to gather children far and wide to attend a single State-provided school in a central place in the district, rather than to permit each hamlet in the area to set up its own private one-room school. But the Scottish highlands and the mountain districts of Kentucky apart, it is difficult to believe that increasing returns to scale in educational systems constitutes a *general* reason for State intervention in the densely populated world of the twentieth century.

The problem of consumer ignorance is much more difficult to deal with. The English classical economists always regarded the protection of children from the incompetent decisions of their parents to be a legitimate ground for State intervention. But John Stuart Mill was nevertheless the first classical economist who thought that the Invisible Hand Theorem broke down with respect to education because of the

1. For details crossing the 't's and dotting the 'i's, see Blaug (1968a, pp. 588–610) or any standard text in welfare economics.

inability of uneducated parents to appreciate the advantages of schooling for their children.[2] It is interesting, however, that despite these misgivings about parental choice in education, Mill followed Adam Smith in refusing to sanction a State-school system on the grounds that it would crush spontaneity and variety. As he said in the famous *Essay on Liberty*: 'A general state education is a mere contrivance for moulding people to be exactly like one another.' And so, in the end, he confined his proposals for State intervention to the requirement that all children should be compelled to pass a public examination at a certain age (Mill, 1909, p. 956).

This illustrates the difficulty of drawing inferences from the existence of consumer ignorance. The question is not whether many parents are uninformed about education and unappreciative of its benefits (who would deny this?) but whether the solution lies in compulsory attendance until a certain age at State schools, or in providing better information that might cultivate the taste for education. The State might set minimum standards that private schools would have to meet, and might even compete with private schools by setting up State 'centres of excellence', and still permit the widest latitude of choice among all educational institutions that come up to prescribed minimum standards. Consumer ignorance *is* a ground for State intervention in education but State intervention need not entail State ownership or State finance. We have State regulations of drugs and medicines because of consumer ignorance but everyone realizes that different arguments are needed to justify nationalization of the pharmaceutical industry.

The essential difficulty about parental ignorance as a ground for State-provided education is that it can so easily become a self-fulfilling prophecy. Perhaps the most obvious reason for the incompetence of many parents and particularly working-class parents in educational matters is the fact that they have rarely been encouraged to exercise choice in education. Surely, the best way to learn to choose is to have to choose? The contrast in this respect between British and American parents is striking and full of lessons about the art and practice of choice. The recent evidence in the *Plowden Report* that parental interest in schooling is a decisive factor in the educational

2. West (1964) gives a fascinating account of the sharp change in attitudes toward education among members of the English classical school around the 1840s.

achievements of children may be a case of the chickens coming home to roost: British parents have been told for so long that they have no right to opinions about educational issues that they have indeed lost almost all active interest in their children's education.

The issue being the actual scope for choice, arguments about parental ignorance in the field of education reduce quickly to philosophical differences about the role of the State in relation to the family. If one really believes that the State should increasingly take over the responsibilities of the family, that the State is somehow more than the sum of the individuals in a community, that all educational decisions should be 'taken out of politics' and handed over to professional experts, there is nothing more to say. If, on the other hand, it is conceded that parents ought to be allowed some choice, however limited – after all, the 1944 Education Act, which is still the legal basis of British education, states that wherever possible, 'pupils are to be educated in accordance with the wishes of their parents' – then parental incompetence cannot become the basis of a case for State education although it may be made the basis of a number of recommendations for specific State actions in the sphere of education.

This leaves us with conditions (c) and (d), namely, absence of externalities and public goods. The concept of Pareto optimality assumes that an efficient allocation of resources can be achieved by comparing the value of output in different uses: a transfer of any factor or product from one use to another alters economic welfare only in so far as it results in a change in the value of output. But suppose the transfer of factors from firm A to other firms gives rise to benefits for which firm A cannot charge, or else inflicts a loss on other firms for which firm A cannot be made to pay? Or suppose a transfer of products to some consumers diminishes the satisfaction of other consumers because the latter are trying to 'keep up with the Joneses'? In all such cases the presence of *externalities* violates the conditions of Pareto optimality. The reason is obvious. If some activities generate external benefits (or costs) which cannot be marketed because they cannot be confined to individual agents, we would all be better off if more (or less) of these activities were carried out; because they are not marketed and registered in prices, the market mechanism provides no signals to guarantee their optimum supply.

Clearly, externalities are a matter of degree. It is useful to think of a continuum at one end of which there are no externalities – economic

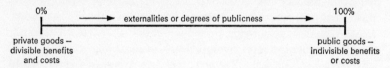

Figure 10   Externalities

agents who render services to others can appropriate to themselves the full value of these services or, if they inflict damage on others, are made to pay a fee to cover the full cost of their nuisance value – and at the other end of which externalities are the only benefits or losses from an economic activity. All actual instances of externalities fall in between. In that case, what is meant by the far end of the continuum where externalities amount to 100 per cent (see Figure 10)? The case where an economic activity generates no benefit or loss that can be assigned to any particular individual is the case of *public goods*. The peculiar nature of public goods is that their consumption is necessarily joint and equal: the more there is for one person, the more not the less there is for someone else (Musgrave, 1959, pp. 8–12). Since the benefits or losses are indivisible, everyone is motivated to avoid payments for public goods. Why pay when the total supply of public goods remains unaffected by the decision? In consequence, public goods will not be provided at all in a perfectly competitive market; a market mechanism is powerless to induce anyone to reveal their preferences for public goods. And yet if everyone were coerced into paying his share of the cost of public goods, everyone would be better off.

It is obvious from the nature of the case that no market test can establish the optimum quantity of public goods. Their provision can only be determined by a political decision through the ballot box. It is important to realize, however, that the concept of public goods is more limited than may appear at first glance. It is not enough to have joint consumption; the condition of equal consumption must apply to all, whether they pay or not. Furthermore, there must be no administrative rationing of the supply of a public good because a limitation on quantities offered, accompanied by something like the issue of ration coupons, is equivalent to a solution by pricing. It is doubtful, therefore, whether roads, police protection, parks, playgrounds, schools and hospitals are really instances of public goods. Public roads, for example, yield divisible and not indivisible benefits, in the sense that 'the more there is for you, the less there is for me'. Similarly, education is not a pure public good because at least some of the economic benefits of education are personal to the educated individual and, therefore, perfectly discriminate. Furthermore, below the school-leaving age, it is usually possible to buy 'more' education in private schools and, above the school-leaving age, the number of places in upper-secondary and higher education are more or less rationed in different countries in accordance with examination results. It follows that neither of the two conditions of joint consumption and of equal consumption apply to the provision of educational services. Education could be privately financed and even privately provided, and every level and type of education is so financed and provided somewhere in the world. Furthermore, in so far as both the inputs and the output of the educational system are either directly or indirectly sold in markets, the 'prices' of teachers, students and buildings do, to some extent, reflect the relative scarcities of resources involved in schooling. This leaves such phenomena as lighthouses, national defence, noise and smoke abatement, and immunization against infectious and contagious diseases as unambiguous examples of public goods.

Nevertheless, not all the benefits of education are confined to those who have paid for it, nor is it possible to exclude the less educated from the various externalities generated by the more educated. Therefore, education represents what might be called a 'quasi-public good' and hence the attempt to provide it by a market process must result in some social underinvestment in education. The operative questions are: how important are the externalities, or, to use any one of the synonyms current in the literature, the 'spill-over effects' or 'neighbourhood effects' of education?; how large is the degree of 'publicness'? Granted that we are somewhere in the middle of the externality continuum, are we nearer to the pole of pure private goods or to the pole of pure public goods? Depending on the answer, private choices and strictly economic calculations will lead us near to or far from an efficient allocation of resources in education.

The idea that the external or indirect benefits of education to society as a whole are enormous in magnitude and vastly exceed the direct personal benefits to the 'educatees' is one of the myths of our times that has gained wide currency in the literature as the one sure basis of an economic case for State education (e.g. Youngson, 1967, p. 88). It is a myth because there is virtually no evidence of any kind to support it and indeed there is great confusion as to what is meant by externalities or spill-overs of education. Before we present the very meagre empirical results that have been achieved to date in this area, we have to do some sorting out of terms and concepts to see just what it is we are trying to measure.

A less than exhaustive compilation of the spill-over benefits of education that have been cited at one time or another in the literature (Bowman, 1962; Peacock and Wiseman, 1968, pp. 349–55*; Weisbrod, 1964, pp. 28–37) yields the following list: (a) the income gains of persons other than those that have received additional education, (b) the income gains of subsequent generations from a better educated present generation, (c) the provision of an efficient mechanism for discovering and cultivating potential talents, (d) the means of assuring occupational flexibility of the labour force, (e) the creation of an institutional environment that stimulates research in science and technology, (f) the encouragement of lawful behaviour and the promotion of voluntary responsibility for welfare activities, both of which reduce the demand on social services financed out of taxes, (g) the tendency to foster political stability by developing an informed electorate and competent political leadership, (h) the emergence of 'social cohesion' by the transmission of a common cultural heritage and (i) the widening of intellectual horizons of both the educated and the uneducated, contributing to enhanced enjoyment of leisure.

Merely to scan the list is to realize something is wrong. The first five items are completely different from the last four, which are more appropriately described as 'atmospheric effects' rather than spill-over effects. Item (f) is in a class by itself: the belief that the spread of education will reduce crime and stimulate private charities is simply old-fashioned sociology. Item (i) is a favourite subject of popular magazines and we will resist the temptation to leap to easy answers. Items (g) and (h) are simply over ambitious. We might as well be asked to quantify all the indirect costs and benefits of industrialization or urbanization. No doubt, a minimum degree of literacy is vital to the very existence of a market economy and it is no less obvious that economic progress is impossible without some degree of political stability. As we saw in the last chapter, these are questions which can be and have been investigated by economists as well as other social scientists, and for all we know they may be crucial to the historical emergence of State-owned educational systems and vital to the role of education in long-term economic growth. But they have nothing to do with an *economic* case for State education and they are irrelevant to the kinds of allocative decisions that have to be made in the normal course of educational planning: the spill-over benefits of a literacy campaign of a given size, yes, but not the spill-over benefits of converting an illiterate society to a literate one, not the consequences of a total transformation of society. This is not to deny the importance of the intangible social and political benefits of education to the community at large. It is simply that these are not economic values at all in the ordinary sense of terms and to assert that they are 'large' or 'small' is merely to dress up a personal value judgement. We all indulge in these judgements – usually without attempting to assess the rather mixed evidence – but we ought to keep them separate from the analysis of measurable economic gains.

To come to grips with the problem, we must begin by distinguishing economic spill-overs from atmospheric effects and confine ourselves to the former. A minimum requirement is that we quantify the effect of better-educated people on the earned income of less-educated ones. Ideally, we would like to quantify the financial benefits to each individual of every other individual having been educated. Unfortunately, it is not immediately self-evident how many rounds of activity will be embraced in such an ideal calculation, with the result that interpersonal and intertemporal effects are straightway confounded. If we go so far as to look at the effects on future generations, it is undoubtedly true that more education for the present generation tends to raise the earnings of the next generation – item (b) in the list – inasmuch as the children of better-educated parents typically acquire more education themselves. But this tendency will be registered in time to come in the form of direct economic benefits and will enter into future decisions to provide educational facilities. The intergeneration argument really amounts to saying that, even if there are no returns today from investing in education, there are bound to be returns some day. This is either a fact that can be shown to be a fact or else is simply an appeal to the uncertain future to cover up ignorance about the present.

Items (c) and (d) raise other questions. Surely, the direct costs and benefits of education already reflect the selective function and vocational aims of educational systems? It is not at all obvious that there is anything left to attribute to the indirect benefits.

The hard core of the list of spill-overs is item (a), namely, the increments in the current earnings of other people due to the additional education of a certain individual. Let us call these the *first-round spill-overs*. If we cannot quantify these, we are not likely to quantify the more ambitious remaining items in the list. It is generally believed that the first-round spill-overs from education are positive. As we saw in Chapter 1, even Marshall thought that this was obviously so. Unfortunately, it is far from obvious and, indeed, little effort has so far been devoted to spelling out the nature of these 'employment-related' external benefits, to use Weisbrod's language. Presumably, they take the form of educated supervision raising the productivity of less-educated members of a working team in industry. The difficulties of isolating this external effect from the observed earnings directly attributable to people's own educational attainments are formidable.

Are the earnings of less-educated people actually raised by the additional schooling of the better educated in other than a purely relative sense? The qualifying phrase is essential: the larger the proportion of an age group that stays on in school to prepare themselves for entry into higher education, the greater the relative scarcity of school leavers with no education beyond the legal minimum age. Everything else being the same, this raises the wages of the less educated relative to the better educated. In short, the diffusion of more education in an economy tends to narrow skill differentials. However, this tendency of skill differentials to narrow has nothing to do with the spill-overs of education. It is the result of changes in the relative *supplies* of people with various amounts of education, whereas external effects have to do with changes in the productivity of individuals other than the 'educatee' which is then reflected in the relative *demands* for such people. Since the relative earnings we actually observe are the outcome of both demand and supply forces, how do we begin to sort out one from the other?

To explain what we mean consider Figure 11 which divides the entire labour force into those with no more than compulsory schooling, labelled 'unqualified', and those with some secondary or higher education, labelled 'qualified'. *DU* and *DQ* are the respective demand curves for the two types of labour, showing the proportions who would be hired at various monthly pay rates; *SU* and *SQ* are the respective supply curves, showing the proportions of unqualified and qualified

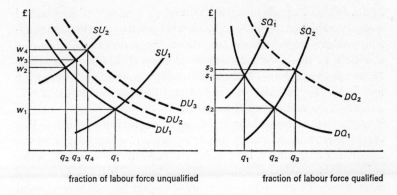

Figure 11   Two labour markets

workers seeking jobs in the two labour markets at various rates of pay. We begin with a situation in which the equilibrium rate of pay is w_1 for unqualified workers and s_1 for qualified workers, at which rates q_1 workers are employed in each of the two markets. Suppose now that there is an increase in the numbers staying on in school after the school leaving age: SQ moves forward from SQ_1 to SQ_2 and, assuming no change in demand, equilibrium salaries for qualified workers decline from s_1 to s_2, while the proportions employed rises from q_1 to q_2. In addition, however, the reduction in 'early leaving' decreases the *relative* supply of unqualified labour: SU moves backwards from SU_1 to SU_2, relative wage rates move up to w_2 and employment moves down to q_2.

Skill differentials have now narrowed ($s_1/w_1 > s_2/w_2$) but the labour force is better educated on average and this may lead to an all-round increase in productivity. This causes demand curves for all types of labour to move to the right, but probably more so for qualified than for unqualified workers: DU_1 moves forward to DU_2 and, likewise, DQ_1 moves forward to DQ_2. In consequence, both the salaries and the levels of employment of better-educated workers increase still further; wage rates and employment of less-educated workers also rise but not enough to recover q_1 levels of employment. In addition to all this, external effects generated by the better educated may bring about another forward shift in DU_2 to DU_3, and thus tend to raise both the wages and the employment of unqualified workers once again. We end up by observing w_4 and q_4 numbers of unqualified workers employed, on the one hand, and s_3 and q_3 numbers of qualified workers employed, on the other. The problem of measuring externalities, therefore, is to sort out this last effect from (a) changes in the relative supplies of labour with different amounts of education and from (b) increases in productivity brought about by capital accumulation and technical progress.

Let us look at the problem in a different way. It is perfectly true that early leavers may eventually benefit from the fact that other students are staying on at school, but this is merely an example of a much wider class of phenomena that economists have labelled 'pecuniary external economies'. That is to say, these are spill-over benefits or costs that do not accrue to the economic agents that have generated them – hence the word 'external' – but that are, nevertheless, reflected in the price system and to that extent are automatically self-correcting. Economies or diseconomies of this kind do not violate the ordinary principles of the market mechanism: for example, the narrowing of earnings differentials between people with different amounts of education, when it does occur, automatically reduces the financial incentive to stay on at school and thus encourages leaving at an earlier age. This is not the case with 'real external economies', consisting of those spill-over benefits or costs that are not transmitted through the price system and hence do not generate counteracting market forces. The full benefits of additions to technical knowledge, to cite a favourite example, are not easily captured by the original inventor, even with strong patents and copyrights, in consequence of which the earnings of inventors as well as the prices paid for inventions are too low to induce the optimum amount of inventive activity. Or to come a little nearer home, it may be that institutions of higher education provide a particularly suitable setting for conducting basic research – item (e) in our earlier list. If so, this benefit is a *real* external benefit in the sense that it is not registered in any obvious way in the earnings of people or the prices of goods and services. Hence, if educational decisions were left entirely in private hands, there might well be social under-investment in pure research because no one would be adequately motivated to bear the cost of conducting it.

We can see that the difficulty of deciding whether education produces spill-over benefits in the strict sense of the term, is that of finding instances where the additional education of one individual raises not only his own earnings beyond what it would otherwise have been, but simultaneously raises the earnings of other individuals who have not acquired further schooling *by less than an equal percentage amount*, thus widening or at any rate not narrowing earnings differentials by levels of education. If it left relative earnings differentials the same by raising everyone's earnings equi-proportionately, we would never be able to separate the direct from the indirect effects of education on earnings. Besides, the *absolute* earnings advantages of the more educated would increase if all earnings rose in the same proportion, so that market forces could be trusted to induce people to stay on in school. On the other hand, if additional education narrowed earnings differentials by levels of education, it would provide its own counter-check and so constitute a pecuniary rather than a real external economy What we are after is the tendency of education to *widen* earnings differentials. An increase in the relative supply of highly educated people, considered in isolation, would never widen earnings differentials by education. Therefore, by a process of elimination, it appears that the examples we are looking for involve changes in the relative demands for people with different educational qualifications *caused* by changes in the relative supplies of educated people. Obviously, it is not going to be easy to find such examples and it is hardly surprising that very few results have yet been reported in this area. We do well, therefore, to maintain a sceptical attitude about the actual magnitude of the real spill-over benefits of education. But a small number is still greater than zero. Even our brief discussion has produced some examples of such spill-overs and there is no reason to think that the real advantage of joining teaching to research at the university level is an insignificant benefit.

Weisbrod has argued that one of the external benefits of widespread elementary education in the United States is that of permitting an ever larger number of taxpayers to prepare their own income-tax returns instead of purchasing the services of a tax accountant; he estimates the value of this benefit in 1956 to be 250 million dollars, or about 3 per cent of the total resource costs of American elementary schooling in that year (Weisbrod, 1964, p. 25). Similarly, he argues that the provision of elementary schools raises the female labour-force participation rate over what it would otherwise be and estimates the value of the child-minding services of American elementary schooling in 1956 to be roughly 2000 million dollars, or almost 25 per cent of the total costs of elementary schools (Weisbrod, 1964, p. 29). Whatever we may think of these examples, the resulting estimates do not involve trivial magnitudes. It is true, of course, that externalities are not always positive. It is very likely that certain kinds of education hinder the discovery of potential ability, impede the ability of the labour force to adjust to changing technology, foster useless academic research, encourage civic disorder and actually increase the pressure on social services. Some of the external economies of additional amounts of education will be offset by the external diseconomies of the wrong kind of education and the net effect may be smaller than might appear at first glance. Therefore, we may reject the proposition that the indirect benefits of education are greater than the direct benefits as being extremely unlikely. But the fact that the net externalities of education are nevertheless positive must be continuously kept in mind.

Have we arrived at long last at an economic argument for State education? Alas, no. Externalities constitute grounds for State intervention but they tell us nothing about the form intervention is to take. Shall we nationalize schools and provide 'free' compulsory education, or shall we confine intervention to financial aid, possibly supplemented by enforcement of minimum educational standards? Obviously, the former is more ambitious than the latter and, therefore, reasons additional to the existence of spill-over effects are required to justify State education.[3] The same thing is true of the principle of parental incompetence to choose, a leading nineteenth-century argument for State intervention in education: it may justify a legal minimum school-leaving age, public inspection of schools, and State expenditures on vocational counselling, but not the actual administration of schools by the State, not nationalization of the education industry. In short, the economist as economist simply has no case to make for State provision of education. His case is one of public subventions to education and to be sure this is enough to explain State involvement in educational planning. Nevertheless, educational systems are almost everywhere owned wholly or in large part by central or local governments. If this has nothing to do with the inherent economic characteristics of education, what is it about education that has brought it so squarely in the public sector?

3. This is a point ignored by some nineteenth-century advocates of State intervention in education (Baumol, 1965, ch. 12).

The Non-Economic Objectives of Education

At some point in the nineteenth century, all the industrialized countries in the world introduced compulsory primary education and met the new demand for school places thereby created either by nationalizing most of their private schools or by setting up a separate State-school system. It is by no means true, as is so often asserted, that the only or even the main motive for the introduction of State schooling was the inadequacy of private education. In Britain, for example, there was a marked spontaneous growth of private voluntary education in the first half of the nineteenth century, long before the introduction of compulsory primary education in 1870 (West, 1965, chs. 10, 11). As we saw in the last chapter, even as early as 1833, when Parliament first began to vote small annual appropriations to assist private schools, more than half of the working class had already achieved rudimentary literacy, something which could hardly have been the simple product of home training. Similar evidence, as well as hard data on the growth of private education, is available for the United States around the middle of the century (Fischlow, 1966; West, 1967a), and in general we may conclude that private education of all kinds was more widespread in the early stages of industrialization than is usually appreciated.

This is not to say that everyone at the time was perfectly satisfied with the quantity and quality of private education[4] but simply that such considerations were minor elements in contemporary arguments for State provision of education. The advocates of State education rested their case more frequently on grounds of equality of opportunity and social cohesion. Both of these became more rather than less important in debates as time passed until now, in the twentieth century, they have become literally everyone's argument for publicly provided education.[5]

Equality of educational opportunities is a somewhat ambiguous

4. Forster, the architect of the English Education Act of 1870, presented evidence to suggest that about half of the children in England in the 1860s were either receiving no education or else education of appallingly low standards. Most historians of English education have agreed with Forster but see West (1965, pp. 145–6).

5. These are what Musgrave (1959, pp. 13–51) calls 'merit wants' which he never in fact defines, except to say that they involve 'interference with consumer preferences'.

concept. Does it mean (a) equal amounts of education for everyone, (b) education sufficient to bring everyone to a given standard or (c) education sufficient to permit everyone to reach their endowed potential (Anderson and Bowman, 1967, pp. 359–60*)? No country has ever adopted the first interpretation at all levels of education. The second interpretation is sufficient to account for compulsory attendance laws but is of no help in making decisions about education above the minimum prescribed level. The third no doubt corresponds to the everyday meaning of 'equality of educational opportunities'. Even so, it must be interpreted negatively to give it any definite meaning. People have potentials in all sorts of directions and even the strictly academic potentials which are encouraged by schooling vary to some extent with the type of curriculum provided. The essence of the third interpretation is that of breaking any connexion between the distribution of education and the distribution of personal income.[6] Inasmuch as education creates future earning capacity, the more education is sold to the highest bidder rather than rationed out in equal amounts, the more the distribution of a good education approximates the inheritance of real wealth systematically favouring the rich. Education must be distributed not in accordance with purchasing power but with reference to differences in capacities to learn.

When carried to its logical extreme, this view of equality implies the concept of a 'meritocracy'. Unfortunately, capacities to learn depend to a large extent on home background which in turn depends on the education of parents. Thus, to distribute education in accordance with so-called 'natural abilities' favours children from well-educated backgrounds which reintroduces the influence of income distribution. Pure meritocracy requires positive discrimination in favour of children with less than average abilities, that is, 'enrichment' programmes for pre-school children or children in the first years of compulsory education, an idea which only the wealthiest countries like the United States and Great Britain have so far dared to entertain.

The goal of equal opportunities to acquire education is frequently espoused without facing up to its logical implications and is, in fact, rarely advocated without serious qualifications: witness the oft-heard phrase 'it just isn't worth while to keep them in school any longer'. Nor

6. Recall Marshall's remarks (quoted above, Chapter 1, pp. 5–6) on the differences between the behaviour of parents in 'the higher industrial grades' as compared to those belonging to 'the lower ranks of society'.

is it self-evident that 'free' State education is the only or even the most effective way of equalizing educational opportunities. Possibly, the most effective way of dealing with the inherent disadvantages of children from low-income families is by direct financial aid in the form of grants, bursaries, scholarships, loans and educational vouchers (see below Chapter 10, pp. 293–316). State provision of education is perhaps a clumsy indirect way of meeting the problem since, as we all know, it is perfectly compatible with a great deal of hidden discrimination against working-class children. In particular, it does nothing to meet the problem of financing the earnings forgone by students staying on in school after the legal leaving age, a factor that alone accounts for much of the bias against working-class students in higher education. To be sure, whatever the egalitarian administration of finance, the cultural advantages of children from richer families would still create inequalities in educational attainment. We are only just beginning to understand how the disadvantages of unfavourable home background may be overcome by compensatory education programmes. Such programmes could become part of the minimum standards that are imposed on all primary schools, whether public or private. But whatever we may conclude about more vigorous use of discriminatory State finance in education, the fact remains that equality of educational opportunity is not by itself a convincing argument for public as against private provision of education. That it was so employed in the great controversies over State education is not to be denied. But that it continues to be so employed, without much effort to become specific about its exact meaning in different contexts, exemplifies the emotional character of popular controversies about education.

The confusion between State provision and State financing is so prevalent in most discussions of the Welfare State that we might pause a moment firmly to establish the distinction. For example, to show that many people cannot afford to educate their children beyond the statutory leaving age at best establishes a case for a cash grant by the State, an income-tax rebate or a personal loan from the public authorities, but has absolutely nothing to do with the issue of private versus public ownership of schools. To make the point clear by analogy: many people in Britain favour the present system of student maintenance grants in higher education because they feel it equalizes educational opportunities. However, the fact that British working-class students cannot afford to support themselves through university without student grants is not a sufficient reason for eliminating the autonomy of universities and bringing them all within the public sector under the care of the Department of Education and Science. Exactly the same argument applies to the lower levels of the educational system except that historical tradition inhibits us from thinking about it in this way.

We have not so far produced a single compelling reason for State-administered education. What we have shown is that there is sufficient lack of appreciation of education and sufficient lack of competence to assess the quality of education to justify both compulsory schooling until a certain age and minimum standards enforceable on all schools; but this is State intervention, not State administration. Furthermore, parental incompetence to choose associated with poverty, as well as the income-generating power of education, leads to the conclusion that the State must provide financial aid to parents in relation to income, not simply in higher education but at all levels of education. It could be argued, however, that this does not go far enough. The inequality of treatment that is required to get equal results calls for much more than discriminatory finance. Positive discrimination will have to be built into the provision of educational facilities and this implies State ownership and administration. This brings us to the question of *social cohesion* which offers a firmer platform from which to advocate State provision.

Education can contribute to social cohesion by inculcating common values and agreement on some fundamental values is clearly necessary for the very existence of a society. The private provision of education would encourage such bodies as religious organizations to set up their own schools. Such schools would disseminate values at variance with one another and in this way, it is argued, education might easily become a disruptive rather than a stabilizing force in society. The creation of a measure of social and particularly national solidarity, therefore, calls for public provision of schooling.

The socialization function of schools is rarely put as baldly as this. No one wants to be put in the position of approving State-directed social cohesion. But the fact of the matter is that education of young children to some extent does amount to 'brain washing' in that it serves to internalize socially accepted attitudes and norms of conduct. The quarrel between the authoritarian and the permissive approach to primary education is about the length to which one should go in inculcating the adult norms of the society, and sometimes about whose norms should be inculcated. At any rate, there is a very thin line between stating that ethnic, religious and racial minorities will be better integrated in the community, the more children attend the same kinds of schools, and denying any choice whatever to parents in selecting appropriate education for their children. Modern writers on education are not as worried as John Stuart Mill was that an educational system wholly controlled by the State could so easily become a 'mere contrivance for moulding people to be exactly like one another', establishing 'a despotism over the mind, leading by natural tendency to one over the body'. Nevertheless, outside the Communist world, all modern societies have struck some sort of uneasy compromise between freedom of choice in education and the community interest in shared values. In consequence, most societies with a State system of education, but a respect for the principle of free choice of individuals as consumers, have allowed a variety of private groups to provide educational facilities outside the State system.

What we face here is a genuine conflict of alternative social goals; this is illustrated by the continued controversy over the segregation issue in the United States and the public schools question in Great Britain. Public schools in Britain are said to exacerbate class distinctions by their exclusiveness and superior social appeal and yet few British critics of the public schools are willing to go so far as to abolish them. Instead, it has been proposed that they should be gradually 'integrated' into the public sector by turning over half of their places to pupils allocated by the State. Be that as it may, it is perfectly clear that this rather tortuous solution would never have been put forward were it not for the desire both to break down the social divisiveness of these schools and to preserve what freedom parents now have to opt out of the State system (see Public Schools Commission, 1968, pp. 6–7, 76–80).

A book could be written illustrating the pervasive conflict in the history of modern education between social cohesion and parental choice. Enough has now been said to suggest that one can make out a perfectly good case for State education based on the role of schools in providing a non-legal type of 'social control'. It is, however, a case whose relevance varies with time and place: it may have had more force in the nineteenth century than in the twentieth; it may hold more for a country like the United States with a large immigrant population and a sizeable coloured minority than for a fairly homogeneous society like that of Great Britain; in general, it is more applicable today to poor countries with largely illiterate populations than to rich countries with stable governments. And, being among those 'atmospheric effects' of education mentioned earlier, it is hardly a question on which economists are particularly authorized to speak. As we have seen, there is, in fact, no convincing economic case for State ownership of the education industry.

Having come this far in indicating some of the non-economic objectives that motivate State provision and State financing of education, we will now sum up by introducing a fundamental distinction that will run through all of the subsequent chapters on educational planning. It is the distinction between 'cost–benefit analysis' and 'cost–effectiveness analysis'.

Cost–Benefit and Cost–Effectiveness Analysis

Of all the techniques of investment appraisal which in recent years have come to be applied to the public sector, none has attracted more attention than cost–benefit analysis. Although the underlying concepts have been familiar to economists since the turn of the last century, the subject as such was only born in the 1950s as a result of attempts to rationalize the large-scale development of major river valleys in the United States. Since then, the technique has been applied to virtually all nationalized industries, health expenditures, housing schemes, traffic networks, land-use and town-planning problems, regional development and, of course, education (where it is better known as rate-of-return analysis) in both the United States and the United Kingdom, and indeed throughout the advanced and underdeveloped countries.[7] In one sense, cost–benefit analysis is an attempt to do explicitly what the price mechanism does implicitly, namely, to choose investment projects in order of their benefits per unit of costs. The need to become explicit arises from the fact that in all countries a whole range of government services are normally supplied without prices being charged for them; even if the inputs into the public service are purchased in markets, the output is not sold in markets and, furthermore, the service in question may not be produced at all

7. For a good survey, see Prest and Turvey (1965).

by the private sector – motorways in Britain (but not highways in the United States) are a typical example. In all such cases, there are no prices in terms of which benefits can be evaluated. Even if comparable services are being produced in the private sector (for example, private medicine in countries that have a National Health Service) the prices generated by the market mechanism will rarely serve as suitable weights for appraising the output of the public sector, for the simple reason that government activity in the field usually arose, in part at least, as a response to market failure.

We will now define *cost–benefit analysis* as a technique for evaluating public investment projects that compete actually or potentially with similar projects in the private sector; that is, the market mechanism generates prices for the activity in question which can be used to translate the benefits of the public project into terms directly comparable to its costs. To be sure, these prices will have to be adjusted to take account of one or more reasons for market failure but, at any rate, they give us a base from which to start. Clearly, if a National Health Service is an attempt to overcome social underinvestment in health resulting from private transactions in medicine, it would be a mistake to evaluate the benefits of public hospitals simply by taking the prices charged by private nursing homes. That is to say, in almost all cases in which the output of the public sector can be evaluated by means of prices of comparable private activity, these prices are not quite the weights we are looking for. Nevertheless, if we are to choose one public activity over another or a public activity over a private one, we must find some way of comparing costs and benefits, and this is only logically possible if they can be expressed in terms of a common denominator. Given the physical heterogeneity of costs and benefits, a satisfactory common denominator will almost always take the form of money. In short, we can hardly get away from prices as measures of costs and benefits of public-sector activity and yet these prices cannot be adopted uncritically from the real world. This is indeed the *pons asinorum* of cost–benefit analysis.

But what if the service in question is not produced at all and never has been by the private sector, so that there simply are no market-generated prices to start from? The appropriate evaluation technique in all such cases is, not cost–benefit analysis, but *cost–effectiveness analysis*. A favourite example is national defence; it is not merely that defence programmes are not bought and sold in markets but rather that consumers would never reveal their preferences for national defence through a market process because it is a pure public good. Man power and hardware for defence programmes can be costed in monetary terms but the benefits of national defence must be expressed in other terms such as military striking power or deterrence value. This example suggests that, for all practical purposes, the distinction between cost–benefit and cost–effectiveness analysis is that the former is concerned only with economic benefits, whereas the latter takes account of all objectives, whether economic or not. This means that in cost–benefit analysis we usually end up with a single decisive cost–benefit ratio or an equivalent thereof, such as an internal rate of return. Cost–effectiveness analysis, however, may yield a number of criteria on different definitions of objectives and, in general, as many criteria as there are different objectives. So, for example, if a defence project ranks high on the criterion of maximizing damage to the enemy but low on the criterion of minimizing loss from attack, there is no way of deciding whether it is worthwhile without ranking the two objectives in order of importance. In so doing, we are willy-nilly eliciting the planners' 'preference function', a problem that rarely arises in cost–benefit analysis where it is simply assumed that economic objectives are given over-riding priority.

A moment's reflection will show that education falls uneasily between the two stools of cost–benefit analysis and cost–effectiveness analysis. On the one hand, in so far as there are private schools and colleges, there is a private as well as a public sector in education. Unfortunately, the existence of private educational institutions does not help us very much in evaluating the output of public education, for the simple reason that most private schools and colleges are heavily subsidized by the State, either directly or indirectly, and hence provide their services at fees below unit costs. However, educational institutions, whether public or private, in one sense do 'sell' their output of services in a market, the labour market, with the difference that payments accrue to the owners of the services and not to the producing units. That is, the case is analogous to that of a nationalized electricity industry that competes on equal terms with private electricity producers. Thus, the earnings of educated people can be used as 'prices' with which to evaluate the output of the educational system; whether these 'prices' correspond to the 'value added' by education is another question.

On the other hand, the tendency of education to raise the productivity and hence the earning capacity of individuals as part of the preparation of students for the 'world of work' is one, and only one, of the objectives of the educational system. If instead we view the goals of education not only as vocational but also as a source of personal enrichment and the cultivation of potential talents ('intrinsic goals' the philosopher might call them) or of fostering social cohesion, say, by equalizing the life chances of different social classes ('extrinsic goals'), then expenditures on education can only be assessed by cost–effectiveness analysis. The social, cultural and political goals must somehow be scaled and the units of the scale then become the required weights to apply to the 'output' of the educational system. Since education everywhere serves multiple goals, only one of which is strictly vocational, both cost–benefit analysis and cost–effectiveness analysis are appropriate techniques for evaluating educational projects. Indeed, in the final analysis all educational projects must be submitted both to cost–benefit analysis and to a variety of cost–effectiveness analyses, one for each separate quantifiable non-economic goal of education.

The distinction we have drawn cannot be rigidly held since the boundary between what is 'economic' and what is 'non-economic' is arbitrary and largely governed by intellectual traditions. An underdeveloped multilingual country may select as its principal educational objective that of imposing a single dominant mother tongue on its people; this will create a sense of national solidarity which in turn will foster political stability conducive to economic development. Is this an economic objective or a non-economic one? It all depends, clearly, on the time horizon of the educational plan. Article 26 of the Universal Declaration of Human Rights declares that free primary education is a fundamental 'human right'. Signatories to the Declaration thus commit themselves to providing free primary education to an entire age group before satisfying demands for education at higher levels. But primary education has all sorts of immediate economic consequences. Shall we call universal primary education as a first priority an economic objective or an ethical one? Questions like this do not have simple, obvious answers. For the sake of clarity, we shall decide here and now to assess 'economic objectives' in terms of effects on the economic activity of educated individuals within the time span of an educational plan granting, however, that over long enough periods of time all objectives take on an economic character.

Cost–effectiveness analysis is clearly the wider of two evaluation techniques, since it is completely neutral about the nature of the objectives themselves. In principle, any objective will serve the purpose, provided it can be expressed in terms of a numerical index or scale. For most purposes, an index or scale that is at least semi-cardinal must be found for each objective, that is, one that has intervals which have meaningful units of width; we must be able to say 'how much more' not simply 'more' or 'less'. Purely ordinal measures will not do because the outcome for one objective will rarely dominate the outcomes for all other objectives and, of course, in almost all cases we will want to satisfy multiple objectives simultaneously. Vaguely stated amorphous objectives, such as 'developing the moral character of students' or 'improving the cultural tone of the community', which cannot be scaled either cardinally or ordinally, cannot be used to evaluate educational projects or programmes; the difficulty is not with these objectives as such but with their deliberate generality. When we decide to spend another pound sterling on education rather than on health or housing, or on one kind of education rather than on another, we do so in the belief that, for the same cost, some stated goal can be more effectively achieved. Since costs are normally expressed in monetary terms and hence easily compared, our decision implies that one consequence is somehow larger than another. But 'larger' suggests at least ordinal measurement, and thus our decision to prefer A over B logically implies not only that the consequences of A and B can be measured but that we have indeed succeeded in measuring them. The oft-encountered assertion that the results of the educational process are so diverse and diffuse that they cannot be measured is either a semantic misunderstanding or pure obscurantism. Indeed, if it were true, educational decisions involving financial outlays would be impossible. This is not to assert that 'what is not measurable is not significant' but rather that when decisions have to be taken in terms of more or less expenditures, the resort to certain unspecified social, ethical and spiritual contributions of education is simply designed to take questions of educational planning out of the realm of rational discourse.

The goal may be a purely educational one: to maximize learning of a body of knowledge over a given time interval. In that case, the educational 'value added' over the time interval is measured by the increment of scores on appropriate educational achievement tests administered at the beginning and at the end of the course in question (see below Chapter 9, p. 269). The goal may be consumption-oriented: to give students as much education as they will voluntarily choose. This objective is easily quantified in terms of available places taken up. Needless to say, this goal has to be specified in terms of given private costs of education since the demand for additional education can be raised to infinity simply by subsidizing students sufficiently (negative fees are perfectly feasible). Satisfying educational demand at cost-covering fees is an economic objective but satisfying it at subsidized fees must necessarily involve considerations that are not strictly economic. The goal may be that of equalizing educational opportunities, which can be measured by, say, the proportion of children of manual working-class fathers who participate in upper-secondary and higher education. The goal may be that of maximizing interoccupational, interindustrial and inter-regional mobility, and again this objective is quantifiable provided we are furnished with data on the labour force cross-classified by the relevant variables. Nothing but lack of ingenuity prevents us from mentioning other objectives of education and different ways of measuring them.

Each objective and each corresponding measure is, of course, *sui generis* and they can only be compared with the aid of the planner's 'preference function' indicating his order of priority among objectives. How this preference function is to be discovered is another question. Certainly it is never written down in so many words even in policy documents. It is, however, implicit in every educational decision and in that sense it should be deducible by a purely logical process from a series of decisions. But that is only strictly true if successive decisions are internally consistent and unaffected by the passing of events or the outcomes of previous decisions. This is unlikely to be the case. Indeed, in so far as educational decisions are decisions made by politicians, the pressures of appealing to an electorate with widely divergent views and interests inevitably lead to a blurring of objectives and the deliberate avoidance of specifying quantifiable objectives: no politician wants to hand his opponents yardsticks in terms of which his policies can be decisively evaluated. In the practical circumstances in which educational planning is carried out, the best we can do is to present the planner with as many cost–effectiveness ratios as we can calculate, leaving it to him to attach the weights that are required to produce a conclusive answer. We may have to go as far as actually demonstrating that some answers are more sensitive to changes in weights than others for even this much is not well understood. In so doing, we are helping to spell out the implications of different views about the goals of education and contributing, by articulating the preference function itself, to more rational decision making. We are talking about educational planning but practically all these remarks are just as applicable to economic planning (Hutchison, 1964, pp. 177–83).

The central principle of educational planning is to maximize the returns, in some sense or other, from given amounts of resources devoted to education, or alternatively expressed, to produce at the lowest possible cost whatever level of educational output is chosen as 'preferable'. When the returns in question take the form of economic variables, the economist comes into his own to apply cost–benefit analysis. When the returns partake of the nature of educational, social and political considerations, the appropriate tool is cost–effectiveness analysis and here the economist is clearly less equipped to speak than other social scientists. Even so, the non-economist does not take easily to systematic comparisons of costs and returns, something which the economist has taken in with his mother's milk. When Robbins, years ago, defined economics as 'the science which studies human behaviour as a relationship between [multiple] ends and scarce means which have alternative uses', he realized that to that extent 'any kind of human behaviour falls within the scope of economic generalizations' (Robbins, 1935, pp. 16–17). What we have here is not simply a subject matter but a technique for thinking about decisions, whatever their character and whoever makes them. 'What, then, is the significance of Economic Science?' Robbins asked.

We have seen that it provides, within its own structure of generalizations, no norms which are binding in practice. It is incapable of deciding as between the desirability of different ends. It is fundamentally distinct from Ethics. Wherein, then, does its unquestionable significance consist? Surely it consists in just this, that, when we are faced with a choice between ultimates, it enables us to choose with full awareness of the implications of what we are choosing.... For rationality in choice is nothing more and nothing less than choice with complete awareness of the alternative rejected. And it is just here that Economics acquires its practical significance (Robbins, 1935, pp. 151–2).

It is indeed one of the peculiarities of economics as a discipline that it seems to furnish a paradigm for a science of rational decision making. For this reason the economist would have contributions to make to educational planning even if the strictly vocational aims of education counted for nothing.

Having distinguished cost–benefit analysis and cost–effectiveness analysis, we put the latter aside for the next few chapters of the book. In other words, until further notice (see Chapter 9) we will proceed as if educational planning were geared solely to economic growth. Having clarified educational planning for economic objectives, we will then come back to cost–effectiveness analysis in an effort to do justice to the many non-economic objectives that undoubtedly influence educational planning.

Budgetary Expenditures on Education

It is useful to think of educational planning as involving a hierarchy of decisions:

1. How much of the total resources of an economy should we devote to education?

2. How much should we spend on education out of the government budget, relying on private finance to fill out the rest?

3. How should we divide public expenditures on education between *formal education* provided by educational institutions and *informal education* provided by industry and various government agencies (subsidies for on-the-job training, off-the-job training, adult education, literacy campaigns, agricultural extension, community development, and so on)?

4. How should we divide public expenditures on formal education between the different levels of the educational system?

5. How should we divide public expenditures on formal education at a particular level between the institutions comprising that level?

This is not to suggest that educational planning actually proceeds rigorously down the list, never taking the next step until a previous one has been determined. In some sense, of course, educational planning amounts to making all the five decisions simultaneously and there is really no reason why planning should not start at step 5 and work backwards. Nevertheless, in discussing educational planning we have to start somewhere and the notion of a hierarchical structure of decisions provides a convenient framework for an analysis of planning decisions in education.

It is true that 'educational planners' so called do not make all the relevant educational decisions. Much depends here on what is going to be included in the definition of 'education'. In measuring the total costs of the 'education industry' in the United States in 1958, Machlup emerges with an enormous figure of 60,000 million dollars or about 14 per cent of GNP, after including education in the home, in the church, in the armed services, training on-the-job, as well as formal in-school education, the latter only accounting for 46,000 million dollars (Machlup, 1962, pp. 104–5). Our definition of 'education' does not go so far as Machlup's although it does extend well beyond formal education. Nevertheless, the focus of the subsequent discussion is, firstly, on total resource commitments to formal education and, secondly, on public expenditures on education, its division between formal and informal education, and the allocation of expenditures on formal education between primary, secondary and higher education. Later chapters will touch on the issue of private finance and the microeconomics of resource allocation at the level of individual educational institutions.

The first question we might consider is not number 1 but number 2 in the list: how much to spend on education out of the public budget. Clearly, if this decision is made irrationally, all subsequent decisions must be sub-optimal, that is, subject to the constraint of a total educational budget that is somehow given at the outset of the exercise. What can the economist say about this grand over-all planning decision? Very little, if the truth is to be told. Consider what is involved. First there is the division of national income between consumption expenditures, investment expenditures and government expenditures net of total tax receipts (the latter can be negative or positive). In a centrally planned economy, this basic division is itself subject to a prior central decision. But even in a mixed economy, the size of the public budget in relation to tax revenues is in part determined by the desire to control the level of aggregate demand, a desire which is independent of the efficiency and equity objectives that may be said to justify public expenditures of any kind. In other words, the size of the public sector is to some extent a function of the desire to stabilize the total volume of private expenditure, an economic objective quite different from any so far considered.

Well and good: we must start with a given level of government expenditures and simply ignore for present purposes the famous Galbraithian question whether the public sector should or should not be larger than it is in most mixed economies. We come now to the allocation of the exogenously determined public budget among the various activities of government. We take it for granted that, in general, there can be no *economic* justification for devoting more resources to any particular use and less to all others unless this results in greater measurable economic benefits per unit of costs. Thus, all we need to do is carry out cost–benefit analysis of each and every area of government activity, dividing the budget in such a way among the nationalized industries and the various public services so as to equalize cost–benefit ratios in all directions. But this is to say that we cannot do educational planning until we have solved the problems of the economics of housing, of health, of social insurance, and so on. This is a philosophy of despair. We cannot wait that long. Besides, experts in the other social services are likewise waiting for us to solve our problems so that they can determine their own optimum level of expenditures.

Whether we like it or not, therefore, we seemed to be doomed to analysing allocative efficiency in education at a sub-optimal level. The constraint with which we are operating – total public expenditures on education – is determined by a political process that is only vaguely connected with any of the objectives we have described as economic and non-economic; the size of the educational budget seems to be largely the outcome of an attempt to maximize electoral support.

It is interesting to ask, however, whether even this over-all strategic decision is not in fact confined within narrow limits which are themselves the product of economic forces. For example, are educational expenditures in fact constrained by the level of income that a country has reached? Is there a sense in which it can be said that countries can only 'afford' to spend so much and no more on education? One way of investigating the question is to examine the role of income constraints as they have operated in the past within countries or as they operate now between countries. Only the most advanced countries possess the appropriate time series for such an analysis and so we are driven back once again to international cross-section comparisons. In so doing, we enter an area of research that seems to have exerted an almost hypnotic fascination on some experts in the economics of education. The problem has been attacked time and time again, apparently in the belief that it would eventually yield a magic formula stipulating the optimum size of the public budget for education as a function of national income. The quest for such a formula, we shall try to show, is chimerical.

The measures that have been used are the correlation between educational expenditures and various concepts of national income, and the change of educational expenditures that is associated with changes in national income, better known as the 'income-elasticity of educational expenditures'. One of the pioneer studies making use of these measures was Edding's *International Trends in Educational Expenditure* (1958). Edding selected eighteen countries 'in which the definition of school expenditure was not too strongly divergent' at three different dates, 1938, 1950 and 1954, and discovered correlation coefficients as high as 0·95 and even 0·99 between *per capita* income (Net National Product at Factor Cost) and *per capita* expenditures on public education. Given these correlations, he concluded that 'the scope of freedom in decisions on education expenditure is more limited than was hitherto assumed' (Edding, 1958, p. 813). However, he conceded that the time series evidence was rather different: from 1900 to 1950, the proportion of education expenditure to national income in these countries rose from 1 to 2 per cent to 4 to 5 per cent (Edding, 1958, p. 814). This hardly suggests a unique relationship between income and public spending on education. A subsequent elaboration of his earlier estimates confirmed the cross-section conclusion of a strong correlation between income per head and educational expenditures per head (twenty-one countries in 1960). Nevertheless, the ratio between educational expenditures and income varied in 1960 among twenty-four countries from a low of 1·85 per cent for India to a high of 7 per cent for the U.S.S.R. Furthermore, the secular upward trend in the ratio since the First World War appeared to have accelerated sharply in the decade of the 1950s (Edding, 1966, pp. 26, 39, 41).

Blot and Debeauvais repeated Edding's analysis on data for ninety-five countries in 1960 and for 104 countries in 1961. They found that $r = +0·93$ for the relationship between *per capita* GNP and *per capita* education expenditures. The correlation coefficient was even higher when they used totals instead of *per capita* values (Blot and Debeauvais, 1966, p. 75). However, dividing the countries into various categories of rich and poor, they found sometimes lower and sometimes higher correlations within the subcategories than in the sample as a whole. They came to the reluctant conclusion that the results depended largely on the particular groupings adopted (Blot and Debeauvais, 1966, p. 77; see also Palm, 1968).

Turning now to income-elasticities of educational expenditures, Blot and Debeauvais fitted a least squares regression of 1960 educational expenditures per head on 1960 income per head, and found an elasticity of 1·24 for their entire sample of ninety-four countries and one of 1·06 for the group of nineteen advanced industrial countries. In short, the elasticity of the poor countries generally exceeded those of rich countries. They repeated their calculations, regressing total expenditures on total GNP, which made very little difference at least for industrialized countries (Blot and Debeauvais, 1966). In all cases where *per capita* values were used, the income elasticity was in excess of unity; a given increase in income per head was always associated with a more than proportionate increase in educational expenditures per head. The same statements held true when population was ignored, at least for the advanced countries of Europe and North America.

Reviewing the results of these and other examples of cross-sectional analysis, one commentator summed it up by saying:

Contrary to Edding's expectation, education expenditures do not appear to be uniquely related to income. Income is clearly *a*, perhaps *the* major determinant, but it is not the sole determinant of educational expenditures. Differences in planning or manner of financing, or any other of a number of factors may, in fact, be operative and of more importance than if there were a unique relationship between income and education expenditures (Sacks, 1967, p. 122).

We have already cited the result that the ratio between educational expenditures and income appears to have increased significantly throughout the world after the First World War. Most historical studies of educational expenditures in individual countries conclude that, in addition, income-elasticities of educational expenditure shifted upwards once-and-for-all in the period after the Second World War. However, this finding may be due to a misinterpretation of the effects of the Great Depression and the process of catching-up in the recent post-war era. During the Depression, educational expenditures did not fall as fast as income, and in some cases did not fall at all. During the Second World War, educational expenditures were deliberately held back as income rose. Since 1945 the rapid growth of educational expenditures, rather than the slow growth of income, seems to have been responsible for the relatively high income-elasticities observed in recent decades. Thus, the instability of income-elasticities over short periods is perfectly compatible with a stable long-term relationship between income and educational expenditures.

Indeed, in some advanced countries, for example, the U.S.A., the U.K. and the Netherlands, there appears to be a steady underlying trend in the relationship, with a constant income-elasticity of educational expenditures of about 1·2 to 1·4, from which departures in depressions and wars are recovered in normal peace-time periods (Sacks, 1967, pp. 126–7). 'For planning purposes this long-term trend is of great consequence', Sacks concluded.

The income elasticities of the developed countries are of about the same order of magnitudes regardless of their rates of economic growth. This raises the conjecture that educational expenditures may have an important internal dynamic of their own, on which past history might throw a great deal of light (Sacks, 1967, p. 134).

Perhaps so, but this is moot comfort for educational planning over the next five or ten years. The Washington OECD Conference in 1961 projected educational expenditures in fifteen European countries by 1970, using past evidence on the income-elasticity of education expenditure within and between European countries (Svennilson, Edding and Elvin, 1962); by 1970, however, it is perfectly clear that all of these projections seriously underestimated the growth of educational expenditures in Europe in the sixties.

It may be doubted, therefore, whether knowledge of past income-elasticities of educational expenditures in a country provides a reliable predictive tool for more than a few years ahead, and it is certainly no golden rule for estimating the optimum level of educational expenditures. This is the more so when it is realized that the results we have just reviewed do not involve either estimates of the income-elasticity of demand for education or of the income-elasticity of supply of education, but a hybrid of both. If we were estimating the income-elasticity of demand for education, we would try to hold constant the 'price' of education in the form of the direct and indirect costs of education to individuals (Schultz, 1963, pp. 8–10). These obviously differ radically between countries and even within countries over relatively short periods of time. If, on the other hand, we were estimating the income-elasticity of the supply of education, we would treat separately those countries that ration higher education (like the U.K.) and those that practise open-door policies and admit everyone with given qualifications (like the U.S.A.). The so-called 'income-elasticity of educational expenditures' ignores all of these factors and appears almost to be the random outcome of a series of relationships between various income and educational variables.

Sensing the difficulties in extrapolating past trends, educational planners have instead opted for normative ratios of educational expenditures to national income. This is sometimes called the 'social demand approach to educational planning', apparently on the grounds that the norm in question is in some sense decided by society as a whole. Unfortunately, it is impossible to discover any ethical or logical foundation for the norms that are usually selected other than the international equivalent of 'keeping up with the Joneses' – because country A spends 5 per cent of her national income on education, country B which now spends 4 per cent should spend more (it is noteworthy that the argument is never used to justify a reduction in expenditures). Now it is true that such comparisons may show that it is possible to spend more, but they can never show that it is advisable to do so, particularly when the comparisons involve countries with unplanned educational systems. In fact, the meaning of this particular Great Ratio of educational planning, educational expenditures as a proportion of national income, is so frequently misunderstood, or rather introduced without explanation, that we might spend a moment on it.

First of all, the ratio is sometimes expressed as a proportion of Gross National Product, sometimes of Gross Domestic Product, sometimes of Net National Product at Market Prices and sometimes of Net National Product at Factor Cost (or National Income), as if it did not matter by what we divide educational expenditures. But as a matter of fact, the ratio expressed in terms of GNP is in most countries 20 to 35 per cent lower than those expressed in terms of National Income, with the other national income measures falling between. Perhaps this does not matter, provided we keep using the same ratio. However, if we are going to compare educational expenditures with national income net of depreciation of capital, should we not make a similar allowance for depreciation of capital invested in educational facilities? Ought we not to treat both numerator and denominator consistently? It all depends, of course, on what we are trying to measure. But what precisely is the point of calculating this particular ratio?

Are we trying to measure a nation's 'educational effort'? If so, it would make more sense to compare educational expenditures at constant prices with government expenditures at constant prices, or the trend in educational expenditures with the cost-of-living index. Are we trying to discover what education 'contributed' in the social accounting sense to national output, or the proportion of national expenditure which is represented by purchases of education as final output? If so, we should be comparing the net output of the education 'industry', after deducting all purchases from other sectors, with GNP at Factor Cost or, alternatively, the sum of wages and salaries, the imputed value of educational buildings and the undistributed profits of private schools. At least, this comparison makes sense in terms of income accounting conventions, whereas the ratio of educational expenditures to national income is neither fish nor fowl and defies economic interpretation.

To show what a difference all this can make, consider some calculations of the famous ratio for the United Kingdom. The leading study of British educational expenditure is Vaizey's *Costs of Education* (1958), recently up-dated by Vaizey and Sheehan in *Resources for Education* (1968). Vaizey and Sheehan define educational expenditure as current plus capital expenditure at current prices, exclusive of transfer payments such as students grants, and national income as Net National Income at Factor Cost; they show that the ratio of the former to the latter rose dramatically between 1952 and 1965 from 3·4 to 5·4 per cent. They then subtract from educational expenditure all outlays on non-educational functions which happen to be discharged by schools (such as catering, boarding and health services), and find that the ratio is still over 5 per cent (Vaizey and Sheehan, 1968, p. 140). But what do these comparisons mean? It is difficult to know because they do not tell us. Adding educational expenditures net of transfers and social service expenditure and dividing by Net National Income does not tell us 'what education took of the National Income': we have included intermediate output in the numerator but excluded it in the denominator. Besides, why *Net* National Income in the denominator when capital expenditure on education is included gross of depreciation?

Furthermore, we are in effect comparing educational expenditure valued at market prices with a factor cost valuation of NNP.

Rigorously deducting intermediate purchases from educational expenditure, Peacock has shown that United Kingdom public and private education 'contributed' in 1963 just over 3 per cent to the gross domestic product at factor cost, rather than 4·8 per cent as reported in the official *Statistics of Education, 1965* or 4·4 per cent as reported by Vaizey and Sheehan for the same year, although the last two figures should have been smaller by virtue of the fact that they refer only to public education (Peacock, Glennerster and Lavers, 1968, p. 22).

One could argue that all this makes no difference to comparisons over time provided one keeps strictly to one or another definition of terms. Perhaps, but it makes the world of difference to international comparisons. For example, there has been a strong swing in British education since the war away from expenditure on labour and towards expenditure on equipment, maintenance of buildings and materials of various kinds (Vaizey and Sheehan, 1968, pp. 133–4). This swing towards capital intensive technology does not affect 'value added' in the education industry for the simple reason that equipment and materials are purchased by the education sector from other sectors. But it does affect figures on total educational expenditures. Thus, when we compare the Great Ratio in Britain and some other country in which the proportion of labour services to tangible inputs in education has remained unchanged, we get an exaggerated picture of the importance of education in the British economy.

It is time to draw a halt to these peregrinations. I think one may agree with Edding when he said in a debate, perhaps after reflection on his own work in the field, that 'educational expenditure as a percentage of GNP should not be used for making international comparisons. Such comparisons were likely to be almost meaningless and it was unfortunately true that the statistics were frequently being misused for the purposes of special pleading' (Edding, 1966, p. 618).

Educational planning begins with a given budget for educational purposes. This means that we deny ourselves the easy remedy of advocating an increase in educational expenditures at the expense of some other social service or of defence spending. This popular gambit is, of course, completely illegitimate. It implies that we have conducted cost–effectiveness analysis of every type of government expenditure and have considered all the economic and non-economic objectives that lie behind expenditures on health, housing, pensions, motorways, the nationalized industries and defence, in the course of which we have come to the conclusion that an *optimum optimorum* is only achievable by shifting expenditures towards education. To decide the issue on the grounds of a personal preference for education and a dislike of military expenditure is socially irresponsible. Unless we are going to pretend an expertise in public-sector economics, we are, in fact, constrained to optimize within the predetermined budget for education.

Our task is to find criteria for allocating the public budget efficiently between formal and informal education, on the one hand, and between levels of formal education and types of informal education, on the other, as well as within levels of formal education, with a view to maximizing economic objectives. The next few chapters are designed to show that cost–benefit analysis is capable of furnishing such criteria. We deal first, however, with an alternative approach to investment criteria for education.

Chapter 5
The Man-Power
Requirements Approach

Shortages and Surpluses of Man Power

Educational planning is as old as state education and much older than
economic planning. Until comparatively recent times, however,
educational planning was haphazard rather than deliberate, a matter
for local rather than central government, concerned with individual
educational institutions rather than entire educational systems, and
little thought was given to the objectives that planning was supposed
to satisfy. The Second World War changed all that: the post-war
explosion in the demand for education, the new interest in central
economic planning, the obsession with growth rates in both rich and
poor countries, all combined to promote a new attitude to the administration of education. Educational planning by the State with the
purpose of promoting economic objectives is now as universally
approved as economic planning itself. However, just as there is a world
of difference between central investment planning in the U.S.S.R. and
'indicative planning' in France and Britain, so enthusiasm about
educational planning has not yet produced any consensus about the
methods and techniques of planning education.

Nevertheless, a recent UNESCO inquiry shows that, out of ninety-
one countries for which data are available, seventy-nine have economic
plans, seventy-three have educational plans, and sixty-four out of the
seventy-three have educational plans that are specifically tied to
development planning; more to the point is the fact that sixty out of
the seventy-three educational plans are based on forecasts of future
man-power requirements, carried out in most cases for the first time
in the early 1960s (UNESCO, 1968, p. 46). In other words, the concept of 'forecasting man-power requirements' is today the leading
method throughout the world for integrating educational and
economic planning. Even the training programmes that international

organizations nowadays run for educational administrators from under-developed countries are completely dominated by the man-power requirements approach.

The essence of the man-power requirements approach is the attempt to forecast the future demand for educated man power, but only in a special sense of 'demand'. The operative term is 'requirements'. Required for what? Required to fulfil a target figure for GNP or industrial output. In other words, forecasts of 'man-power require-ments' are conditional forecasts, not predictions of what will actually happen. To clarify subsequent discussion, we will now draw a rigid distinction between 'forecasts' and 'projections'. Henceforth, a *forecast* will always refer to a prediction that depends on the achieve-ment of definite growth targets, that is, a statement of *what would happen* if economic growth were deliberately manipulated by govern-ment policy. In one sense, therefore, a man-power forecast simply spells out the implications of an economic plan with respect to some characteristics of the labour force. *Projections*, on the other hand, predict the outcome of purely spontaneous forces, that is, *what will happen* in the normal course of events in an unplanned economy, where 'normal course of events' is so defined as to include the infor-mation made available by the projection. We will speak, therefore, of man-power projections in the American or British economy but of man-power forecasts in the Soviet or Indian economy, because in the former case the central government does not commit itself to a growth target but in the latter case it does. Clearly, there are hybrid cases where it is not obvious whether we are faced with a projection or a forecast. Nevertheless, the distinction will usually be self-evident from the nature of the prediction.

Armed with this distinction, we can now ask why anyone would want to make man-power forecasts. The basic rationale for man-power forecasting, particularly of the long-term variety, is the length of time that is normally required to produce skilled professional people. Train-ing a scientist or an engineer takes about fifteen years and the effective production period may be even longer because the educational system is a hierarchical input–output structure; it is usually necessary first to feed back an intermediate output of teachers if we want to obtain a higher final output of scientists and engineers. This is something of an exaggeration as we do not usually start out *de novo*; if we want to produce more scientists and engineers, we can always make use of students already in the pipe lines of the educational system. Still, depending on the age of specialization in the country in question, it does take three to six years to turn a secondary-school pupil into a qualified professional engineer or scientist. In consequence, it is likely that labour markets for highly qualified man power are subject to 'cobweb cycles'.

When excess demand for a specialized skill raises its relative earnings, the increase in the supply of that skill, assuming students are made aware of and respond to the rise in prospective earnings, takes five or ten years to materialize. Because of this lag in the adjustment of supply, there is every chance that market forces will overshoot the equilibrium, so that what was a shortage turns suddenly into a glut. As earnings fall, the reverse effect takes place. This dynamic adjustment process may never produce market clearance in any one period but rather continuous fluctuations in earnings associated with successive phases of labour shortages in one field and labour surpluses in another. Given the strong probability that there will be structural disequilibria in the distribution of educated man power among occupations, and the high cost of such disequilibria when they occur, it is imperative that some central agency should try to forecast the demand for scientific or technical man power at least five or ten years ahead, in the same way that a nationalized electricity industry would forecast the demand for electric power before it committed itself to building a hydro-electric dam that takes almost a decade to complete. Even if we could predict relative earnings five or ten years hence, this would be of no help to rational investment decisions in the field of education, because observed earnings simply reflect disequilibrium situations. So runs the central argument of the advocates of man-power forecasting (e.g. Bombach, 1965).

The fact that the lead time for the production of scientific man power is fairly long, and hence that markets for this type of man power are characterized by cobweb cycles, does not itself prove that market forces never converge on equilibrium. So much is clear from the elementary theory of cobwebs. It is rather that long lags on the supply side are combined with short lags on the demand side and that, in addition, the utilization of qualified man power is likely to be dominated by customary and conventional behaviour. When excess demand for, say, engineers leads to a rise in unfilled vacancies, business firms become aware that they must pay higher salaries to obtain additional engineers. Time is required, however, to check whether technicians can be trained on-the-job to carry out the tasks previously performed by trained engineers, or whether new equipment can be purchased to replace some technically qualified labour. When the decision is finally made to hire more engineers at higher salaries, it takes still more time to recruit engineers away from other firms who are likely to retaliate by matching the rise in salary offers. As the higher salaries are extended to all engineers, whether already employed or newly hired, the cost of the salary rise begins to exceed the firm's original calculations, leading to a reassessment of their total demand for engineers. Once again, this final adjustment requires time-absorbing consultations with various department managers in the organizational hierarchy. In this way, even highly efficient firms may take six months or longer to work out the full implications of a decision to raise engineering salaries (Arrow and Capron, 1959, pp. 323–5*).

These lags on the demand side are, of course, as nothing compared to the lags on the side of supply: apart from the length of time it takes to educate new engineers, there are the well-known difficulties of rapidly diffusing information about salaries and vacancies throughout labour markets, the inadequacies of vocational counselling in schools and the weight of non-vocational factors in choosing careers (Arrow and Capron, 1959, p. 331*). In addition, the relatively high cost of obtaining information about conditions in the labour market on the part of both employers and job applicants encourages the use of short cuts, such as the labelling of skills by paper qualifications. This can have the result of further slowing down supply responses as students take extra time to acquire meaningless educational qualifications; it may also lead to the neglect on the part of employers of potential substitutabilities between skills. If we now think of underdeveloped countries, a host of additional considerations having to do with traditional hiring practices and status-oriented job hunting come into play to inhibit market clearance for specialized skills (Leibenstein, 1965).

Enough has now been said to show why man-power forecasters have no faith in the free play of demand and supply forces that are supposed to bring a labour market automatically into equilibrium. But even all this is not enough to justify long-term man-power forecasting. Lags in labour markets and imperfections in adjustment processes can be overcome to a considerable extent by 'active man-power policies' designed to improve information channels and to shorten the time required for skill preparation (see Chapter 7, p. 221). Other concepts lie behind the notion that every rate of economic growth entails definite skill requirements and that these skill requirements in turn make definite calls on the educational system: these are (a) the concept of fixed input coefficients, and (b) the associated idea of a rigid connexion between occupation and education.

The fundamental axiom of the man-power requirements approach is that highly qualified man power constitutes a bottleneck to economic growth: since highly qualified man power is an indispensable input into the productive process and since it takes a long time to produce them, shortfalls of such people must impede growth. We might call this 'the pilot analogy': it takes one more trained pilot to fly an extra plane and, by analogy, highly qualified man power is 'required' to produce extra output. The daring leap in this argument is not so much the denial of any scope for substitution between people with different skills or between human skills and capital equipment, but rather the definite link that is postulated between an industrial task and an educational qualification.

It is a truism to say that satisfactory performance in an occupation is a complicated function of native intelligence, psychomotor skills, work experience, on-the-job training, off-the-job training and formal educational preparation. The great question for the economics of education is how much the latter contributes to the total mix. It would be vain to pretend that we can yet answer this question decisively. It is clear, however, that the optimum education for an occupation depends as much on relative earnings as on the actual skills imparted by a course of schooling. This is because there appear to be three possible relationships between occupation and education: (a) there is a minimum educational qualification for each occupation, below which the task in question cannot be carried out at all but above which additional qualifications have no economic value; (b) the output of workers in particular occupations increases with their educational qualifications, very gradually at first, then at a sharply increasing rate beyond a certain threshold level, after which it levels off again; and (c) the productivity of workers in particular occupations increases monotonically with their educational qualifications, first at an increasing rate and then at a decreasing rate, but it never levels off. These three cases relating to a specific occupation are illustrated in

Figure 12 with educational qualification measured as a single dimension on the horizontal axis and productivity or any other index of performance in the occupation measured on the vertical axis. The three possibilities mentioned above correspond to the three numbered curves.

If the real world is correctly depicted by a or b, it makes sense to talk of a minimum educational qualification that is required for a job. But if case c is representative of the real world, the optimum amount of education for an occupation depends on the earnings associated with additional education and cannot be defined independently of

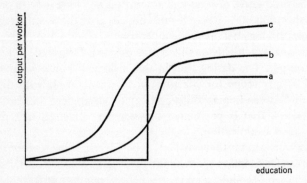

Figure 12   Performance in an occupation

them: a draughtsman with sixteen years of schooling may be twice as productive as one with twelve years, but if he costs the employer three times as much, the optimum amount of education for the job is nevertheless twelve years.

Only empirical research can tell us whether most occupations in the real world correspond to those in the mind of man-power forecasters, cases a and b, or instead to case c. Unfortunately, virtually no direct evidence has yet been gathered on this question. There is, however, a great deal of indirect evidence that education and occupation are only loosely related. In Chapter 3 we showed that there is sometimes no relationship whatever between occupation and education across countries; even when there is, as with professional and sales workers, it is only a systematic relationship for very broadly defined occupations. Within countries, it is well established that there is considerable variance in the mean number of years of schooling observed in two-digit and even three-digit occupational categories (Anderson, 1965b, pp. 321–4; G. B. Baldwin, 1965, p. 147; Parnes, 1962, pp. 112–13). To put the matter differently, whenever the stock of highly qualified man power is identified in an economy, a fair proportion of such people are found working in occupations where their qualifications, however useful in themselves, do not appear to be directly required for the job (e.g. Moser and Layard, 1964, pp. 299–302*).

Oddly enough, the man-power forecasters themselves are the first to admit the failure to observe any unique relationship between educational background and occupational affiliation, except for professions such as medicine, law and teaching where custom or legislation imposes a minimum entrance qualification. While insisting that the essence of the man-power requirements approach is 'the rather rigorous link that has been assumed between productivity levels and occupational structure on the one hand, and between occupation and educational qualification on the other' (Parnes, 1962, p. 51), they concede that the possibilities of substitution among people with various educational qualifications are such that very detailed forecasts of demand are meaningless. The argument is rather that long-term forecasts even of the crudest kind, distinguishing merely between occupations requiring general academic education and those requiring scientific and technical preparation, are useful in guiding the allocation of educational expenditures among levels and branches of the educational system. The appeal to higher levels of aggregation is perfectly sound, since it is generally true that substitutability diminishes as we define the relevant factors more broadly: it is difficult to automate an industry by substituting physical capital for labour of all kinds but it is easy to substitute a particular worker by a particular machine, or a worker with twelve years of schooling by one with fourteen years.

But even for such broad categories as arts graduates, science graduates, teachers, technicians and engineers, the man-power requirements approach is subject to criticism on the grounds of inconsistency. It is a common practice in such forecasts to make allowances for *up-grading*, that is, for higher educational qualifications across all occupations in the target year than are observed in the base year of the forecast. However, if the relationship between occupation and education corresponds to cases a and b in Figure 12, this extra education is simply wasteful from an economic point of view. Certainly, it is unnecessary to achieve the growth target for output. If, on the other

TEOE–F

hand, it is alleged that it will contribute to output to some extent – the case approximating to c rather than to a and b in Figure 12 – the question of how much it will cost the employer to obtain this extra output immediately arises. Either educational up-grading contributes to growth and, therefore, relative earnings must be considered in the fit between education and work, or else it does not, in which case it is nonsense to build up-grading into forecasts of man-power requirements. One cannot have it both ways.

Man-power forecasts inevitably derive the educational distribution of the labour force in the target year from observations in the base year or from extrapolations of past trends. But the schooling currently associated with each occupation is as much the outcome of the supply of educated people in the past as of the history of the demand for qualified man power. In any economy with a high level of aggregate demand, qualified man power, however irrationally produced, will somehow be absorbed into employment: what we observe today may simply represent the outcome of educational expenditures in the past (see Chapter 3, p. 73). Thus, if we want to forecast the demand for educated people, we cannot simply start from the existing connexion between occupation and education. The task we face is to find an independent method of estimating the optimum amount and type of education for each job group. This task has yet to be tackled by man-power forecasters. So far it has hardly been adequately recognized as the principal difficulty.

The whole point of man-power forecasting is the notion that the present situation represents a poor utilization of educated people. After all, if it does not, ordinary market forces may be trusted to produce results as satisfactory in the future as in the present. By implication, therefore, man-power forecasters must assume that the market has so far failed to allocate man-power resources optimally. In other words, businessmen are suffering unnecessary losses by employing men who have too much or too little education for the jobs which they are presently carrying out. But in that case, it would seem to be more important to tighten up the utilization of highly qualified man power than to perpetuate poor utilization by projecting the existing fit between education and occupation into the future. It would also seem to be as important to avoid man-power surpluses as man-power shortages. On the contrary, however, the emphasis in the man-power requirements approach is heavily biased towards discovering impending shortages. Perhaps that does not matter when the approach is applied to very poor countries with extremely low stocks of qualified people. But surpluses are dismissed just as cavalierly in rich countries.

A recent British forecast, for example, distinguished between 'demand' and 'need', the former referring to 'willingness and ability to pay', the latter to 'stated objectives of an organization or a community', and went on to note:

Objections have been raised to taking steps to meet need which is appreciably greater than or ahead of demand, on the grounds that this would mean that the number of qualified people becoming available would exceed the number to whom the community would be prepared to offer commensurate jobs. In practice such difficulties rarely occur because employers can be expected, when there is better educational supply, to revise their views about the importance of employing new skills, and also because the emergence of such skills duly creates its own demand – not only in the disciplines in which the individuals concerned were educated but more widely in management, the professions and employment generally (*Jackson Report*, 1966, p. 17).

Here is a kind of Say's Law with reference to technically qualified man power: supply creates its own demand but, apparently, demand does not create its own supply. It is a curious argument which starts off from poor utilization to argue that 'need' exceeds 'demand' and then concludes that supluses can always be absorbed because 'demand' will keep in step with 'need'.

It is worth noting that the term 'need', which crops up so frequently in the man-power literature, almost always marks the appearance of special pleading in what otherwise appears to be a purely objective assessment of man-power shortages. To speak of the necessity for public action because the 'needs of industry' are not being met is to imply, at least in the context of a mixed economy, that businessmen cannot be relied upon to know their own interests. This may be true, but if so we want to be doubly sure that alternative criteria of 'industrial needs' have been carefully specified. To appeal in these circumstances to the concept of the 'needs of the community', when the community has never in fact voted on the issue, is simply arrogant paternalism. It is a useful rule to regard all references to 'man-power needs' with the suspicion we usually accord to the emotive argument of special-interest groups.

Methods of Man-Power Forecasting

Having considered the theory underlying man-power forecasting, we can now ask: how are such forecasts actually made? At the risk of oversimplification, we may summarize the wide variety of forecasting techniques employed in different countries under five headings: (a) the employers' opinion method, (b) the ILOR-trend method, (c) the density ratios method, (d) the international comparisons method and (e) the Parnes-MRP method.

We will discuss each of these methods in turn, citing representative examples as we go along, without however attempting to provide an exhaustive survey of all the possible forecasting methods that have ever been employed somewhere in the world.[1]

The simplest method of all is to ask employers how much and what kind of labour they expect to hire in the next few years. Aggregating over all employers and subtracting estimated deaths and retirements over the relevant period, we arrive at a forecast of the increase in effective demand for labour by the target year. This method has been used in the United States, the United Kingdom, Canada, Sweden, France and a number of underdeveloped countries, frequently with reference to technical and scientific man power where the connexion between the nature of the job and a specific educational qualification is clearly established by occupational licensing agreements or by professional traditions. Nevertheless, on the whole, the method is more popular for purposes of making short-term general employment forecasts (periods up to one year) than for medium-term (three to five years) or long-term forecasts (ten to fifteen years) of the demand for highly qualified man power. As such, they may throw light on the present trends in the labour market but they hardly begin to touch on the problems of planning the future output of educational systems.

Even as a technique for short-term forecasting of employment trends, however, the employers' opinion method is seriously deficient. First of all, it assumes that employers themselves make such forecasts; if they do not, it is very likely that they will fill out the questionnaires at least cost, that is, by guessing. But the evidence suggests that the

1. For similar efforts, see Mehmet (1965) which is focused exclusively on developed countries, and Goldstein and Swerdloff (1967) which is actually confined to methods of projecting employment opportunities rather than to methods of forecasting man-power requirements.

forecasting of personnel requirements at the firm level is a very recent development and that few firms make a regular practice of it even in advanced countries.[2] Secondly, unless employers are asked to forecast their production levels as well as their demand for labour, which is rarely the case with this method, the answers cannot be checked for internal consistency. Thirdly, even if expected growth rates of industrial output are stipulated in the questionnaire, employers in industries that are oligopolies cannot deduce from these their own needs for labour without knowing their future market shares, that is, without knowledge of the actions of rival firms; this argument applies, however, to each firm in turn. In short, whenever the market structure of an industry is characterized by competition among the few, employers' estimates of future employment cannot be consistently aggregated.

These objections to the method of surveying employers are well known. Nevertheless, they continue to be ignored by intrepid manpower forecasters. The United Kingdom Committee on Scientific Manpower under the chairmanship of Sir Solly Zuckerman made three man-power forecasts in 1956, 1959 and 1962, by asking a sample of employers how many people with scientific and engineering qualifications they 'would aim to employ in three years' time, assuming ... that the required number of recruits will be available' (quoted in Moser and Layard, 1964, p. 303*). Notice that no mention is made of relative salaries, trends in industrial output, or rates of growth of national income. Testifying before the Robbins Committee in 1963, Sir Solly admitted that 'we have discovered in our successive inquiries that one of the least reliable ways for finding out what industry wants is to go and ask industry' (*Robbins Report*, 1963, evidence, pt 1, vol. B, p. 432). Nevertheless, the Committee on Manpower Resources for Science and Technology, which succeeded the Zuckerman Committee in 1965, has continued to conduct triennial surveys of employers' views on likely recruitments of engineers, technologists and scientists, and has not hesitated to use the results to indicate a persistent shortage of scientific and technical man power in Britain (*Jackson Report*, 1966, fig. 1).[3]

2. One study of the metal manufacturing and metal using industry in the U.K. shows that only one out of four British metal firms make systematic forecasts of their employment needs for more than two years ahead and only one out of forty do so for all categories of labour (Ministry of Labour, 1965, p. 2).

3. For more detailed critical accounts of the work of these two British forecasting committees, see Gannicott and Blaug (1969), Moser and Layard (1964)*, Payne (1960, ch. 3) and Peacock (1964).

We pass on to the somewhat more promising method of extrapolating trends in ILOR, the *incremental labour–output ratio*, where 'labour' refers to a particular type of man power in an occupational category and 'output' to industrial output or national income. In the Netherlands, for example, forecasts of the future demand for engineers have been produced by extrapolating a linear regression of the number of engineers on national income, using data for the period 1900 to 1956 (De Wolff, 1963, pp. 96, 103; Netherlands, 1967, pp. 102–7). Similarly, linear trends in output per engineer and the proportion of engineers in the labour force of different sectors of the economy have been used in Sweden to forecast the sectoral demand for engineers (Döös, 1963, p. 36; Moberg, 1960, pp. 53–4). Obviously, this is a method that is applicable only in advanced countries that have time series on output per man cross-classified by sector, occupation and educational qualification. In the absence of time series evidence, the method is usually unreliable owing to the short-period instability of ILORs. In Britain, for example, the Zuckerman Committee in 1956 produced a ten-year forecast of the number of scientists and engineers 'required' to realize a 4 per cent growth in total industrial output by assuming a fixed ALOR, the *average* ratio of scientists and engineers to output; three years later, this ALOR was four times what it had been in 1956, implying a sharp rise in ILOR (Moser and Layard, 1964, p. 296*). Elsewhere too, forecasts using this method continue to be based on observations of ILOR over periods as short as five years (Zschock, 1967).

Reference to the proportion of engineers in the labour force of a sector brings us to the *density ratios method*, which deserves special mention as the favourite Soviet method of making long-term man-power forecasts. Known in the U.S.S.R. as the 'ratio of saturation' method, it consists, firstly, of estimating stable fractions of qualified man power in the labour force of an economic sector (L_{ij}/L_j in the notation of Chapter 3) and, secondly, of applying this fraction to demographic forecasts of the total labour force as distributed among the various sectors. Thus, for example, a leading American forecast extrapolated the ratio of scientists and engineers employed in a given industry to total employment in that industry up to 1970, on the basis of a linear trend in the relevant density ratio between 1954 and 1959; subsequent investigations, however, threw doubt on the assumption of a stable employment fraction for scientific man power in both the chemical and the electrical equipment industries (Bureau of Labor Statistics, 1961, pp. 3, 16–17, 21–4; 1963, p. 5; also Folger, 1967a, p. 211). Similarly, the density ratios method together with the ILOR-trend method has been used in Austria to forecast 'requirements' for engineers up to 1980 (Austria, 1968, pp. 132–43). Britain's second long-term forecast for scientific and technical man power estimated density ratios in individual manufacturing industries by assuming that the highest densities observed in 1961 among the 'best firms' in an industry would become the pattern for all firms in the industry by 1970 (Moser and Layard, 1964, pp. 297–9*); it was taken for granted, of course, that the highest densities of scientific man power were 'best'.

A variant of this third method of forecasting man-power requirements is to estimate stable density ratios between different types of man power, such as the ratio of scientists to engineers or engineers to technicians, so that a forecast of one type leads directly to a forecast of the other. In the U.S.S.R. for example, the 'ratios of saturation' are used to forecast ten to fifteen years ahead; over the period of a five-year plan, however, forecasts are based on the concept of 'staffing norms'. So-called 'labour balances' are drawn up for firms, industries and sectors in terms of such categories as unskilled, skilled, middle-level and high-level man power, having regard to the average work load of workers as determined by their supervisors. These are then adjusted for up-grading of hiring standards over the plan period in the light of best-practice levels in leading enterprises. This method of forecasting, first used in 1930, is now regularly applied in the U.S.S.R. to 300 occupations normally staffed with higher-educated personnel and 360 occupations normally staffed with secondary-educated workers. The fact that half of all higher-educated workers in the Soviet economy are either teachers or doctors simplifies the problem of estimating work loads. Soviet legislation requires all doctors and teachers in upper-secondary schools to have university degrees. Work loads in the medical and teaching professions are then specified in practice by widely accepted standards-of-service as measured by doctor–patient ratios and pupil–teacher ratios.[4]

The fourth method is that of employing international comparisons, sometimes as the only method but frequently in conjunction with other methods. Thus, the French have long made use of time series in

4. Two excellent references on Soviet forecasting methods are DeWitt (1967) and Skorov (1964); for an account by a leading Soviet forecaster, see Nozhko (1964).

other advanced countries to help forecast the distribution of the labour force among twenty-five sectors of the French economy; since 1960, these have been extended into forecasts of educational requirements by applying normative density ratios (Fourastié, 1963, pp. 63, 69). A comprehensive application of the international comparisons method is afforded by Puerto Rico's 1957 forecast of the distribution of the labour force by occupation and education up to 1975. In the absence of Puerto Rican time series, it was decided to use the educational attainments observed in American occupational categories in 1950 as a model for Puerto Rico in the target year 1975, the argument being that the productivity of labour in Puerto Rico would continue to lag about twenty-five years behind that of the U.S.A. and 'to achieve equivalent levels of productivity, parallel occupation groups in two economies must have equivalent educational characteristics' (Puerto Rico, 1959, p. 32; see also Knowles, 1965, pp. 134–5). Similarly, an Italian study in 1960 forecast the distribution of the Italian labour force among sectors fifteen years ahead by assuming that Italian productivities in 1975 would match the levels reached in France in 1960 (Martinoli, 1960, p. 90). Since then, analysis by OECD (see Chapter 3, p. 84) has thrown doubt on all such crude comparisons between countries.

The thoroughly discredited Harbison rule-of-thumb (see Chapter 3, p. 73) has been applied by Hunter and Harbison to forecast high-level man-power requirements up to 1971 in three East African countries (Hunter, 1963, pp. 59–60; 1965, p. 336) and in seven South-East Asian countries (Hunter, 1967, p. 23). The Tinbergen Regressions, stipulating a constant ILOR between higher-educated man power and national income (see Chapter 3, p. 74), have been enthusiastically taken up in several African countries (Rado and Jolly, 1965*; Zambia Cabinet Office, 1966, pp. 28, 110–11). It also forms the basis for the twenty-five-year forecast of the Indian Education Commission Report: ILORs of unity were applied to each sector of the economy, apart from certain public services such as defence, education and health where normative staffing ratios were used (Burgess, Layard and Pant, 1968, pp. 7–13; *Kothari Report*, 1966, pp. 92–6).

We come, finally, to the most general technique of all, the *Parnes-MRP method*. This method travels under a variety of guises but is perhaps best represented by OECD's Mediterranean Regional Project (MRP), an effort to produce educational plans for Portugal, Spain, Italy, Greece, Yugoslavia and Turkey within a common conceptual framework. The MRP approach is to proceed in stages from an initial projection of a target GNP in some future year, exogenously determined by an economic plan, to a supply of educated man power 'required' to achieve the target (Parnes, 1962). The stages are as follows:

1. The target GNP in, say, 1980 is broken down by major sectors, such as agriculture, manufacturing, transport, distribution, etc., which may be further subdivided by industries.

2. An average labour–output coefficient (ALOR), the reciprocal of the familiar concept of the average productivity of labour, is applied to the sectoral or industrial GNP targets, yielding a forecast of labour requirements by sector or industry.

3. The labour force is now distributed among a number of mutually exclusive occupational categories.

4. The occupational structure of the labour force is converted into an educational structure by applying a standard measure of the level of formal education required to perform successfully in each occupation.

Allowances are then made for deaths, retirements and emigration, that is, for replacements as well as additions to the stock of educated man power. The final result is a forecast of the demand for educated people in 1980 conditional on the achievement of the GNP target.

The entire method is neatly summed up in the identity involving the multiplication of a scalar (1) by a row vector of fractions of GNP originating in different industries (2) by a column vector of labour–output coefficients (3) by an industry–occupation matrix (4) by an occupation–education matrix (5):

$$(X)\left(\frac{X_j}{X}\right)\left(\frac{L_j}{X_j}\right)\left(\frac{L_k}{L_j}\right)\left(\frac{L_i}{L_k}\right) \equiv \text{a matrix of required workers of educa-}$$

(1) (2) (3) (4) (5)

tion i in occupation k in industry j, where

$X = \text{GNP}$,

$X_j = \text{GNP originating in each industry} \ (j = 1, \ldots, n)$,

$L_j = \text{the labour force in each industry}$,

$L_k = \text{the labour force in each occupation} \ (k = 1, \ldots, m)$,

L_i = the labour force with each level of education ($i = 1, \ldots, t$),

and $\sum_{j=1}^{n} \sum_{k=1}^{m} \sum_{i=1}^{t} L_{jki} \leqslant L.$

The difficulties in this method centre largely on steps (3) and (5), although step (4) also raises controversial questions. As we have seen, the standard procedure for forecasting ALORs, step (3), is to extrapolate past trends, either as a function of output or a function of time. An alternative device is that of adopting the ratio observed in more advanced countries, on the notion that there are definite man-power growth paths that all economies follow in the course of development (see Chapter 3, p. 82); a variant is to take the ratio ruling in the most advanced sector of the economy in the hope that the best-practice technique of that sector will eventually become the average-practice technique of all sectors. We shall return to these estimating procedures later. For the moment, we simply take note that the problems involved in forecasting the productivity of labour are perfectly familiar to economists. This is not so with the difficulties encountered in step (5) of the exercise, namely, the translation of a matrix of labour requirements by occupation into a matrix of labour requirements by education. The simplest method of converting occupation into education is to apply the mean number of years of schooling currently observed in each occupation or job cluster. Unfortunately, the concept of educational attainment is not adequately expressed by a simple index such as years of schooling. In any case, this is not the only thing that the educational planner wants to know: he also has to make decisions about different types of education. The problem, therefore, is that of specifying a measure that combines varying amounts and kinds of formal education required in different occupations. So far, despite many attempts to develop such a measure, it cannot be said that this difficulty has been satisfactorily resolved. The difficulty is not merely technical; as we shall see, it is at the root of the inadequacy of the man-power requirements approach as it is now conceived.

More ambitious input–output models than the MRP have been developed in a number of countries for purposes, among other things, of forecasting man-power requirements. The 'Cambridge model' of the British economy, for example, starts with a detailed social accounting matrix for thirty-six sectors of the economy and ends up, after

allowing for different trends in technical progress in different industries, with a sectoral distribution of the labour force by seven occupations for 1970 (Brown, Leicester and Pyatt, 1964). However, the one
attempt to translate this forecast of skill requirements into one of
required educational attainments produced results based on nothing
more than purely arbitrary equivalences (Leicester, 1964; but see
Jones, 1964). We might just as well confine our discussion to the M R P,
therefore, always keeping in mind that most of the elements of an M R P
forecast appear in many other forecasts of the input–output type.

This completes our survey of man-power forecasting methods. We
must now attempt to evaluate these methods. Before doing so,
however, we digress briefly to examine the problem of classifying
occupations.

The Classification of Occupations

We have so far employed the term 'occupation' as if it raised no
special difficulties. Now we all know what is meant by a 'job' but the
cluster of jobs represented by an official occupational classification
is an aggregation of specific tasks carried out in industry or government. There are millions of jobs in an economy but a one-digit classification of occupations divides all of these into a dozen or so categories;
even a three-digit classification goes no further than about 200 jobs.
The U.S. Dictionary of Occupational Titles distinguishes as many as
20,000 occupations but even this level of disaggregation is still highly
aggregate. When we encounter occupation–education matrices in
man-power forecasts, however, these rarely go beyond two-digit
classifications, or about seventy-five different occupations; thus, the
occupations which are translated into educational categories in man-
power forecasts are themselves gross clusters of jobs rather than
specific skills.

The literature reveals a clash of opinion between man-power experts
about the appropriate method of classifying occupations for purposes
of man-power forecasts. Debeauvais suggests that the labour force
might be classified at the outset of the forecasting exercise into six
successive levels of educational attainments; in short, he proposes to
define occupation by education (Debeauvais, 1963, pp. 87–8). Parnes,
on the other hand, argues that it is conceptually impossible to group

occupations by educational qualifications, at least if 'occupation' is defined, as it usually is, in terms of the tasks customarily performed by workers, independently of the industry or economic sector in which the workers are employed. It is true, of course, that it is possible to draw up an educational profile of the labour force in terms of equivalent levels of educational attainment and then to study the distribution of this profile among industries and sectors. But for purposes of forecasting the educational 'requirements' of a growing economy, it is necessary to relate this profile to the actual functions carried out by people with different amounts and types of education, which reintroduces the need for a genuine occupational classification (Parnes, 1963, pp. 78–9*). The point is that whenever we classify the work people actually do into more or less homogeneous job clusters, these clusters or skill categories turn out to be distributed among several educational levels. We need, therefore, to keep occupational classifications separate and distinct from educational ones. Engineers are people who perform similar tasks; they are also people who have received a special type of education leading to an engineering degree or diploma.

The fundamental objection to defining 'occupation' by the level of education and training required is simply that, even if it were feasible, it would preclude asking questions about the optimum utilization of educated man power. If an engineering *occupation* is simply all jobs held by people with an engineering qualification, any questions about trained engineers working as salesmen, or technicians designing and constructing machinery, are ruled out by definition. In the same way, all problems about substitutability between people with different amounts and types of education are eliminated or rather turned into problems of measuring occupational mobility.

We conclude that occupations must be defined in terms of the nature of the job that is to be performed, without any reference to the characteristics of the people who take them up. Unfortunately, most official occupational classificatory schemes fail to satisfy this criterion. For a variety of historical reasons, the occupational census of most advanced countries groups occupations partly by the type and level of skill required to carry out the job, partly by the prestige rating of the work performed and partly by the formal qualifications possessed by typical job incumbents (Scoville, 1965); in other words, occupations are to some extent defined by the types of people commonly observed in them.[5] For example, in the 'Notes on coding occupations' attached to the British General Register Office's *Classification of Occupations* (1960), a paragraph is devoted to the difficulty of defining professional and technical occupations. The rule laid down for engineering jobs contradicts the claim that occupational classifications only take account of functions as set out in a job title: 'If the specific title is prefixed by the term professional, chartered, advisory, chief, consultant, consulting, designing, development, research, senior, superintending or membership of a professional institution is stated, e.g. AMIEE, it is assumed that the person is a professional engineer. In cases of doubt, the person is regarded as non-professional.' The same criticism applies to the *International Classification of Occupations*, devised by the International Labour Office. The ILO has taken great pains to define 1345 five-digit occupations in terms of the functions and duties involved in the work itself, without reference to the educational qualifications normally associated with them. In practice, however, educational qualifications contaminate the definitions of certain higher-level technical jobs. Thus, with respect to the first one-digit category 'professional, technical and related workers', it is admitted that 'many of the definitions of professional occupations refer to the possession by workers in the group of a diploma or university degree or equivalent qualification' (ILO, 1958, p. 7; on engineers, see p. 28).

The question is: can higher-level work be classified at all into different categories without resorting to educational qualifications, given the fact that these jobs have so many different facets? Executive work, for instance, has been classified along ten dimensions, covering both the degree of authority exercised and the spheres in which the work falls (Hemphill, 1959). According to the use that is to be made of the classification, one may select one or another of the various characteristics of a managerial occupation to define it. At one extreme, the managerial function may be defined by a single parameter such as educational attainments, but only at the cost of omitting information relevant to

5. It is amazing how frequently occupational classifications are accepted without questioning by those investigating the structure of occupational earnings or the occupational mobility of the labour force. Routh writes a whole book on occupation and pay in Great Britain but spends only a few pages on the official definition of occupation (1965, pp. 3–5, 155–7); Duncan and Blau (1967), in what is undoubtedly the most sophisticated study of occupational mobility ever published, nowhere define exactly what is meant by 'occupation'.

man-power planning. At the other extreme, one may take account of a whole group of parameters and convert them to a single scale by a points system; in that case, however, educational qualification is likely to count for less than half of the total points for an occupation (Blaug, Peston and Ziderman, 1967, p. 47).

Perhaps one reason why most occupational classificatory schemes include education and training among the criteria for grouping together occupations is the reluctance to face up to the difficulties of *job analysis*, the science of listing the tasks involved in an occupation.[6] Job analysis is the first step towards *job specification* (a list of the skills or abilities required of the person who is to perform the job successfully) and *job evaluation* (the process of determining the relative worth of a job for the purpose of salary grading).[7] Needless to say, the conversion of occupation into education can only be an inspired piece of guesswork without job analysis and job specification.

It is hardly surprising, therefore, that a purely subjective element enters into virtually all man-power forecasts precisely at the point where occupation is translated into education (Berg, 1965, p. 248; Döös, 1963, p. 33; Hollister, 1966, pp. 60–61, 81–3; Platt, 1964, pp. 119–20; Seltzer, 1965, p. 278; R. L. Thomas, 1965, pp. 303–4). One sympathizes with those forecasters who refuse arbitrarily to up-grade the educational requirements of jobs over the planning period and so find themselves projecting a fixed distribution of education by occupation over a period as long as twenty years (Edding, 1967, pp. 111–12; Riese, 1966; Widmaier, 1967, p. 176).

The United States has gone further than any country in the world in basing occupational classifications firmly on job analysis and the functional requirements of jobs. In 1955, the U.S. Department of Labor published *Estimates of Worker Trait Requirements for 4000 Jobs*, defining a long list of attributes which, in the view of experienced labour placement specialists, were required for an average level of successful performance in four thousand different occupations (extended in 1960 to 14,000 jobs; see Fine, 1968). The attributes are divided into seven 'specific vocational preparation (SVP) categories' and three 'general educational development (GED) categories', the

6. For a brief description of job analysis, see National Institute of Industrial Psychology (1951).

7. For a description of methods of job evaluation and an indication of its use in British industry, see National Board for Prices and Incomes (1968).

latter being deliberately measured, not in years of schooling, but in terms of levels of reasoning ability and standards of literacy and numeracy. Ignoring the last point, Eckaus has translated the GED categories into equivalent years of schooling and combined these with the training times specified for the SVP categories; applying these estimates to the occupational census of 1940 and 1950, he classified the entire labour force in each sector of the economy by its 'education and training requirements' in the two census years (Eckaus, 1964, pp. 184–5; also Scoville, 1966). This showed that actual employment of high-school graduates in 1950 exceeded the numbers 'required' for successful performance in jobs, while actual employment of college graduates fell below the numbers estimated to be necessary (Eckaus, 1964, p. 186).

Eckaus frankly conceded that his conversion of GED categories into years of schooling was based on personal judgement and took no account of the actual variability in quality among school systems in the United States. Furthermore, since the same job descriptions were used in the occupational censuses of 1940 and 1950, his method only revealed the effects of movements between jobs in the decade of the 1940s, not the possible up-grading of education requirements within jobs over the ten-year period. This is a serious deficiency, since others have shown that the association between occupation and education. in the United States loosened over the years 1940 to 1960 and that most of the change that did take place was attributable to up-grading, that is, to the rise in educational attainments within occupations, rather than to a shift towards jobs requiring more education (Folger, 1967b, pp. 165–73; Folger and Nam, 1964).

Furthermore, it appears that the GED categories straddle more than one conventional school level and, given the way they were prepared, they cannot be translated into equivalent years of schooling by any defensible method (Horowitz and Herrnstadt, 1967; Ross, 1966). Nevertheless, in principle if not in practice, the Eckaus approach marks an advance over the crude and arbitrary conversions of occupation into education that have so far characterized most man-power forecasting exercises. The difficulty is that no other country has yet even began to calculate performance requirements for jobs in such detail.[8]

8. But see Wilkinson (1965, ch. 3) for an application of American job titles to Canadian occupational data.

It is becoming abundantly clear that the problems posed by man-power forecasting call for a drastic overhauling of occupational censuses throughout the world. It is also evident that what is really needed is a double set of categories, classifying occupations in terms of particular combinations of skills required for successful perfor-mance and classifying workers in terms of their capabilities to perform assigned tasks (of which educational attainment is but one ingredient). That is to say, occupations should be classified from the employers' standpoint, depending fundamentally on the technical characteristics of the production function in the industry in question, and workers should be classified from the standpoint of employees, depending fundamentally on their acquired skills and on their willingness to carry out particular functions. It has been suggested that such a double classificatory system could be based on the rates of pay which employers offer and employees do or do not accept for different jobs (Cain, Hansen and Weisbrod, 1967; Scoville, 1967, p. 9). But this is likely to do more harm than good. By introducing relative earnings into the classification of occupations, it would undermine the purely technical basis of present-day classificatory schemes and thus prevent investi-gation of the ease with which particular jobs and particular workers may be substituted for one another to obtain a given output. If job A is to be distinguished from job B merely because it carries a higher rate of pay, we cannot ask at which trade-off ratio job A would be replaced by job B? If Smith is to be distinguished from Jones merely because he earns more, we cannot examine the conditions under which Jones would replace Smith. Besides, under this scheme, most occupa-tions and workers would have to be frequently re-classified. The fact is that rates of pay associated with different occupations do vary over time in response to changes in the demand and supply of different types of labour. For example, Meltz has shown that the pattern of relative earnings of twelve one-digit Canadian occupational groups shifted continually between 1931 and 1961, with relative supplies sometimes shifting more than and sometimes less than relative demands (Meltz, 1965, pp. 35–49, 104–9).

The basic use of occupational classifications in the field of man-power planning and forecasting is to provide information about substitution possibilities. For that reason, occupation must be defined in terms of the skill content of jobs, a requirement that is not satisfied by any of the standard classificatory schemes. It is high time, therefore, that man-power forecasters abandoned once and for all official statistics on occupations as worse than useless for their purpose.

Assessing the Accuracy of Man-Power Forecasts

There are upper limits to the elasticity of substitution of certain critical skills, that is, skills involving long formal preparation and training. And no matter how late we postpone specialization in higher education, the effective lead time of technical and scientific man power is sufficiently long to create the possibility of unstable cobweb effects. It takes years to put up a complex of school buildings and, obviously, foresight is indispensable to the decision to begin building. In addition, students base their career decisions on today's market forces and only a forecast can reveal the situation that they will confront when they eventually enter the labour market. There can be no question, therefore, about the necessity of trying to take a forward look at man-power demands. In principle, of course, one should look forward as far as possible. However, the period over which we can reliably predict the demand for man power in the present state of knowledge is much more limited than is usually admitted. All the existing evidence shows that we do not yet know how to forecast beyond three or four years with anything remotely resembling the margins of error that are regarded as tolerable in general economic forecasting. Indeed, at a time when economists are just beginning to take pride in their ability to forecast GNP fairly reliably one or two years ahead (Zarnowitz, 1968, pp. 435–6), the eagerness with which man-power forecasters make detailed predictions over a period as long as ten or twenty years borders on 'social science fiction'.

After forty years of experience with medium-term and long-term man-power forecasting, the Soviet Union is no nearer today to any accurate method of forecasting man-power 'requirements' than it was in 1927. Krushchev himself told a conference in 1959 that 'we do not have any scientifically reliable method of estimating how many and what kind of specialists we need in different branches of the national economy, what the future demand will be for a certain kind of specialist and when such a demand will arise', a statement that has since been echoed by a number of Soviet man-power experts (DeWitt, 1967, p. 230).

Elsewhere, the record is equally discouraging and yet it is difficult to cite conclusive evidence to that effect. One of the problems is that all man-power forecasts to date have provided single-valued predictions rather than a range of estimates based on various assumptions about the magnitudes of the critical variables and coefficients. Single-valued forecasts, however, can rarely be falsified by a simple comparison of forecast with outcome. The point is that unless the GNP target itself is achieved, we cannot be sure where the fault lies. In the vast number of cases where single-valued man-power forecasts were made, the economic growth rate fell for one reason or another below the target growth rate, with the result that even with hindsight it proves impossible to say whether the forecast was accurate or not.

Table 6

The Man-Power Requirements Hypothesis

GNP target	Hit	Miss
Man-power target		
Hit	Forecast confirmed	Bottleneck other than manpower?
Miss	Forecast falsified	?

Hence, repeated failures to forecast reliably have taught us little, and despite twenty years of experience with man-power planning in both centralized and decentralized economies we are not much wiser today about the nature of the changing demand for educated man-power.

To appreciate the difficulties of assessing the accuracy of man-power forecasts of the conditional variety, consider the Mediterranean Regional Project, which has been evaluated in its early stages by its sponsor, OECD. The document in question, *A Technical Evaluation of the Mediterranean Regional Project* by Hollister, is one of the most significant critical works to have emerged from the vast man-power literature of the last decade (for a summary, see Hollister, 1967*). It is recommended by OECD as demonstrating that 'the man-power requirements approach is both rational and applicable to educational planning' (Hollister, 1966, p. 4) but, if the truth be told, it marks the death knell of the man-power requirements approach as it has been traditionally understood. Hollister concedes that changes in labour productivity over time and among economic sectors have never been satisfactorily explained and hence 'that it is not likely that estimates of future productivity levels will be accurate' (this is confirmed by international cross-section comparisons: OECD, 1970, p. 262). Furthermore, 'no sound empirical basis' has yet been discovered for linking the advance of productivity to changes in either the occupational or educational composition of the labour force.[9] Lastly, substitution possibilities at given levels of technical knowledge as well as the effects of technical progress itself mean that presently observed occupational inputs are as much influenced by the relative supplies of various types of labour as by relative demands (Hollister, 1966, pp. 19–22, 60). Indeed, comparisons of occupational coefficients between the six MRP countries – the number of workers in particular occupations in a sector per unit of sector output (L_{kj}/X_j in our notation) – show a wide range of values for almost all occupations in all sectors. While these variations might have arisen because different countries operate on different production functions (this is highly likely as we are looking at huge sectors rather than individual industries), the presumption is that some of the variation is in fact due to the possibilities of substituting labour within and between occupations (Hollister, 1966, pp. 36–8, 60). Using 'sensitivity analysis', Hollister shows that the MRP forecasts for 1980 are, in fact, highly sensitive to very small changes in both the labour–output and occupational coefficients but not, surprisingly enough, to the disaggregation of total GNP into its sectoral com-

9. It is worth noting that popular discussions of man-power problems frequently do assume a simple relationship between productivity changes and employment changes. In recent years, for example, America has witnessed an outburst of hysteria over the effects of automation: the rapid introduction of computer control in industry in the near future, it was said, would lead to the massive displacement of labour and, in particular, to the virtual disappearance of a demand for workers with less than high-school qualifications. As a matter of fact, however, automation, as distinct from increased mechanization, has made few inroads in American industry even now and tentative evidence suggests that automated factories create a demand for semi-skilled workers at the expense of both skilled and unskilled labour (Jaffe and Froomkin, 1968, ch. 5, §2; Terborgh, 1965). At the level of individual industries, American data show no systematic relation between labour productivity, occupational composition and educational densities (Jaffe and Froomkin 1968, pp. 2, 4, 74, 91).

ponents; apparently, disaggregation must be carried down to the industry level to yield significant improvements in forecasting (Hollister, 1966, pp. 44, 60). In conclusion, Hollister notes that,

educational strategy should be formulated with the uncertainties engendered by technological change clearly in mind. In the light of such uncertainties, objectives of labour force flexibility may receive more stress in the formulation of the structure and content of education. Man-power requirement estimates which conceal these uncertainties, by presenting single value estimates of requirements rather than ranges of alternatives, may do a great disservice to formulators of educational policy (G. Hollister, 1966, p. 62).

It is not difficult to see that when 1980 rolls around it will be impossible to state unambiguously whether the hairpin forecasts of the MRP were accurate or not.[10] We have spoken so far exclusively of man-power forecasts in the sense defined earlier (see p. 138). Some additional insight is gained from experience with man-power *projections* in mixed economies such as the United Kingdom and the United States that have no definite commitment to a national economic plan. We have already said enough to suggest that the British record of man-power projections is one of endless failures, revisions and renewed failures. The American record is more difficult to judge: the methodology of American man-power projectors is highly eclectic and short-term errors in prediction have been as common on the side of enrolments as on the side of employment (Folger, 1967a, pp. 205–15). Nevertheless, little comfort is derived from the various American efforts at predicting the demand for scientists, engineers and technicians, not to mention teachers, doctors and dentists. Eclecticism in projection techniques raises further problems in conducting post-mortems on past projections. French man-power projections, for example, have combined so many different forecasting methods, held together by generous doses of ad hocery (Vimont, 1964, pp. 238–9), that the final results literally defy assessment.

Forecasts or projections for teachers and doctors around the world have fared no better than the more comprehensive estimates. This is somewhat surprising as minimum entry requirements for entry into

10. In extending the MRP exercise to Argentina, OECD went over to multi-valued forecasting, in line with Hollister's recommendations (Argentina, 1967).

these professions would seem to solve the usual problem of specifying the minimum educational qualification for the job. In the case of teachers, the poor record of forecasting is largely due to the mis-specification of factors on the supply side, such as the tendency of students to enrol in teacher training colleges or of remaining in the profession after acquiring their qualification; the use of administra-tively determined staff–student ratios in effect turns forecasts of the demand for teachers into demographic forecasts of the supply of children of school-going ages (W. Lee Hansen, 1965b). In the case of physicians, on the other hand, the forecasting errors of the past stem rather from the naïve view that the productivity of doctors always remains constant, or that para-medical personnel are of no importance to the total output of health services (see Appendix, p. 321).

The general picture is a depressing one and poses a central dilemma: do we brush all criticisms aside and forecast as best we can or do we revise our basic ideas about man-power forecasting? Parnes, the architect of the MRP, is in no doubt that we must make the best of such forecasting methods as we have.

The sceptics call attention to the large margins of error that are likely at virtually every stage of the forecasting process: the estimate of GNP fifteen years in advance; the distribution thereof among the various sectors and branches of the economy; the estimation of future man-power structure within each of the branches; and the equation of occupations with required educational qualification.

But 'so long as one grants that man-power considerations are one of the elements that *ought* to influence educational decisions, then all such decisions, if they purport to be rational, involve man-power forecasts, whether or not they are explicitly made' (Parnes, 1963, pp. 74–5*; see also Rado and Jolly, 1965, pp. 76–7*). This misses the point. If long-term forecasts of the traditional kind are really as subject to error as Parnes himself admits they are (1963, pp. 13, 30*), it is difficult to see how they can be justified; the fact that all educational decisions have man-power implications makes errors more serious, not less.

The question is not whether to forecast or not to forecast, but rather whether to forecast inaccurately as much as ten or fifteen years ahead, or to forecast three or fours years ahead with a much better chance of being accurate. The case for long-term as against medium-term forecasting is usually made on the basis of the actual production period of scientific man power. But the fact that it takes fifteen years to educate an engineer from start to finish does not imply that we must predict the demand for engineers in 1985. After all, there are usually students in the pipelines who can be induced to study engineering as they enter higher education, or even after they have started it. On the other hand, if we are making forecasts, not for scientists or engineers, but for all those with higher education, it would be preferable to create new intermediate qualifications than to settle for a four-to-five-year university cycle with the consequent need to forecast five years ahead. Strangely enough, the insistence on *long*-term forecasting is the one critical assumption of the man-power requirements approach that has never been questioned by man-power forecasters, not even by Parnes and Hollister who between them mention literally every objection to the approach that has ever been raised.

The need to guide students' career choices is sometimes given as the reason that man-power forecasts must look at least six or seven years ahead. Certainly, students, and particularly British students, must think about career opportunities six or seven years later when they come to choose their major fields of study. Suppose they were furnished with a completely accurate forecast of the demand for a particular profession by 1975; would this improve their subject choice? Not necessarily, as they would still have to estimate how many other students would react to the forecast. This is true, of course, of every student in turn. Students are in the same position as oligopolists who cannot decide what price to charge without knowledge of the prices that rivals will be charging. It is not enough, therefore, to be told about the demand for engineers by 1975; one also needs to know the probable supply of engineering students by 1975. Provided the student is furnished with both sides of the question, he is indeed better off. If a shortage is forecast, he need not worry much about his aptitude for engineering, as he is likely to find employment in any case; if, on the other hand, the forecast suggests that there will be a buyers' market, he must pay stricter attention to his own occupational aptitudes. This argument shows that even completely accurate medium-term man-power forecasts are not by themselves sufficient for purposes of vocational counselling. In practice, however, even these are rarely accurate. Furthermore, they say nothing about prospective earnings, which are certainly an important consideration for many students. There is a world of difference between stipulating the minimum levels of educated people required to realize a G N P target, as in the typical man-power forecast, and predicting the employment opportunities that will most probably materialize in various fields of specialization so as to help students in planning their careers. The confusion between the two may perhaps account for the poor quality of vocational guidance in most countries.

Despite everything that we have said, advocates of man-power forecasting will probably continue to insist that some knowledge of the future ten or fifteen years hence, however hazy, is better than nothing. Put like this, one can only agree. However, the implication of this view is that we ought to build the admitted haziness of long-term forecasts directly into the forecast itself. For instance, one plausible hypothesis is that the variance around the estimated mean of a forecast increases with the square of the length of time over which we are forecasting, producing a margin of error that steadily widens as we look farther into the future. Thus, the margin of error in predicting the demand for man power might be ± 2 per cent of the 1970 figures by 1971, $\pm(0.02)^2$ of 1970 figures by 1972, and so forth, amounting to an error of ± 22 per cent in 10 years and ± 35 per cent in 15 years. The same argument, possibly with a different margin of error, applies to the supply of man power. The growth paths for a particular type of educated man power might then look as follows:

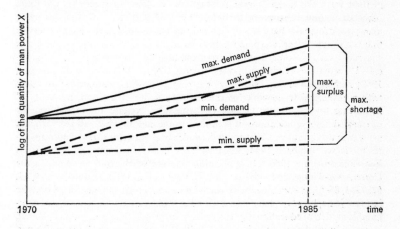

Figure 13   Growth rates of demand and supply of man power

In this case, we would have to be satisfied by the undramatic conclusion that there will be a shortage of X by 1985 if we have underestimated the demand for X and overestimated its supply, and not otherwise. Figure 13 is, of course, purely illustrative. I do not know whether the future supply is more uncertain than the future demand, whether the errors are symmetrical around the forecast, as in Figure 13, and whether the compounding error-term should be 1, 2 or 3 per cent.[11] However, until some such conception of discounting the uncertain future in terms of declining 'confidence levels' enters explicitly into man-power forecasting, the case for long-term man-power forecasting even of the multivalued type lacks intellectual foundation. Surely, there is some point at which the penumbra of doubt associated with a forecast becomes so large that the forecast itself misleads rather than informs?

In Conclusion

There can be no *economic* justification for allocating more resources to education and less to some other activity unless this results in greater

11. Nor do I know whether the path that is pursued to reach the target actually takes an exponential form, as in Figure 13. There are clearly a large number of possible paths that will achieve a target at some distant date. We can start off slowly and then speed up as we approach the target year; we can grow at a uniform rate over the entire planning period; we can grow quickly at first until we reach a plateau and then move gradually towards the target, and so on. By whatever method we make a man-power forecast, the problem of specifying a definite sequence of annual changes up to the target year of the forecast still remains. Most man-power forecasts have simply ignored this question or have opted for a path that is a simple linear interpolation between starting date and target date. It was squarely faced, however, first by Correa and then by Tinbergen and Bos: the so-called 'Correa–Bos–Tinbergen model' (Correa, 1963, ch. 14; Correa and Tinbergen, 1962; Tinbergen and Bos, 1965*) is one attempt to provide man-power forecasters with a numerical framework for calculating possible 'transition disequilibria' in moving towards future targets. Unfortunately, because the model consists of linear difference equations, it is limited to the case in which all the variables grow over all time at constant and indeed identical rates (for useful comments on the model see Bombach, 1964; Sen, 1964*; for further extensions, see Netherlands Economic Institute, 1966c). In application to several Mediterranean countries, the Correa–Bos–Tinbergen model gave inconsistent results (OECD, 1965, pp. 39, 43, 52, 72–3, 85–6), in consequence of which interest in it seems to have dried up. The last few years, however, have seen a veritable proliferation of less ambitious computable models of educational systems which can project the actual path of planned increases in enrolments (Armitage and Smith, 1967*; Armitage, Smith and Alper, 1969; Redfern, 1967; UNESCO, 1966).

measurable economic benefits per unit of costs. Few man-power planners would disagree with this fundamental rule of resource allocation in education. Nevertheless, the man-power requirements approach seems to be cast in an entirely different mould. Apparently, it regards the economic benefits of education as a matter of expediting economic growth by providing indispensable man-power with particular skill attributes. The costs of producing this educated man-power do not determine the outcome of a man-power forecast, presumably on the grounds that the returns in the sense of realized economic growth are certain to exceed the costs. Not only are the costs of education ignored as critical variables in the man-power requirements approach, but so also are the wages and salaries of educated people. In fact, prices are simply left out of account altogether in this brand of educational planning and what we have instead are physical requirements for a certain structure of occupations, associated with corresponding physical requirements for a certain structure of educational attainments. All this makes good sense if there are, in fact, no substitutes whatever for particular skills and if these skills can be produced in schools in one and only one way. Unfortunately, the approach itself provides no means of testing this strong assumption. At present, forecasts of man-power requirements cannot be made with any reliablity beyond periods of three to four years – and even three-year forecasts have frequently proved inaccurate – and yet the time perspective of almost all man-power forecasts is as long as ten to fifteen years. In other words, the assumption of low substitutability between highly qualified people has become an 'article of faith' that is inherently non-falsifiable.

Educational planning cannot get away from the need to make *ex ante* estimates of the likely future changes in the demand for skills – man-power projections in fact – but not ten or fifteen years ahead without the slightest reference to changes in earnings. It should be obvious now that the man-power requirements approach is simply an illegitimate extension of Leontief input–output models to periods so long that the assumption of fixed coefficients becomes an absurdity. The fact is that our ignorance of the distant future introduces an element of uncertainty into educational planning that no juggling with vectors and matrices can ever dispel. But the deterministic nature of long-term man-power forecasting is not an accidental feature that can be easily amended, reflecting as it does the degree to which the whole approach is steeped in engineering rather than economics. Someone once described man-power forecasting as 'a flourishing practice with virtually no theory'. This is unfair, I think. There is a theory of some sort. It is just that it is far-fetched. If educational planning is ever to grow up and to become integrated with economic planning, it must repudiate this modern form of crystal-ball gazing.

Chapter 6
Cost–Benefit Analysis:
The Private Calculus

The Private Demand for Education

Cost–benefit analysis of educational investment begins with a cross-tabulation of the labour force by age, earnings and educational attainments, from which are derived age–earnings profiles for particular educational cohorts. As we saw in Chapter 2, the internal rate of return on investment in education can be calculated as the discount rate which equates the present value of the extra lifetime earnings attributable to a certain amount or type of additional education (after the legal school-leaving age) to the present value of the costs of that extra education. It is an application of the 'discounted cash-flow technique' to human capital formation and as such is sometimes referred to as 'rate-of-return analysis' of educational investment. When earnings are taken after tax and costs are confined to out-of-pocket costs and earnings forgone, we obtain the private rate of return; when earnings are taken before tax and all resource costs are taken into account, we obtain the social rate of return. For purposes of educational planning, it is the social rate of return that is directly relevant. But the private rate of return also constitutes an important statistic for the educational planner if – and it is a big if – students and parents are attentive to employment opportunities and career prospects associated with various amounts and types of education. If the private rate of return on, say, university education is higher than the yield parents could earn on their financial assets, if any, or would have to pay for money they borrowed, if they can borrow, there will be a buoyant demand for university education. Whether households behave in this way is still an open question. But if they do behave like this, even if only approximately, the private rate of return may be almost as important for educational planning as the social rate.

In this chapter we will explore the implications of the idea that households choose education on rational economic grounds, deriving the private demand for education as a function of the private rate of return on educational investment. It may seem that this discussion is relevant only to rich countries. On the contrary, however, few indeed are the poor countries whose authorities have firm control over the supply of educational facilities; more often than not, it is the private rather than the social rate of return that drives the system forward.

Let us begin by considering what we will call *the education market* in a country like Britain. The decision to stay at school beyond the present legal-leaving age of fifteen is a voluntary decision and, therefore, one would think that the quantity of extra education demanded could be usefully regarded as a functional relationship between the willingness to purchase educational services and the 'price' of education. This is not the way the question of 'staying on' is usually posed in the literature. Nevertheless, it might be illuminating to follow the traditional line of thought of economists to its logical conclusion.

If we think of extra education after the age of fifteen as just another consumer good, its 'price' is simply the cost of remaining at school, consisting principally of earnings forgone since no fees are charged in secondary schools. It appears, however, that very few parents and even fewer students regard additional education as just another consumer good to be enjoyed for its own sake. Social surveys of the attitudes of parents and students reveal a keen awareness of the vocational opportunities opened up by additional education; job expectations are almost always ranked above all other motives in the decision to stay at school beyond the compulsory leaving age.[1] In other words, education is regarded as an investment good as much as a consumer good, because everyone recognizes the fact that extra education generates a stream of financial benefits in future years (see Chapter 1, p. 19). Viewed as an investment good, however, the 'price' of education necessarily involves a comparison of the costs and benefits of extra education with the costs and benefits of alternative investment opportunities. Is it possible to collapse this pair of cost–benefit

1. For Britain see *Crowther Report* (1959, II, pp. 25–6), Furneaux (1961, pp. 58–62), *Gurney-Dixon Report* (1954, pp. 41–8), *Robbins Report* (1963, vol. 2 (B), pp. 167–89) and Schools Council (1968). For the United States see Cole (1956, pp. 145–6, 163), Holinshead (1952, pp. 135–85), Lansing, Lorimer and Moriguchi (1960, pp. 119–46), Morgan *et al.* (1962, pp. 356–7), Roper (1949, p. xxi) and Rosenberg (1957, pp. 11–16).

streams into a single variable, the 'price' of education, so as to draw a demand curve for education as a function of price? This is the main question to which this section will be addressed.

The private rate of return on investment in education reduces the first pair of cost–benefit streams to a single number. The yield of the best alternative investment option available to households likewise reduces the second pair to a single number, ignoring for the moment what yield in the real world corresponds to it. The decision criterion is: remain at school if the private rate of return on the next increment of education exceeds the yield of the best alternative investment option, and not otherwise. In other words, we are assuming that people acquire extra education only when the job opportunities and the associated lifetime income stream that it is expected to create outweigh the value of the time and resources that will have to be invested, due allowance being made for the fact that income forgone in the present is worth more than equivalent income accruing in the future. Rigorously expressed, we are postulating the existence of a rational educational calculus according to which students or their parents act *as if* they were equalizing rates of return on all possible investment options available to them.

Put like that it sounds absurd. But let us spell it out concretely; suppose a fifth former aged sixteen is wondering whether to leave school at the end of term with a few GCE O-levels or to continue into the sixth form in the hope of eventually obtaining two A-levels, the minimum requirement for university entrance. The cost, including earnings forgone, of two additional years of schooling at that age is about £500 per year; this much he has no difficulty in discovering. More difficult is the question of benefits. There are even now virtually no relevant statistics that he can consult. What he does is to form some crude notion of the contribution that the additional years of schooling would make to his lifetime earnings by talking to friends, his parents, his teachers, vocational counsellors and Youth Employment Officers. It has been suggested that most students can realistically estimate only two points on their lifetime earnings profile, namely, their starting salary and their earnings at the age of about forty-five, being the typical age of their parents (Schultz, 1967, pp. 303–4). In other words, instead of a smooth profile observed after the event, as depicted in Figure 1 (p. 24) we get a kinked expected profile (Figure 14a). Alternatively, students obtain an impression of earnings over the next ten years, that is, up to the age of twenty-eight, so that the *ex ante* profile has the appearance of Figure 14(b). In either case, the fact remains that the student projects a prospective stream of extra future earnings associated with two more years of schooling. It is an open question whether he makes an implicit allowance for differences between his own native ability and that of the average student. Similarly, he may or may not take account of the likelihood that he will

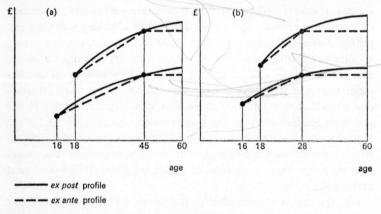

ex post profile
--- ex ante profile

Figure 14   Private estimates of lifetime earnings

complete the additional years of education; failure to do so will usually imply that costs have been borne that never yield a commensurate return. At any rate, having projected an expected net returns stream, he may at this point be said to discount it at his own subjective 'rate of time preference',[2] the market rate of interest or the yield of the next best investment option, whichever is higher, the last two only being relevant if he or his parents have borrowing power or funds to invest. That is to say, he calculates the private rate of return on the additional years of schooling and compares it with an alternative rate of return.

This stylized version of educational choice would appear more convincing if capital markets were perfectly competitive and freely accessible to individuals for loans to finance additional education: each household's time-preference rate would then have been brought

2. The rate at which an individual prefers present over future income when both are available to him on the same terms; for details, see Blaug (1968a, pp. 503–7, 533).

into equality by borrowing or lending at the market rate of interest, and the latter would then provide an accurate measure of the marginal profitability of investment opportunities in the economy. Under existing circumstances, however, the student's discount rate may well exceed the market rate of interest, particularly when it dawns on him that he should be adding a premium to his time-preference rate to make up for the considerable uncertainty of the pay-off from education, not to mention the peculiar illiquidity of the capital asset so acquired (Becker, 1964, pp. 111–13). This is true even if we suppose that the decision to remain at school is made by parents and not by students (see Chapter 1, p. 21) and that the ability to borrow (via hire purchase) will tend to raise the pattern of interest rates up to the marginal rate of time-preference of households. Nevertheless, credit rationing creates a spread of rates such that some households can borrow at 8 per cent while others have to pay up to 25 per cent (Becker, 1964, pp. 114–16). Suffice it to say, therefore, that it is perfectly possible that students, acting like rational investors, will reject additional years of schooling despite the fact that the investment in education would have been profitable if discounted at the market rate of interest. In rate-of-return language, the yield of two years in the sixth form might exceed the market rate of interest but that is not to say that it need exceed the subjective discount rate which students or their parents are using.

The upshot of these considerations is that evidence about rates of 'staying on' after the age of fifteen can never by itself tell us whether we are justified in postulating the existence of a rational educational calculus. Different students and parents have different time-preference rates and these themselves can never be observed. We have to infer what they are from behaviour and so long as people behave differently in acquiring additional education, we can always 'explain' all observed behaviour in terms of differences in the time-preferences of households, or indeed by the absence of a rational educational calculus. Nevertheless, it is reasonable to argue that more students would stay on at school if the costs of extra education declined and/or the future lifetime earnings differentials associated with extra education increased; and evidence to the contrary would indeed be a refutation of the assumption of a private calculus. In other words, we assume that the quantity of extra education that individual households demand is a positive function of the private rate of return on the increment of education. Furthermore, the best alternative investment option available to

British parents is unit trusts, which permit a minimum initial investment as low as £15 and have yielded returns since the war of about 12 per cent after tax at current prices and about 8 per cent after tax at constant prices (Merrett and Sykes, 1963, pp. 73–4). At the real rate of 8 per cent, some parents will demand zero amounts and other parents will demand positive amounts of extra education, depending on their subjective rates of time-preference and, of course, their 'taste' in education. Summing horizontally over all individual demand curves, we obtain the market demand curve for education as a negative function of r/i, where r is the yield of the best alternative investment option and i is the internal rate of return (see Figure 15).[3] What we are saying is: any combination of a reduction in the costs of voluntary education, an increase in the net earnings stream associated with additional education and a fall in the yield of alternative investment opportunities will lead to an increase in the demand for education *at the margin*; not that everyone will demand more education, but that some will.

The market demand curve for education, like all demand curves, is drawn on the assumption of 'other things being equal': firstly, the current incomes and 'tastes' of households and, secondly, the prices of other goods and services and particularly the spread of personal borrowing and lending rates. Taste is frequently a rather mystical element in the theory of consumer and investment behaviour. In the case of education, however, taste has been thoroughly investigated and, as a matter of fact, forms the subject matter of a rich literature in the sociology of education. That is to say, incomes and tastes are parameters of the demand curve from the viewpoint of the economist but dependent variables from the viewpoint of the sociologist. For our purposes, the most important sociological finding is that something like an intergeneration ratchet effect tends constantly to shift the demand for education irreversibly to the right as succeeding generations achieve ever higher terminal education ages (Brazer and David, 1962; see also Anderson, 1967a).[4] Projections of future enrolments in upper-secondary and higher education involve, therefore, in addition to projections of the private rate of return to education, an analysis

3. The market demand curve for education is analogous to the demand curve for investment in Keynesian macroeconomics, except that textbook diagrams of the investment-demand curve define r as the market rate of interest and ignore i, taking it for granted that the investor has already ranked all feasible investment projects in terms of their internal rates of return.

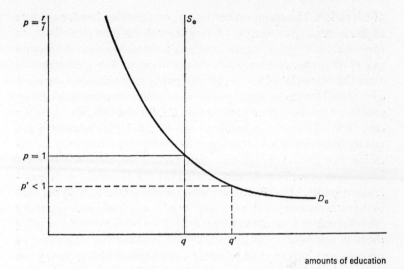

Figure 15   The market demand and supply curve of education

of the 'other things' that are held constant when we draw the demand curve for extra education.

If the supply of education were a function of the 'price' of education, as defined above by r/i, excess demand would cause the price to rise, that is, cause the rate of return on investment in education to fall, and equilibrium would be found at $p = 1$ where $r = i$. But it is doubtful whether the supply of educational services provided by the State is a function of the rate of return; even if it were, it would be a function of the social and not the private rate of return. The private rate of return, it will be recalled, involves a comparison of lifetime earnings differentials *after tax* associated with extra education with the *private* costs

4. Campbell and Siegel (1967) estimate the demand for higher education in the United States in the period 1919 to 1964 by regressing the fraction of the age group enrolled in institutions of higher education on time series of (a) real disposable income per household and (b) real tuition costs. They note that there has been no consistent trend in student enrolment ratios over the period 1919–64 from which they conclude that 'tastes' have not changed and that all observations fall along a single demand curve: the proportion of the age group entering higher education in any particular year is only different from another year because the supply curve has shifted. Apart from the failure to include opportunity costs as an independent variable in the regression, the argument about the identification of the demand curve is not very convincing.

TEOE–G

of education. The social rate of return, on the other hand, contrasts the same earnings differentials *before tax* with the *total* resource costs of education. Usually, the social rate of return is less than the private rate of return because tax payments out of extra lifetime earnings are more than outweighed by the excess of public over private educational costs; that is to say, voluntary education is almost everywhere heavily subsidized by the central government. So, for example, about 90 per cent of total financial expenditures on British higher education are met from public funds and the figure is even higher in secondary education. For students in full-time higher education, even indirect costs in the form of earnings forgone are heavily subsidized through maintenance grants. Thus, British university students bear only 25 per cent of the total resource costs of university education, whereas secondary school students bear about 65 per cent of the total costs of educating them. In consequence, British students in 1963 were earning about 14 per cent on what they had privately invested in obtaining three years of secondary plus three years of higher education: investment in these six years of additional education paid itself off in about seven years. On the other hand, the corresponding social yield on this investment to the community was only about 8 per cent (Henderson-Stewart, 1965, p. 260). Assuming that the State is aware of the social rate of return on educational investment, and even assuming that it entirely ignores the various non-economic benefits of education, the fact is that the supply curve is a function of different variables from those that govern the demand curve. We have expressed this fact by drawing a perfectly inelastic supply curve (Figure 15).

The *Robbins Report* demonstrated the existence of excess demand for higher education in Great Britain in 1963, defined as an excess of secondary school leavers qualified for admission over the number of student places available.[5] Lumping secondary and higher education together, and defining $p' = r/i = 8/14$, where r is the figure supplied by Merrett and Sykes and i the figure supplied by Henderson-Stewart, the quantity of extra education demanded in 1963 was q', whereas the

5. The situation has improved somewhat since then, but without eliminating excess demand. To some extent, further education acts as a safety valve, absorbing the demand not satisfied by universities and colleges of education. At the moment, about 60 per cent of those with two or more A-levels now obtain a university place, with another 20 per cent ending up in the public sector of higher education, that is, technical colleges and colleges of education (Layard, King and Moser, 1969, p. 72).

quantity supplied was q (Figure 15). In the normal case, we would expect this excess demand to be eliminated by the demanders bidding up the price of the investment good. Applied to the problem before us, the implication is that students would offer to pay higher fees to competing educational institutions, thus lowering the private rate of return on educational investment. Since this is impossible under existing arrangements, excess demand persists and q amount of places are rationed out by adopting appropriate standards of educational selection. Moreover, p is an equilibrium price from the point of view of the State, being the price at which rates of return on social investment in voluntary education are equal to the target rate of return of 8 per cent which nationalized industries since 1961 are expected to earn on their total assets. From the private point of view, however, q amount of places available implies p', which is a disequilibrium price because the demand for extra education at that price is not being satisfied (see Figure 15). And yet the attempt to satisfy the demand forthcoming at p' would make education socially unprofitable. The reason for this curious contradiction is simply that p' is itself a policy variable owing to the existence of student grants in higher education: excess demand for places could always be eliminated by cutting grants and thus raising the private costs of education.[6]

So much for the static picture. Surely, even with a given level of student grants, excess demand for additional education will lead to an adjustment of supply in the long run? Let us begin by observing that the static picture depicted above correctly describes the English situation, but it misrepresents the American educational scene. Most of the American state universities are required by law to admit all applicants; some of the others do not exercise their legal rights to be selective. Private American universities are largely privately financed and, while controlling their own rates of expansion, tend to add facilities in the wake of the number of applications. In general, nearly

6. It is significant that the shortage of university places in Great Britain first made itself felt in 1945/6 as a direct result of substantial grants for ex-service men and women under the Government's Further Education and Training Scheme (the British analogy to the American G.I. Bill). This extra demand had hardly been absorbed when the recommendations of the Minister of Education's Working Party on University Awards (1948) were put into effect, increasing the number and amounts of grants available to intending students to more than twice the pre-war levels, and thus sharply raising the private rate of return on investment in education.

all American students wanting to go to college in recent years have been able to find an institution willing to accept them. Similarly, there is no shortage of high-school places to accommodate students who want to remain in school.[7] Thus, the short-run supply curve of places in the United States shifts to the right from period to period so as to eliminate excess demand for places. The fundamental axiom of the *Robbins Report* is that 'courses of higher education should be available for all those who are qualified by age and attainment to pursue them and who wish to do so'. This is a far cry from the American 'open-door policy', inasmuch as the expansion contemplated in the *Robbins Report* is contingent upon maintaining the existing standards of admission and the existing levels of student aid. Nevertheless, it is tantamount to advocating a shift of the short-run supply curve to the right so as to increase the amount of education supplied to something like q'. This will, however, make investment in education socially unprofitable unless, of course, it is argued that rate-of-return calculations do not capture the spill-over benefits of education (see Chapter 4, p. 108), or that it takes time to add to the plant and equipment of colleges and universities, by which time the demand from industry and government for educated man power will have increased. As soon as the problem is posed in this way, it becomes apparent that we cannot meaningfully discuss the private demand for education without bringing the demand for labour into the picture. If we confine ourselves for the moment to higher education, this new consideration can be illustrated graphically by an extension of the demand-and-supply diagram for the education market.

The Education Market and the Labour Market

In the first quadrant of Figure 16, we simply reproduce Figure 15. In the second quadrant, we draw the demand curve of industry and government for university graduates as a function of their relative starting salaries (w), an upside-down version of a familiar diagram. One

7. The ones who do go to college, about 40 per cent of the relevant age group, turn out to be largely although not exclusively middle class (see above, Chapter 2, p. 38). The basic reason for this, in the U.S.A. as in the U.K., is the high private cost of attending college; it is perfectly possible to get through college in America without any help from parents, by virtue of the ample opportunities available to work part-time, but it requires more than average drive to do so (Jencks and Riesman, 1968, pp. 115–21).

difficulty with this demand curve is that it is only partly composed of profit maximizers; at the time of the *Robbins Report*, about 45 per cent of university graduates were public servants, that is, worked in education, health, civil service, local government, armed forces, nationalized industries and government research establishments, and in recent years about one-third of all pure- and applied-science graduates and about 40 per cent of arts graduates have found employment in the public sector. What we will assume, however, is that the private sector sets the pace for remuneration offered by the public

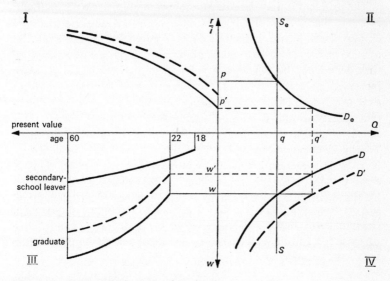

Figure 16 Demand and supply of graduates

sector. In the third upside-down quadrant, we depict the typical age–earnings profiles of graduates and secondary-school leavers (see Figure 1, p. 24). To complete the story and to remind us of the calculation of rates of return, we show the present value of the net returns stream of graduates in the fourth quadrant; this simply reproduces the argument of Figure 5 (p. 59), except that the vertical axis in the fourth quadrant is r/i instead of i.

We are now in a position to see the effects, everything else being the same, of the Robbins recommendations to increase the supply of graduates from q to q'. The impact effect is to lower starting salaries from w to w', to shift down the entire age–earnings profile (towards the horizontal axis), to shift and tilt down the curve of present values (away from the horizontal axis) and, as a summary statement of all these changes, to decrease the private rate of return on investment in education. All this is simply common sense expressed in jargon. The difficulty is that industry's demand for graduates is likely to increase over time, so that starting salaries may remain at w, or even rise beyond it, despite the increase in the supply of graduates to q'. Clearly, long-run equilibrium is possible but only perhaps as a tendency which is always approached but never actually reached.

The problem is that the educational production cycle of graduates is longer than the average production cycle of the industries that will employ them. Hence, industry's demand curve for, say, graduates in applied science is likely to move about considerably in the period of time in which the effective supply of science graduates is being increased. Even if it stays put, the demand curve for education is an *ex ante* function of the ratio of future benefits to present costs. A current scarcity of applied science graduates leading to an upward trend in salaries may shift the demand curve for higher education to the right. This builds up pressure to add to the number of available science places, whereas in the meantime industry is moving down a given demand curve by substituting cheaper technicians for expensive technologists. By the time the science students in the pipelines of the educational system have graduated, the total number of technologists that private industry wishes to hire may have declined. In other words, cycles of years of high salaries and years of low salaries are very likely to occur for highly qualified man power (see Chapter 5, p. 139).

In point of fact, the range of possibilities is even greater than that suggested so far. The figure of 14 per cent for the private rate of return to six years of secondary and higher education is an average for all faculties and subjects. But what little evidence we have suggests that, while the private costs of education are more or less the same for all students, the financial benefits of higher education are greater for science than for arts graduates (Craig, 1963, p. 35; Nottingham University, 1962, p. 1; Political and Economic Planning, 1956, pp. 133, 210–11, 227–33). While it is reasonable to argue that the average student is motivated by the private yield of education in deciding to stay on at school in order to qualify for higher education, it has sometimes been denied that the distribution of students among faculties in higher education is so motivated. It is obvious that prospective salaries are an important influence on the graduate's choice of subject but possibly his personal abilities and interests play an even greater role.[8] If this is the case, and recalling the difficulty of switching faculties in British universities, this means that the private rate of return on investment in higher education could vary between 13 and 15 per cent depending on the distribution of students among faculties, with no guarantee that the number of, say, technology graduates will conform to the quantity of technologists demanded by industry at current salaries. Furthermore, since the social costs of educating a science graduate are twice those of educating an arts graduate, the social rate of return on investment in science places is considerably less than that on investment in arts places. Even if the total supply of university places were governed by cost–benefit calculations, which may be doubted, the policy on faculty balances or broad subject groupings in universities has long been based, not on comparisons of costs and benefits, but on the results of man-power forecasts (Bowen, 1964, pp. 58–65; Layard, King and Moser, 1969, pp. 45–9). However, students have had their own views on the subjects they have preferred to study – witness the present glut of technology places.

Whatever the reason for this gap between the supply of and demand for technology places, the fact is that the number of students that will graduate in applied science in future years is only subject to control by the State at one remove, via the number of places made available. At the same time, it may well be true, as we just noted, that the demand for a particular type of education, as distinct from the demand for an additional amount, is not closely related to the differential economic benefits of one or another vocation. In consequence, the mechanism which overcomes a shortage of a particular skill by raising its rate of reward, and so attracting additional people to acquire that skill, works at best indirectly and inadequately for that range of skills requiring

8. There is little direct evidence on this question. In 1953, the University Grants Committee took the view that 'Any impression that men choose the faculty in which they would propose to read mainly by reference to the salaries to be expected on completion of training receives little support from the figures which show the pressure to enter the various faculties' (University Grants Committee, 1953, p. 20). In 1958, however, they forecast the demand for places in various faculties over the next five years, but observed that 'as long as prospective students are allowed freedom of choice any forecast of this kind can only be tentative. On the other hand, student choices have shown themselves to be remarkably sensitive to prospective demand' (University Grants Committee, 1958, p. 75).

higher education. And so long as student grants do not vary with the subject that is being studied, there may be very little the educational authorities can do to improve the situation. For example, more efficient vocational counselling might help but only if the root of the problem were inadequate information. If instead the problem is that students allow personal inclinations to dominate financial consider- ations, additional guidance on career choices alone would not alter the present picture.

All these difficulties disappear in the American context owing to the tradition of the 'liberal arts college' which militates against any tendency towards specialization at an early age. This tradition, coupled with the lack of rationing of places, gives credence to the notion that students by and large obtain additional schooling prim- arily because it leads to occupations with relatively higher earnings. Indeed, we find that the private rate of return on investment in American high school and college education over the last thirty years, as well as separate private rates of return to additional years of high- school and college education for white males, white women and Negroes, are in conformity with observed changes in school atten- dance rates and with differential rates of entry to college on the part of different sorts of students (Becker, 1964, pp. 91–3, 95, 101, 103). But in Great Britain, evidence of excess demand for university places, accompanied by relatively high private rates of return on invest- ment in higher education, proves nothing one way or the other about rational educational choice. The fact remains that if industry demands more technologists in 1970 and is prepared to pay more to obtain them, there is no guarantee that additional technologists will be forthcoming by 1973. The number of university students will increase only if the State decides to invest in additional places; even if ad- ditional places are created, a 'swing' from science to arts in fifth forms may actually reduce the number of technologists forthcoming.[9] Clearly, considerations such as these, in conjunction with the volatility of demand for educated man power on the part of industry, reduce the likelihood of rational intertemporal choice on the part of stu- dents and so throw into doubt the meaning of the demand curve drawn in quadrant I.

9. The crucial decision to specialize in science rather than in arts must be made at about fifteen on entering fifth form. Apparently, about half of all secondary- school children make the decision even before they reach the age of fifteen.

Indeed, the demand curve in quadrant II is subject to some doubts. It is true that an arts graduate is unsuitable for certain industrial occupations calling for technical knowledge and, similarly, that science graduates function poorly in most commercial occupations. There are jobs which only an engineer can fill; similarly for economists, accountants, doctors and lawyers. There is a sense, therefore, in which we can talk of a demand curve for a particular skill. But for a fair proportion of the occupations in a modern economy, what is required is not a special skill but rather a certain level of ability and drive. In large part, the function of an educational system is to provide employers with a costless selection device of ability and motivation. Not that the educational attainment of a job applicant serves merely to indicate his native ability, schooling having added absolutely nothing to his genetic endowment – this argument is extreme to the point of absurdity (see Chapter 2, p. 30) – but rather that people differ both in native ability and in the extent to which schooling improves their effective performance. To the extent that the educational system promotes students in accordance with measured ability, the expansion of the system may draw on students of lower abilities. When this is the case, an increase in the supply of graduates simply deflates the value of a university degree as an index of measured ability and, therefore, automatically increases the demand for graduates by relaxing hiring policies; alternatively, it tends to dry up the supply of less qualified people and hence forces employers to hire graduates to handle jobs which had previously been filled by secondary-school leavers. Demand and supply are now interdependent and, whenever this happens, the apparatus of demand-and-supply must be abandoned: when demand and supply shift about in unison, it is misleading to talk about price being determined by demand and supply.

The relevance of this argument depends on the facts of the case: as it happens, the 'pool of ability' is not always in imminent danger of being depleted (see Chapter 2, p. 43). In general, we are perfectly justified in regarding the demand for educated people as being independent of the quantities supplied, particularly when we are thinking not of all graduates but of people with particular professional qualifications. We reach the position that even if the total supply of educated people were geared to perfectly accurate predictions of the demand for educated man power, the failure to control the demand for education would cause the employment of educated people to be a function of the pattern of earnings. The argument involves four variables: demand and supply in 'the education market' and demand and supply in the labour market. All of these are policy variables, in the sense that they are subject to a measure of control by the public authorities. But only one of them, supply in the education market, is a policy variable pure and simple. It is precisely this which creates problems for educational planning.

The *scale* of higher education in Britain is not, of course, determined in accordance with man-power forecasts; except for a brief interlude after the war, it has been consistently based on what is quaintly called the 'social-demand approach', that is, on projections of the private demand for places. These projections, first carried out systematically by the Robbins Committee, simply take for granted most of the elements that underlie the private demand for higher education, namely, (a) the level of provision of upper-secondary education, (b) the standards of admission into higher education, (c) the level of student grants, and (d) the earnings of educated people in the labour market. But the demand-for-places approach to higher education has in practice come to be combined with the man-power requirements approach, in a way that is even now not adequately understood.

A man-power forecast would tell the educational planner how many scientists, engineers, technicians, and so on, he should supply by, say, 1980, without regard either to their prospective earnings or to the relative costs of producing them. In short, it would provide a forecast of one point of the 1980 demand schedule for a particular skill, if indeed the concept of a demand curve for labour is acceptable in this context. If, for any reason, the supply target stipulated in the man-power forecast is not met, so that relative earnings change, the educational planner will have no way of knowing whether the error was due to an inaccurate forecast of the shift in the demand curve between 1970 and 1980, or simply to the mistaken assumption that students choose to study particular subjects without regard to earnings prospects. Take the case of scientists; the forecast states that the demand for scientists in 1980 will be q (see Figure 17). As no reference is made to the earnings of scientists, the notion seems to be that the supply of scientists is entirely a matter of the facilities made available for the study of science; hence, the supply curve is depicted as perfectly inelastic. In 1980, however, instead of q scientists at salaries w, q' scientists are forthcoming at salaries w'; that is, we observe intersection

B instead of *C*. Are we on the 1980 demand curve, the error being due to the failure to meet our educational supply target, or are we on a different demand curve?

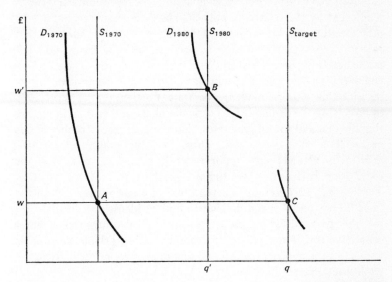

Figure 17   Man-power forecast for scientists

A projection of the private demand for education, on the other hand, predicts the number of students with different types of professional preparation that will be forthcoming by 1980. The educational planner has no way of knowing whether these students can be absorbed in the labour market without a change in the pattern of relative earnings. If relative earnings alter, it is possible that this will affect the structure of the private demand for education by fields of specialization. At this point, planners may be tempted to combine the demand-for-places projection with a man-power forecast by trying to provide enough places in higher education to meet the demands of students qualified for entry, while allowing the distribution of places among faculties and subjects to be governed by a forecast of man-power requirements. Indeed, this is exactly the approach that was adopted by the Robbins Committee in planning higher education in Britain: the Robbins projections embodied the principle handed down from previous man-power forecasting exercises, that two-thirds of the additional places outside medicine and agriculture should be in science and technology. But a moment's reflection will show that this really combines the worst of both worlds: it assumes that economic growth is affected by the relative supply of skilled professionals but not by their absolute supply; and it treats the fraction of the labour force that has received higher education as a consumption-decision best left in the hands of parents and students, whereas the ratio of scientists to engineers, or engineers to technicians, is taken to be an investment-decision that must be made by the State. Furthermore, it is precisely in projecting the demands for particular skills, rather than in projecting the demand for all graduates, that the man-power requirements approach is most vulnerable. Thus, this combination of the two approaches actually makes poor use of the advantages of man-power forecasting, such as they are. In any case, the outcome is a policy that is neither *laissez-faire* nor intervention, but a curious mixture of the two. To be sure, it is not difficult to find an ideological justification for the demand-for-places approach in a decentralized market economy. But if the policy of accommodating private demand is applied to the choice of additional schooling, why not equally to the choice of subject?[10]

It is perfectly clear that man-power forecasters have in mind the case in which both the demand and supply of educated man power are perfectly inelastic: this is evident from their inclination to define man-power shortages in physical terms, such as the number of unfilled job vacancies, while assuming as a matter of course that shortages can only be remedied by increasing supply. The difficulty with this view is that of explaining why the relative earnings of highly qualified man power change at all, since the changes that do take place cannot apparently affect anything. Similarly, projections of the demand-for-places that invariably ignore earnings give comfort to the view that

10. The University Grants Committee has recently relaxed the policy of faculty balances but it has not abandoned its schizophrenic attitude to the principle of student's sovereignty. In their 1968 *Memorandum of General Guidance* to the universities, they say, firstly, that 'in the light of the present A-level trends the major increase must be in the number of arts-based, rather than science-based students' and, secondly, that 'it would be valuable if the universities collectively made a further deliberate and determined effort to gear a larger part of their "output" to the economic and industrial needs of the nation' (University Grants Committee, 1968, app. C).

the private demand for education is perfectly inelastic. This encourages the tendency to discuss educational supply in total isolation from conditions in the labour market. But if there is anything to the idea of a rational private calculus with respect to education, enrolment projections that neglect to consider earnings, and with it the price-elasticity of demand for education, are almost certain to go wrong. The connexions between the education market and the labour market make it impossible to consider adjustments in either without reference to the other.

At this point, the argument clearly calls for empirical support. What evidence is there that swings in the earnings of particular types of educated man power feed back to the demand of students to read particular subjects? Alas, as we already noted, there is virtually no British data that can throw light on these questions. Figures on earnings by level or type of education are not collected by any official agency in Great Britain, and even the need to collect such data is not generally recognized. Some tentative evidence on engineers is now beginning to emerge (Richardson, 1969; also Peck, 1968, pp. 453–64), but it is as yet unrelated to the demand for engineering education. There is, of course, a vast body of social survey data which does indicate that British students and parents are principally motivated by vocational considerations in making educational choices (see p. 170). But the method of testing hypotheses by inquiring directly into personal motives is inherently unsatisfactory, since it fails to distinguish between marginal and intramarginal choices.[11] Besides, it is not

11. The point is so little understood that an illustration may be helpful. Suppose we ask whether an increase in the salaries of teachers would increase the supply of teachers, either by motivating students to acquire teaching qualifications or by inducing trained teachers who have left the labour force to come back into teaching. The social-survey approach to this problem would be to submit a questionnaire to a random sample of the relevant population, asking them to place weights on the pecuniary and non-pecuniary attractions of teaching. No doubt what we would find is that some teachers care more about salaries than about anything else, whereas others care more about the type of children they are teaching, the subject they are teaching, the atmosphere of the school, etc. But what we wanted to know is the cost in terms of total salaries of producing a given increase in the supply of teachers. It is a matter of indifference to the authorities whether every potential teacher responds to an increase in salaries, provided enough of them do. The fundamental lesson of economics that 'prices are determined by the *marginal* buyer and seller' has never been grasped by those who go about dealing with social problems by conducting opinion surveys.

what people think they are doing that concerns us, but what they actually do. It is always preferable to check assumptions about motives by looking at the behaviour that is predicted by the assumptions. Unfortunately, we know so little about the behaviour of households with respect to education. It is perfectly possible, therefore, to account for the whole post-war 'enrolment explosion' in Britain in terms of a radical shift in the taste for education as a consumer good, while remaining agnostic about the causes of the 'swing from science to arts' which, after all, no one has yet succeeded in explaining satisfactorily (*Dainton Report*, 1968, pp. 46, 77, 81, 86). The data, such as it is, is not yet capable of definitely rejecting such interpretations. All that we can say at this stage is that it appears that students and parents choose more education and different types of education *as if* they were making a rational investment response to certain monetary returns. At any rate, no evidence has yet been produced that would falsify this assumption.

For the United States, however, the evidence is much more persuasive. In the case of engineers, for example, an excess of unfilled vacancies over applicants in the early 1950s led to widespread complaints of a 'shortage' of engineers. In a well-known study, however, Blank and Stigler showed that the salaries of engineers had risen less between 1946 and 1955 than those of other professional groups, suggesting a market surplus rather than a shortfall (Blank and Stigler, 1957, pp. 22–33). Their definition of a shortage is a situation where 'the number of workers available (the supply) increases less rapidly than the numbers demanded *at the salaries paid in the recent past*'. However, when we recall the lags that are likely to characterize labour market adjustments for highly qualified man power (see Chapter 5, p. 140), it is immediately apparent that the Blank–Stigler definition is ambiguous: salaries of engineers lagging behind those of other wage and salary earners could mean either (a) that a previous shortage was being eliminated, (b) that a previous shortage was turning into a surplus or (c) that a previous surplus was getting worse (Arrow and Capron, 1959, pp. 333–5*). Indeed, after breaking down the salaries of engineers by subcategories, distinguishing between older and younger engineers, Hansen found evidence that the surplus of the late 1940s and early 1950s had turned into a shortage around 1953 or 1954. The finding of a decline in all engineering salaries up to 1953, followed by a rise particularly for new engineers, proved to be consistent with information on trends in engineering enrolments and the output of engineering degrees: the number of graduates in engineering fell from an absolute peak of 53,000 in 1949–50 (16 per cent of all first degrees awarded to men in that year) to a low of 22,000 in 1953–4 (11·9 per cent of all male degrees); by 1958, however, the output of new engineers had increased to about 35,000 or 14·5 per cent of all male degrees (W. Lee Hansen, 1961, pp. 255–6). These sharp changes in both absolute numbers and proportions begin to suggest the degree of responsiveness that typifies both American students and American educational institutions.

So far we have argued as if individuals take account only of relative earnings in selecting an occupational career. But the costs of acquiring a professional qualification may vary independently of changes in earnings, thereby altering the relative attractiveness of one occupation to another. This suggests that comparisons among rates of return would provide better criteria of shortages or surpluses than comparisons among earnings. Following this train of thought, Hansen has enforced his earlier conclusions of the appearance of a shortage of engineers in 1953: he shows that the private rate of return to all college graduates, which stood at 14 per cent in 1939, remained unchanged at about 12 per cent between 1949 and 1956, whereas the rate to engineers fell from 20 per cent in 1939 to 12 per cent in 1949 and then rose to 17 per cent between 1949 and 1956 (W. Lee Hansen, 1967, pp. 211–12; see also Bumas, 1968). Similar trends have been observed in private rates of return for doctors and dentists, with rates to doctors falling absolutely and relatively to all college graduates between 1939 and 1956 (W. Lee Hansen, 1965a, p. 86). Clearly, both the relative training costs and the relative earnings of particular professions do vary significantly over fairly short periods of time in the United States, bearing all the earmarks of a dynamic adjustment to shortages and surpluses. On the whole, the American system of higher education appears to be amazingly responsive to economic 'needs' as manifested in the labour market (Folk, 1967, pp. 126–36).

It is worth saying once again, however, that all this is only confirmatory evidence which by itself 'proves' nothing. The demand for years of schooling may be a positive function of expected earnings and a negative function of costs, but from this it does not follow that choice of subject is likewise a matter of rates of return. Much more detailed work on particular professions and occupations is needed before we can conclude that the private calculus plays a part in determining both the scale and the composition of the output of higher educational systems.

The discussion so far may have encouraged the belief that occupational choice is entirely a matter of pecuniary advantages and disadvantages. Long ago, however, Adam Smith argued that the exercise of occupational choice tends to equalize, not the pecuniary rewards, but the 'net advantages' of different occupations to different individuals, that is, the sum of the monetary and non-monetary attractions. Occupations, he observed, differed in (a) agreeableness, that is, conditions of work and degree of effort; (b) the costs of acquiring the skill to carry them on; (c) the degree of regularity of employment; (d) the trust reposed in those employed in them (deemed to be irksome); and (e) the degree of uncertainty attaching to anticipated earnings (Smith, 1776). Therefore, he concluded, differences in pecuniary earnings constitute 'compensating differences', in the sense that they compensate individuals for the positive or negative psychic income from a job. We may quarrel with some of his categories and to the list we would now want to add fringe benefits, paid holidays, non-contributory pensions, expense accounts, subsidized housing, etc. Nevertheless, the implication of Adam Smith's argument is as clear today as it was then: in general, we do not expect private rates of return on investment in education and training to be equalized between occupations. This does not necessarily invalidate comparisons between occupations over time, since the non-pecuniary attributes of occupations are not likely to alter radically in periods of less than ten years. But at any moment of time, identical rates of return on educational investment by occupation could only mean that educated people are indifferent about the non-pecuniary aspects of work.

Wilkinson has made use of the 1961 Canadian Census to examine private rates of return to education by six occupational categories: labourers, carpenters, typesetters, draughtsmen, technicians and engineers. He found that rates of return to various levels of education are equalized within each occupation but not between occupations (Wilkinson, 1966, pp. 563, 567). The former result suggests that individuals do respond to differences in expected net lifetime earnings when deciding upon the amount of education to acquire before entering an occupation. The latter result, however, suggests that other factors intervene in the final selection of an occupation. Wilkinson denies that the explanation can be found in the non-pecuniary disadvantages of higher-paying occupations. He suggests that variations in knowledge regarding opportunities in the better-paying jobs, unemployment rates for persons of different skill levels and differences in bargaining power account for most of the differences in rates of return between occupations. In addition, he raises the question of whether there is a positive association between formal education and on-the-job training received, so that comparisons in terms of the cost of schooling alone ignore an element that generates higher lifetime earnings (Wilkinson, 1966, pp. 567–9). Be that as it may, it should be obvious now that economic theories of occupational choice are inherently difficult to test; the central problem is that at least one element in the choice process, non-pecuniary advantages and disadvantages, can never itself be directly observed (Reder, 1955; Rottenberg, 1956).

The Economics of Labour Training

We will now round off our discussion of the private calculus by introducing the notion of investment in labour training, a type of human capital formation that is practically, although not conceptually, distinct from investment in formal schooling. At first glance, it may be difficult to conceive of individuals investing in their own training: most of us are inclined to think of labour training as something provided by business firms for reasons which individual workers cannot affect by their own action. But when entering the labour market, workers are usually free to choose between jobs with relatively high pay which offer no prospects of learning from experience, and jobs which pay less but provide both on-the-job training in the form of experience in certain skills and off-the-job training in the form of instruction programmes. Since either type of training may be expected to raise the productivity of workers and hence their future earnings, the choice is actually between income streams differing in starting levels and in rates of increase over time.

It appears that 'training' is actually a somewhat vague term. It may comprise one or all of three things: (a) 'on-the-job learning from experience', some of which is unavoidable and hence does not constitute training, (b) 'on-the-job training' under the supervision of a foreman or an older worker and (c) 'off-the-job training', involving the provision of formal training programmes inside the factory (Machlup, 1962, pp. 57–61). Cutting across these three types of training is Becker's powerful distinction between 'specific training' and 'general training' (Becker, 1964, pp. 11–12, 18–19*). *Specific training* is training which enhances the future productivity of a trainee in the firm providing it, and either does not increase his productivity in other firms or at least does not increase it to the same extent. *General training*, however, raises the trainee's productivity irrespective of which firm he works for. Now, in perfect competition, wage rates reflect the marginal productivity of workers, that is, their productivity in any firm whatever. Thus, firms operating under competitive conditions have no incentive to pay the costs of general training because they cannot guarantee that they will be able to retain workers who have received training. This does not mean that general training will not be provided. What it does mean is that the costs of general training programmes are passed on to trainees in the form of reduced earnings during the training period. In short, firms do not finance general training, they only provide it. Firms will bear the burden of training expenses only when the training is specific. Eventually, of course, workers pay for it anyway as the training expenses are recouped out of their increased productivity; nevertheless, specific training must raise earnings if the trained worker is to have incentive to stay on with the firm. Obvious examples of specific training are (a) formal orientation programmes for newly hired workers, (b) initial rotation of new workers among departments, (c) probationary periods of supervision, and the like, whose costs consist largely of output forgone for several days or weeks.

To the extent that training is largely general rather than specific, workers themselves invest in training by choosing jobs that pay less now but promise opportunities for training and hence promotion at a later date to better-paying jobs. It is almost obvious that general training is likely to be a more important phenomenon than specific training. After all, the best example of general training is formal education itself, which like all general training is largely paid for by trainees themselves in the form of earnings forgone. But even ignoring formal schooling, it is probably true that the bulk of expenditures on training are devoted to general rather than specific on-the-job and off-the-job training. But a statement like this carries conviction only if we interpret the distinction between two kinds of training as a matter of the nature of the training provided. But what if a firm, after providing training that produces skills useful to any firm in the industry, discovers that trained workers rarely leave? In that case, it may be tempted to bid for labour by paying above the competitive rate, in effect sharing the cost of training with the trainees, knowing that it can always recoup these later by paying trained workers less than their improved marginal product. What started out as general training has become, at least in part, specific training simply because, for some reason or other, there is little mobility in the relevant labour market. Reflection on this example suggests immediately that the distinction between general and specific training actually has little to do with the content of training. If a firm were certain that a trainee would never leave, the question of the generality of the training becomes irrelevant and the firm can behave as if the training were specific. Turned around and expressed in the form of a theorem: the higher the mobility of labour, the more training is general rather than specific, paid for in the first instance by workers rather than firms (Oatey, 1970).

Becker recognizes the significance of labour mobility in distinguishing between the two kinds of training[12] but fails perhaps to emphasize it sufficiently. In consequence, he has been misunderstood as formulating a theory that holds only in perfectly competitive labour markets (Eckaus, 1963*), whereas the distinction he drew is perhaps even more useful in labour markets characterized by monopsony and oligopsony. All that needs to be assumed to make Becker's theory applicable to the real world is that (a) general trainees are paid less than the going rate for performing some skilled task and that (b) specific trainees tend to be paid above the going rate in the firm providing specific training. Becker has also been attacked for implying that training in industry typically involves off-the-job training. Most training, it has been argued, is simply 'learning on-the-job' and hence an unavoidable joint input with capital equipment in a particular investment project; in that sense, there are no identifiable training costs that can or cannot be shifted to trainees (Eckaus, 1963*).

12. He observes that 'very strong monopsonists might be completely insulated from competition by other firms, and practically all investments in their labour force would be specific. On the other hand, firms in extremely competitive labour markets would face a constant threat of raiding and would have fewer specific investments available' (Becker, 1964, pp. 19–20*).

But except for training that is absolutely specific to a single firm (such as an induction course given to new employees), it is almost always possible to avoid training costs by directly recruiting workers with the required level of skill. Whether a firm recruits or trains for a skill depends simply on the costs of the two alternatives. If a skill is in abundant supply, it will usually be cheaper to recruit for it; as the skill becomes scarcer, however, search costs will increase to the point where it is cheaper to train for it, assuming the job cannot be re-designed so as to eliminate the need for this particular skill. Even when training takes the form of informal experience on-the-job, it does not follow that the costs of this kind of training are, therefore, inseparable from production costs. So long as it is possible to compare the output of experienced and inexperienced workers in the same department, the costs of on-the-job training in the form of output forgone can be estimated. In general, despite a good many difficult cases, there is no reason to think that firms cannot identify and measure the costs of providing unavoidable 'learning from experience' (Oatey, 1970).

A much more telling criticism of Becker is that firms are likely to treat labour training as a fringe benefit; although it may be initially introduced to deal with the costs of a high rate of labour turnover, training soon comes to be regarded as a welfare service to which the cost–benefit calculus is not applied. It can be no accident that few firms keep accounts of the direct costs of training programmes and that even fewer firms make attempts to measure the benefits of train- ing. In the light of such non-optimal attitudes to training, it is doubtful whether firms do, in fact, pass on the true costs of training to workers. Nevertheless, even casual observation shows that apprentices are invariably paid less than fully skilled workers, while performing much the same tasks, a fact which is neatly explained by Becker's distinction between general and specific training. Even if Becker's theory is only partially applicable, it provides a powerful framework for uniting various aspects of labour economics – wage determination, training, recruitment, pension schemes, labour contracts, fringe benefits – which up to now have been treated as separate problems

Becker spells out several implications of his theory which illustrate its fecundity in illuminating well-attested features of labour markets (Becker, 1964, pp. 11 ff.*). Among the most important of these is that the 'general' component of any training will give rise to age–earnings profiles that are initially convex from below: during the early years of the profile, the worker is paying for all or a good part of the training by forgoing earnings; during the later years of his working life, he receives returns on his investment in training and hence the profile becomes concave from below. Thus, the tendency for earnings to rise with age in the early phases of working life, which we found to be one of the dominant characteristics of age–earnings profiles (see Chapter 2, p. 27), is in conformity with Becker's theory, assuming that general training tends to outweigh specific training.

Having come so far, we must now face up to the problem that the earnings differentials we observe to be associated with various levels of educational attainment include the monetary returns to training that may have been provided to workers. In using age–earnings profiles to calculate rates of return on investment in schooling, are we not in fact confusing the effects of schooling with the effects of training? Indeed, if all labour training is general training, the age–earnings profiles we observe systematically understate earnings attributable to formal education in the early years of employment and overstate them in the later years; likewise, even if training is specific, there is a general tendency to overstate earnings attributable to schooling. We can convey the argument, by considering an age–earnings profile associated with a certain number of years of schooling when no training is given, and then adding to this the effect of either general or specific training (see Figure 18). In the case of general training, the worker voluntarily sacrifices earnings during the training period for the sake of higher earnings after being trained. In the case of specific training, the firm pays for the training provided and only pays the worker a little more after he is trained in order to retain his services so that the costs can be recouped; specifically trained workers, therefore, will earn less in later life than generally trained workers. The age–earnings profile we actually observe compounds all these effects and the problem we now face is that of somehow removing the effects of training, so as to leave us with the age–earnings profile attributable to schooling alone.

The point we have just made is perfectly general and applies in turn to every other form of human capital formation: for example, the profiles we observe also confuse the effects of investment in medical care with those of investment in education and training. In the circumstances, how can we ever hope to isolate the income benefits of education?

Contrary to intuitive impression, however, the phenomena of

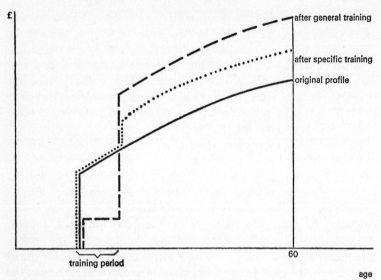

Figure 18   Effects of training

multiple investments in human beings only bias our estimates of the rate of return on education in situations of disequilibrium. In conditions of general equilibrium, when all investments have been carried to the point where rates of return are equalized in all directions, expenditures on labour training or medical care simply add as much to the costs as to the returns to human capital formation. That is to say, if the individual has decided to terminate his education because additional amounts of education would yield less than 8 per cent (which we assume to be his cut-off rate), he will choose an occupation providing general training if and only if the immediate earnings he thereby sacrifices will yield 8 per cent in the form of higher earnings in later life. In other words, investing in yourself does not stop when you leave school but continues when you enter the labour force; the choice between jobs with different provisions for training continuously creates new opportunities for self-investment. In full equilibrium, the present value of the earnings forgone will be equated to the present value of the extra lifetime earnings generated in this way, when both are discounted at 8 per cent. And provided all investments are carried out until the margin of indifference is reached, estimates of rates of return on education from observed age–earnings profiles will not be biased by the effects of other types of human capital formation (Becker, 1964, pp. 89–90).

On the assumption that all training is general training and that the yields of all investments in human beings are, in fact, equalized, Mincer manages to calculate the total amounts invested in on-the-job and off-the-job training in the United States in 1939, 1949 and 1958 without ever resorting to accounting data at the enterprise level (Mincer, 1962). The procedure is simple enough: starting with actual age–earnings profiles, he constructed net returns streams by three levels of education and calculated the corresponding private rates of return on investment in schooling (see Chapter 2, p. 47). He then applied these rates to each successive profile to determine what earnings would have been if individuals had not invested in training. These forgone earnings constitute the costs of general training and hence measure the investments individuals make in training. Let us illustrate the argument for high-school and college graduates (see Figure 19). Suppose the private rate of return on going to college at the age of eighteen is 8 per cent. Since all rates of return are equalized, this means that high-school graduates are investing in general training which yields 8 per cent. Thus, if they refused to invest and instead chose to enter higher-paying jobs which provided no training, their earnings would compound at 8 per cent over the four years that is required to complete a college course. An identical argument holds for college graduates aged twenty-two. All we have to do, therefore, is to build up the successive annual layers of earnings forgone compounding through time at 8 per cent (the shaded areas in Figure 19) and sum over all individuals to obtain the total sums invested by individuals in training; the series converges on actual earnings around the age of forty by which time further opportunities to invest in training have been exhausted (Mincer, 1962, pp. 526–8 and table A4).

Although Mincer's results have all the appearance of pulling a rabbit out of a hat, they involve nothing more than a straightforward application of the basic assumption that long-run equilibrium under conditions of perfect competition implies 'that the rate of return is the same on each year's investment whether at school or on the job' (Mincer, 1962, p. 526). Furthermore, it is well known that the internal rate-of-return approach to capital budgeting decisions only provides the correct decision-rule in any and all cases if (a) capital markets are perfectly competitive, (b) all available investment options are com-

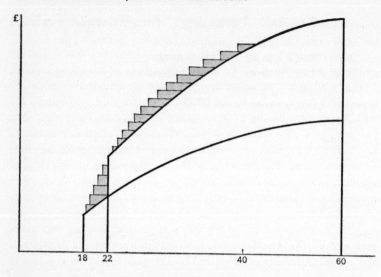

Figure 19   Investment in general training

pletely divisible, (c) all investment options are independent of each other and (d) all net returns from options can be reinvested at their own internal rates of return up to the terminal date of the most durable option available. The availability of jobs providing general training is precisely what secures conditions (b) and (d), and indeed the best way of understanding what Mincer did is to consider the implications of condition (d). Mincer's principal conclusion is that investment in general training for the male labour force is as great as investment in formal education. Secondly, investment in training has been increasing since 1939, both in the aggregate and per worker employed, although not as quickly as investment in formal education. Thirdly, women undertake only about one-tenth as much training as do males, although investment in schooling is roughly the same for the two groups. And, fourthly, better educated males undertake more training than less educated males, a surprising result inasmuch as it makes training complementary to, rather than a substitute for, formal schooling (Mincer, 1962, pp. 530, 532, 535, 539).

Mincer discusses various shortcomings in his calculations: age-earnings profiles are not standardized for differences in native ability and home background; all rates of return to investments are assumed to be constant throughout working life; no reliable evidence on the costs of specific training is available, and so on. But more important than any of these is the assumption that rates of return on schooling are not very different from those on training. He does make an effort to check his results by examining data on the costs and returns of particular training programmes in the United States. For example, comparisons of craft apprentices' and operatives' earnings gave an average private rate of return to apprentice training for three industries well below the private rate of return on college education, although social rates of return were not very different in the two cases (Mincer, 1962, pp. 533–4). However, from the point of view of Mincer's calculations, it is the private rate of return that is important. Since the private rate of return on schooling seems to exceed the rate on training, the implication is that his estimates of the costs of training are actually on the low side. Likewise, it follows that calculations of the rates of return on schooling from observed age–earnings profiles are, in fact, biased downwards: if we could truly separate the costs and returns from training, rates of return on schooling would rise – a surprising result.

We have reached what is perhaps the central weakness in the armoury of educational planners. We may as well confess that we know almost nothing about the economics of training, its incidence, its costs and its benefits. Although some material has recently appeared on government retraining schemes (Gordon, 1965; Lester, 1966, ch. 7; Somers, 1965, 1968; Weisbrod, 1966; and a review by Ribich, 1968, pp. 38–50), Becker's book seems not to have stimulated much research on the phenomenon of training in industry (but see B. Thomas, Moxham and Jones, 1969). To this day, we appear to have to make do with rates of return on investment in education which are actually averages of rates of return to schooling and rates of return to training. Since it is difficult to sustain the belief that rates of return on all types of human capital formation are more or less equalized, all our results are subject to an indeterminable bias.

This chapter may seem inconclusive but the notion of the private calculus, and its extension from schooling into training, marks what in time may come to be regarded as a watershed in the history of economic thought. Becker's *Human Capital* is perhaps one of those seminal works whose full impact is the greater for being long delayed.

Chapter 7
Cost–Benefit Analysis:
The Social Calculus

An Omnibus of Objections

We switch gear now to consider the social rate of return on investment in education. This statistic must be judged in terms different from those invoked in the last chapter on the private rate of return. There is no question now of 'explaining' how people make decisions about education, or of testing behavioural assumptions about educational choice. Rather the issue is: assuming that economic growth is the maximand of educational policy, do social rates of return on educational investment provide relevant criteria for policy makers? We are still in the realm of positive rather than normative economics because doubts are raised, not about the objectives of educational policy, but about the means of securing these objectives. Nevertheless, the social level of discourse raises all sorts of difficulties not encountered at the level of individual decision making.

These difficulties may be summarized in the form of a number of objections which critics have advanced against the notion of basing educational planning on rate-of-return analysis (Balogh and Streeten, 1963*; Danière, 1965; Eckaus, 1964; Merrett, 1966; Shaffer, 1961*; Vaizey, 1962, ch. 3):

1. Endowed ability, individual motivation, social class origins, educational attainment, occupation taken up and training received are all so highly intercorrelated that the pure effect of education on earnings cannot be satisfactorily isolated.

2. Social rates of return are consistently underestimated because no allowance is made for the consumption benefits of education and the non-pecuniary attractions of certain occupations that are accessible only to the highly educated.

3. The direct benefits of education are quantitatively less important

than the indirect spill-over benefits and the latter are not taken into account in what is called 'the social rate of return'.

4. Existing earnings differentials in favour of educated people reflect, not differences in their contribution to productive capacity, but long-established social conventions in an inherently imperfect labour market.

5. The calculations depend on the projection of future trends from cross-section evidence, thus neglecting historical improvements in the quality of education as well as future changes in the demand and supply of educated man power.

We will now discuss each of these objections in turn, dwelling longer on those which have not yet been discussed in earlier pages of this book.

Psychic Returns and Spill-Overs

The possibility of attributing a definite portion of observed earnings differentials to the effect of education alone was canvassed in some detail in Chapter 2 (p. 32). All that need be said here is to remind the reader of the conclusions we reached. It appears that the bulk of earnings differentials associated with educational attainment can be statistically attributed to education, and that the so-called 'alpha coefficient' which expresses this fact typically varies from 0·6 to 1·0, rising as we move up the educational ladder through secondary to higher education. Whether we should actually adjust observed earnings differentials for differences in ability and family environment before calculating social rates of return depends on the policy action that we are contemplating. For marginal changes in enrolments, new students may be expected to share the personal and social attributes of existing students and hence no adjustment is called for; if, however, we intend to expand the demand for a certain level of education by eliminating fees or by subsidizing students directly, an ability adjustment is clearly warranted. In the context in which the problem frequently arises, such as that of an underdeveloped country considering a non-marginal expansion of education, there may be no data from which the alpha coefficient can be estimated. In all such cases, sensitivity analysis is called for: rates of return must be calculated on the basis of several alpha coefficients, so as to check whether the results are sensitive to the ability adjustment. Examples of this way of resolving the difficulty are given below.

Earnings differentials attributable to education include the monetary returns to associated medical care and on-the-job training. Whether this introduces a bias in estimates of the rate of return on educational investment depends entirely on determinants of expenditure on these other forms of human capital formation. As we noted earlier (Chapter 6, p. 196), no bias results if the social yield on investment in health and training is the same as the social rate of return on investment in formal education. In the absence of any evidence of these other yields, therefore, there is no way of knowing whether we have overestimated or underestimated the rate of return on education. In general, it is difficult to say more than this except to underline the fact that educational planning cannot afford to ignore the incidence of medical care and on-the-job training for the labour force.

This brings us to objection 2 having to do with the psychic returns to education. The standard method of dealing with consumption benefits of education is either to subtract a notional consumption component from costs or to add an estimate of the consumption benefits to the monetary returns (Schultz, 1963, pp. 54–6); in either case, of course, the effect is to increase the rate of return on investment in education. We have already thrown doubts on this argument in so far as the private rate of return is concerned (see Chapter 1, p. 21). From the point of view of policy, however, the assertion that education is to be valued for its own sake amounts to a denial, not of rate-of-return analysis as such, but of economic growth as the principal objective of educational planning. The problem cannot be resolved simply by adding to the social rate of return on investment in education a figure which reflects the intrinsic value of education (Bowen, 1968, pp. 89–90). When objectives are in different dimensions, every addition of values implies a set of weights and it is precisely these weights which constitute the problem of decision making (see Chapter 4, p. 126). The point of calculating the social rate of return is simply that it provides a summary of the measurable economic effects of education. If it is decided that other effects are more important, the only question is: how much more important? This would be a difficult question to answer even if we knew all about the financial profitability of education to the country as a whole. It is an impossible question to answer, however, if we do not.

The non-pecuniary benefits of certain white-collar occupations that are accessible only to better educated people constitute another psychic income from education, and in this case a psychic income that is bound to give rise to lower earnings than would otherwise be observed. No doubt, neglect of this factor leads to a tendency to underestimate the private rate of return (see Chapter 6, p. 191). But it is questionable whether the magnitude of this bias is very large: if it were, we would not always observe a positive correlation between education and earnings for all age groups. Non-pecuniary alternatives, however, create no bias whatever for the social rate of return. Since they affect only the supply and not the demand for labour, they do not distort the relationship between earnings and the marginal revenue product of labour (Bowen, 1968, pp. 83–4). It is true that employers can offer less for particularly attractive jobs; thus, two jobs differing in their non-pecuniary attractions, but otherwise the same, will differ in relative earnings but this difference will accurately reflect the relative scarcities of labour available for the two jobs. The argument is unaffected by the fact that non-pecuniary attractions may take the form of fringe benefits that impose extra costs on employers, provided these costs are no greater than what employers would have had to pay in higher earnings to attract the same amount of labour. In point of fact, employers may save money by offering fringe benefits instead of higher earnings, at least if it is true, as is so often asserted, that better-educated people attach a higher than average value to the non-pecuniary aspects of work. Therefore, if it is indeed true that fringe benefits are more common in education-intensive industries, a modest upward adjustment is required in the social rate of return to education.

Objection 3 concerns the vexed question of spill-overs which we have already discussed at some length in Chapter 4. We recall that the core of the problem is what we have called the 'first-round spill-overs', that is, the tendency of better-educated people to raise the incomes of less educated people who are working alongside them. If these first-round spill-overs are positive, we have underestimated the social rate of return twice over. That follows from the fact that the earnings differentials we observe do embody the first-round spill-overs. If we can somehow remove them, the absolute earnings differentials attributable to education must increase and, hence, the calculated social rate of return must rise; adding them back in, however, raises the rate of return once again.

In addition to the first-round spill-overs, there are a number of second-round spill-overs in the form of encouragements to research and reduced demands on social services. These second-round spill-overs have so far defied measurement but, in principle of course, they are measurable. In *Human Capital*, Becker (1964) argues that we can get an idea of their probable magnitude without measuring them directly. He begins by deriving the social rate of return in the usual way from pre-tax earnings differentials as a percentage yield on the total resource costs of education. This figure, construed as a lower limit to the true social rate of return, comes to 12·5 per cent for the 1949 cohort of white male college graduates. As an upper limit, Becker takes the value of 'advancement in knowledge' in Denison's residual (see Chapter 2, p. 96) and attributes all of it to education. This gives him an upper limit of 25 per cent. The difference between 12·5 and 25 per cent, he concludes, measures our ignorance of the external effects of education (Becker, 1964, pp. 119–21).

Some of the second-round spill-overs clearly involve the dissemination and not the creation of new knowledge. Hence, these are already reflected in the lower limit of 12·5 per cent. Becker's procedure, therefore, amounts to attributing another 12·5 per cent to the side-effects of university-based research and the incidence of self-help promoted by schooling. That may well be correct (Villard, 1960, pp. 376–7) but it seems difficult to believe. But these are quibbles. Becker's calculation of the upper limit implies more confidence in the numerical accuracy of Denison's model of economic growth than is warranted. The upper limit of 25 per cent may serve as a bench-mark for further argument but it has little significance in its own right.

For better or worse, the direct economic benefits remain at present the only ones capable of fairly accurate measurement and this is the chief, if not the only, justification for concentrating on them. To be sure, rate-of-return analysis ignores indirect economic benefits in the form of spill-overs. But so do all the other competing approaches to education planning, such as the man-power requirements approach or the 'social-demand' approach. We simply do not know how to quantify external effects and all economists, whatever approach they have used, have been guilty of ignoring these benefits. Nevertheless, rate-of-return analysis has the virtue of posing the issue sharply and thus opening the door to its successful resolution, whereas the other approaches virtually preclude, by their very formulation, the quantification of spill-over benefits. For example, in the man-power requirements approach it is all too easy to forget that primary schooling is just as likely to generate spill-overs as higher education, and that indeed all forms of social expenditure generate external effects. It is very unlikely that the indirect benefits of education exceed the direct benefits, at least when benefits are interpreted in a strictly economic sense. It is even more unlikely that these indirect benefits exceed the indirect benefits of expenditures on health and housing. And within the educational budget, there is no general presumption that one level of education systematically generates larger indirect benefits than another.

Earnings and the Marginal Product of Labour

The question whether earnings differentials between more and less educated individuals reflect differences in their contributions to national income might be fairly said to constitute the 'Achilles' Heel' of rate-of-return analysis. In most countries, a high proportion of qualified man power is employed in the public sector at administered salaries. More often than not, however, the public sector gears its pay scales to relative rates of reward in the private sector. But salaries in the private sector may in turn be influenced by traditional hiring practices and a variety of social conventions about the relative worth of different kinds of labour, not to mention the restrictive practices of trade unions and professional associations. In view of these facts, can we assume that earnings are related to the marginal revenue product of labour or, to express the same technical proposition in ordinary language, that the structure of wages and salaries corresponds closely to the relative scarcities of people with different skill attributes? A negative answer to this question necessarily implies that social rates of return on educational investment furnish misleading signals for policy-making purposes.

A firm's demand curve for labour is the marginal revenue product curve, that is, the schedule of the marginal physical products of labour multiplied by the corresponding marginal revenues. This means that the demand curve for labour in an industry is ultimately derived from an underlying production function. To ask whether earnings correspond to the marginal revenue product of labour is equivalent to asking (a) whether employers are maximizing profits and hence operating on the boundaries of their production function, and (b) whether the labour market functions competitively. That is to say, so long as employers pay identical workers the same and strive to minimize costs of production for a given level of output, excess demand for a particular skill leads necessarily to a rise in the earnings of that skill, and vice versa for excess supply. The rivalry between firms in bidding for labour acts to drive employers continuously back on to their demand curves for labour and in this way is forever tending to bring wages and salaries into line with relative marginal productivities.[1]

In meeting the fourth objection to rate-of-return analysis, therefore, we may fall back on the general notion that earnings by and large do reflect the push and pull of market forces. But such a defence is so vague that virtually no observation could refute it. The major testable implications of a competitive theory of wages and salaries are (a) that positive excess demand for a skill leads to a rise in its price and (b) that the price of a skill varies directly with the cost of acquiring it. If these implications were refuted by experience, we would indeed be justified in asserting that earnings have nothing to do with marginal productivity. But there is a good deal of evidence to show that earnings do rise in a seller's market (see Chapter 6, p. 188) and, in addition, the very data in question show that higher earnings do accrue to people who are relatively scarce because they have invested in acquiring special skills. In other words, the shoe is really on the other foot: if relative earnings reflect not relative contributions to national output, but family connexions, traditional conventions, the snob-value of a university degree, nepotism, entry restrictions in trade unions and professional organizations, politically administered pay scales or any other market imperfection one might care to mention, how is it that

1. It is worth noting that the question whether labour is paid in accordance with the principle of relative scarcity is only meaningful in terms of the marginal productivity theory of employment, that is, in the context of microeconomic production functions. The notion of an aggregate production function and something called 'the marginal productivity theory of distribution' has lately come in for much criticism, but it is not clear whether these criticisms are also meant to apply at the microeconomic level. At any rate, the wholesale denial of marginal productivity theory would mean that, among other things, we could never raise questions about the contributions of individual workers to output: since all inputs participate in producing output, only a production function can identify the contributions of a particular input. For further clarification, see Blaug (1968a, pp. 431–46) and Machlup (1963, pp. 207–10).

so large a proportion of gross earnings differentials associated with education turns out to be due to education alone?

The issue before us, however, is not actually whether there are imperfections in the labour market (who would deny it?) but whether these are so significant as to invalidate rate-of-return calculations. Indeed, the only imperfections that really matter in this connexion are those that are directly related to the educational attainments of the labour force. For example, suppose it were true that trade unions raised wages in unionized industries relative to those in the unorganized sectors of the economy. Since the majority of union members have received little education beyond the legal school-leaving age, this sort of departure from a competitive labour market would not affect the marginal rate of return to higher education, although it would affect that to secondary education. On the other hand, rate-of-return comparisons in the United States between professions with similar educational requirements but different conditions for entry into employment show that American physicians have succeeded in creating monopoly rents for themselves, although not always with the same degree of success (Friedman and Kuznets, 1946; W. Lee Hansen, 1965a; H. G. Lewis, 1963, pp. 114–24). Clearly, this is a result that matters for any conclusions we might draw from social rates of return on higher education in the United States. Similarly, if it were demonstrated that business firms really do practise 'conspicuous consumption' of university graduates for reasons of prestige, paying them more than they are really worth, we would not be inclined to attach any significance to the social rate of return on investment in higher education.

Two further points are worth mentioning. Whenever there is a market shortage for a particular type of labour, earnings are necessarily less than the marginal revenue product of labour and the corresponding social rate of return on educational investment is inevitably underestimated; this follows from the fact that employers are driven off the demand curve for labour whenever they want to hire more labour than is available at the going rate (see Figure 20a). Contrariwise, if the public sector rewards labour on the same terms as the private sector but then disguises unemployment by overstaffing, the result is that the social rate of return is now overestimated (see Figure 20b). Considerations such as these must be kept in mind in interpreting rates of return: separate biases are not always in the same direction.

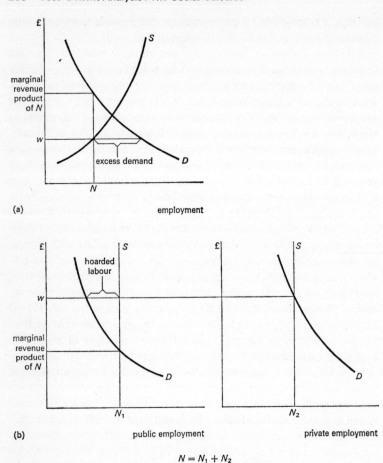

Figure 20   Earnings exceeding the marginal product of labour

It is obvious, therefore, that it is not possible to give a general blanket reaction to objection 4. It all depends on time, place and circumstance. It is the critics who in fact adopt a dogmatic position, dismissing out of hand all educational planning that makes the slightest reference to the earnings of educated labour, without however facing up to the destructive implications of their argument. Once we take it as an article of faith that firms are constitutionally incapable of maximizing profits and that there are no competitive pressures in labour markets that can impel firms to remove slack, all prices of both inputs and outputs lose their meaning as indices of relative scarcities. If we are consistent, we must now reject not just rate-of-return analysis but all cost–benefit analysis of government activities. Nor can we logically recommend man-power forecasting as an alternative to rate-of-return analysis[2] because this would be to assume that firms will always hire labour when it is technically required to produce additional output. But why should firms stop at technical requirements when they are not interested in maximizing profits? They are very likely to hoard labour, in which case a man-power forecast that simply extrapolates observed labour-output coefficients runs the danger of recommending the production of skills that make no contribution whatever to economic growth.

It is only with reference to underdeveloped countries that objection 4 carries real force. In many African countries, as much as 50 to 60 per cent of all highly educated man power is employed in the public sector and it is salaries in the private sector that are tied to government pay scales, rather than the other way around. Thus, for all practical purposes, the earnings of college graduates in these countries are never effectively submitted to a market test. In such cases, the social rate of return on investment in higher education reflects, not the productivity of college graduates, but simply the strength of their control over their own earnings.

What follows? Do we throw away earnings and with it the rate-of-return approach to educational planning, or do we meet the problem head on by attempting to reform the salary structure? When the price system is irrational, in the sense of failing to reflect relative scarcities, textbooks on economic planning tell us to impute 'shadow prices' to resources. In the present context, this implies that we should impute specific scarcity-prices to people with different educational qualifications. This is easier said than done. Short of developing a complex

2. Educational planners who attack rate-of-return analysis on the grounds of the inherent imperfections of labour markets invariably end up advocating the man-power requirements approach: see, for example, Balogh and Streeten (1963, p.392*) and Balogh (1967, p. 104) who suggests that 'the most promising approach [to educational planning] is that adopted by Mr Pitambar Pant of the Indian Planning Commission'. This 'promising' approach in fact involves the questionable use of Tinbergen Regressions to make long-term man-power forecasts (see above Chapter 5, p. 150). See also Myrdal (1968, vol. 3, pp. 1548, 1812–13, 1956–61) who combines a diffuse attack on the concept of 'investment in man' with an equally vague approval of man-power forecasting.

dynamic programming model of the economy, the duals of which would furnish shadow earnings of labour, there would seem to be no way of estimating shadow prices.[3]

Rate-of-return analysis itself, however, provides us with a point of departure. Suppose, for example, that a medium-term man-power forecast in some underdeveloped country indicates that college education should be expanded at the expense of primary and secondary education. Putting this forecast aside, we look at the same question via social rates of return calculated from current age–education–earnings data. If these give us the same answer, well and good. But suppose they do not: let us now add to or subtract from earnings by education until we get the same answer from both approaches. We have now learned something: either the actual earnings of educated people diverge in a particular way from the true shadow prices of educated labour or else the man-power forecast is wrong. In this way, jogging back and forth between the two indicators until all inconsistencies are ironed out, we must by the nature of the procedure improve the quality of educational planning. At the same time, we may in this way contribute to the reform of salaries, a reform that is bound to make a significant contribution to general economic planning in underdeveloped countries (Skorov, 1968, pp. 21–3).

An illustrative example may help to clarify the argument. Smyth and Bennet (1967) calculated the following social rates of return to four levels of education in Uganda, using 1965 government salary scales (the entry points of which are defined in terms of educational qualifications) grossed up by the estimated excess of salaries in the private over the public sector:

1. Higher School Certificate (upper-secondary)   = 78 per cent
2. Primary schooling   = 66 per cent
3. Cambridge School Certificate (lower-secondary) = 22 per cent
4. University Degree   = 12 per cent

The lifetime earnings of university graduates in Uganda are two to three times those of secondary-school leavers and twenty times those

3. A halfway-house to such a dynamic programming model of the economy is a simplified linear programming model of two-sector economy, education being treated as one of the sectors and the rest of the economy as the other. Some progress is now being made in developing such models (see Adelman, 1966; Bowles, 1967*; 1969, chs. 4 and 5; Huntsberger, 1968; Psacharopoulos, 1970).

of primary-school leavers, but the total resource costs of university education, even ignoring the cost of secondary education leading up to it, is almost sixty times that of primary schooling. In consequence, the rate of return on university education in Uganda is only a fifth of the rate of return on primary education. Although these results are subject to some reservations because they are not based on actual earnings-by-education data (Knight, 1968, pp. 286–9), they are undoubtedly of the right order of magnitude in suggesting substantial underinvestment in Ugandan primary education. All the man-power forecasts that have been made in Uganda, however, point instead to severe 'shortages' of higher-educated man power (Rado, 1967, esp. pp. 284, 291–2). Assuming these forecasts are accurate, how is it that we nevertheless obtain a social rate of return on higher education of only 12 per cent? Is it due perhaps to the artificially inflated salaries of university graduates, which in turn inflates the costs of university education because teachers in universities are themselves university graduates?

We can test this proposition by assigning a 'shadow price' to university graduates below their actual earnings. Once we have fed back the new price into the accounting costs of teachers, we can then calculate rates of return in the standard manner. We now proceed by a process of trial-and-error, cutting the earnings of graduates by 10 per cent, 20 per cent, etc., until we obtain rates of return on higher education in excess of 66 per cent.[4] The object of the entire exercise is to find the critical range of salary differentials between university graduates and primary-school leavers that reverses our initial ranking of the two educational levels; this critical range places limits on the true shadow price of university graduates, at least if we can rely on the results of man-power forecasts and not otherwise. In the case of Uganda, it turns out that even when we have reduced the salaries of university graduates to those of secondary-school leavers, in effect staffing the universities with secondary-school leavers, primary education still yields a much higher rate of return than university education. We must perforce conclude, not that Ugandan graduates earn just what

4. Although we seem to be cutting off our nose to spite our face, cutting rather than raising graduate salaries is the correct policy in this case. This follows from the fact that (a) teaching costs dominate total costs, (b) the teachers are themselves graduates, and (c) present costs have a much larger impact on the rate of return than future salaries.

they are worth, but rather that man-power forecasts in Uganda have gone wide of the mark.

The problem of educational planning is ultimately one of determining the potential economic value of different amounts and types of education. Therefore, why not confront the problem directly by imputing economic values and calculating the effects of these imputations on decisions about educational expenditures? This is not to suggest that such as-if calculations can by themselves establish what is, in fact, the shadow price of educated labour. Only job analysis and job evaluation in government departments and business enterprises can ever settle this question (see Chapter 5, p. 156). However, there is reason to think that job evaluation will be considerably assisted by the kind of sensitivity analysis of earnings differentials that we are advocating. In most underdeveloped countries, teachers' salaries are held well below the salaries of equivalently educated people, so that the feedback problem in recalculating rates of return is not as serious as might be assumed at first glance: so great are the difference between the costs of different levels of education that the ranking order of levels is, in fact, insensitive to a wide array of salary scales. In consequence, investment criteria in education are frequently unaffected by the possibility that salaries for certain grades of labour are 30 to 40 per cent more or less than they should be. This sort of information is well worth having. All too frequently, critics of rate-of-return analysis write as if cost–benefit calculations are worthless the moment the labour market is characterized by the slightest degree of imperfection.

Predicting Future Rates of Return

Rate-of-return analysis does not mean slavish adherence to actual earnings and actual costs in total disregard of what earnings and costs mean in a particular situation. So much is clear from the last section. There remains a final objection to rate-of-return analysis which we have not yet considered: rate-of-return analysis is marginal analysis which can only suggest the direction but not the appropriate magnitude of change. Both forecasts of man-power requirements and projections of the demand-for-places provide educational planners with exact magnitudes to aim at. Rate-of-return analysis, on the other hand, merely provides a signal of direction: invest more or invest less. But how much more or less? To this question the approach gives no other answer than 'a little bit more or less', after which yields will have to be recalculated. Rate-of-return analysis does not even make the attempt to predict future demand and supply of educated man power. At best, it indicates how the two are matched at present. But for educational planning the present is simply a bygone, and knowledge of the present is not of much use in making decisions whose effects will not be felt until several years from now; so runs the criticism.

Besides, the quality of education has improved in the past and may be expected to go on improving. A cross-section analysis of age–education–earnings data, however, includes some people who were educated thirty or forty years ago. Thus, a time-series projection of lifetime earnings from cross-section data is bound to underestimate the expected rate of return on education. Rate-of-return analysis, therefore, is not only a myopic technique for moving forward one step at a time, but one which stands condemned as extrapolating the obsolete education of the past.

Both of these criticisms are damaging but not quite so damaging as critics imagine. It is perfectly true that the rate of return is calculated from projected lifetime earnings but this is not to say that the figures are equally sensitive to the earnings of older and younger workers. Let us suppose, for example, that sixty-year-old members of the labour force are paid 50 per cent more than they are really worth because of respect for their seniority rights, unrelated to their actual economic performance. But when we apply this assumption to the standard British or American age–earnings profiles, we lower rates of return on investment in education by only about 1 per cent, for the simple reason that the later years get very little weight in the final calculation. Rates of return are extremely sensitive to the first ten or fifteen years of lifetime earnings; provided we correctly project earnings over the next ten years, significant shifts in earning patterns twenty or thirty years from now do not substantially affect the results. The same argument holds for the effects of past investment. The education some workers received in the 1930s has virtually no impact on the rates of return that we would calculate from cross-section data in 1970; moreover, while each new cohort of school leavers is no doubt better educated than the last, it would be naïve to expect that the quality of education normally improves so rapidly as to invalidate all results based on current earnings (see Chapter 9, p. 278).

American calculations show that rates of return are remarkably stable from decade to decade. The problem of predicting future rates of return, therefore, is one of predicting the rate at which a set of demand and supply curves will continue to shift to the right with the passage of time. Man-power forecasts, as we know, are concerned with the demand side of the picture. Demand-for-places projections are concerned with the supply side; and the intersections of the two curves determine the pattern of earnings that enters into rate-of-return calculations. If both demand and supply are responsive to earnings, there is a feedback effect that complicates estimates of the slopes of these functions. But estimates of the slopes are only one difficulty. The way in which demand and supply shift over time is determined on the demand side by the pace of technical change, and on the supply side by the incomes and 'tastes' of households and by administrative decisions about educational facilities. In short, the shifts of the demand and supply curves, as well as the slopes, are also influenced by the pattern of earnings and by the costs of educational provisions. All this is to say that if the demand and supply functions in a particular labour market are correctly predicted for the years ahead, the consequence is necessarily an implicit prediction of the marginal rates of return on educational investment. We are, therefore, driven to the conclusion that either all three approaches to educational planning are valid when used in conjunction with one another, or there is something wrong with man-power forecasting or 'social-demand' projections or both. To deny this conclusion, one must assert that both the relative earnings of highly qualified man power and the costs of different amounts and types of education vary little over time and hence can be left out of account. But this is precisely what man-power forecasters argue. We have come at last to what really lies behind the quarrel between man-power forecasters and rate-of-return advocates: it is nothing less than a totally different view of how economic systems work.

Two Views of the State of the World

Suppose we had an educational system that did not permit students to specialize until their second or third year of higher education, that provided a perfectly general education for everyone until the ages of nineteen or twenty, that made full use of team teaching and new educational media in the interest of keeping pupil–teacher ratios as flexible as possible and capable of ranging from 10:1 to 300:1. Suppose also that vocational counselling was so efficient that students were extremely well informed of career opportunities. Suppose, further, that employers' demand for different skills was highly elastic, that capital was an almost perfect substitute for labour and that, in addition, workers with different skill characteristics were good substitutes for one another. In short, there were always many people who could perform a given job and, as a last resort, the job itself could always be displaced by a machine. Lastly, suppose that most specialized skills were acquired on-the-job, not learned in schools, and that technical change demanding new and hitherto unfamiliar skills proceeded smoothly without fits and starts. In that case, would it really matter that education is an extremely durable asset and that highly qualified man power can only be produced with a lag of five or ten years? To forecast man-power requirements under these circumstances would be almost meaningless: in this sort of world educated man power could never be a bottleneck to economic growth. Projections of the private demand for education and calculations of the rate of return, however, would be perfectly meaningful in such a world and, as a matter of fact, the only guides available for decision making in education.

We can now go to the other extreme and imagine a world created in the image of man-power forecasting. Students and parents would be poorly informed of career prospects and more interested in acquiring education for consumption than for investment reasons; specialization by subjects would start very early; pupil–teacher ratios would be fixed and unalterable and all school buildings and school equipment would be indivisible and highly specific in each use; the demand schedules for separate skills would be highly inelastic and the elasticity of substitution between labour and capital as well as that between men with different skills would be well below unity; industry would provide virtually no training and the pace of technical change would be so rapid that the demand for people with different skill attributes would shift through time unevenly and irregularly. Obviously, in this sort of world, the private demand for education would be so unstable as to make it impossible to extrapolate existing trends and all rate-of-return calculations would be irrelevant; labour-output coefficients would be largely technically determined and earnings associated with education and even the costs of supplying various skills could be ignored.

To fix the distinction firmly in our minds, Table 7 reiterates the contrast we have been drawing: items 1 to 4 cover what might be called the 'education market' (see Chapter 6, p. 170), whereas items 5 to 7 deal with the labour market in which educated people are hired.

Table 7

Fixed Versus Variable Coefficients

The Man-Power Forecasting View of the World	The Rate-of-Return View of the World
1. Students acquire more education for consumption reasons.	1. Students acquire more education for investment reasons.
2. Students choose major subjects in ignorance of, or with no regard to, career prospects.	2. Students are well informed and attentive to career prospects.
3. All education is specialized and specialization starts early.	3. All education is general and there is no specialization at any age.
4. All input-coefficients in schools are fixed: complete indivisibility and specificity of teachers, plant and equipment.	4. All input-coefficients in schools are variable: complete divisibility and non-specificity of teachers, plant and equipment.
5. The demand curves for different skills shift discretely.	5. The demand curves for different skills shift smoothly.
6. Near-zero elasticities of substitution between skilled men.	6. Almost infinite elasticities of substitution between skilled men.
7. Near-zero elasticities of demand for different skills.	7. Almost infinite elasticities of demand for different skills.

And so the quarrel really is about the real world![5] What we have is a picture of a continuum: to the right is the sort of neo-classical universe that we meet in textbooks on economic theory, characterized by substitutabilities in both the educational system and the productive process; to the left is a Leontief-type universe of fixed input-coefficients, characterized by extreme complementarities in both the education market and the labour market. Needless to say, the real world lies somewhere in between. To resolve the conflict that we are examining, therefore, we must decide whether the world lies nearer to the right

5. As Anderson and Bowman put it (1967, p. 374)*: 'Evidently both man-power planning and rate-of-return approaches have severe limitations. The contrasts between them have roots deep in the ways men look at political-economic systems and in the controls over those systems that are attempted in practice.'

or to the left end of the continuum, and if to the left end, whether so far to the left that educational planning can safely ignore costs and earnings. But is this really all we can say? Must educational planning stand aside until further research shows whether the world is, in fact, characterized by fixed or by variable input-coefficients?

In an earlier chapter, we defined educational planning as the process of preparing a set of decisions for action to be taken in the future (see Chapter 4, p. 101). Since it is oriented to the future, educational planning partakes of all the difficulties inherent in sequential decision-making under uncertainty. Furthermore, even the present relationship between the supply and demand for educated people is little understood, particularly in underdeveloped countries. In the circumstances, it seems desirable to build into the educational system the kind of flexibility that allows it to adjust automatically to bottlenecks and surpluses. In short, educational planning should consist in large part of action designed to move the real world closer to the right end of the continuum, characterized by a multiplicity of alternatives in producing and utilizing educated man power. For whatever is the state of the world in a particular country, such action ensures a smoother adjustment of the educational system to the labour market and improves the chances of market clearance.

Take as a case in point: the man-power situation in Great Britain and the United States. Although it can be asserted out of hand that both countries approximate a neo-classical rather than a Leontief-type universe, it is apparent that Britain lies well to the left of the United States along the continuum (McCarthy, 1968). First of all, specialization in schools starts much earlier in Britain than in America. British students begin to concentrate on their major fields (arts or science) by the age of fifteen, and sometimes as early as thirteen; by the age of fifteen or sixteen, the science students have largely ceased to study arts subjects and vice versa, and by the sixth form extreme specialization even as between pure and applied science is almost universal. Early specialization is said to be caused by university entrance requirements and excessive competition in sixth forms for a limited number of places in universities. But whatever the reason, the undisputed fact that British students specialize at an earlier age than almost anywhere else means that the supply of, say, scientists and engineers in 1975 is already determined in Britain, whereas in the United States it will be possible to make a substantial impact on the 1975 supply by policies adopted in 1972 or 1973. Thus, the lead time required to produce skilled man power in Britain is at least twice as long as in the United States, in consequence of which there is a much stronger probability in Britain of periodic shortages and surpluses of scientists and engineers.

Added to the first consideration, and directly related to it, is the chronic excess demand for higher education in Great Britain ever since the war, in contrast to the open-door policy of American colleges (see Chapter 6, p. 176). Furthermore, not only is the over-all supply of places in higher education rationed in Britain but so is the allocation of places between faculties, in consequence of which, applicants for arts places are frequently denied entry while there are still vacant places in science and technology. Although it is sometimes admitted that student choices have shown themselves to be sensitive to prospective demand, the policy on faculty balances continues to be based squarely on man-power forecasts. But, clearly, either students are poorly informed of career prospects, in which case they can be better informed, or else they are well informed, in which case the argument must be that the labour market fails to produce signals of impending man-power shortages. In that case, one would think that the State would adopt a differential student-grant policy so as to encourage students to take up those professions in which there is known to be a prospective shortage. This view implies considerable confidence in man-power forecasts and, no doubt, a lack of conviction about forecasting accounts for the present inconsistent policy.

In the United States, on the other hand, students are allowed freely to choose their own subject once they have gained admission to university. They are kept informed of trends in the labour market by means of vocational counselling, and full use is made of special scholarship programmes and student loans restricted to particular subjects or fields of study that require encouragement.

It seems obvious that the supply of highly qualified man power is more rigidly predetermined in Britain than in the United States, that students' educational choices are less firmly linked to job opportunities and that, in general, the demands of the labour market have less influence on the structure of higher education in Britain than in the United States. If we add to this the contrast between the British tripartite secondary education, with a university stream separated from the rest by the age of twelve, and the comprehensive high schools of America that allow over 40 per cent of the sixteen to eighteen age group to pass on to college, as well as the rigid paths of British technical education in which professional qualifications are only obtainable by passing the examination of a particular professional institution, albeit by part-time as well as full-time study, and the extraordinary variety of trade and vocational high schools, technical institutes, two-year junior colleges, four-year technical colleges and the like in the United States, we are forced to conclude that there is much less scope for short-run adjustments in the demand and supply of man power in Britain and, therefore, the much stronger probability of imbalances in the labour market. It may be that all this is offset by differences in the provision of industrial training in the two countries, but even here casual impression runs against Britain.

These differences between the two educational systems go a long way to explain the American preoccupation with rate-of-return analysis and their sceptical attitude to man-power forecasting, and exactly the reverse attitude in Britain. Faced with a rigid and highly structured educational system and aware that as much as two-thirds of university graduates and probably a similar fraction of those with G.C.E. O- and A-levels are employed by the public sector – the State in respect of education combining monopoly with monopsony – educational planners in Britain have seen no alternative to man-power forecasting with all its admitted shortcomings. But the price of rigidity is that errors are more disastrous. This is the great paradox of the man-power forecasting approach: the very lack of synchronization between the educational system and the labour market which is invoked to justify man-power forecasting also leads to waste that cannot be easily remedied when forecasts go wrong. In a Leontief-type economy, there is a premium on the accuracy of forecasts and yet inaccurate forecasts can aggravate instead of improve the situation. In contrast, if the economic system is sufficiently flexible to adjust to erroneous forecasts, even crude estimates of man-power requirements can serve as useful guides, but at the same time there is, so to speak, less need to forecast in the first place.

The way to cut through this Gordian knot is to create a safety-valve against forecasting errors by strengthening the automatic adjustment mechanism of the market. In the British context this means attacking the problem of early specialization and, since this is in turn related to keen competition for a limited number of university places, encouraging further expansion of higher education to accommodate the unsatisfied demand, possibly outside the universities through the development of polytechnics. Hitherto, early specialization has been attacked on purely educational grounds. What has not always been realized is that early specialization is also one of the major causes of man-power difficulties in Britain.

Further, every effort should be made to allow students freely to choose their faculties, concomitant with heavy investment in vocational counselling in schools. Indeed, the provision of career information both in schools and in labour exchanges ought to be a principal activity of the educational authorities. Unfortunately, in most countries this function is divided between the Ministry of Education and the Ministry of Labour, and hence there is little communication between schools and employers. In Britain, for instance, the Youth Employment Service is still in part under the umbrella of the Department of Employment and Productivity, and this division of control may help to explain why facilities for vocational guidance are so poorly coordinated and why the level of provision is well behind the United States and most other European countries (Lester, 1966, pp. 59–75).

More broadly, any policy action that increases the flexibility with which resources are combined within the educational system must improve the capacity of schools to adjust to shortages and surpluses of various types of man power. That is, any action that encourages educational innovation in school, such as constructing school buildings easily adaptable to various class sizes, training teachers to use new educational media such as closed-circuit television and programmed instruction, tends to ease the burdens of man-power planning. Of course, the case for new educational media is not one to be decided solely or even largely on man-power grounds, but the fact remains that the more teachers are replaced by mechanical aids, the easier it is to expand enrolments or to adjust pupil–teacher ratios.

Turning to the labour market, we recall that shortages of particular skills, that is, the existence of unfilled vacancies at current salary levels, are overcome in the short run either by raising salaries, by lowering minimal hiring standards or by providing more on-the-job and off-the-job training. There is much less scope here for public policy than in the case of the educational system. Nevertheless, in the absence of specific knowledge of the extent of shortages, it is always possible for the State to alleviate the situation by adopting a flexible policy with respect to pay scales in the public sector, by furnishing better information about the future output of the educational system to personnel officers in business enterprises in the hope of encouraging an adjustment of hiring standards, and by offering financial incentives to industry to expand its training programmes. Recent attempts to experiment with public provision for training and retraining of adult workers, as in the Industrial Training Act in Britain and the Manpower Training and Development Act in the United States are, of course, precisely along these lines. The more we avoid placing all responsibility for man-power development on the schools alone, the less we need to pay the consequences of unemployable school leavers or economic growth held back by shortages of various skills.

The picture of educational planning that is beginning to emerge is quite different from that usually projected in the literature. It consists, as we have seen, of attempts to reform the educational system, on the one hand, and of what is sometimes described in America as 'an active man-power policy', on the other. Educational planning, and particularly educational planning in underdeveloped countries, should concern itself more widely than it does with the reciprocal impact of the educational system and the labour market. It is a fallacy to think that there can be no man-power planning without man-power forecasting and that, in the absence of forecasting, educational planning must consist of a passive attitude towards the economic returns from education. Rather than accepting existing educational patterns and prevailing hiring policies as data in the planning process, much of the effort of educational planning should be directed at altering them. Tanzania, for example, recently shortened the length of medical courses and now produces doctors in five instead of seven years; this makes Tanzanian doctors less qualified than British doctors but that is all to the good. The aim of a poor country is not to maximize the numbers of highly skilled people but to minimize the costs of producing the flow of essential skills, skills that can be produced in a variety of ways. Indeed, the task of re-examining all specialized professional education to see if it is really necessary to produce these skills in formal institutions has hardly begun to be tackled in most underdeveloped countries. On the whole, there is much less reliance on training in industry in the underdeveloped than in the developed world and as yet no underdeveloped country has seriously entertained the idea of subsidizing private industry to undertake more on-the-job and off-the-job training. English-speaking Africa, for example, has imitated almost every feature of British education except the practice of producing technicians by 'sandwich courses' or 'day release', that is, by part-time courses for people already employed in industries. Along the same lines, there is a case to be made for more emphasis on adult literacy campaigns, particularly if they are work-oriented (see Chapter 8, p. 260). If all this should mean less reliance on forecasting and other mechanical techniques for gearing the educational system to long-term targets, so much the better. It is high time that educational planning faced up squarely to the utter inability to foresee the consequences of big, lumpy decisions. Rational planning can never be much more than what Popper has called 'piecemeal social engineering' and the maxim of educational planning should be 'avoid binding commitments'.

Let us try now to draw together the strands of the discussion. There seems to be little point in continuing to waste resources on long-term single-valued forecasts whose results are suspected even by the forecasters themselves. These resources could be much more profitably invested in improving our knowledge of the utilization of the current stock of qualified man power and disseminating this knowledge to students and employers. It is no accident that after two decades of considerable activity in man-power forecasting, no country besides the United States and Canada has anything like adequate data on the distribution of the labour force by sectors, occupations, earnings and years of schooling. Such data are not even expensive to collect since they can be gathered by sample surveys. The truth is that the mystique of long-term forecasting has discouraged investigations of the current stock of man power, while convictions about the imperfections of labour markets in countries have inhibited research on the earnings of educated people to determine the precise degree of imperfection.[6]

Faced with the difficulties of man-power forecasting, difficulties that seem to increase at a progressive rate the longer the time period

6. The steadfast reluctance to collect earnings data continues to limit the value of many educational planning exercises in poor countries. A recent study of Nigeria, directed by F.H.Harbison, for example, described its approach as 'an assessment of the confrontation between man-power supply and demand', sharply condemned 'present techniques of man-power planning' and conducted an extremely useful survey of the 'educational and training content of occupations' in all sectors of the Nigerian economy (Education and World Affairs, 1967, pp. 13,

over which we are forecasting, the remedy is to begin modestly with short-term forecasts which are then extrapolated with a compounding margin of error (see Chapter 5, p. 165). As we accumulate more experience, we can begin to adjust the margin of error, gradually producing more and more reliable medium-term and eventually long-term forecasts. As a check on such forecasts of demand, we ought to make continuous year-by-year projections of the future supply of educated people.[7] Indeed, the forecasts of demand ought to be of the type that provides a range of alternative estimates, given different estimates of the projected supply. If the demand for educational inputs depends in any way on their prices, and this will necessarily be so if there is any substitutability between educated people, changes in supply are just as capable of altering prices as changes in demand and, therefore, the quantity demanded of educational inputs is not independent of its supply. It follows that man-power forecasts must always be combined with projections of the demand-for-places. As we combine forecasts of demand for man power with projections of the supply of man power, we start thinking quite naturally of earnings associated with education as possible indicators of impending shortages and surpluses; and since the costs of training various types of specialized man power differ considerably, we shall be led to consider variations in earnings in relation to variations in the costs of education. This is rate-of-return analysis, whether we call it that or not. If earnings are inflexible and fail to reveal shortages and surpluses of man power, the remedy lies in imputing 'shadow prices' to labour of different skills and calculating the critical rates of return that lead to definite investment priorities in education. By making such calculations on a year-to-year basis, we keep a continual check on labour markets for highly qualified man power and gradually develop insights into the ways in which education interacts with economic growth.

Rates of return as such can never provide more than an *ex post*

34–40). Nevertheless, the earnings of educated people are never mentioned in the study: all that we are told is that 'the difficulties in quantitatively estimating expected benefits make a cost–benefit exercise for Nigeria of questionable value' (Education and World Affairs, 1967, p. 88). But working entirely on his own in Northern Nigeria, Bowles (1967)* managed to collect representative data on earnings by education in only a few months.

7. Recall the earlier distinction between 'forecasts' and 'projections' (Chapter 5, p. 138).

check on the efficiency of investment already embodied in different kinds of educational facilities and, of course, a signal for a possible direction of change in the pattern of educational investment. By supplementing rates of return with *ex ante* estimates of the likely changes in the demand and supply of skills over the planning period, however, we convert them into tests of the validity of predictions of demand and supply. If we get different answers from rate-of-return calculations than from man-power forecasts, it may be that (a) earnings are divorced from the marginal productivity of labour, (b) the costs of education are artificially inflated, (c) future rates of return will diverge from present rates or (d) the man-power forecasts are wrong. Which of these four factors or which combination of them is responsible for the difference in answers cannot be settled on *a priori* grounds. What we have been trying to do is to build up a framework in which such factors can be systematically considered. The message of this framework is that the man-power requirements approach, the 'social-demand' approach and rate-of-return analysis are reconcilable and, in fact, complementary techniques of educational planning, but not as these approaches are presently practised around the world. Above all, they must be combined with educational reforms and an active interventionist attitude to all forms of producing educated man power, whether by formal or by informal methods. Economists do have a contribution to make to educational planning, but not by pressing the claims of one particular panacea, not by pretending to foresee the future accurately ten or fifteen years ahead, not by presuming to know how to promote exactly so much economic growth by just so much education. There is no reason to be apologetic about the fact that in most cases all that we can safely recommend is movement in a particular direction for a limited period of time.

Some Results

It is time to come down to earth and to review results. In Chapter 2 we presented age–earnings profiles by years of schooling or levels of education for the United States, Great Britain, India and Mexico (see Figure 1, p. 24). The American profiles for males in the year 1949 were used by Hansen to compute both private and social rates of return to years of schooling (Table 8). What was earlier called one to four years of elementary schooling, corresponds here to row (2); likewise eight

years of elementary schooling corresponds to row (3), four years of
high school to row (5), one to three years of college to row (6) and
four years of college to row (7). The diagonal elements in Table 8
represent marginal returns, while the off-diagonal elements are average

Table 8a

Private Rates of Return, United States, Males, 1949

				(1)	(2)	(3)	(4)	(5)	(6)	(7)
	From:	Age		6	8	12	14	16	18	20
			Grade	1	3	7	9	11	13	15
(1)	To:	7	2	+	—	—	—	—	—	—
(2)		11	6	+	+	—	—	—	—	—
(3)		13	8	+	+	+	—	—	—	—
(4)		15	10	27·9	33·0	24·8	12·3	—	—	—
(5)		17	12	25·2	28·2	22·2	14·5	17·5	—	—
(6)		19	14	17·2	17·5	13·7	9·4	8·5	5·1	—
(7)		21	16	17·2	17·3	14·4	11·5	11·4	10·1	16·7

Source: W. Lee Hansen (1963, table 5).
Note: + indicates an infinite rate-of-return, given the assumption that education
is costless to the individual through the completion of eighth grade.

Table 8b

Social Rates of Return, United States, Males, 1949

				(1)	(2)	(3)	(4)	(5)	(6)	(7)
	From:	Age		6	8	12	14	16	18	20
			Grade	1	3	7	9	11	13	15
(1)	To:	7	2	8·9	—	—	—	—	—	—
(2)		11	6	12·0	14·5	—	—	—	—	—
(3)		13	8	15·0	18·5	29·2	—	—	—	—
(4)		15	10	13·7	15·9	16·3	9·5	—	—	—
(5)		17	12	13·6	15·4	15·3	11·4	13·7	—	—
(6)		19	14	11·3	12·1	11·1	8·2	8·2	5·4	—
(7)		21	16	12·1	12·7	12·1	10·5	10·9	10·2	15·6

Source: W. Lee Hansen (1963, table 3).

returns. In other words, suppose that an individual aged six has just completed grade 1 and his parents are considering keeping him at school through two years of college (grade 14); the average rate of return on the required investment would then be 17·2 per cent. If, however, he has completed one year of college and is now considering a second, he can expect a marginal rate of return of only 5·1 per cent. Similarly, the average social rate of return on investment in college education for a cohort of high-school graduates (grade 12 completed) is 10·9 per cent, but once they have been in college for two years the marginal social rate of return on the last two years required to graduate is as high as 15·6 per cent.

The meaning of the terms 'average' and 'marginal' in this context are sometimes confused. The marginal rates in Hansen's tables are marginal in the sense that they refer to an increment of schooling but since they are computed from age cohort data they are averages for particular age groups: they do not show what would happen if an additional student were provided with an extra year of education; they are not rates of return on increments of schooling for the marginal student. This is a serious limitation from the point of view of the individual since he can never be sure whether he is himself representative of his own age cohort. It is no drawback, however, for social policy which in any case cannot be framed for each and every individual case.

It is evident that both private and public decisions based on rate-of-return analysis depend critically on whether average or marginal rates are deemed to be relevant. It is clear that individuals must base their decisions to continue education on marginal rather than average rates of return. In the case of public policy decisions, however, consideration of the full range of investment options available to the State calls for a computation of both rates of return. It has been suggested that we ought really to add at each stage of the educational ladder the cash-value of the option to obtain still more education, suitably weighted by the probability of the option being exercised. In other words, we must attribute to one level of schooling the expected value of the financial rewards obtainable from the next level to the extent that these rewards actually exceed the next best alternative investment opportunity (Weisbrod, 1964, pp. 19–23, 138–43). But the traditional method of dealing with interdependent investment projects is to lump them together and to calculate a rate of return on the aggregate (see Ribich, 1968, app. C). This is precisely what is meant by 'average' rates of return in Hansen's tables. But despite the fact that different levels of education are successive investments for the individual, they are not interdependent investment projects from the standpoint of social policy; provided sufficient numbers of students are actually enrolled in the various levels, each level can be marginally expanded or contracted independently of every other. Thus, marginal rates of return are usually more pertinent in evaluating public expenditures on education by levels or years of schooling.

Hansen's figures are not ability-adjusted (see Chapter 2, p. 54). However, Becker has used the same data to calculate private rates of return to white male college graduates of about 11·5 per cent, after allowing for differences in native abilities and family background and for the expectation of future economic growth (Becker, 1964, pp. 78, 82).[8] Similar ability-adjusted rates were calculated for white male college drop-outs in 1949 (8 per cent) and urban Negro male college graduates in 1939 (8·3 to 12·3 per cent); the unadjusted rate for high-school graduates in 1949 was 20 per cent (Becker, 1964, pp. 93, 94 and 124).

The U.K. figures for 1963 adjusted for ability differences produced a private marginal rate of return on secondary education (terminal education age sixteen to eighteen) of 13 per cent, and one on higher education (terminal education age nineteen or over) of 14 per cent; the corresponding social rates were 12·5 and 6·5 per cent respectively. The average rates on both secondary and higher education taken together were 14 per cent for the private calculus and 8 per cent for the social calculus (Henderson-Stewart, 1965). The pilot study of five British firms at about the same time (see Figure 2, p. 28) yielded somewhat lower figures than the national sample, particularly after adjusting the results for ability differences.

The Indian rates of return were calculated on two different assumptions about the magnitude of the ability-adjustment (Table 9). In addition, all the age-earnings profiles were adjusted for the probability of 'wastage' at each stage of education, the probability of unemployment associated with each educational qualification and the expectation of a 2 per cent growth rate in Indian incomes. Rows (1) to (4) present marginal rates of return; rows (5) to (7) present average rates

8. For other American evidence on ability-adjusted rates of return see Hirsch and Segelhorst (1965), Morgan and David (1963), Morgan and Lininger (1964) and D. C. Rogers (1969).

Table 9

Private and Social Rates of Return, Urban India, Males, 1960

		Private Rates			Social Rates		
Level of Education		Un-adjusted rate	Adjusted for $\alpha=0\cdot65$	Adjusted for $\alpha=0\cdot5$	Un-adjusted rate	Adjusted for $\alpha=0\cdot65$	Adjusted for $\alpha=0\cdot5$
(1)	Primary over illiterate	24·7	18·7	16·5	20·2	15·2	13·7
(2)	Middle over primary	20·0	16·1	14·0	17·4	14·2	12·4
(3)	Matriculation over middle	18·4	11·9	10·4	16·1	10·5	9·1
(4)	First degree over matricu-lation	14·3	10·4	8·7	12·7	8·9	7·4
(5)	Matriculation over illiterate	21·4	16·5	14·7	18·1	13·9	12·2
(6)	First degree over illiterate	18·5	13·9	12·3	15·9	12·0	10·3
(7)	Engineering degree over illiterate	21·2	17·0	15·2	17·3	13·8	12·3

Source: Blaug, Layard and Woodhall (1969, tables 9–1, 9–2).

or return. The unadjusted rates of return in the first column represent a maximum, while those adjusted for $\alpha = 0\cdot5$ in the third column represent a minimum. For the individual, the true *ex ante* rate of return is likely to fall between these values, depending on how students estimate their own chances of dropping out and of being unemployed after entering the labour market. For the Indian authorities, the true rate likewise falls in between the two extreme values, depending in this case on the particular policy that is being considered and on estimates of future demand and supply relationships. Table 9 is a summary of a much more comprehensive menu of possible alternative rates of return prepared by the authors of the Indian study (Blaug, Layard and Woodhall, 1969, ch. 9).

Lastly, there are the Mexican data for 1963, from which rates of

Table 10

Private and Social Rates of Return, Urban Mexico, Males, 1963

	Private Rates		Social Rates	
Years of Schooling	Unadjusted rate	Adjusted rate	Unadjusted rate	Adjusted rate
2–4	21·1	15·2	17·3	12·8
5–6	48·6	44·9	37·5	34·5
7–8	36·5	31·0	23·4	20·6
9–11	17·4	15·2	14·2	12·3
12–13	15·8	14·6	12·4	11·4
14–16	36·7	39·5	29·5	31·5

Source: Carnoy (1967a, table 6).

return were calculated both gross and net of variations in father's occupation. It will be noticed that here, for the first time, we get a case where an adjustment for family background actually increases rather than reduces the rate of return: for reasons not yet explained, coming from a family of high occupational status in Mexico actually lowers the net returns from the last years of university education.

It will be noticed that all the figures cited above refer to males only. There has been some reluctance to calculate rates of return to investment in the education of women, partly because of the belief that there is discrimination against women in all labour markets, but perhaps more because of the recognition that there are no markets which place a value on the efforts of housewives or on the contributions of educated mothers: the years in which married women are actively engaged in the labour force cover only a small part of their total lifetime contributions to national income. Since better-educated women are more likely to marry better-educated men, Becker has suggested that the returns to women from additional schooling should be measured by family earnings classified by the wife's education rather than by personal earnings; even so, he finds lower rates of return to American women college graduates than to men college graduates (Becker, 1964, pp. 100–102). Not too much should be made of this result. It may be that the education of women must be considered in terms of intergeneration effects, but much more work on female education must be done before we can usefully speculate on such questions.

So much for hard data. Lack of space inhibits presentation of additional results for other countries. Reference should be made, however, to the calculations of unadjusted rates of return for the United States in 1959 (cross-classified by sex, race and region: Hanoch, 1967; Lassiter, 1966, pp. 37–45; Psacharopoulos, 1969b), for Canada in 1961 (Podoluk, 1965, pp. 60–65; also Wilkinson, 1966), for Denmark in 1964 (N. B. Hansen, 1966), for Greece in 1964 (Leibenstein, 1967), for Israel in 1957 (Klinov-Malul, 1966, ch. 6), for Uganda in 1965, already mentioned above, for Zambia in 1960 (R. E. Baldwin, 1966, pp. 207–13), for Kenya in 1968 (Thias and Carnoy, 1969), for Puerto Rico in 1960 (Pacheco, 1963, pp. 27–9), for Venezuela in 1957, Chile in 1959 and Colombia in 1961 (Carnoy, 1967b, table 7; Selowsky, 1968). In addition, ability-adjusted rates of return to levels of education have now been calculated for the Netherlands in 1965 (De Wolff and Ruiter, 1968). Further results for Germany, Ghana, Japan, Jordan, Malaysia, New Zealand, Nigeria, Norway, the Philippines and Sweden so far remain buried in unpublished manuscripts, government reports and doctoral dissertations.[9] Certain broad conclusions emerge from all of these studies:

1. Private rates of return are almost always higher than corresponding social rates (American college drop-outs are an exception), reflecting relatively high levels of State subsidies to education which are, in fact, never completely recouped by the application of the progressive income tax to the higher lifetime earnings of more educated people.

2. Private rates of return are invariably well in excess of what individuals can earn from stocks, bonds and savings accounts, but not always of borrowing rates on personal loans even in the well-organized part of the capital market.

3. In most underdeveloped countries, primary education produces unusually high social rates of return; in all developed countries,

9. No results have ever been reported for the Soviet Union, although the idea that education is a form of private investment is explicitly recognized in the Soviet literature. Most Soviet scholars follow Strumilin's pathbreaking essay (Strumilin, 1925) in calculating the social returns to education without resorting to discounting of any kind. Like Strumilin, they simply measure the productivity of skilled workers in terms of the ratio of their earnings to the standardized wages of unskilled workers, ignoring the fact that this ratio typically increases with age; this ratio is then applied as a coefficient to national income and what emerges is said to be 'the economic value of additional education' (Jamin, 1966) If this is not nonsense, it is so close to nonsense as to be indistinguishable from it.

secondary education produces higher social rates of return than tertiary education.

4. Social rates of return on higher education are either roughly the same as the yield of alternative public and private investment (as in the U.S.A. and the U.K.), or are sometimes clearly below alternative yields (as in Israel and India).

5. Both private and social rates of return on additional levels of education generally decline monotonically (Canadian higher education is an exception), indicating something like diminishing returns to increments in the quantity of schooling; but the generalization breaks down for additional years rather than levels of schooling, suggesting that the labour market prizes documentary proof of the successful completion of a course.

It is evident that, if equilibrium denotes equality of yields in all directions, educational investment is almost everywhere characterized by disequilibria.

It may be convenient at this stage to recall all the factors that we have mentioned as tending to produce biased estimates of rates of return (see Table 11).

It will be remembered (see Chapter 4, p. 135) that educational planning is usually conducted within the constraint of an exogenously determined educational budget. Whenever this is the case, there is no need to look beyond social rates of return on educational investment for decision criteria. But what if we drop the budget constraint? Since the issue is now one of allocating resources among *all* alternative uses, the problem is that of finding an appropriate comparison with the rate of return on education. What we are after is the social opportunity cost of education: the value to society of the next best alternative use of the resources invested in education. But what about the social time preference rate – the value that society places on the consumption stream that would be created by releasing the resources now invested in education – which is unlikely to be the same as the social opportunity cost rate? And so which is it to be, the social opportunity cost rate, the social time preference rate or both?

Becker used the after-tax yield on American business capital as the alternative rate of return; since this fell within the same range as the social rate of return on investment in college education, he concluded that but for externalities there was no social underinvestment in

Table 11

A Check List of Biases in Rates of Return

	Downward Bias (too low)	Upward Bias (too high)
Private Rates of Return	1. Lower rates of return to other types of human capital formation (training, health, etc.)	1. Higher rates of return to other types of human capital formation
	2. Future consumption benefits (?)	2. Present consumption benefits (?)
	3. Non-pecuniary occupational preference of educated people	
	4. Improved quality of education	
	5. Earnings differentials include first-round spill-overs	
Social Rates of Return	1. As 1 above	1. As 1 above
	2. Future consumption benefits (?)	
	3. Non-pecuniary occupational alternatives taking the form of fringe-benefits	
	4. As 4 above	
	5. Earnings below marginal private product (?)	5. Earnings above marginal private product (?)
	6. Excess demand for labour	6. Over-staffing in public sector
	7. Externalities (first-round and second-round spill-overs)	

college education in the United States (Becker, 1964, p. 121). Denison has argued, however, that even if the yield of education is actually less than the yield of business capital, the diversion of resources from private industry to education would nevertheless raise national income simply because private investment tends to be financed out of savings, whereas additional private and public funds for education tend to be financed out of consumption expenditures (Denison, 1962, pp. 77–8). Given the way in which education is financed in the United States, that is, with heavy reliance on local property taxes, Denison is perhaps right. However, the nub of his argument is that additional funds for education do not necessarily displace an equivalent amount of investment in physical capital. This provides us with a clue to answer the question posed earlier. The alternative rate of return is a weighted sum of the social opportunity cost rate and the social time preference rate; in so far as educational expenditures are financed by taxes whose incidence is on consumption, we should apply the social time preference rate, and for the rest, the social opportunity cost rate.[10] This neat analytical solution to the problem can be a nightmare to apply in practice. In Britain, for example, it is simply impossible to associate any portion of educational expenditures which are financed by the central government (which is two-thirds of the total) with any particular tax so as to distinguish the tax-elasticity of saving from that of consumption. Nevertheless, that is what we have to do if we want to argue about the optimum allocation of resources between all possible private and public uses.

In the past, rate-of-return analysis has been almost exclusively concerned with evaluating the yield of extra years or levels of education. But analysis of the economic effects of various *amounts* of education must be considered only a first step in a more comprehensive approach which would include the effects of various *kinds* of education. Becker argued, for example, that there is no striking evidence of social underinvestment in college education but agreed that there may well be high returns to improvements in the quality of American college education, or to expanding low-cost at the expense of high-cost institutions (see also Jencks and Riesman, 1968, pp. 128–9). The evidence on types of education, it must be admitted, is still very thin. There is Hansen's work on American engineers, doctors and dentists, and Mincer's analysis of labour training referred to earlier (see Chapter 6, pp. 189 and 197). There is the effort of Hirsch and Marcus (1966) to evaluate junior college programmes in the United States. Carroll and Ihnen (1967) have examined the graduates of a

10. This is an oversimplified account of a very difficult subject; for a fuller account, see Henderson (1965, pp. 96–118) and Marglin (1967, pp. 47–71); for an application in the context of rate-of-return analysis of education, see Blaug, Layard and Woodhall (1969, ch. 1).

two-year post-secondary technical college in the United States, and American post-graduate education has recently received increasing attention (Ashenfelter and Mooney, 1968, 1969; Butter, 1966; Hunt 1963). Most encouraging of all is the interest that is beginning to develop in measuring the returns to improvements in the quality of education (Morgan and Sirageldin, 1968; Welch, 1966) and particularly the returns to compensatory education programmes (Ribich, 1968, ch. 4).

It is too early to say what all these bits and pieces add up to and there is almost nothing to report on outside the United States. Rate-of-return analysis is still too young to permit final appraisal but its fecundity in opening up new lines for exploration promises well. The great bottleneck in extending the approach, however, is lack of data. Unless more countries become convinced of the importance of collecting statistics on personal earnings cross-classified by age and education, little more can be done to convey the significance of rate-of-return analysis. We are caught here in a vicious circle: because the approach is suspected, no figures are collected; because no figures are collected, no results are reported; and because no results are reported, suspicion feeds on itself. Clearly, any hope of progress in this area now depends critically on persuading governments to raise the relevant data.

Chapter 8
Applications of Cost–Benefit Analysis

Educated Unemployment in India

This chapter is intended to illustrate the application of cost–benefit analysis to certain educational problems that have arisen in under-developed countries. It is a small sample of an almost infinite list of such problems. The problems selected are the phenomenon of educated unemployment, the flight from farming into the cities, and the conflict between schooling for children and literacy campaigns for adults.

We begin with educated unemployment, taking India as a case in point, although Pakistan, Korea, the Philippines, the United Arab Republic or Argentina would have served just as well.[1] The number of 'educated unemployed' in India in 1967 is conservatively estimated at half a million; the estimate is conservative because it counts only men who are out of work the entire week, and does not allow for about an equal number doing casual or part-time work for several hours a day on two or three days in the week; it also excludes educated women who show much higher unemployment rates than men. The term 'educated' refers to all those who have at least completed secondary education, or in Indians' parlance, 'all those who are matriculates and above'. Half a million is undoubtedly a relatively large figure; it is equal to 6 to 7 per cent of the total stock of 'educated labour' in India in 1967. Expressing it in other terms, it is equivalent to nearly two-thirds of the annual output of matriculates and graduates from schools and colleges. If Britain faced similar problems of unemployment among people with one or more A-levels and with one or more university degrees, educated unemployment in Britain would amount to over 100,000.

That a poor country should suffer from a chronic surplus of labour is hardly surprising. But general unemployment is one thing and

1. This section is a terse summary of Blaug, Layard and Woodhall (1969).

educated unemployment is another. The Indian economy has been growing at about 3·5 per cent per annum since Independence, a sufficient rate of growth, one would have thought, to absorb all of its best-educated people into employment. Nevertheless, educated unemployment, which was already a serious problem in 1947, has remained a more or less constant proportion of a rapidly growing stock of educated labour. And yet matriculates and graduates constitute only 4 per cent of the labour force in India. Even among this relatively small group of highly educated people, however, the unemployment rate exceeds anything normally experienced in advanced countries. Clearly, here is something of a mystery, difficult to square with popular notions of the crying man-power 'needs' of underdeveloped countries.

Why then is there educated unemployment in India? Because there are too many matriculates and graduates relative to the number of job opportunities that require these qualifications. But this answer only throws up more questions. Why do so many students rush headlong into secondary and higher education when they know that on average one out of fifteen of them will be unemployed? They may not know the precise figures for educated unemployment but they are perfectly familiar with the phenomenon. Besides, why is it that the existence of educated unemployment does not cause salary differentials to fall, so as to increase employment in the short run and to reduce the financial advantages of acquiring more education in the long run?

The standard retort to this line of questioning, so standard as to have become the stock-in-trade of foreign visitors to India, is to point to the self-defeating search for status which drives Indian students to seek education without regard to career prospects. Instead of acquiring qualifications in technical and vocational subjects, like science, engineering and medicine, they pursue traditional academic subjects like law and literature, or commercial subjects like book-keeping and accounting. In other words, the fault lies partly with the educational system for not imparting technical and vocational education, and partly with educated invididuals themselves for preferring white-collar to manual and industrial occupations, the implication of the argument being that educated unemployment would soon vanish if only education were vocationalized and if only educated people were willing 'to get their hands dirty' (Myrdal, 1968, vol. 2, pp. 1124–31).

This conclusion receives support from the fact that educated unemployment is greater among graduates in arts and commerce than among graduates in science and engineering. Even among B.Sc.s and M.Sc.s, however, high rates of unemployment are not uncommon and in the last year or two, unemployment has appeared among engineers and technicians. Besides, whose fault is it that so many more students study academic rather than vocational subjects? It is certainly not what students want. We know from attitude surveys and from application rates that every second Indian student would like to study medicine or engineering, probably because employment prospects in these fields are excellent; they end up in arts and commerce only because they cannot gain admission into medicine and engineering. The reason is quite simple: while technical education has been deliberately restricted in the light of anticipated demand for technically qualified people, secondary and general higher education have been allowed to grow at a pace determined by the pressures for admission.

In point of fact, there has been so far no real attempt in India to gear the scale of secondary and higher education to forecasts of man-power requirements, this despite the fact that two-thirds of all graduates and nearly two-thirds of all matriculates work in the public sector. The enrolment targets that have appeared in the three Five-Year Plans since 1950 have been mere extrapolations of past trends in the private demand for education and hence predictions of what is considered likely rather than what is considered desirable. By and large, Indian secondary and higher-educational institutions have practised an 'open-door policy' and only medical and engineering colleges have rationed their places in accordance with admission quotas. The fact that over half of all Indian university students are enrolled in arts and commerce courses is not evidence that they are addicted to purely academic pursuits: it is simply a consequence of restrictive entry into colleges of medicine and engineering.

But why is there any demand at all for arts and commerce degrees if the incidence of unemployment among graduates with these specializations is as high as it is? The answer is that a B.A. can earn more than a matriculate, although much less than a B.Eng., even after allowing for the possibility of unemployment; the adjusted private rate of return to B.A.s is less than that to a matriculate qualification (see Table 9, p. 228) but it still compares favourably with the rates which urban Indians could earn on their personal savings or which they would have to pay if they borrowed capital to finance education (borrowing to enable children to continue their schooling is much more common among Indian parents than among British or American ones). Thus, an arts degree is a vocational degree in Indian circumstances and this is not really surprising because a growing economy needs administrators and clerks with B.A. qualifications, just as much as it needs doctors and engineers.

As for educated unemployment, can we really explain it all away by the unwillingness of matriculates and graduates to take up blue-collar occupations? In one sense, of course, it is tautologically true that unemployment would always disappear instantly if only the unemployed were willing to accept any job whatever at any rate of pay, however low. The question is one of degree: are the educated unemployed in India really less willing than unemployed professionals in advanced countries to accept a cut in pay and a decline in status? The first thing that must be said is that unemployment among the educated has, in fact, led to a reduction in their relative earnings, exactly as predicted by economic theory: the notorious stickiness of occupational rates of pay in underdeveloped countries has not prevented a decline in the real earnings associated with educational qualifications in India at a rate of about two to three per cent a year. There has been widespread and persistent upgrading of minimum hiring standards in India ever since Independence. In other words, jobs that used to be filled by matriculates now increasingly call for graduate qualifications, and so on for jobs lower down the occupational hierarchy; in consequence, highly educated people have constantly tended to drift down to lower-paid jobs. Nevertheless, upgrading has failed to clear the market for educated man power. Earnings have never declined fast enough to reduce the incentives to acquire still more education. Indeed, the supply of educated people has so persistently run ahead of demand that, as we mentioned earlier, educated unemployment as a fraction of the total stock of educated manpower has remained relatively constant for at least twenty years.

The persistence of educated unemployment ever since 1947, and probably ever since the 1920s, can be explained only by certain features of Indian labour markets that slow down the process of adjustment to unemployment and, in particular, the rate at which the unemployed lower their 'reservation price' (the price at which they offer themselves for employment). Educated unemployment in India constitutes, as it were, a revolving queue: it is not that some are permanently employed and others are permanently unemployed, but rather that large numbers are made to wait years before finding a first job. The number of jobs is growing all the time and everyone will eventually find employment if they are prepared to wait long enough. The 'average waiting time' in 1967 for matriculates was just under a year and a half and, for graduates, just over six months. There are strong taboos in India about changing jobs to enhance one's prospects and this alone puts a premium on a lengthy search for work. In addition, however, searching for work can be a full-time occupation in a poorly organized labour market. Despite the rapid growth of labour exchanges around the country since 1950 and despite the increased use of newspapers as sources of information about vacancies, Indian labour markets still rely to this day to an extraordinary degree on personal contacts as a source of job offers, which again tends to lengthen the period of search. Lastly, the institution of the 'joint family', with its creed of pooling resources, reduces the incentive to cut down on the length of search: the unemployed Indian student can rely almost indenifitely on some support from his family.

When we put all these factors together, it is hardly surprising that the 'average waiting time' of the educated unemployed is much longer in India than it is in advanced countries even for school leavers. Nor is it surprising that, despite the incidence of unemployment, the supply of matriculates and graduates goes on growing faster than the demand for them; as we noted, additional education is a good investment for individuals even though they take 6 to 18 months to find employment. But it does raise the question whether it is also socially advantageous that people should continue their education in the face of so much unemployment. Surely, the implied waste of resources would be reduced if fewer educated people competed for the limited pool of jobs? To cut down on college places, however, would simply increase the number of unemployed matriculates; to cut down on secondary-school places, would simply increase the number of unemployed primary-school leavers, and so on. Is there no advantage in keeping people off the labour market as long as possible, particularly as the incidence of unemployment does seem to fall with every additional educational qualification after matriculation?

Unfortunately, resources are used up in producing more educated people, a social cost which is only partly borne by individuals themselves.[2] Indian secondary and higher education is subsidized, inasmuch as fees are set below unit costs, and scholarship finance is made available to some students. Although four out of five arts and science colleges and two out of three secondary schools are private institutions, they receive substantial grants from state governments who are, in turn, supported by the central government. In fact, three-quarters of total educational expenditure in India comes from government funds. Levels of subsidization fall below those in Great Britain but generally exceed those prevailing in the United States. Furthermore, the government recovers little of the extra earnings of the better educated by taxation; income tax in India is surprisingly light and beings to apply at levels of income that are only attained by graduates after the age of 30 or 35. The result, as we might expect, is that social rates of return on educational investment in India invariably fall below private rates. More to the point, however, is the fact that social rates of return to secondary and general higher education are considerably less than rates of return to primary and middle-school education (see Table 9, p. 228). This fact alone argues for a re-allocation of educational expenditure towards primary education. Even if we drop the assumption of a given budget for education and compare the rates of return on education with the yield of other public investments, it is impossible to justify continued expansion of general higher education. The social opportunity cost rate of capital in India is estimated to be about 20 per cent; the social time preference rate appears to be about 5 per cent; since about half of total outlays on Indian education displace private investment, with the other half displacing private consumption, the 'composite social discount rate' for appraising investment in education (see Chapter 7, p. 233) is 12·5 per cent. While the argument leading to this conclusion is at best crude and ready-made, the resulting figure compares reasonably with the target rates of return of at least 11 to 12 per cent required of public sector enterprises in the Fourth Five-Year Plan (1966–71) document. If this much is accepted, it follows that there is social underinvestment in primary and middle schooling and social overinvestment in secon-

2. This is what some authorities forget when they recommend that poor countries 'ought to produce more educated people than can be absorbed at current prices, because the alteration in current prices which this forces is a necessary part of the process of economic development, (W. A. Lewis, 1962, p. 38).

dary and general higher education (see Table 9, p. 228, assuming $\alpha = 0.65$ or $\alpha = 0.5$).

Have we left anything out of the comparison? Social rates of return on educational investment ignore the consumption benefits and the externalities of education, but provided the magnitudes of these two effects is identical at all levels of education, our central finding is unaffected by these considerations. Although cogent arguments can be produced on both sides of this question, it is difficult to sustain the view in a largely illiterate country that higher education necessarily generates a greater sense of personal enrichment, as well as greater indirect benefits for the less educated, than primary education. Furthermore, the bulk of graduates are employed in the public sector which tends to disguise unemployment by overmanning, causing earnings to exceed the marginal private product of labour (see above Chapter 7, p. 207), whereas the bulk of primary-school leavers are employed in the private sector which is more likely to pay labour no more than its marginal private product. This means that even if primary-school leavers and graduates generate identical spill-overs, we have, in fact, overestimated the social rate of return on college degrees. This doubles the force of our previous conclusion: higher education is badly overexpanded relative to primary education.

To be sure, education serves other ends than that of economic growth. The objectives of educational planning may include, apart from maximizing the contribution of education to the growth of national income, equality of educational opportunity, political stability and national solidarity. The social inequality that exists between an illiterate and someone with primary education, however, is much greater than the inequality between a matriculate and a graduate. If the goal were equity rather than efficiency, therefore, there is no doubt that too much of the educational budget has gone to the higher levels and too little to the lower levels of the educational system. Similarly, it is difficult to argue that political stability and the reduction of regional and religious strife in India would be better served by producing more unemployed matriculates and graduates than by increasing enrolment rates in primary education and thus producing more people with at least three or four years of schooling. In short, if equality, political stability and social cohesion in India can be secured by educational policies (which is doubtful), the optimum policy is once again to divert resources from secondary and higher education to primary education, middle schooling and perhaps adult literacy (see Myrdal, 1968, vol. 3, pp. 1669, 1817–18, which argues along these lines to reach identical conclusions).

It is interesting to contrast the results of rate-of-return analysis with those of man-power forecasting in India. The Indian Education Commission, which published its recommendations in 1966, made use of a man-power forecast based on the assumption of rate of growth of GNP of 6·5 per cent per annum over the years 1961–76, compared with 4·1 per cent actually realized over the decade 1951–61 (see above Chapter 5, p. 150). It recommended that the *stock* of matriculates and graduates in employment should grow by 8 per cent per year, compared with a growth rate of slightly under 6 per cent a year experienced in the 1950s which, nevertheless, implied that the proportion of middle-school leavers who went on to matriculation, as well as the proportion of matriculates who stayed on for a first degree, would have to be reduced below current levels. By way of contrast, rate-of-return calculations for 1961, had they been available to the Commission, would have indicated reducing the rate of growth of the *stock* of higher-educated man power below 6 per cent with correspondingly sharper reductions in the rate of growth of the *flow* of matriculates and graduates.

The work of the Education Commission was nearly completed before the recession of 1965–8 set in but even at that stage it was doubtful whether any reasonable acceleration of the Indian growth rate could have outweighed the low observed rates of return on secondary and higher education. By 1969, however, these rates have fallen still further and by now even engineers are in oversupply. In other words, the events of the last few years have thrown into relief the folly of basing educational planning on forecasts of the man-power requirements of unrealistic targets for national income.

The case for cutting back the growth of secondary and higher education in India is overwhelming but the instruments for actually enforcing this policy are few. In Indian circumstances, it would be suicidal for a government to deny higher education to students who would have qualified for a degree if only they had been born earlier. However, there is more than one way to kill a goose. One possibility is gradually to raise the real values of fees in an effort to lower the private rate of return to secondary and higher education; another is for the public sector to adopt a policy of maximum rather than minimum educational qualifications for a job; still another is to select people for public service jobs before they go to college, making their appointment conditional on their getting a satisfactory degree; lastly, there are a number of curriculum changes that have been proposed by the Indian Education Commission, such as diversification of secondary courses, vocationally oriented education at post-primary level, and so on. Space does not allow discussion of the relative merits of these proposals (but see Blaug, Layard and Woodhall, 1969, ch. 10). The fact is that no easy remedy is available: the causes of educated unemployment in India run deep in the functioning of Indian labour markets, the hiring practices of the government, and from there to the institution of the joint family and the attitudes of educated Indians. The basic thread, however, is the Malthusian-like tendency of higher education in India to grow faster than the ability to absorb graduates into employment. For a while, the progress of upgrading minimal hiring standards disguises the problem. By the time the labour market is saturated, however, the scramble of students for higher and higher qualifications has built up a pressure that few governments can resist. The process has probably gone further in India than anywhere else, but India is the mirror in which the rest of the underdeveloped world can see the problems they may well be facing in the decade of the 1970s.

The difficulties of eliminating educated unemployment in India are essentially those of taking policy decisions which run against the grain of private rate-of-return calculations. Whatever remedies are eventually adopted must take the form of altering the terms on which private decisions are made – or fail. This is merely one illustration of a general thesis: the private rate of return is no less a vital statistic for educational planning than the social rate of return. Indeed, educational planning in underdeveloped countries could be considerably improved merely by paying due attention to the economic benefits of education to the individual, even when private rates of return are not actually calculated. The much-debated question of agricultural education in Africa provides an example of how a standard investment decision about types of education immediately takes on a new complexion when approached in a cost–benefit framework.

Agricultural Education in Africa

The role of agricultural science in the curriculum of primary and secondary schools has been a bone of contention among African educators for almost fifty years.[3] Experts have argued again and again that African schools themselves are responsible for the exodus from rural areas to towns and for the emergence of urban unemployment among school leavers, problems which have already reached alarming proportions in West Africa and are now beginning to be matters of concern in East and Central Africa (Callaway, 1963, 1965, 1967). Imitating the academic type of instruction of Europe and America, African education, it is alleged, generates unrealistic expectations of clerical employment, fosters a disdain for manual occupations and, in consequence, inhibits rather than promotes rural progress. Since most Africans are dependent on agriculture, so the argument runs, the only way in which schooling can make a significant contribution to the economic development of Africa is by imparting an agricultural bias to the curriculum at all levels of the educational system, followed on by the expansion of junior agricultural colleges at the upper-secondary level (Balogh, 1962; Dumont, 1964; 1966, chs.7, 14; 1968).

This thesis has been examined with respect to Ghana in a remarkable book by Foster, who labels it the 'Vocational school fallacy in development planning' (Foster, 1966, esp. pp. 137–9, 294–5; and 1965*). Foster shows that proposals to increase the provision of agricultural and technical education in Ghana formed an essential element in every major document relating to education in the Gold Coast from as long ago as 1847 to the grant of independence in 1957. Nevertheless, none of these proposals was ever fully implemented; whenever an attempt was made to implement them in some fashion or other, the experiment soon had to be abandoned. The question that immediately arises is: why, despite a century of effort by successive colonial governors and educational missions to establish agricultural schools and to devise special agricultural curricula, do African schools continue to this day to favour academic education along Western lines?

The answer that Foster provides is as simple as it is penetrating. Throughout the period of colonial rule, the subsistence sector of

3. The origins of the debate date back to two reports of the Phelps–Stokes Fund, published in 1922 and 1923 (L. J. Lewis, 1962).

agriculture (defined on p. 253) held out few prospects for school leavers and the primary function of formal education was to provide the more able African youngsters with entry into the European-dominated modern sector. Within the modern sector, however, there was relatively greater demand for clerical and commercial skills than for technical skills. In view of the slow rate of expansion of the modern sector, the financial rewards and employment opportunities for technically trained individuals, whether in farming or in manufacturing, were never commensurate with those in clerical occupations. Thus, the graduates of the academic schools were always at an advantage compared to the graduates of vocational or vocationally oriented institutions. In the circumstances, the pressure for an academic type of education was nothing else than the familiar mechanism of demand and supply in the labour market transmitting an influence on the private demand for education. African students, far from being irrational in insisting on bookish education, correctly appraised the actual job opportunities that were available; paradoxically enough, the teaching of the three 'R's provided a 'vocational' education in the best sense of the word, allowing entry to the most prestigious and better-paid occupations in the economy.

This picture has changed very little since Independence. In 1965, only about 15 per cent of the total employed labour force of 2·5 million were fully employed in the modern exchange sector of the Ghanaian economy. Wage employment opportunites have been growing at about 4 per cent per annum, creating 25,000 new jobs every year; but the annual output of middle schools alone has now risen to about 30,000 students a year. The only reason this has not led to unemployment of middle-school leavers is the fact that employment in the public sector has been growing faster than employment in the exchange economy. Government jobs, however, are largely of a clerical and administrative nature. The progressive enlargement of the public sector has, therefore, led to an even greater demand for academic secondary-school education than in the days before Independence. It is not the schools that are the culprits but rather the modern sector of the economy which has not grown rapidly enough to create a demand for technical skills. On the basis of a number of sample surveys of secondary-school pupils in Ghana, Foster concludes that African schoolchildren have remarkably realistic job expectations. His findings have been confirmed by a follow-up study in the Ivory Coast and by another similar investigation in Tanzania (Heijnen, 1968, ch. 6). The Ivory Coast study also examined the employment histories of secondary-school graduates and discovered that unemployment was largely confined to graduates of technical and agricultural schools, rather than to the graduates of academic-type schools (Clignet and Foster, 1966, pp. 185–9). If such findings are representative of Africa as a whole, the popular notion that the curriculum is a major determinant of the vocational aspirations of students will have to be abandoned, and with it the idea that one can generate economic development by according high priority to agricultural and technical education without a corresponding change in employment opportunities.

The fact of the matter is that few African teachers are properly qualified to teach an ordinary syllabus; to add to their burdens by asking them to introduce farming into the time-table or to operate a demonstration garden-farm attached to the school is, in effect, to ensure a dilution of educational standards. Perhaps one can get round this problem by adding an agricultural specialist to the staff of each school, but this only means that fewer graduates in agriculture would be available to staff the Extension Service of the Ministry of Agriculture. Unfortunately, there are already too few agricultural extension workers in most African countries: the typical ratio in Tropical Africa of one extension officer to 1500 or 2000 farming families is well below the threshold level at which an Extension Service might make an effective contribution to the productivity of agriculture (B. F. Johnston, 1964, pp. 177–8; Yudelman, 1964b, pp. 578, 580; see also p. 255). The failure to invest heavily in agricultural development is indeed the chief problem and nothing that is done in schools will of itself make much impact on the monetary rewards of farming (Griffiths, 1968; Hunter, 1966, 1968; W. A. Lewis, 1962, pp. 38–9; Skorov, 1968, pp. 43–5, 195–208). The alarms which are forever being raised about agricultural education in Africa spring quite simply from totally exaggerated expectations of what schools by themselves can be expected to contribute to economic development. This is not to say that it would do no good if reading material in African schools were systematically infused with rural idiom and even with a few basic principles of good land use and sound animal husbandry (Evans, 1962). It is just that the addition of a rural flavour to the curriculum, or even the teaching of agriculture as a constituent subject in schools, cannot keep African school leavers in the countryside and cannot eliminate urban unemployment among primary-school leavers; this can only be done by making the countryside a better place to live and work in, that is, by a concerted national effort to promote investment in rural training and development.

Besides, it is one thing to dream up ideal curricula and another thing to enforce them. Experience throughout the underdeveloped world has shown that it is impossible to alter the school syllabus unless the change keeps touch with what parents wish their children to learn (Anderson, 1967b, pp. 27–31). Radical departures from the educational aspiration of parents simply founder upon a rising rate of absenteeism as parents begin to boycott the schools. In the face of prevailing conditions in African agriculture and the persistent tendency of government pay scales to be rigidly defined in terms of educational qualifications, one can hardly blame African parents for bitterly resisting anything that smacks of vocational education oriented to farming. Whatever educational planners may think, African parents have not misread the signals provided by casual rate-of-return calculations.

This is a convenient point at which to note that much of the confusion in the debate on rural education is created by the conventional distinction between academic and vocational education. This distinction, which is actually grounded in the nature of the two curricula, is allowed to carry the implication that some education prepares students for the 'world of work' and some does not. All too frequently, however, those who have taken courses of study generally called 'academic' (think of a degree in classics in Britain until recently) reap substantial financial returns from their education, returns which may even be higher than those to 'vocational' education, thus producing the paradoxical conclusion that academic education has a greater 'vocational' value than vocational education. The traditional distinction was developed by educators but the labour market has its own way of appraising qualifications. There is need to be on guard, therefore, when encountering passionate claims in favour of vocational education.

Adult Literacy in Poor Countries

In this section, we go beyond formal education in schools to ask: should educational planners in poor countries devote a fraction of their scarce resources to adult literacy programmes and, if so, what fraction? In so doing, we fulfil the promise that was made in Chapter 4 to furnish criteria for dividing the total educational budget between formal and informal education.

It must be conceded at the outset that the question has no definite answer in the present state of knowledge. What we will do in effect is to show how one could go about answering it. The general approach is once again cost–benefit analysis, but new problems are encountered in applying it to adult literacy.

The principal effect of literacy (of which numeracy is an important component) is to provide people with an additional means of communication. In this way, literacy may contribute to economic development by (a) raising the productivity of new literates; (b) raising the productivity of individuals working in association with literates – the so-called 'first-round' spill-overs of literacy; (c) reducing the cost of transmitting useful information to individuals (say, about health and nutrition) by creating, as it were, a new channel for disseminating knowledge; (d) stimulating the demand for vocational training and technical education; and (e) strengthening economic incentives, meaning the tendency for people to respond positively to a rise in the rate of reward for their efforts. This is not an exhaustive list of all the direct and indirect economic benefits of promoting literacy in poor countries, but it seems to cover the more obvious points made in the literature (Bertelsen, 1965; Doob, 1961, pp. 173–9; Schuman, Inkeles and Smith, 1967; Wharton, 1965). Unfortunately, an enumeration of the economic benefits of increasing enrolment rates in primary and secondary schools would yield an almost identical list. How is the planner to choose between more adult literacy and more school education?

The difficulty is that adult literacy and primary schooling are not all-or-nothing alternatives. Of course, universal primary education would in time cut off illiteracy at its source. It appears to be impossible, however, to achieve even 70 or 80 per cent enrolment rates in primary schools in a largely illiterate community. So long as parents are illiterate it is difficult to secure attendance of children in schools and even more difficult to keep them there for six years or longer. In short, the efficiency of a school system is dependent on some minimum percentage of literate parents in the community.

On the other hand, to promote adult literacy to the point of neglecting formal schooling, quite apart from the fact that it is not politically feasible in most underdeveloped countries, would ignore the prima facie case in favour of school education. The child is typically educated for six to eight years, gaining competence in reading and writing over a period of time sufficiently long to develop disciplined study habits. The illiterate adult typically attends classes for six or twelve months, learning to read, write and calculate after a day's work in the field or factory. In the circumstances, it seems reasonable to suppose that school education makes a greater impact on the development of economically useful knowledge than adult literacy. There are considerations which run the other way: the adult already possesses a skill, however simple and crude, which is improved by knowledge of the three 'R's, whereas the child is acquiring no specific skill whatever. Nevertheless, in the absence of any concrete evidence to settle the question, it seems reasonable to conclude that the economic returns to school education, whatever they are, exceed the returns to adult literacy.

However, even if the initial economic benefits of school and adult education were identical, the two benefit streams do not accrue over equal time periods. A child in an underdeveloped country who leaves school at the age of thirteen or fourteen can generally expect to look forward to a productive life of thirty-five years. The average adult who has attended literacy classes will have no more than fifteen to twenty years to enjoy the benefits of literacy. Thus, the productive life-span of an educated child is typically more than twice that of a literate adult and, for that reason alone, school education would appear to promise the greater yield.

But the superior economic benefits of school education are in all probability more than offset by the cost differential between school and adult education. In most countries, it costs as much to keep a child in school for a year as to provide twelve months of literacy classes for an adult (the lower cost of part-time teachers and the part-time use of buildings in literacy campaigns is just about matched by the greater cost of publicity, books and materials, not to mention the diseconomies of operating on a small scale). Although the annual unit cost of the two types of instruction is more or less identical, the fact remains that school education typically takes six to eight years and involves some output forgone, whereas literacy courses usually take one or at most two years, and, if confined to evenings, involve no output forgone. Therefore, the economic benefits of school education would have to be four to five times greater than the economic benefit of adult literacy to produce identical cost–benefit ratios for the two types of education. When costs are brought into the picture, the presumption that school education is the more profitable investment loses much of its force.

Up to this point, we have been arguing as if the planner were indifferent about time, treating costs and benefits in year one as perfectly equivalent to costs and benefits in year eight. In fact, he will always weigh earlier years more heavily than later years, if for no other reason than that a pound's worth of goods and services can always be reinvested in a growing economy to produce more than a pound's worth later on. As we saw, a pound's worth of investment in school education on average begins to yield an economic return in six to eight years, whereas a pound of investment in adult literacy starts to pay off in one or two years, an average difference of five years. At a social opportunity cost rate as low as 9 per cent, a sum will double itself in just over eight years, or increase by one-half in five years. Therefore, even if the arithmetic sum of all the lifetime economic benefits of school education were one and a half times greater than that of adult literacy, either by virtue of its greater initial impact or because of the longer productive life-span of the educated child, the discounted present value of these benefits would be the same, simply because the returns from investment in literacy accrue on average five years earlier and can therefore be reinvested at compound interest for five years. The argument applies equally on the side of costs but with opposite consequences for the comparison between schooling and literacy classes: the present value of the unit costs of a primary-school expansion programme is *not* three and a half times greater than the unit cost of an adult literacy campaign because the later costs are incurred, the lower their real burden.

It is not possible to produce a neat conclusion from all this. The arguments in favour of school education are that its impact on the future productivity of the individual is probably greater and that it lasts longer; but it also costs more, not perhaps per year but over the whole cycle of instruction. The arguments in favour of adult literacy are that it yields an early return and that its costs are soon liquidated; when economic growth is mandatory, patience is at a premium. This is not enough to tell us that the rate of return or the discounted cost–benefit ratio of adult literacy exceeds that of school education. Suffice it to say that the case for investing more resources in literacy campaigns at the expense of formal schooling is stronger, (a) the

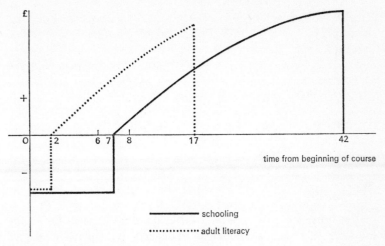

Figure 21   Comparative cost–benefit profiles

smaller the differential benefit of school education, (b) the greater the annual unit cost differential of adult literacy, (c) the younger the adult literate, and (d) the higher the social discount rate of the planner. We can summarize the problem in a conjectural diagram (Figure 21) assuming that the child leaves school at fourteen years of age after seven years of schooling and is then employed for thirty-five years; that the adult acquires literacy at the age of thirty after a two-year course and then works another fifteen years; and that the benefits of literacy and schooling mature gradually at the same rate with work experience (ignoring for the moment how to measure these benefits).

The present values of these two net benefit streams (net in the sense that both are compared to the benefits of a totally illiterate worker), when calculated at successively higher discount rates, might look like Figure 22 (see also Chapter 2, p. 59). The question of which one has a higher present value depends entirely on the social discount rate; if the planner insists on a relatively short pay-off period, that is, a relatively high discount rate reflecting an extreme preference for present income over future income, the discounted benefits of a literacy campaign are likely to exceed those of school education, and vice versa for a relatively long pay-off period and a low social discount rate. It is true that, in the example before us, the internal rate of return on adult literacy is greater than that of school education; if the educational

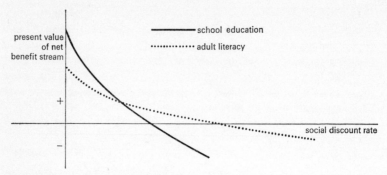

Figure 22   Comparative present value curves

budget is exogenously determined, this decides the issue. But in the more general case, the outcome must depend on the planner's degree of impatience.

All this is no doubt very interesting but it is purely speculative. The educational planner may be in a position to cost the two types of education and even to estimate the average length of the two benefit streams, but he rarely has a clue about their particular shape over time. At this point, he is inclined to turn for help to the research worker – to little avail. As we have seen, not much has so far been accomplished in measuring the impact of formal schooling on the productivity of individuals under different economic conditions, and virtually nothing is known about the economic effects of raising literacy in poor countries. The only general result that we can draw on is the finding that a 40 per cent literacy rate represents a critical threshold level for rapid economic advance (see Chapter 3, p. 64).

Even if we accept the idea that a literacy rate below 40 per cent constitutes a barrier to self-sustaining economic growth, it is not immediately evident how illiteracy actually impedes the rise in incomes. As anyone who has travelled in underdeveloped countries can testify, much can be accomplished with illiterate farmers and workers. It is sometimes possible to double or treble crop yields by persuading an illiterate farmer, after a few visits to a Demonstration Farm, to make use of improved seeds and chemical fertilizers. Occasionally, the same effects are achieved merely by building an irrigation dam or by providing for the efficient storage of rainwater. Highly mechanized textile factories are found in several Asian and Latin

American countries which are entirely staffed by illiterate workers. On the west coast of Africa, economic transactions on a considerable scale are managed by illiterate women, and, indeed, throughout Tropical Africa it is not uncommon to find trading companies, employing fifty or more workers, run by illiterate entrepreneurs who keep records with the aid of a simple abacus. It is simply not true that illiteracy is an absolute barrier to economic progress. What is true is that there are definite limits to what can be accomplished with an illiterate population.

To get any further we must distinguish between 'subsistence economies' (regions in underdeveloped countries where market transactions are still relatively unimportant) and 'exchange economies' (regions where exchange activities more or less permeate every aspect of economic life). In subsistence economies, the tendency of literacy to stimulate economic change largely depends on its capacity to transform traditional man into economic man: it has an economic impact only to the extent that it fosters the cash-nexus. In exchange economies, however, people are already conscious of money-earning opportunities; here literacy may also strengthen economic motives directly but, more importantly, it is likely to contribute indirectly to more efficient cultivation and marketing in agriculture and to the further training of skills in industry. Nothing but confusion is created by discussing 'subsistence economies' and 'exchange economies' under the single heading of 'underdeveloped countries' (Myint, 1964, pp. 43–50, 58–60).

We begin with the case of subsistence economies. The term 'subsistence economies' is apt to be misleading, suggesting that the people of an entire country are living at a physiological minimum level of existence without knowledge of money or money prices. A more descriptive phrase might be 'non-exchange economies' but even this fails to convey the central idea of households largely dependent on the goods they themselves produce and only marginally on the sale of cash crops or on earnings from wage labour. This situation characterizes the economies of East, Central and West Africa and, to a lesser extent, India, Pakistan, South-East Asia and Latin America. Despite the mines of Zambia and the Congo, despite the sugar plantations of the Cameroons, despite the cocoa farmers of Ghana, most of Tropical Africa consists of islands of exchange activity entirely surrounded by an ocean of peasant subsistence economies. The root cause of the persistence of subsistence economies is not so much lack of pecuniary motivation on the part of African farmers, but rather geographical remoteness and inadequate local opportunities for earning money. This is evident from the standard pattern of regional development in Tropical Africa: some hitherto inaccessible area in a country is brought into contact with a leading town or port by means of a new road or railway; this immediately produces a flow of migrant labour into the towns which within a few years carries the seeds of change back to the outlying rural area; there follows the introduction of cash cropping, possibly stimulated by extension work on the part of the Ministry of Agriculture; community development projects and village improvement schemes now add yeast to the brew. At this point, occupational aspirations begin to rise and pressure develops for additional primary schools to educate the young. Depending on the economic potential of the soil in the area, this stage is accompanied either by the further export of labour or by the rapid spread of one or two profitable cash crops for overseas markets, associated with more diversified food cropping. By now, the subsistence economy has all but disappeared; agricultural productivity is still low but all activity is focused on the market.

It follows from what has been said that literacy is no panacea for the subsistence economy. At best, a literacy campaign can accelerate the process of transition to an exchange economy, once the process is under way. Even so, there are reasons to believe that the extension of agricultural credit on generous terms, or the stabilization of crop prices via marketing boards or, best of all, improvements in the means of transportation, are more effective ways of spending money to ensure expansion of the exchange economy. However, once money-earning activities have become a normal feature of the area or country in question, literacy comes into its own as a possible policy instrument to raise incomes and productivity. We need now to consider this second case.

Exchange economies characterize most of Latin America and are also found here and there throughout Africa and Asia. To grasp the complexity of the problem, we must consider the role of literacy in agriculture separately from its role in industry. It is self-evident that even a 100 per cent literacy rate is not a sufficient condition for agricultural development: reading and writing alone do not produce water in a semi-arid region or tractors for overgrown, stony ground. Conversely, some underdeveloped, largely illiterate countries have achieved remarkable improvements in agricultural productivity by means of heavy investment in agricultural extension, agricultural credit, demonstration farms, free tractor-repair stations and a variety of subsidized seeds and implements. Nevertheless, so long as the farming population remains illiterate, instructions on preparing the land for water, on methods of ploughing and seeding, on techniques of using fertilizers, on the purchase and maintenance of tools and implements, and on the packing and shipping of produce have to be imparted orally, again and again, until the farmer remembers them. If it were possible to issue printed *aides-mémoires*, the work of agricultural extension could be considerably speeded up. Experience with agricultural extension in Africa and elsewhere suggests that an average extension offcer can effectively service about five villages, each of which contains 100 farm households (King, 1967, p. 26). If the officer could distribute simple instruction leaflets to the farmers, or specially prepared pamphlets reminding them of what they had just witnessed in their visit to the demonstration farm, he might be able to service as many as fifteen or twenty villages, or 1500 or 2000 farmers. This sort of argument leads to the conclusion that illiteracy is a barrier to efficient agricultural extension. The principal economic benefit of literacy in the commercialized rural sectors of underdeveloped countries is that of improving the effectiveness of agricultural extension or, to put it differently, reducing the cost of the extension service. When it is remembered that agricultural extension is the key to all agricultural development, this benefit of literacy is not unimportant. Added to this is the direct advantage to the farmer himself of being able to calculate crop yields and to keep accounting records.

It is obvious that the economic returns of literacy campaigns ultimately take the form of increasing the productivity of farmers. Nevertheless, there is value in emphasizing that the direct impact effect of literacy on individual productivity is probably small: even a literate farmer is afraid to take a chance on a new crop without some visible evidence of its yield and he is reluctant to finance a new implement without assurance that credit is available to keep it in running order. Furthermore, written communication is not inherently more efficient than oral communication. On the contrary, while oral communication may be wasteful of time, written communication may be equally wasteful of resources devoted to affecting a change of behaviour (this is the argument for radio and television as new educational media). The best method of communicating knowledge involves oral demonstration and written reinforcements. Thus, it is largely indirectly and in association with the quality and quantity of agricultural extension that literacy is capable of promoting development in the rural sector (Montgomery, 1967; Schultz, 1964, pp. 199–205; Yudelman, 1964a, pp. 146–9, 209–10).

This brings us to the question of literacy in industry. Here the ground is more familiar and we can expect to learn something from experience in the industrialized nations. The first problem is that of deciding whether literacy has a significant effect on the productivity of individual workers. The obvious way of testing this hypothesis is to compare the age-specific earnings of literate and illiterate workers, subject to the proviso that the labour market functions competitively. This sort of information is easy to collect, at least for a sample of the population, and provides a basis for more detailed investigations based on job analysis (see Chapter 5, p. 156). For example, some limited income data for a number of African countries suggest that mere literacy makes virtually no difference to a person's earnings in urban industry; a worker with four or five years of primary schooling earns no more than someone with only one or two years; the better-paying occupations seem to be filled almost exclusively by those who had at least six years of schooling (Pons, Xydias and Clement, 1956, pp. 269, 641; Sofer and Sofer, 1955, pp. 46–8). Such findings have led African educators to conclude that about six years or more of primary schooling are required to achieve 'functional' as opposed to 'rudimentary' literacy.[4]

We have hardly begun to exploit the potentialities of studies that link literacy with earnings and the skill content of occupations. In most underdeveloped countries, the requisite data have never been collected. The fact that a literate worker earns twice as much as an illiterate worker does not, of course, prove that he is twice as productive; it creates a presumption that he is more productive, a presumption which can then be strengthened by further analysis of the characteristics of the particular labour market in question.

4. Other studies in Tanzania, the Philippines and Colombia on the retention of literacy among primary-school leavers (Flores, 1950; Heijnen, 1968, pp. 42–5, 62–4, 150–51; Myrdal, 1968, vol. 3, pp. 1681–3; E. M. Rogers and Herzog, 1966) confirm the view that it takes at least six to seven years of schooling in most poor countries to make a student functionally literate in adult life.

Once we throw away evidence about earnings, we are faced with the more difficult task of measuring productivity in physical terms. If the product turned out by a group of literate and illiterate workers is not homogeneous, we are almost doomed at the outset because we cannot compare like with like. In some cases, there may be a number of such multiproduct firms producing goods of a similar range with different mixes of literate and illiterate workers; in that case, interfirm analysis may reveal the specific effects of literacy. As a last resort, we can try asking supervisors and foremen what would be produced if more of the workers in a plant were literate. It is doubtful whether we would get meaningful answers. A plant with illiterate workers is not laid out, operated and organized in the same way as an establishment staffed with literate workers; the average productivity may be higher in the latter case but there is no way of working back to the particular impact of literacy on an individual worker. Of course, if we are willing to settle for averages, the physical measurement problem, even when the product is heterogeneous, is perfectly manageable. We might use the ratio of supervisors to operatives, the average orientation period of newly hired workers, the length of time needed to complete on-the-job training schemes of a given quality, the cost of preventing accidents, even the amount of capital equipment per worker, as alternative proxy indicators of the effect of raising literacy standards in a factory.

Research along these lines into the economic benefits of literacy in underdeveloped countries is still in its infancy. Nevertheless, it is at the level of the individual firm, and at this level alone, that one can come to grips with the impact of literacy on productivity. It is all very well to talk about literacy contributing to a favourable climate for economic development via its spill-over benefits. In view of the fact that literacy campaigns take time and that much else is happening in a growing economy, the global approach to literacy research yields little beyond vague generalizations. What is needed now is hard data on the output, earnings, aptitude and achievement of literate as opposed to illiterate workers; there certainly are spill-over benefits but these cannot be traced without first measuring the direct effects on new literates.

We could go on in this fashion, sketching the nature of the investigations that would illuminate the economic benefits of literacy, but perhaps enough has now been said to indicate how little we know and how much work remains to be done. Fortunately, UNESCO's new

Experimental World Literacy Programme provides for evaluation and research as an integral feature of literacy projects in a number of countries over the next four or five years. A brief description of UNESCO's programme will allow us to carry the argument one step further, indicating the kind of literacy projects that are most likely to yield substantial economic benefits.

In 1962, UNESCO published an important document entitled *World Campaign for Universal Literacy*. This document contained a survey of the situation with respect to literacy rates in the decade of the fifties, a set of recommendations for national literacy programmes, an analysis of the costs and benefits of a world literacy campaign and a programme of international support for a ten-year campaign designed to eradicate two-thirds of the illiterate population of the world between the ages of fifteen and fifty (about 330 million people). It was estimated that the cost of literacy training per person ranged from $7·35 in Africa to $5·25 in Asia, with teachers accounting for about half the costs. On this basis, the total cost of the world campaign would be just under $2 billion, or $190 million a year for ten years, of which $33 million would be met from external sources.

For a variety of reasons, this mass assault on illiteracy was abandoned some time in 1964. It was not, as is sometimes alleged, that the costs of a mass programme were beyond the resources of the underdeveloped world. After all, the annual outlay of $190 million was in 1963 approximately 0·1 per cent of the combined GNPs of the underdeveloped countries. It was rather that more and more evidence had become available in the late 1950s on the poor results of mass literacy campaigns: first of all, it proved difficult to enrol more than 10 or 20 per cent of the illiterate population; secondly, wastage rates as high as 50 per cent were not uncommon; and those that did receive literacy certificates after a course of nine to twelve months tended to lapse back into illiteracy after a few years. The causes of the failure of mass campaigns are obvious: lack of adequate publicity before the literacy classes open; use of untrained volunteer teachers who soon lose interest in teaching; unimaginative literacy primers in the fashion of reading books for children; and a total lack of follow-up materials for new literates. All of these are the results of trying to do too much with too few resources, that is, of a mass attack on all age groups.

It must be admitted, however, that the Soviet Union did succeed in eradicating illiteracy in less than twenty years by means of a concerted attack on the problem with the aid of volunteers from the trade unions and the Young Communist League. Why did the mass approach succeed in Soviet Russia when it appears to have failed in India and Pakistan? Too little is known about the Soviet campaigns to give a definite answer, but we shall not be far wrong if we say: Communism and rapid economic growth.[5] It is not the ideology of Communism as such that makes the difference but rather the ability of a Communist régime to mobilize and effectively direct social pressures; hence, the recent success of Castro in dramatically raising literacy rates (Jolly, 1964, pp. 190–219). Ecuador, Indonesia and Turkey now actually make literacy compulsory for all citizens but this has had little effect on enrolment in literacy classes in these countries. The Soviet Union, however, utilized all the media of communication to induce people to attend literacy classes, sometimes supplemented by monetary prizes for new literates, while pressing all educated people into teaching them. It is difficult to conceive of any non-Communist country asking its university students to volunteer for evening teaching and ensuring compliance by the threat of social excommunication. But all the instruments of mass persuasion would not have sufficed in the Soviet Union without an 8 per cent annual growth rate and all that this implied in the way of new jobs and possibilities of promotion. It is not claimed that people are motivated only by economic opportunities. No doubt, it is more often traditional religious beliefs or the social status of a literate, rather than expected financial returns, that first motivate illiterate adults to learn to read and write. What we are saying is that it is always easier to get illiterates to attend classes and to complete courses when it is obvious that literacy will benefit them immediately and directly. When a country is developing rapidly and incomes are rising sharply, social prestige tends to accrue to those whose incomes are rising fastest, and these are invariably literate adults. Thus, social and economic motives coincide in the context of a growing economy. The lesson of the Soviet experience, therefore, is to provide literacy campaigns within the framework of a total development effort in order to insure the creation of jobs for literates in step with the issue of literacy certificates.

5. It must be remembered, however, that the rate of literacy of the entire population in Tsarist Russia in 1913 was approximately 33 per cent and that even at the turn of the century the literacy rate for urban adults was as high as 55 per cent (DeWitt, 1961, pp. 71–2).

Prodded by some cogent criticisms of the World Campaign for Universal Literacy (e.g. Curle, 1964b), UNESCO in 1964 went over to what they candidly described as 'a new approach to illiteracy: the selective, intensive strategy' (UNESCO, 1964). This new programme has now been launched on an experimental basis in Algeria, Ecuador, Iran, Mali, Tanzania and Venezuela, financed in part by the countries themselves and in part by the United Nations Development Programme (except in Venezuela where the entire project is nationally financed). The strategy proposed is selective in two senses: literacy campaigns are to be confined to areas that are already experiencing economic growth and the effort will be concentrated on younger people in the age range fifteen to twenty-nine; the strategy is intensive in the sense that it aims to provide not only reading and writing but also elementary civic, health, technical and vocational education.

What lay behind the new approach was a fundamental distinction between 'rudimentary literacy' and 'functional literacy'. A person who has imbibed the rudiments of literacy may be able to read street signs and posters and even to decipher a letter, but he still cannot read a newspaper with anything like reasonable comprehension. He has achieved the standards which a child reaches after three or four years of primary schooling and, like such a child, he tends to read less and less as the years go by, eventually lapsing back into illiteracy. Functional literacy, on the other hand, approaches the standards of a primary-school leaver after six years of formal education. It implies the ability to read a newspaper in an hour or so, to follow a leaflet or a simple pamphlet issued by the Ministry of Agriculture, to absorb a well-written instruction manual for a technical appliance or a machine, in short, to make productive use of reading and writing. The aim of a functional literacy campaign is to bring illiterates to a level where they can make profitable use of vocational and technical training, whether in industry or agriculture. This entails a new approach to almost every aspect of literacy work. The course will have to be longer than the nine or twelve months sufficient to acquire rudimentary literacy. The teachers will have to be specially trained or retrained to teach elementary health instruction, technical knowledge and agricultural science, cooperating continuously with the staff of the various Ministries of Health, Labour and Agriculture. Modern audiovisual techniques (slides, film strips, radio and closed-circuit television) will have to be employed to stimulate discussion and to provoke interest in attending class after work. By concentrating on agricultural regions where successful development projects are already raising crop yields, or on industrial regions where the expansion of productive capacity is already widening job horizons, the difficulty of providing a motivation to adults to attend classes is partly if not wholly overcome. Similarly, by limiting attendance to the productive age group, the temptation to teach reading and writing unconnected with the acquisition of useful skills is likewise minimized.

In a nutshell, the new UNESCO approach is intensive rather than extensive, selective rather than diffusive, work-oriented rather than culturally oriented. It emphasizes continuous adult education fusing into genuine vocational instruction, rather than once-and-for-all teaching of the three 'R's. It favours the use of diversified primers rather than single primers, in conjunction with follow-up materials embodying specific knowledge of nutrition, sanitation, industrial arts and agricultural science. It regards literacy programmes as investment rather than consumption. It is, to say the least, a more than literacy Literacy Programme.

From our point of view, the most important feature of the Experimental World Literacy Programme is built-in evaluation and research. In each country where the programme is adopted, several international experts working together with national counterparts will be assigned to undertake base-line studies in the opening phases of the project. Each illiterate attending classes will be given a battery of intelligence and vocational aptitude tests. These tests will be repeated at the end of the course and their respective results will be compared. Furthermore, the base-line studies will measure and record crop yields, industrial output per man, the salaries of literate and illiterate workers, and similar economic indicators of the productivity of individuals working in the area in question. These, too, will be repeated at a later stage to help determine the benefits of literacy. In addition, studies of quality of agricultural extension in the region and of the scope of industrial training in local factories will be undertaken to throw further light on the pay-off from literacy campaigns.

Needless to say, the selective, intensive strategy costs a good deal more per literate than the mass extensive approach. The sorts of figures that have been quoted in the past for literacy campaigns ($7 to $10 per literate) need to be multiplied by a factor of two or three to give a realistic assessment of the costs of the new approach. Nevertheless, there will still be wide variations between countries owing to international differences in the real costs of teachers and buildings, as well as widely differing practices concerning the training and remuneration of part-time literacy teachers. The chief factor that raises the costs of selective intensive literacy campaigns is simply the length of the course compared with the average duration of classes in a mass extensive campaign. Since it takes about eight months of daily classes of one hour each to achieve rudimentary literacy, it is intended that the new programme would carry the literates for a further cycle of eight months to bring them to the point where literacy becomes functional. This implies the use of trained teachers, for example, qualified primary-school teachers who have received an accelerated retraining course of four to six weeks to acquaint them with the principles of teaching 'functional literacy'. To motivate the teacher, it will be necessary to pay him or her on a *pro rata* basis for teaching in the evening. The temptation to cut costs by using volunteers will be resisted: there is now sufficient evidence to indicate that untrained volunteer teachers are ineffective in teaching adults to read and write, and functional literacy teaching is even more demanding of the teacher's skill than rudimentary literacy.

In addition, there is the cost of preparing primers and follow-up materials specifically designed for the particular needs of the particular area in which they will be used. An excellent idea for improving the pedagogic efficiency of a literacy course is a monthly newspaper for new literates, in bold print and with plenty of photographs. In some countries, it may be possible to persuade commercial newspapers to print a special daily column for new literates, using a simplified vocabulary. Whatever the device employed, however, an extra cost will be incurred. Then there is the use of radio both to liven up the literacy class and to supplement the teacher. An ideal arrangement is to subsidize the local radio station to transmit a nightly programme of twenty minutes having to do with the subject matter of that week's lesson, possibly in association with special broadcasts to teachers to provide guidelines for getting the material across to adults. This is not as costly as it might appear at first glance, inasmuch as it reduces the length of time required to train teachers. Even a closed-circuit television network in towns or densely populated agricultural areas is not beyond the resources of many underdeveloped countries and, indeed, is now being used for educational purposes throughout the underdeveloped world. When the capital costs of textbooks, literacy kits, audiovisual equipment and teacher training are added to the recurrent costs of keeping primary schools, factories and meeting halls open in the evenings, paying school teachers and inspectors a premium for teaching and supervising adult literacy classes, and maintaining all equipment in running order, not to mention the costs of evaluation and research, it is hardly surprising that the World Experimental Literacy Programme may cost on average $35 to $40 per effective literate, or $17 to $20 per literate per year. This last figure is roughly comparable to the annual costs per pupil of primary education in an average underdeveloped country. Since the length of primary education is at least twice and frequently three times that of a literacy course, intensive, selective literacy programmes are still cheaper than formal education as a method of producing an economically useful member of the community.

The World Experimental Literacy Programme will make about 700,000 people in six countries functionally literate over the next three years. In view of the fact that there are now about 450 million illiterate adults in the world, this may seem like a ridiculously small effort. In fact, the picture is worse than that since the number of functionally illiterate people in the world is much larger than the figures for rudimentary illiteracy collected by UNESCO. But of course this is an experiment and the aim of this initial phase of the operation is to gather experience and insight for a subsequent assault on illiteracy in other countries. Nevertheless, the old idea of eradicating illiteracy in ten years was misconceived. It is perfectly feasible to teach every adult in the world to read and write by 1975, or at least to set up classes through which all the world's illiterates will pass by 1975, but the social and economic benefits of that kind of campaign would be negligible. It has become increasingly evident that there is no cheap way to diffuse either education or literacy throughout the underdeveloped world.

We return at the close to our original question: should educational planners in poor countries allocate part of their scarce resources to adult literacy programmes and, if so, what part? We saw that the first part of the question depends largely on the planner's time horizon or, to put it in jargon, on the social discount rate: clearly, the impatient planner will not neglect the quick pay-off of adult literacy. In the absence of reliable evidence, we agreed that the economic benefits of school education probably exceed those of adult literacy; the case for investment in literacy campaigns rests mainly on the short period of production of a new literate. There is some evidence, however, that three or four years of primary education have very little additional impact on the future productivity of individuals beyond providing rudimentary literacy that is soon forgotten, and three or four years is still the average duration of formal schooling in most underdeveloped countries. On the other hand, if literacy teaching in the underdeveloped world becomes truly 'functional' in the new UNESCO sense, its development value is very likely to be greater than that of primary education. Thus, the balance of choice in the future points to additional expenditures for adult education in the form of selective, intensive literacy campaigns.

What of the fraction of available funds that should be allocated to adult education? In 1961, the Addis Ababa Conference on the Development of Education in Africa recommended that 5 per cent of educational expenditures should be devoted to literacy and adult education, and this figure was then regarded as a definite improvement on the existing situation; but even now very few African countries spend as much as 5 per cent of their educational budget on adult literacy (for Tanzania, see King, 1967, pp. 12–13, 21–4). Is 5 per cent too low? We deceive ourselves if we pretend that we know enough to answer yes or no. We are only now at the beginning of a world-wide experiment that may eventually provide us with the evidence on which to base rational investment decisions in the area of informal education.

This chapter has furnished us with some examples, actual or potential, of cost–benefit analysis of educational investment decisions in underdeveloped countries. Its message is that the scarce resources available for education in each country should be husbanded according to a scale of priorities which reflects the estimated costs and expected benefits of educational projects. Due account must be taken of the fact that the economic benefits of education consist largely of the enhanced productivity of educated people and that enhanced productivity more often than not leads to enhanced earnings. The positive association between productivity and earnings, however, is a working hypothesis, not an article of faith. Spill-overs, non-pecuniary economic returns and even non-economic objectives can all be incorporated into the framework, provided there is a firm commitment from the outset to the principle of quantification. To insist immediately on cardinal measurement of all the variables, however, is a counsel of perfection. In many cases, we may have to be satisfied with a purely ordinal ranking of costs and benefits (see Cash, 1965*). In consequence, our answers will lack the quickly comprehended, numerical precision of something like a man-power forecast or a projection of places based on 'social demand'. Still, it is better to be vaguely right than precisely wrong. Planning consists of choosing between alternatives and cost–benefit analysis has the virtue of never letting us forget this.

Chapter 9
The Microeconomics
of Education

Efficiency for What?

When the education budget has been optimally allocated between various levels of the educational system and between formal in-school and informal out-of-school education, there remains the problem of how to apply resources within individual educational institutions. Should we have expensive buildings which are cheap to operate or cheap buildings which incur heavy maintenance charges? Should we distribute schools evenly around the country or try to reap economies of scale by transporting children to a smaller number of very large schools? Should we opt for large classes with well-qualified teachers or for small classes with untrained teachers? Should we rely solely on human instructors or should we try to replace teachers wherever possible by classroom television, programmed-learning machines and other audiovisual aids? Why should all teachers be provided with the same kind of training? Perhaps it would be better to combine a few highly trained teachers with a large number of untrained or semi-trained ancillaries into so-called 'teaching teams'? There is no end to the list of such questions; the possible alternative combinations of buildings, equipment, materials, teachers and students are almost infinite, and at first glance none of these is obviously superior to any other. If we are to make any progress, we must begin by carefully specifying our objectives.

In the last few chapters we have been assuming that the educational system is geared to a single aim, namely, that of maximizing the expected lifetime earnings of students net of costs when both costs and earnings are discounted to the present. Applied to the problem before us, it suggests choosing that combination of inputs into schooling that would maximize the discounted value of the net lifetime benefits of the participants in the educational system. It is time to recall, however, that education serves multiple objectives, some of which involve 'benefits' that cannot be measured in units directly comparable to the resource costs of education.

At some stage in the decision-making process, therefore, cost–benefit analysis must give way to cost–effectiveness analysis (see Chapter 4, p. 120). Provided objectives can be specified in operational terms, we can always find that combination of inputs which will accomplish any objective at least cost. Each objective will require separate analysis and we will end up with as many cost–effectiveness ratios as we have objectives. To combine them all into a single decision criterion we must somehow attach weights or 'prices' to the objectives. In other words, we must resort to an 'objective function' or 'social welfare function' that orders the different objectives in terms of priorities. In the final analysis, we can still say that the choice among competing means has been made under criteria of efficiency in the use of resources, but 'efficiency' now refers not just to the choice between means to achieve a single end but to the choice between ends themselves.

These remarks apply to all aspects of educational planning and arise just as much in deciding between investing in secondary or higher education as in considering the choice between larger and smaller classes. It is simply that the problem is dramatized when we contemplate the problem of combining inputs within educational institutions. The general rule laid down in economic textbooks to the effect that 'inputs should be allocated with maximum efficiency to achieve given ends' is not very helpful when the ends themselves are in question. Should a school attempt to maximize the measured gain in the performance of students in basic subjects from the time they enter to the time they leave ? Should it care less about achievement and more about examination results, judging itself not so much by its own assessment of student performance as by how well its graduates perform in the next successive level of education ? Should it treat all students alike, maximizing the 'value added' of the average students or should it try to 'equalize educational opportunity' by concentrating its resources on culturally deprived students ? Should it prepare students for the 'world of work' or devote itself instead to 'building moral character' ? No doubt, all of these aims are normally pursued simultaneously. Unfortunately, some of them actually conflict with each other and cannot be simultaneously satisfied. For example, a secondary-school system which attaches high priority to equality of opportunity may be less successful in satisfying other goals such as the attainment of high standards in specific skills, than a highly selective system which ensures high standards for a minority but a lower over-all average standard performance. Furthermore, there is likely to be some conflict over the priorities that are attached to different objectives. A recent survey in Britain, for instance, designed to find out what school leavers, parents and teachers thought were the most important objectives of secondary schools, found that,

both fifteen-year-old leavers and their parents very widely saw the provision of knowledge and skills which would enable young people to obtain the best jobs and careers of which they were capable, as one of the main functions that a school should undertake. Teachers, however, very frequently rejected the achievement of vocational success as a major objective of education (Schools Council, 1968, p. 45).

Not only is there lack of consensus on the 'social welfare function' that would rank different aims in order of importance, but frequently there is also a lack of knowledge of how to achieve any aim by purely educational means. We might agree that schools should be judged solely in terms of scores on standardized achievement tests and still disagree whether this objective could be best accomplished by training a larger number of teachers or by improving the quality of the teachers we already have. We might agree that every child should have an equal chance to acquire higher education and still be uncertain whether to invest in 'head start' programmes in primary schools, comprehensive reorganization of secondary schools or generous student grants in higher education. Even if the electorate voted overwhelmingly to confine education from now on to narrow vocational aims, it would be difficult to know whether such aims are better achieved by teaching students a specific skill or by providing them with a sound general education on the basis of which they can later acquire specific skills by on-the-job training. The fact is that we know so little about how people learn effectively and what role schools play in the learning process that we can not be sure about means even when we are sure about ends. A prominent economist has said that most of the disagreements between economists derive from differences of opinion about the positive effects of economic policies, not from differences in ultimate values or norms (Friedman, 1953, pp. 5–7). Whether this is true of economics or not, it is almost certainly true of education. Most of the really controversial questions in education are capable of being settled by an appeal to the facts, except that the relevant facts have not been gathered. Of course, this is not true of all disagreements between educators. No facts can convert those who believe that higher education should be confined to the gifted few: a belief in an educated élite may be good or bad but it cannot be true or false. But the vast range of educational issues that are heatedly controverted appear on close examination to involve quarrels about positive statements between people who are actually in agreement about ends.

Put somewhat differently, we face a pervasive ignorance about the production function of education, that is, the relationship between school inputs, on the one hand, and school output as conventionally measured by achievement scores, on the other. Throughout this book, we have been examining the relationship between scholastic achievement and economic performance, taking it for granted that scholastic achievement is somehow efficiently secured in the education 'industry'. We now turn to the industry itself to discover that the 'technology' of the industry, particularly at the level of the individual unit of production, is imperfectly understood. The inputs are complex: the physical facilities of the school, the quantity and quality of teaching services, a variety of materials and equipment and a 'raw material', students' time, through which other inputs, such as environmental influences on learning outside schools, are transmitted. It is not that we lack piecemeal evidence: the psychological and sociological literature on the educational process is so vast that few of us could command it in one lifetime. The difficulty is that of reducing the mass of evidence to systematic generalizations. What we lack is a framework for organizing all the bits and pieces that we know. In language familiar to economists, we cannot specify the educational production function or even begin to distinguish unambiguously between parameters and variables. In the circumstances, this chapter can only provide the flavour of some of the work that is now in progress on measuring the 'efficiency', in various senses of the term, of resource allocation within the educational system.

The Productivity of Educational Systems

If educational administrators are consistently maximizing some single educational objective such as the scores of students on a set of achievement tests, we ought to be able to estimate the parameters of the implied production function of the system by observation of the inputs and outputs either over a period of time, or between different parts of the system at a point in time. As an example of this approach, Burkhead, Fox and Holland (1967) estimated production functions in large-city high schools in Chicago and Atlanta for a wide range of input variables (median family income of students, average daily attendance, age of school building, textbook expenditure per student, materials expenditure per student, teacher experience, teacher qualifications, teacher–pupil ratio and administrator–pupil ratio). The general finding of the study is that variations in test scores in these large-city high schools are almost wholly conditioned by factors external to the school system, such as family income and the character of the neighbourhood (Burkhead, Fox and Holland, 1967, pp. 56, 72, 88). Similarly, Katzman (1968) estimated both the production and the cost functions of the elementary-school system of the city of Boston, Massachusetts, after adding examination results to achievement scores on the output side. Bowles (1970) provides yet another example, this time for Negro students enrolled in their last year of high school throughout the United States in the year 1965.

But suppose educational administrators pursue multidimensional objectives, or worse still, fail to maximize any well-defined function of school inputs? In that case, we will never discover the educational production function by mere observation; if we think of the production function as a frontier, the educational outcomes that we observe lie in fact within the frontier. This means that we must either conduct controlled experiments in schools, or else fall back on productivity measurement, that is, measurement of the relationship between inputs and output over a period of time on various assumptions about the nature of 'output'. What we are then doing, in effect, is to test the notion that educational administrators do adopt systematic optimizing principles: inputs may not be 'efficiently' combined at any moment in time, but as time passes efforts are made to achieve given objectives with fewer inputs.

A recent effort to measure the trend in total factor productivity in British secondary education for the period 1950–63 exemplifies this approach (Woodhall and Blaug, 1968). A trend in total factor productivity denotes a time series of outputs per units of combined inputs, all variables being measured in terms of physical units of constant quality. Inputs are conventionally defined as (a) the services of buildings and equipment as measured by imputed real rents and real expenditures on materials, (b) the services of teachers and administrative staff as measured by their real salaries and (c) the time of students as measured by real earnings forgone. These measures are then combined into a weighted index of inputs, the weights being the relative contribution of each input to the total direct and indirect outlays on the system in question. Output, on the other hand, is evaluated in terms of different concepts of educational effectiveness or objectives, ending up with as many total factor productivity trends as there are discernible aims or goals of education.

We start with the output side: the annual outflow of school leavers from maintained secondary schools in Britain rose by 30 per cent between 1950 and 1963. However, only 22 per cent of fifteen year-olds remained at school in 1950 whereas 34 per cent did so in 1963. If we assume that one of the aims of schools is to foster a desire for education, we ought to measure output, not just in terms of crude numbers produced, but in terms of the numbers persuaded to stay at school beyond the statutory age. By weighting school leavers by the length of their education, the index of output rose by 38 per cent between 1950 and 1963 compared with an increase of 30 per cent in the unweighted index. Nothing has yet been allowed, however, for academic achievement, nor for the type and variety of courses followed. Despite all the criticisms levelled at examinations, one of the accepted objectives of schools is to prepare pupils successfully for examinations. Unfortunately, the only measure of academic achievement which can be applied to school leavers throughout this period in Britain is attainment in the General Certificate of Education examinations. When these were first introduced in 1951, they were expressly designed for the top 20 per cent of the ability range and standards of marking may have declined over time in response to the tendency for schools to enter ever larger numbers of candidates, each sitting for more subjects. Be that as it may, when school leavers since 1953 are weighted according to the number of O- and A-level passes they have achieved, the output of secondary schools rose by 67 per cent between 1953 and 1963, in contrast to an increase of 26 per cent in unweighted index over the same range of years.

We now introduce a strictly economic evaluation of output by considering the earnings which a school leaver can expect to command in the labour market, on the notion that schools pursue vocational aims as one of their multiple objectives. In the absence of better data, we resort to evidence for 1961 and 1962 on the average incomes of men and women of different ages in three age groups: those with a terminal education age (TEA) of fifteen, sixteen to eighteen, and nineteen and over. Unfortunately, no comparable data are available for the period before 1961 or after 1962; in effect, we have to assume that the earnings differentials associated with an extra year of education have remained unchanged between 1950 and 1963. Thus, those who entered employment at fifteen in each of the thirteen years are weighted by the relative earnings of men or woman with a TEA of fifteen; those who entered employment at sixteen to eighteen, or who went on to further education at fifteen or sixteen, are weighted by the earnings of those with a TEA of sixteen to eighteen. The remainder, who went on to further or to higher education at seventeen or over, or entered employment at nineteen, are weighted by the earnings of those with a TEA of nineteen or over (this deliberately credits the marginal returns from higher education to secondary education). The weights are rough but even these reveal a considerable increase in the economic value of secondary-school output: whereas the unweighted index of output rose by only 30 per cent between 1950 and 1963, the 'economic' index rose by 46 per cent, reflecting the increasing tendency for secondary-school students to stay on at school beyond the legal leaving age.

To sum up: the output of secondary schools, crudely interpreted as numbers of school leavers, rose at an annual rate of 2 per cent over the period 1950–63. However, output adjusted for the length of schooling rose by 2·6 per cent per annum, output adjusted for the increasing academic qualifications of students rose by 4·7 per cent per annum and output adjusted for increased lifetime earnings expectations rose by 2·5 per cent per annum. Expressed in different terms, the 'quality' of educational output of secondary schools rose between 0·6 and 2·7 per cent per annum, depending on the view we take of the aims of secondary education: students in 1963 on average stayed at school longer, more of them were qualified to enter higher education by obtaining GCE passes and they looked forward to higher lifetime earnings as a result of more and better education. But what of those who left school at the age of fifteen? The only evidence there is of the improved quality of secondary schooling in the twelve to fifteen age range comes from several National Reading Surveys, conducted by the Ministry of Education, which showed that between 1948 and 1961 there had been an average increase of 14 to 24 per cent in the standard reading age. But achievement in one subject alone cannot be used as a general measure of educational output since subjects compete with one another for a limited amount of class time: a rise in reading skills is frequently achieved at the expense of performance in other, more complex subjects. It is possible, therefore, that some part of improved quality in lower-secondary education has escaped the nct.

So much for output. We turn now to the measurement of inputs. All inputs must be measured in physical terms making allowance, where necessary, for any changes in quality. Since the inputs are heterogeneous, it is impossible to find a single physical unit in which they can all be expressed. We deal with the problem of valuation and aggregation in the standard way, measuring each input in terms of constant base-year prices. In other words, we take the money value of each input and divide this by a specially constructed index of the price of that input, arriving at a measure that is independent of changes in the purchasing power of money over the relevant inputs employed in schools. Some money values had to be imputed because schools do not purchase all their resources. For instance, schools do not buy the time of students, nor do they rent buildings. Yet neither of these inputs is free.[1] For purposes of measuring productivity trends, we need to calculate the total opportunity cost of education, that is, the total value of any goods and services used in the educational process that have alternative uses. Both the time of students over the age of fifteen and school buildings could be deployed elsewhere, so that both have a positive opportunity cost. Our final estimate of total inputs is therefore greater than total public expenditure on maintained secondary education because of imputed values. At the same time, some items of school expenditure are excluded, such as expenditure on meals and milk and on health services, because these do not contribute to the *educational* activities of schools, and therefore are unrelated to the output of school defined in terms of their teaching function.

1. Students' time below the age of fifteen is a tricky case: in one sense, it is free because it has no opportunity cost, either to society or to individuals; in another sense, it is not free because a cost is incurred by having one compulsory leaving age rather than another. It clearly depends on the problem we are posing. For present purposes, we take the legal fact of a leaving age for granted and hence treat students' time below the age of fifteen as a costless input.

The first input we will consider is teachers' time as measured by outlays on teachers' salaries. The size of the total salary bill is determined by three factors: (a) the number of teachers, (b) their age and qualifications and (c) current salary scales which depend entirely on age and qualifications.[2] In order to estimate the real input of teachers, we must take account of both (a) and (b), since (b) reflects changes in the quality of the teaching profession (a large number of studies have shown that pupil achievement is highly correlated with the length of experience and qualifications of teachers). Teachers' salaries in real terms are estimated by deflating current money expenditures on teachers by a weighted index of teachers' salary rates. In real terms, teachers' salaries more than doubled between 1950 and 1963, although the numbers of teachers increased only 72 per cent; the difference between the two figures indicates the rise in the average quality of the teaching staff as reflected in a shift in the composition of the salary structure towards the upper end of the spectrum.

The second input, students' time after the age of fifteen, is valued in terms of earnings forgone. In the absence of better data, two official estimates of the earnings forgone by students in secondary schools in 1957 and 1963, and published evidence on the trend in the average earnings of all young people over the decade of the 1950s, are used to estimate the age–specific earnings of school leavers in every year between 1950 and 1963. The imputed money value is deflated by an index of juvenile wage rates to provide a final estimate of the real value of students' time. Between 1950 and 1963, the total real value of

2. It is worth noting that the Burnham scale makes no distinction between teachers in terms of competence to teach particular subjects. As a result, mathematics and science teachers, who are in short supply, are treated as equivalent to English teachers, who are only too plentiful – a perfect example of a labour market imperfection that creates rather than alleviates man-power shortages. The standard argument of the teaching profession against salary differentials in accordance with subject qualifications is that it would undermine the *esprit de corps* of teachers in a school. The practice of rewarding people in accordance with the relative scarcity of their skill has not, however, shattered morale in either private business firms, government departments or non-profit research organizations. Studies of American experience with multiple-salary schedules do not suggest that subject differentials create morale problems in schools (Kershaw and McKean, 1962, pp. 147–8). Nevertheless, most teachers find it difficult to accept the elementary economic fact that pay differentials in either a capitalist or socialist economy mean that some people are scarcer than others, not they are more worthy or more important.

students' time increased by 185 per cent; this substantial increase is partly due to the upward trend in staying at school beyond the minimum leaving age and partly the increased real earnings of young people over the period.

Since the measure of student input is based on the opportunity cost of students' time, it measures some changes in the quality of students: student input in 1963 was of higher quality than in 1950 since it included a higher proportion of sixth-form students, and this is reflected in the index. It is sometimes said that the average level of intelligence of school children is rising, but a search of the literature did not reveal any convincing evidence for this hypothesis. Similarly, no striking evidence has yet been produced of any change in the quality of primary-school output. In the circumstances, we are not justified in making any other allowances for improvements in the quality of students over the period.

Thirdly, there are the services of school buildings. The standard method of valuing the use of buildings is by annual rental charges, but educational buildings are not rented, so that once again a money value must be imputed. What we must do is to estimate the annual cost which would be incurred if school buildings were rented, instead of being owned by local authorities. The method employed was similar to that used by the Robbins Committee for higher education, namely, to begin with the current replacement cost of buildings and then to calculate an annual rate of amortization, assuming that the buildings depreciate at 6 per cent per year for sixty years. This yields an estimate of imputed rents of £20 million in 1950 and £50 million in 1963. Building costs have risen since 1950, but due to increased efficiency in school construction, the cost of a new school has risen less than building costs in general; in fact, during the early part of the period, the average cost of a new school place was actually falling. If we deflate the estimate of money rentals by an index of average school-building costs, the real value of the services of school capital rose by 120 per cent between 1950 and 1963.

The last main category of educational inputs includes the time of non-teaching staff, the use of books, stationery and other materials, equipment, heating and light. All these inputs can be estimated by current expenditure, deflated by suitable price indices. Between 1950 and 1963, real expenditure on administrative staff and on maintenance of school buildings, heating and light rose by 140 per cent, real expenditure on furniture and equipment rose by 130 per cent and real expenditure on books, stationery and other materials rose by 100 per cent.

All the inputs are now combined into a single weighted index, the weights being the relative base-year shares of each input in the total resource costs of secondary education. Summing up, the various inputs increased as follows:

Table 12

Rates of Increase of Inputs, 1950–1963

	1950–1963 (1950 = 100)	Percentage Change Per Annum
Students' time	285	8·4
Administrative staff and maintenance	241	7·0
Equipment and furniture	233	6·7
Services of buildings	220	6·3
Teachers' time	210	5·9
Books and stationery	203	5·6
Weighted combination of inputs	235	6·8

Source: Woodhall and Blaug (1968, table 7).

If the index of total inputs is divided into the various indices of output, we arrive at a measure of total factor productivity for secondary education. Output, we recall, rose by either 30, 38, 46, or 67 per cent (the last figure referring to 1953–63 rather than 1950–63 because GCE results are not available before 1953). A glance at Table 12 leads immediately to the conclusion that the productivity of secondary education fell drastically between 1950 and 1963, irrespective of the view we take of the goals of secondary education; in fact, productivity declined at an annual rate of at least 2 per cent a year over the thirteen-year period.

It is, however, slightly misleading simply to relate the output of one year to the inputs in the same year: the 'period of production' of secondary education is long and variable. Pupils stay at school from four to seven years, so that the outputs in any one year have consumed inputs during the previous four to eight years. Since the trend of inputs is constantly rising, the inputs directly related to a particular year's output may be lower than total inputs in that year. To avoid this possible downward bias in the index of total factor productivity, the figures were recalculated by relating the output of school leavers of different ages to inputs lagged four to seven years. The output of sixteen-year-old leavers in 1963, for instance, is related to a proportion of total inputs in each of the previous five years, the whole of their secondary-school life. The proportion itself is determined by assumption, namely, that each age cohort consumes inputs according to the proportion the cohort constitutes of the total secondary-school population. This assumption is probably incorrect because older pupils on average consume more inputs than those below the school-leaving age; unfortunately, we have no information whatever about the age-specific costs of educating students in secondary schools. However, even this imperfect adjustment for the lagged relation between inputs and output illustrates the importance of the problem: when the ratios of output to inputs for the years 1957 to 1963 are recalculated on a cohort basis, the annual decline in productivity is reduced by about 0·5 per cent on all three interpretations of output. This is not enough, however, to convert the decline of productivity into an increase.

Similarly, it might be argued that the output of school should be related only to those inputs over which the school or local authorities exercise control. Therefore, although earnings forgone no doubt reflect an actual input of resources in the educational system, they should be ignored for purposes of measuring productivity trends. To test the sensitivity of the results to the inclusion of students' time, the total factor productivity index was recalculated leaving out earnings forgone. Once again, this reduces the annual decline in productivity but nevertheless leaves productivity falling between 1950 and 1963 by at least 1 per cent per annum. Unless the quality of those who left school in this period has increased in a way that no one has yet been able to measure, or unless there are aims of education in terms of which output may be said to have risen significantly although no one has yet been able to quantify these aims, we may conclude that it took more resources to produce a standard secondary-school leaver in 1963 than in 1950.

The hypothesis that British secondary education achieves given objectives ever more effectively as time passes is rejected. We must, however, resist glib explanations of the findings: measurement never explains anything; it only tells us what there is to explain. Undoubtedly, throughout this period students in secondary education were provided with more teaching and administrative staff, more equipment and materials, and better-maintained buildings only in the belief that these would increase the quality of the education they received. It is simply that what evidence there is suggests that quality did not improve in due proportion to the application of additional inputs. Effectiveness in education is still thought of in terms of 'what is put in' rather than 'what is achieved'; it is assumed as a matter of course that every increase in inputs automatically raises the quality of education. It is widely believed, for example, that smaller classes mean better education, although a considerable body of research in both America and Britain suggests that class size alone has relatively little influence on pupil achievement. As one American economist has said:

Over the years we have had hundreds of experiments testing the effectiveness of teaching in small and large classes. Despite the fact that in the vast majority of instances these tests show either that the advantage (as shown by tests) lies with the large class or that there is no significant difference, the folk-lore of the small class persists (Harris, 1962, p. 530).

Of course, if the quality of education is a function of class size – and past studies throw doubt even on this general proposition – the functional relationship is probably not a monotonic one but rather a discontinuous step-function with more than one maximum and minimum, varying with the nature of the subject, the type of teaching method and the age and ability of students. No single generalization could cover all the different situations in which quality sometimes rises and sometimes falls with variations in class size. The point is, however, that 'the folk-lore of the small class', a folk-lore shared alike by teachers and parents, is precisely the sort of belief that leads to expenditure patterns divorced from all considerations of effective outcomes. Perhaps there really is nothing to explain: declining productivity is just what we would expect to find in an 'industry' where all the 'managers' fervently believe that *every* increase in inputs necessarily raises the quality of output.

A similar exercise for British university education over the period 1938 to 1962 produced similar conclusions: total factor productivity steadily declined on all three alternative interpretations of output (Woodhall and Blaug, 1965). In the absence of any acceptable way of evaluating the output of university research, 'output' was defined solely in terms of the teaching function of universities, with some attempt to allow for differences between subjects. Likewise, only the time of staff and the buildings and equipment specifically devoted to teaching were counted as inputs. This immediately raises difficulties inasmuch as teaching and research are at least to some extent complementary activities, so that the very division of staff time into hours devoted to teaching, research and administration may not be a meaningful one. Nevertheless, according to the *Robbins Report*, university staff members in 1962 devoted about half of their time to teaching and it was, therefore, assumed that roughly half of all inputs in universities in 1962 were applied to carry out teaching activities. There has been a significant increase in research activity since 1938, due to the development of specialized research units in some universities. Working backwards, it appears that about 60 per cent of inputs were devoted to teaching in 1938 as against 52 per cent in 1962. The evidence for these numbers is rather weak but the final results are fairly insensitive to wide variations in the actual division of inputs between teaching and research at the beginning and close of the period. Everything else being the same, a decline in the proportion of outlays on teaching as distinct from research should have produced an increase in the productivity of university teaching. In fact, even if the proportion of university outlays on teaching is assumed to have fallen from 65 to 45 per cent, or from 60 to 40 per cent between 1938 and 1962, rather than from 60 to 52 per cent, productivity still shows a tendency to decline.

The measurement of multiple productivity trends of the type just described is simply cost–effectiveness analysis applied in a new way. Cost–effectiveness analysis is usually applied to a variety of projects at one moment in time to determine which one is to be preferred at that moment. Here, however, we are looking at trends in the cost–effectiveness ratios of a single 'project' to ascertain whether resources are being more or less effectively applied to that project as time passes. The striking implication of the two studies reviewed above is that, from the point of view of trends in effectiveness, it does not seem to matter whether education is valued in terms of intrinsic or in terms of instrumental goals; the finding that the productivity of secondary and higher education has declined over the decade of the 1950s is fairly robust in the sense that it stands up under a wide variety of weighting schemes for evaluating output. This conclusion cannot be reversed by appealing to the rising cost of staff or of equipment; since all the inputs are measured in units of constant purchasing power, total factor productivity is *not* the reciprocal of money costs per student. Everyone knows that unit costs in British secondary and higher education have risen sharply since the war. This rise has either been explained as inevitable – the scope for technical progress is necessarily limited in education and yet schools and universities must compete with other more dynamic industries for staff, equipment and buildings – or positively justified by the rising 'quality' of the education provided. However, all the existing evidence about improvements in the quality of British secondary and higher education over the relevant years has already been taken into account in the measures of inputs and output.

It is true that the existing evidence about educational quality is far from satisfactory and it can be argued that the observed decline in productivity is simply due to the failure to take account of quality factors that have so far defied measurement. For example, British university students do not sit for nation-wide educational attainment tests at the time of graduation; thus, even if we suppose that GCE A-levels are uniformly administered by all the examining boards throughout the country, there is really no *direct* evidence to estimate the 'value added' by British universities in the form of increments in student performance between admission and graduation. Similarly, it is conceivable that the quality of university research has risen over time and this has in turn raised the quality of university teaching in a way that is not reflected in the class of degrees awarded, or in the numbers of students staying on to take second and third degrees, or even in the enhanced occupational prospects of students. But if there are quality improvements that have so far escaped detection, it throws doubt not only on the finding that productivity has declined but also on the standard justification of the rising unit costs of higher education. The shoe is now on the other foot: what has been established is not so much a set of reliable numbers as a general presumption about long-term trends in the productivity of education. Unless new evidence is produced about the rising quality of education, the presumption must be that productivity or effectiveness per unit of costs in British secondary schools and universities has, in fact, declined in the decade of the 1950s.

Would our answers have been different if we had taken account of other objectives of education, such as the creation of new knowledge in addition to dissemination of the old, the promotion of social mobility, the transmission of cultural values, the inculcation of desired behaviour and attitudes, and so forth? The question is not whether these are appropriate functions or inevitable by-products of education – they clearly are – but whether such open-ended aims are amenable to measurement. If they are not, they are of no help in making hard choices between alternative means (see Chapter 4, p. 124).[3] It is clear, therefore, that productivity measurement or cost–effectiveness analysis amounts to little more than a framework for research, challenging us to explore new ways of converting quality into quantity and directing our attention to critical gaps in knowledge (on British universities, for example, see Blaug, 1968b*). The magic numbers that have so far been generated must be regarded as purely provisional, calling for and indeed inviting falsification by further attempts at 'measuring the unmeasurable'. Perhaps they suffice to dispel the belief that schools are operating on the boundaries of some production function relating inputs to output, or that educational administrators are maximizing some complicated objective function which they refuse to reveal to us. In all likelihood, the outcomes we observe are simply the net result of a whole series of unrelated decisions, each of which is itself not necessarily optimal. Future work is probably well-advised to steer clear of attempts to evaluate entire levels of education in terms of a few over-all goals, and to concentrate instead on problems of sub-optimization (Kershaw, 1965, pp. 309–10*). The continued agitation for the introduction of 'educational technology' is already proving to be a useful stimulant in provoking more cost–effectiveness analysis of specific changes in the structure of educational systems (see e.g. Schramm, Coombs, Kahnert and Lyle, 1967 – a series of case studies of new educational media).

3. One explanation of the persistent demand of educationists for smaller classes is that smaller classes increase the satisfaction of teachers, students and parents, even if no significant increase in students' attainments results. Of course, it is perfectly conceivable that classes do improve student achievement indirectly by raising the sense of well-being of students and teachers. However, if this is the true aim of educationists in advocating smaller classes, should it not be made explicit? One virtue of making aims explicit is that it permits comparisons of the effectiveness with which different policies achieve desired objectives. It is not obvious, for example, that reducing the average size of classes is a better way of improving teacher satisfaction than increasing the salaries of those who teach in large classes.

The Advent of Programme Budgeting in Education

We have already mentioned the idea that education is an activity that is unlikely to experience the rapid technical advances that characterize modern industry. Indeed, education may be a victim of what has been dubbed 'Baumol's Disease': Baumol (1967) has argued that there exists a wide variety of labour-intensive economic services, like restaurants, the performing arts, municipal government and education, where the purely technical difficulties of increasing productivity result in a cumulative increase in both the money and real costs incurred in supplying them. These are services where the quality of labour is both a major input and, in some sense, an important element of output; the necessity to bid labour away from other industries that can always afford to pay more for labour leads to a steady upward pressure on the costs of supplying such services. The argument is most clearly seen in relation to the performing arts, and although its application to education (Baumol, 1967, pp. 416, 420–21) is somewhat forced – Baumol implicitly assumes perfect knowledge of technical possibilities in producing educational services, negative income elasticities for education and perfect wage diffusion throughout the economy – there can be little doubt that we are not going to witness dramatic increases in the total factor productivity of education in the near future, whatever happens to the movement to promote so-called 'educational technology'.

Since costs per unit of product must be expected to increase relative to average costs in the economy as a whole in any industry whose productivity increases more slowly than the average, it is certain that the unit costs of education, and particularly of the unit costs of higher education, will continue to rise even on the most optimistic assumptions (Bowen, 1968, ch. 2). This follows if productivity in education rises by, say, one or two per cent a year, which is a good deal less than the average rate of increase of productivity in most economies. Clearly, the situation is still more serious if educational productivity is actually declining. While a low or even zero rate of productivity increase in an industry proves nothing at all about its 'efficiency', a *decline* in productivity is a certain sign of waste and misallocation. Some writers have denied that there is any clear evidence of waste in British universities. Carter (1965)* asks 'Do the teachers work hard enough? Do the teachers work efficiently enough? Do the teachers do too much external work? Do the teachers spend too much time on university work other than teaching?' and answers all four questions in the negative on the basis of what may be fairly described as personal judgement. Even he concedes, however, that it is irrational to determine the volume of research carried out in universities by applying a fixed coefficient to the total number of students in universities (how often is it realized that this is how it is done?) and that the present system of finance gives universities no incentive whatever to economize on the use of buildings and equipment. Others have explored the possibilities of raising university productivity by increasing the plant load, rearranging the time table, increasing supporting staff and by lengthening the academic year (Williams, 1963), without however coming to any definite conclusions. There is indeed very little firm evidence of 'inefficiency' in British universities for the simple reason that there is almost no firm evidence of any kind. Perhaps what is worse is the failure to experiment with different teaching methods, different course structures and different methods of finance. By and large, the fundamental issues such as the optimum balance between teaching and research, the appropriate mix of full-time and part-time students, and the merits and demerits of creating seniority rights by the tenure system, are deliberately avoided as subjects too uncomfortable to discuss. A case in point is the general tendency to ignore the dramatic growth in recent years of higher education outside the universities, involving the deliberate attempt to emphasize teaching at the expense of research. By and large, the critical attitude that is supposed to be the hallmark of the university teacher has not been extended to the structure of his own 'industry'. If this is the state of mind in the universities, we should not be surprised to find resistance in the schools to the concepts of 'productivity', 'cost–effectiveness' and indeed all notions of evaluation in terms of systematic comparisons between efforts and results.

Recent years have seen a growing interest in a new tool of management science, sometimes called 'programme budgeting', sometimes 'performance budgeting' and sometimes 'output budgeting'. In essence, programme budgeting is a method of recasting the accounts of a government department in such a way that the entire budget is distributed among a number of specific programmes, a 'programme' being defined as an activity that has a unique objective. The purpose of such a budget format is to permit measurements of the success or failure of the various programmes in attaining stated objectives. Thus, 'programme budgeting' leads by its very formulation to 'performance budgeting' and the latter is indistinguishable from what we have earlier defined as cost–effectiveness analysis (see Chapter 4, p. 121); 'performance budgeting' is simply cost–effectiveness analysis confined to the broad functional objectives of the programme that makes up a departmental budget. A still more ambitious version of the same idea is the so-called 'planning-programming-budgeting system' announced by President Johnson in 1965, in which all essentially similar services administered by different government departments are grouped together to facilitate comparisons of costs and effectiveness in achieving common objectives.

In 1967, three-quarters of American state colleges and universities employed some form of programme budget (Rourke and Brooks, 1966, p. 69) and the use of programme budgets is gradually spreading to the public-school system in the United States (Benson, 1968, ch. 9; Hartley, 1968). Programme budgeting is no panacea for the management problems of education and real difficulties stand in the way of replacing the old accounting budget by programme budgets (Schwartz, 1968). But the attempt to introduce programme budgeting must of itself lead to a more explicit delineation of goals and may provide an acceptable framework for formulating educational decisions in terms of accomplishing stated objectives. We need say no more than that. Simply stated, programme budgeting is a process which formulates objectives in meaningful and concrete terms, analyses the alternative means to accomplish these objectives, calculates the costs of all the alternative inputs involved, assigns priorities to the various objectives and then maximizes the value of this 'objective function' subject to budgetary constraints. If this were a description of what Ministries of Education do, instead of a pious hope of what they may be gradually induced to do, this chapter would have been superfluous.

Chapter 10
Issues in the Finance of Education

Selectivity in Education

The finance of education, as popular opinion has it, is the true domain of the economist: first educators decide what is to be done and then economists work out how much it will cost and how the money is to be raised. Finance is just an afterthought, a necessary evil, which should not affect the decisions one has to take except by placing limits on what can be accomplished in a given time. In short, from the point of view of the structure and character of the educational system, it does not matter whether education is financed centrally or locally, publicly or privately, solely out of taxes or out of taxes supplemented by user charges.

This notion of the 'veil' of finance is, of course, completely untenable. An educational system that is entirely financed out of general taxes without fees or user charges of any kind produces relatively high private rates of return on investment in voluntary education; in consequence, both the scale and composition of secondary and higher education is different from what it would be if cost-covering fees were charged. An educational system that is largely locally financed, even if the central government later reimburses local governments, is more likely to be subject to popular pressure about, say, the quality of amenities provided and the type of curriculum adopted than a system that is centrally financed. Almost the whole of the vast differences in the character and tone of British and French primary education is due to the fact that schools are locally administered and financed in Britain and centrally administered and financed in France. The particular way in which education is financed in a country can largely determine who it is that will be educated and in what fashion. Surely, financial questions come not after but before the critical planning decisions?

In closing this book with a chapter on finance, we may have inadvertently given comfort to the superficial view that finance is only a second-order problem. It is true that the total resource costs of a given volume of education are generally unaffected by who pays for what. The private returns from education, however, are almost certainly influenced by the precise distribution of the cost burden between tax-payers and parents; therefore, the social rate of return on educational investment is inevitably affected by the pattern of educational finance. Thus, the only justification for postponing discussion of finance until now is the well-known difficulty of saying everything at once, of expounding all aspects of an interdependent system at the same time. So much is true even if educational planning is geared to narrow economic objectives. When we take account of social and cultural objectives, the question of finance looms even larger: it is precisely in the area of finance that so many of the nobler aims of educators are defeated. To attempt to achieve equality of educational opportunity merely by eliminating fees and other school charges is bound to fail: these are simply not important elements in the private costs of education to parents (see Chapter 2, p. 49). To assign all educational finance to central governments may deprive local school administrators of any incentives to experiment and innovate. To adhere to single-salary schedules in the face of shortages of science teachers may keep down expenditures, but is likely to influence the quality of science teaching. The undesirable by-products of different patterns of educational finance are innumerable and what is a rational system of finance for one set of objectives is not so for another.

To attempt to do justice in one chapter to the range of questions that arise in financing an educational system is literally impossible. Rather than to roam far and wide at a high level of abstraction, we shall select a few issues that are now topical in Britain (and to some extent in the United States), indicating the kind of considerations that must always enter into a final assessment of alternative methods of educational finance.[1] In so doing we shall have ample opportunities to illustrate one of the central themes of this book, namely, that the careful formulation of objectives is the *sine qua non* of efficient planning of education.

We begin by sketching the background of current controversy in Britain over the financing of the social services, a controversy which

1. The reader will have to refer elsewhere for discussions of educational finance in underdeveloped countries (e.g. OECD, 1968).

is frequently depicted as a struggle-to-the-death between 'selectivists' and 'universalists'. 'Selectivists' believe in the principle that social benefits should be distributed in relation to 'needs' as revealed by some form of income assessment or 'means test'. 'Universalists', on the other hand, are in favour of a system of making social benefits available freely to everyone, regardless of needs. The arguments on both sides are well known. The refusal to concentrate limited resources selectively on improved benefits for those who need them most is said to lead to inadequate expenditures on welfare for everyone; furthermore, since the capacity to make use of free social services is not equally distributed, the effect is frequently to provide free social services for those who need them least. By way of contrast, the defence of the universal principle is couched in egalitarian rather than in financial terms: universalism is intended to eradicate the stigma that attaches to the discriminatory receipt of public assistance and to destroy once and for all the social privilege that is inherent in the juxtaposition of a private sector with and a public sector without charges.

The polar extremes of selectivity and universalism, however, fail to do justice to all the subtleties of the debate. Within both camps, there is, so to speak, a 'right' and a 'left' wing. Some advocates of selectivity urge a selective system on grounds of fundamental values and not merely of financial imperatives: they look forward to the growth of private welfare services that would compete with the State sector because they believe that this would expand the scope of choice and serve to restore 'consumer's sovereignty' in welfare. This point of view is perhaps best represented by the staff publications of the Institute of Economic Affairs but is widely shared by many who vote Liberal and Conservative (see Collard, 1968; Seldon and Gray, 1967). Similarly, while the Labour party as a whole may still be said to subscribe to universalism, some party spokesmen have recently come out in favour of selective charges *within* the State sector, administered with the aid of income codes for everyone (Houghton, 1967). They point to the impossibility of raising standards and expanding existing services out of general taxation, given the firm expectation of a relatively low growth rate for the next five or ten years. The fact that Britain enjoys an unusually high average propensity to consume (personal consumption as a percentage of GNP), they contend, is an opportunity to enlist private contributions, an opportunity that is lost under a universalist system because people as consumers always demand more 'free' social services than they are willing to pay for as voters. Besides, the principle involved is not new: supplementary benefits, rate rebates, council rents in some areas, subsidized school meals, student grants, legal aid and the new mortgage option scheme are all geared to means as measured by earned income. Indeed, the dominant Labour argument is no longer that of pure universalism, but one of grafting additional selective benefits on an essentially universalistic structure of welfare services.

What controversy remains within the ranks of the Labour party is whether to extend the selective principle so far as to introduce, say, charges for State nursery schools or charges within the National Health Service, not only for prescriptions but also for consultations with specialists and for short stays in hospital. However, while some are convinced that the coding system of P A YE can be carried below the point of no tax liability, so that everyone will receive a code number either for purposes of taxation if income exceeds tax allowances and exemptions, or for allocating selective social benefits if allowances and exemptions exceed income, the 'high priests of universalism' – Titmuss (1967) and Townsend (1968) – continue to deny the administrative feasibility of a 'negative income tax'. Now, it is true that the incidence of unemployment, disability, adversity and dependancy is not conveniently synchronized with the Inland Revenue financial year, thus necessitating some payments in advance of the coding that would justify them. It is also true that a negative income tax would have to be so devised as not to create a disincentive effect for heads of households working in low-paying occupations.[2] But all that this proves is that a negative income tax is not a perfect device for administering selective benefits; it is merely the best that we can think of. Provided it is agreed that there really is a case for deliberately discriminating between people in providing tax-financed public services, the argument reduces to differences over the appropriate extensions of the selective principle and over practical ways of improving the assessment of income. It has been said that the real obstacle to putting welfare benefits on a reverse-P A YE basis is the inability of the Inland Revenue to cope with universal income coding. But this is merely to say that a negative income tax would have to be accompanied either by comprehensive tax reform or by an overhaul of the Inland Revenue.

2. The scheme proposed by Lees (1967) is perhaps open to this objection; but so is the present system of supplementary benefits.

Until it is shown how we can select those in need of social benefits without investigating their income, all attacks on means tests as such are simply refusals to face unpleasant economic realities.

What continues to divide the Labour party view from radical thinking about welfare outside the party is the notion mentioned earlier, namely, that choice between public and independent provision should be facilitated by encouraging voluntary private expenditure on welfare services. Even when there is common ground in the view that additional purchasing power should be drawn into welfare at the expense of personal consumption, there is no agreement on whether this should be accomplished by charges for State health services or reductions in subsidies for council housing, on the one hand, or by something like the issue of vouchers (see p. 307) to assist low-income families to purchase private medical insurance and private housing, on the other. This particular dispute is much more difficult to resolve than the one between the friends of Labour about a little bit more or less selectivity: it involves basic value judgements such as leaving people to choose social services in their own best interests, and it requires specific predictions of the consequences of new and hitherto untried social arrangements. In one sense, everyone favours 'competition for excellence' and giving people more opportunities to cultivate the art of choice in welfare. But would it work out that way?

The great fear is that the State services will be denuded and impoverished as those who opt out increasingly refuse to subsidize those who are forced to stay in. That this is not a groundless fear is indicated by the contrast between 'public squalor and private affluence' in even so wealthy a country as the United States. Nevertheless, there is valuable experience in other European countries where more use is made than in Britain of privately provided but publicly subsidized welfare services. The precise effects of underwriting private initiative in the provision of social services depend critically on the particular methods that are adopted, and little thought has yet been given in this country to the wide variety of alternative welfare systems that are available. Debates on selectivity quickly degenerate into arguments about sources of finance: can we divert defence spending to the social services or must we take more money out of private pockets? The questions that ought to be asked, however, are: should people be given the wherewithal to visit private doctors? Should parents be allowed to send their children to private schools if they have the means and, if so, should we concentrate on equalizing means? Is something like the mortgage option scheme a better answer to housing needs than additional council houses? Do we want to give aid to the underdeveloped countries in the form of indiscriminate subsidies to overseas students? Would the quality of State services improve if the State had to compete with rival suppliers? These are the basic issues which have so far been neglected in favour of mere penny-pinching arguments.

The last few years have seen a strong swing towards selectivity in British education, the most prominent example of which was the recommendation of the *Plowden Report* on primary schools to establish 'educational priority areas', that is, to spend an extra £11 million to discriminate positively in favour of socially deprived areas in an attempt to bring primary schools in these areas up to the level of the best. In other respects, however, the *Plowden Report* shied away from the full implications of selectivity. For example, it recommended the extension of 'free' nursery schools to the tune of £29 million, and it was left to a minority of the Plowden Committee to argue the case for means-tested charges in nursery education as the only practical means of getting some State nursery schools started at long last (*Plowden Report*, 1967, pp. 487–9).

Another indication of the trend toward selectivity is the recent increase in charges for school meals, combined with the abolition of free milk in secondary schools. The new charge is 1s. 6d.[3] a meal which is still well below the gross cost of 2s. 6d. for producing a meal. The subsidy on school meals and on free milk in primary schools is currently running at about £90 million a year, or almost 5 per cent of total public expenditures on primary and secondary education. The increase of the charge to 1s. 6d. per meal will increase income from private contributions by almost £20 million, if we assume that the increased charge will not reduce the number taking meals. In fact when charges were raised in 1957 by 11 per cent, the numbers taking dinners fell by 4 per cent; in other words, the price elasticity of demand for school meals was 0·35. However, it is certain that the elasticity will be higher for the 50 per cent increase that recently took effect. If the cost price of 2s. 6d. were charged, with suitable remissions for children from poor families, the total saving in public expenditures might be as high as £50 million.

3. Charges were raised again by 3d. in the early part of 1970.

Any further increases in charges for school meals and primary-school milk will adversely affect those children and families who need the services most, unless a means test for purposes of remitting charges can be cheaply and efficiently administered. What we need to know to tackle the problem are the proportions of children from each income group and from each family size now taking school dinners. The existing evidence is difficult to interpret but one multiple regression analysis revealed that the female labour-force participation rate in different areas explains 'dining rates' (proportions of children taking school meals) better than the poverty, population density and average family size of the areas (Davies and Williamson, 1968). On the other hand, about 300,000 children received free meals in 1968, which was about 7 per cent of all children taking school dinners in that year, but the estimated number of children under the age of sixteen in families with incomes below the National Assistance Board scale rates was about 500,000. Unfortunately, we do not know whether the difference of 200,000 is due to lack of information about the remission of charges, the reluctance of poor parents to be means-tested, the actual willingness to pay the nominal sum of 1s. 9d., or, of course, a preference for feeding children at home. In the present state of knowledge, there would seem to be little warrant for pontificating on the injustice of raising charges for school meals and milk.

Further indication of the trend toward selectivity is provided by the raising in 1967 of fees for overseas students (from £70 to £250 a year) and for some non-vocational adult education courses. In both cases, the new fees are still well below the average costs of providing the service (the average running cost per student in British universities is about £700 per year). Nevertheless, there was furious opposition to both increases, most of which was unrelated to the actual aims of the subsidies in question. The increase in the fees of overseas students was no doubt badly managed from the start; nevertheless, the case for raising fees never received a fair hearing. The move was widely interpreted as a blow to the underdeveloped countries and a betrayal of Britain's traditional obligations to her ex-colonies, ignoring the fact that about 30,000 out of the 72,000 overseas students in Britain in 1967 came from advanced countries, such as Canada, Australia and the United States, and that about half of the 42,000 overseas students from underdeveloped countries were recipients either of awards from their own governments, a British official source or an international organization. In other words, for the sake of 20,000 students, Britain subsidized and to a large extent still subsidizes 70,000 students. Would it not be preferable to extend all foreign aid to governments instead of to students? After all, an important category of beneficiaries of subsidized fees for overseas students are the children of well-to-do families in underdeveloped countries. If instead it were argued that we ought to assist individuals rather than governments, would it not be better to raise fees all round and at the same time to institute a scholarship programme to aid those that cannot obtain the approval of their governments?

Similarly, the addition of only a few shillings to the charge of 25s. for certain evenings courses that are alleged to cost almost £13 per student should really have been criticized as being too small. Further increases in 1968 and 1969 have still done no more than to raise fees to a little over £2 per course per year. Adult education in Britain is, on the whole, badly staffed and there are few prospects of obtaining better staff without a significant rise in salaries which in turn is more likely to happen when fees have been raised. This is quite separate from the issue of evening degree courses for mature students in full-time employment. A strong case can be made for the creation of more institutions of the Birkbeck pattern outside London with low fees and generous financial aid on the same terms that are now available to full-time university students. This brings us to higher education in general, which is perhaps the one level of education which now most stands in need of drastic financial rethinking. Before turning to this question, however, we must pause a moment over some tendencies in secondary education which have come to be regarded as manifestations of the tenets of 'universalism'.

The tendencies in question are comprehensive reorganization, the trend toward unstreaming and the scheduled raising of the school-leaving age to sixteen in 1973. But these have actually little to do with the bone of contention between the selectivists and the universalists which is, as we said, whether to distribute social benefits in relation to income or not. It is important to notice that one may be a selectivist and still disagree violently with other selectivists, and with universalists for that matter, about the appropriate scale of higher education, the methods now used to select students for admission to higher education, the educational and social effects of streaming in secondary schools and the desirability of keeping young people off the labour market until sixteen rather than fifteen. Moreover, one may take one position on these questions in principle and another in practice, given the present supply of teachers, and the present distribution of school buildings between local authorities. From almost every point of view, comprehensive reorganization, streaming, secondary-school leaving examinations and the statutory leaving age are much more important issues than that of means-testing. However, they are not issues on which economists can speak with authority.

This is not to deny that, say, comprehensive secondary schools would constitute a much more substantial selective benefit to working-class parents than cheap school meals, nor that the £100 million we will be spending in the next few years in preparation for the raising of the school-leaving age in 1973 will not, in fact, be better spent selectively on poorer areas and on older, understaffed schools, but simply that so much more is involved here than distributing benefits universally or selectively. The same thing is true of the issue of public schools, which at first glance appears to provide a fertile field for the application of the selective principle. In other words, when we opt either for the selective or universalist approach to the finance of education, there is still much left to argue over. To press all the participants in educational controversies into either of these two camps is to transform a difference of emphasis into a Procrustean bed.

Student Loans in Higher Education

Student grants in higher education conform in essence to the principle of selectivity, inasmuch as the value of the grant declines with the taxable income of parents. The fact that the parental contribution is means-tested suggests that the purpose of the grants system is to assist the less affluent to keep their children in full-time education after eighteen. In short, its purpose appears to be that of equalizing educational opportunities in the face of unequal means to postpone employment. If all that was required for higher education was finance after the age of eighteen, the system would succeed admirably in achieving this objective. Unfortunately, what is also required is at least two A-level passes, and this implies full-time attendance in school between the ages of fifteen and eighteen; it is precisely this that tends to undermine any equalizing effects that grants after eighteen might have.

The roots of social-class differences in educational attainments go back to the first years of schooling and, indeed, most of the disadvantages of working-class children have already made themselves felt before they enter primary schools. In the course of primary schooling, working-class children decline steadily relative to middle-class children in terms of measured ability; thereafter, the eleven-plus hurdle, streaming in secondary schools and the unequal provision of grammar-school places in different areas reinforce the tendency for working-class children to fall behind middle-class children. At fifteen we reach the next decisive bottleneck. Parents who want to keep their children at school in order to qualify them for entry into higher education face indirect costs of about £450 to £500 per year. These indirect costs are simply the earnings that fifth and sixth formers forgo by staying on at school. When the father is earning £1100 per year (the average annual income of male manual workers in 1969), an addition of £450 to the family income is no mean consideration. To be sure, most local authorities pay a maintenance grant in exceptional circumstances for children staying on after the statutory leaving age but this rarely exceeds £70 a year. As a matter of fact, total expenditures on this item are now only about £1 million which works out to a little more than £2 per fifth or sixth former per year. In short, the bulk of working-class parents receive no financial aid to cover the direct costs of schooling from fifteen to eighteen, although, of course, fees are zero, and little or no aid to compensate them for the earnings their children sacrifice by staying on at school. Is it any wonder that working-class children leave early?

A policy designed to equalize educational opportunity should start with maintenance grants in fifth and sixth forms and end with financial aid after entry into higher education. No one would pretend that this would wipe out all the disadvantages of working-class children, since much of the damage is already done by the age of fifteen. But as one of the principal reasons for early leaving is low parental income, there can be no doubt that sixth-form scholarships or generous maintenance allowances for secondary-school pupils would significantly alter the social-class characteristics of entrants into higher education.

There is nothing new in this idea. It has been broached again and again by various writers and committees but so far nothing has been done about it for the simple reason that it would roughly double present expenditures on student grants. A crude calculation suggests that a grant of £200 for all fifth and sixth formers, accompanied by a means test similar to that now employed for grants in higher education, would add a net sum of £100 million to the present bill for schooling of £2000 million. Unwilling to face up to the costs of true equality, we have instead created a system in which education between fifteen and eighteen is effectively distributed in accordance with the purchasing power of parents – the absence of fees still leaves parents paying indirectly for two-thirds of the total costs of secondary education – after which we award those who have survived the race with an average prize of £300 per year, equivalent to 60 per cent of what they could earn at that age in productive employment. The total cost of this bonanza in 1966–7 was over £100 million, or 25 per cent of total expenditure on further and higher education.

It is true that student grants are means-tested but every student receives at least £50 per year and gross parental income has to reach about £4000 before the grant falls to the minimum figure. No data have ever been published of the actual family incomes of students in higher education, nor even of the 'balance of incomes' which are used by local authorities to assess the parental contribution to the grant. The 'balance of income' is determined by deducting from the gross taxable income of both parents such items as (a) £200 per dependent child other than the student in question, (b) mortgage interest, if any, (c) life insurance premiums, if any, and (d) educational expenses for brothers and sisters (school fees up to £200 per student and fees for further education up to £350). Thus, if a student has brothers or sisters and his parents are buying their own home, gross taxable income may be £250 to £600 higher than the 'balance of income'.

It is known that about 3 per cent of students in higher education receive no grant (these are mainly overseas students); about 48 per cent receive the full grant because the 'balance of income' of their parents falls below £900; and the rest, 49 per cent, receive scaled-down grants, of which seven per cent lose the grant altogether but receive £50 nevertheless. We may conjecture that the 48 per cent that receive full grants come from homes where gross taxable income probably does not exceed £1100 to £1200. With the average incomes of male manual workers running to £1100 per year, these are certainly parents who are not well off, which is not to say that they are necessarily blue-collar workers. However, the remaining 49 per cent have parents earning anywhere from £1200 to £4000 per year, with 7 per cent, or roughly

20,000 students, receiving £50 a year despite the fact that their parents have a taxable income of at least £4000. About £40 million out of the £100 million spent on student support, therefore, goes to students whose parents could perfectly well pay for their own maintanence. Without splitting hairs, it is fair to say that almost half of the grants system simply gives to those who already have. There is nothing wrong with this if we really believe in supporting an educational élite. But to defend grants in higher education on grounds of social equality is a monstrous perversion of the truth.

The whole of the last two paragraphs rests on an inference from uncertain facts. We do not know how much the parents of students in British higher education actually earn. Perhaps the reason that these figures have never been revealed, and that no voices have been raised to demand that they be revealed, is that their suspected implications would be deeply destructive of traditional beliefs about university finance. Judged in terms of effectiveness per unit of costs, the present grants system is perhaps the least efficient method conceivable of increasing working-class participation in higher education.

In an ideal world, we would give grants an inverse proportion to parental income, or even better to students' income, to all those who stayed on in full-time education beyond the age of fifteen right up to the Ph.D. level; in that world, we would never have to make difficult policy choices either because the electorate could always be persuaded to vote in favour of more public expenditures or because defence spending could always be cut to release funds for educational purposes. In the real world, however, education must compete with the other social services in face of budgetary restraints.[4] Even within the educational system, there is no dearth of improvements that await action for lack of additional resources: more day nurseries, more State boarding schools, new primary schools, more teachers and better pay for the teachers that we have, more comprehensive secondary schools, Plowden 'priority areas', etc. etc. Surely, if we are going to make use of student aid to equalize educational opportunities – which in some sense is like locking the stable door after the horses

4. In the United States, for example, the adoption of a system of maintenance grants and tuition allowances for all of America's six million college students would have cost in 1966–7 about $12,000 million, requiring a fourfold increase in tax supports for higher education or an increase of 2 per cent of GNP devoted to higher education (Jencks and Riesman, 1968, p. 136).

have bolted – we ought to reduce public subsidies in higher education and apply the funds released thereby to subside upper-secondary education? The gradual introduction of a system of financing students in higher education by loans, beginning with postgraduates and then gradually extending downwards, seems to be the least painful way of accomplishing this. Within about fifteen or twenty years, the scheme could become entirely self-financing, making perhaps as much as £50 million to £75 million available for maintenance grants to fifth and sixth formers.

Student loans schemes of one type or another already exist in the United States, Canada, Western Germany, the Netherlands, Sweden, Norway, Denmark, Finland and a significant number of under-developed countries, although of all these countries, Sweden and Norway are the only ones that rely on loans as the principal source of student finance. British opinion has so far been unalterably opposed to the very principle of student loans: at various times in the last few years, the National Union of Students, the National Union of Teachers, the Association of University Teachers, the Association of Teachers in Technical Institutes, the Committee of Vice-Chancellors, the Trades Union Congress and both major parties have lined up against the idea. In their evidence to the Robbins Committee on Higher Education, some economists, such as Peacock, Wiseman and Prest spoke out in favour of a system of financing students by loans, but the report itself dismissed the suggestion, at least for the time being. Since then all three have developed the theme at greater length (Peacock and Wiseman, 1964; Prest, 1966) and Mishan (1969) has added his voice to theirs. Nevertheless, in contrast to American economists (Danière, 1964, pp. 109–14; Harris, 1962, chs. 17–22; Vickerey, 1962) the vast majority of British economists apparently remain unconvinced by the case for loans. This is perhaps less surprising when it is realized that the discussion so far has been conducted at cross purposes. Peacock, Wiseman, Prest and Mishan argue the case essentially on the basis of the benefit principle of taxation. Higher education in Britain, as we have seen (see Chapter 7, p. 227) confers substantial financial benefits on those who have been privileged to receive it. Is it equitable, they ask, to give 10 per cent of an age group free annuities paying 14 per cent interest per year for the rest of their working lives, out of taxes largely paid by those with less income? The requirements of distributive justice would be satisfied, so the argument continues, if we provided eligible students with necessary finance, not as an outright gift from public funds, but in the form of a personal loan repayable after study out of earned income. But the central argument put forward for giving the subsidy in the form of grants rather than loans runs on completely different lines: no one with ability to benefit from education should be barred from it on financial grounds; since the willingness of students to incur personal debts is directly related to the income of their parents, a loans scheme would act as a deterrent to working-class students.

Clearly, when one side attacks the grants system because the incidence of taxes should be as closely related as possible to the incidence of benefits, while the other side defends it because it gives working-class children a better chance to take up higher education, fruitful debate becomes impossible. If the grants system is vulnerable it must be criticized on the same grounds on which it is defended, or else the grounds themselves must be challenged. After all, the fact that the recipients of grants are being subsidized for an activity which is likely to increase their lifetime income is no more an argument against student grants than the fact that business firms profit from the installation of capital equipment is an argument against tax incentives to promote investment. We subsidize what we like to subsidize. The only question is: are we subsidizing effectively?

No doubt, there is much humbug in the popular appeal to equality of educational opportunity. It is not clear why it should be considered more egalitarian to provide 'free' higher education to all those who are clever enough to benefit from it, rather than to all those who want it and are willing to incur a debt to undertake it (Merrett, 1967, p. 297). However, since the grants system is defended as favouring able but poor students, it must be judged in these terms. The standard Pareto optimality arguments are simply irrelevant. For example, it may be true that the benefits of widespread higher education spill over to the whole community and that therefore public subsidies are required to avoid social underinvestment in higher education. But interest-free loans or fees below costs constitute just as much of a subsidy as student grants. Unless we know the magnitude of the spill-overs, the concept of externalities is of no help in choosing between loans and grants.

Does the present system of grants serve to equalize educational opportunities? We have seen that about half of all students in British higher education come from families where the parents probably would experience great difficulties in supporting their children until the age of twenty-one. Of course, if students were provided with opportunities to work in vacation time, even these parents might manage. However, so long as students are expected to complete the course in three years, the present system of grants appears to be defensible, at least as an expensive way of fulfilling the objectives of equality. It is only when the matter is seen in a historical and comparative perspective that real doubts begin to creep in. In recent years, we have heard repeatedly of the Robbins statistic that 25 per cent of students in British universities (and 34 per cent in further education) come from manual working-class homes, a figure unmatched anywhere else in the world except possibly the U.S.S.R. Since we subsidize students more generously than any other Western country, it follows that the grants system must be responsible for the relatively high proportion of working-class students in British universities.

However, the proportion of one in four has not changed significantly since 1938, although at that time we extended rather niggardly grants to only about half of all university students. As the *Robbins Report* put it: 'There was little change between 1928–47 and 1961 in the proportions of students coming from working-class backgrounds, in spite of the fact that the number of students at university had more than doubled during this period' (*Robbins Report*, 1963, app. 2(B), p. 4).

Maintenance grants on a significant scale were first introduced in Britain in 1948, although grants as such were not unknown in the 1920s and 1930s. The principle of awarding a grant as of right to every student accepted for a first degree course (or its equivalent) was first laid down in the *Anderson Report* of 1960. Between 1960 and 1967, the number of students receiving awards from public funds at institutions of higher education more than doubled, while the costs of making these awards more than trebled.

From all impressions, data for the years 1938 to 1960, if they were available, would show a similar discrepancy between the growth of numbers and total expenditure on awards – that is, more and more students received awards and the level of the awards rose steadily. Nevertheless, working-class participation in the university sector (we have no data on trends in further education over these years) showed little change between the 1930s and the 1960s. After an authoritative review of all the available evidence, Westergaard and Little (1967, p. 224) concurred with the *Robbins Report*:

There are certainly no indications of any narrowing of class differentials in access to universities over the generations. In terms of the broad categories distinguished here, the social class composition of the student body in the universities has remained roughly the same during the past three to five decades – this despite expansion, despite maintenance grants for students and the changes which have occurred in secondary-school provision.

It follows from all this that an international comparison of working-class participation in universities in the 1930s would show Britain in the lead then as now.[5] Why this should have been true even in the 1930s is not clear, but it is difficult to believe that grants as they were then administered had much to do with it. It is conceivable, of course, that the 6000 or so scholarships that were awarded in 1938 by the State and by local authorities were so carefully means-tested that they did encourage working-class boys and girls to go to university. But it is clear that since 1938 the extension of grants to additional students, and the increases in the absolute amount of grants awarded has done little to increase the relative chances for working-class students of reaching higher education.

Unwilling to rest the entire case for grants on grounds of equality, defenders of the grants system sometimes fall back on what are actually élitist arguments. Since British students do not have to seek part-time employment to supplement their incomes, Britain can produce a high-quality graduate in only three years with a wastage rate well below that of any other advanced country. In short, the cost of the grants system is really much less than appears at first glance: without it, the course would last for four to six years as on the Continent, and wastage would be two to three times what it is.

Wastage rates for students in higher education holding full value

5. This statement is based on casual evidence: no attempt has ever been made, either for 1930s or for the 1960s, to carefully verify the popular impression that Britain enrols a larger proportion of working-class students in higher education than other countries. International comparisons of this kind are full of traps for the unwary and the results are sometimes surprising. For example, Pryor (1968, pp. 479–80) has adjusted the percentage of students in higher education with parents in manual and farming occupations in the U.S.A. and the U.S.S.R. for the proportions of such groups in the total population; he found that, measured in this way, there were no significant differences in the class composition of students in higher education in the two countries.

awards in England and Wales in the academic year 1964–5 averaged 24 per cent: 18 per cent for universities and 31 per cent for further education. These are undoubtedly among the lowest wastage rates found anywhere in the world. But can we attribute this superiority to the grants system?

University education in Britain is a privilege: half of those with two or more A-levels are turned away. To be sure, 80 per cent of those not admitted now enrol in some kind of full-time or part-time further or higher education, but wastage rates in further education are 31 per cent, which is uncomfortably close to American wastage rates where students are largely self-financed. On the Continent and in the United States, university or equivalent-level higher education is a right rather than a privilege and everyone with a *baccalauréat* or a high-school diploma is entitled to a university place. Once university education is made a right, a positive wastage rate, however deplorable in itself, constitutes a price that must be paid to achieve the objective of an open-door policy.

Considering that Britain rations higher education to an unusually small proportion of the relevant age group, it ill behoves British commentators to look complacently at the higher wastage rates of foreign systems of higher education. The British educational system screens students carefully before they enter higher education, whereas other countries weed students out one or two years after entry. Little wonder then that wastage rates are low in Britain. But comparisons of wastage rates over entire cycles of higher education between open and closed systems are completely spurious. Since qualified students in Britain have completed at least one year of education more than European or American students (because entry into school is at the age of five rather than at the age of six or seven), and since the British degree course lasts three not four years, a fair comparison would have to consider the last year of the sixth form as well. It is immediately obvious that this would wipe out much of the British advantage in wastage rates. Actually, an open system of higher education should be judged in terms of its success in giving longer education to the largest possible absolute number of students, not in terms of its success in carrying a fixed number to completion. Thus, the fact demonstrated by Robbins that the cost per completed graduate is actually lower in Britain than in most other countries is beside the point: the more relevant statistic is the annual cost per student.

Furthermore, Robbins showed that wastage rates differ between faculties for no objective reasons that the Committee could discover. Clearly, British universities keep wastage rates low because of the belief that high enough hurdles have already been created at entry. In other countries, where the entry hurdles are low, they are much stricter about allowing students to go on. That is all, or almost all, there is to comparative wastage rates.

It may be conceded that a loans scheme would give students an incentive to work in vacation periods and in some cases to take up part-time rather than full-time higher education. Surely this is all to the good or, at any rate, it is not self-evident that it is bad? Without fully accepting the Soviet principle of polytechnic part-time education, it can be argued that vacation work has values of its own in bringing largely middle-class students into contact with manual workers. Besides, we now give grants to cover a portion of maintenance during vacation, on the notion that students need the time to study. Everyone has ignored the findings of the 1964 Hale Committee on University Teaching Methods which discovered that 'for a large proportion of students the long vacation is, academically speaking, time largely wasted. ... One hour a day or less of study was claimed by 53 per cent, more than one hour but less than three by 31 per cent, more than three but less than five by 11 per cent, and more than five by 5 per cent'.

The implicit British assumption that short, intensive full-time education without any outside employment is best for all students good enough to be admitted into universities ought to be considered afresh. At any rate, if British higher education is maintained at its present scale or allowed to expand gradually in accordance with the Robbins targets, there is actually little reason to think that wastage rates would be significantly higher with a loans scheme than with a grants system, and they might even be lower.

However, the most appealing feature of a loans scheme is that it would make the expansion of higher education more likely, because it would alleviate the burden of student grants on the Exchequer after a certain number of years. Now, a vastly expanded system of higher education would probably mean more failures as a proportion of total intake; this is a price that would probably have to be paid if we are going to have comprehensive higher education on a much larger scale than now exists. After all, if the argument is that wastage rates should be reduced regardless of the scale of higher education, the most effective way of accomplishing this is to contract the system. The rule seems to be that the degree of wastage people are prepared to accept varies directly with the scale and type of higher education that they favour.

All the leading advocates of student loans schemes in Britain, with the exception of Mishan (1969), have proposed repayments over a graduate's working life that are either proportionate to or a definite percentage of personal income. Thus, no income, no tax, which takes care immediately of the hoary old charge that a loans scheme would impose 'negative dowries' on female graduates contemplating marriage.[6] But this is merely to say that it would have been more clarifying to have talked of a graduate tax rather than a loans scheme: it was never intended that students should repay a loan as if it were a personal debt.

It has been shown (Glennerster, Merrett and Wilson, 1968) that the level of the graduate tax could vary from £30 per year (if full maintenance grants at current levels were repaid interest free over a forty-year working life) to £270 per year (if the average graduate repaid maintenance grants and the full teaching cost of his course at 8 per cent interest over his working life). At one extreme, this would represent a tax of about 3 per cent of a graduate's starting salary. At the other extreme, it would represent a tax of about 25 per cent of his starting salary although, of course, a somewhat smaller proportion later on in life, in effect removing on average about one-third of the salary differential that British graduates now enjoy over those who leave school at eighteen. If universities expanded in line with the Robbins targets and if the graduate tax went into operation in 1970 – all undergraduates receiving a full grant of £370 without a means test but becoming liable to the new tax on graduation – the revenues raised by the tax would vary once again between two extremes: if graduates were only taxed to recoup maintenance grants and no interest were charged, the system would only become self-financing by 1996 (with interest at 4 per cent, implying a tax of £60 per year, the system would be self-financing by 1991). On the other hand, if the tax involved

6. Actually, the 'dowry' which an educated woman gives to her husband is positive: even though her services as a housewife, child-minder and general factotum are not saleable on the market, an adequate substitute is purchasable in the market at the price commanded by female graduates. Thus, a debt burden would at most reduce the value of this positive dowry. There is no warrant whatever for thinking that it would reduce it so much as to render it negative.

repayment of both maintenance and tuition costs compounded at 8 per cent over forty years (£270 p.a.), revenues would equal appropriate outlays (research would still have to be paid for out of taxes) by 1981.

A wide range of policy options is now opened before us and clearly nothing that has been said implies approval of the extreme case for a tax of 25 per cent of graduate earnings so as to eliminate all public subsidies to the teaching functions of universities. Even a gentle tax of £60 per year, designed merely to recoup maintenance grants, would involve a subsidy to the extent of interest forgone by the State. Nevertheless, it would generate annual revenues of £30 million to £45 million by 1985. Furthermore, the widespread fear that any prospect of a debt burden would deter working-class children from continuing their education is alleviated at its roots: with a graduate tax there is no burden of debt that must be paid; this is indeed why a graduate tax is a superior scheme to personal loans. Besides, it is doubtful that a sum of £60 per year, equal to 6 per cent of a graduate's present starting salary and equal to about 3 per cent of this peak salary at the age of forty, would deter anyone that had stayed on in school until the age of eighteen.

It will be recalled that a graduate tax of £60 per year implies full maintenance grants to everyone. If the grants were means-tested as they now are, they could be repaid at a 4 per cent interest rate with a graduate tax of only about £45 per year. Smaller revenues would then be generated and it would take until the year 2000 before the tax would finance all grants. Nevertheless, in the meanwhile we could be slowly raising maintenance grants for fifth and sixth formers. Can there be any doubt that equality of educational opportunity would be better served by this arrangement than by our present system of nothing at all between fifteen and eighteen and generous support thereafter?

Could a rich father avoid the tax by paying off the liability on graduation, or better still by simply refusing to accept a maintenance grant? If so, would this not deny equality to working-class students? Almost certainly: short of levelling all incomes, no conceivable system of university finance can eradicate all the advantages of the rich. Surely, all we can do with any scheme of student support is to raise up, not to level down? Besides, the graduate tax would fall on gross income, while income tax would be levied on income net of graduate tax. Thus, the rich father who opted out on behalf of his son would saddle his son with higher income taxes than will be paid by a poor student who accepted the maintenance grant.

But what about 'brain drain'? No doubt, graduates enjoy higher lifetime incomes than non-graduates but by going to America they can do better still. If British graduates paid the full costs of their own education, there might still be some national loss from brain drain, although it is doubtful. But as long as higher education in Britain is heavily subsidized, there is almost certainly a national loss from brain drain. In other words, concern about brain drain strengthens the case for loans rather than grants. This is not the way the argument is usually put. On the contrary, the possibility of emigration is said to make a loan scheme administratively unworkable and, indeed, it is alleged that the debt burden would stimulate brain drain.

It would be very simple to devise an administrative arrangement to tax British graduates working abroad; in practice, the only two countries that matter are Canada and the United States and there are already bilateral agreements with both countries to force British nationals residing there to pay surtax owed to Inland Revenue. It would be sufficient merely to extend the same principle to work permits given by the Canadian and American governments to British graduates working in North America: failure to pay the graduate tax would then lead to withdrawal of the permission to work. Even the sole use of the power to withdraw passports might suffice to to guarantee repayment of loans, as it takes five years to become an American citizen. Furthermore, if we were interested in reducing brain drain, a loans scheme would provide an almost perfect instrument for controlling it, without interfering with the right to emigrate. The loans would carry interest charges, presumably at subsidized rates, which would be embodied in the calculation of the graduate tax. We might remit all interest charges on graduates working at home while levying them only on graduates who go to work abroad. If this had no effect, we could simply raise the graduate tax on emigrants. I am not recommending a tax on brain drain but simply suggesting the manifold policy uses of a graduate tax.

A strong ancillary argument for a graduate tax is that it would facilitate an increase in university fees, perhaps to the extent of covering most of the cost of teaching additional students (Bowen, 1964, pp. 81–3). If the 'grant' so-called were then paid to students instead of institutions, the consequence would be that the entire system of higher education would become more flexible and responsive to the demand from students and their families. Universities would have an incentive to expand whereas under present arrangements every additional student increases their dependence on public funds, and to diversify their courses in the effort to appeal to students with different tastes and interests. Fees might vary considerably between universities and so might entry standards, but universities would broadcast these differences in the effort to compete for students, instead of hiding them as they now do. If this were coupled with a modified credit system on the American pattern, say, in the form of certification for each year of course work, students could begin to choose between alternative routes to the final degree by moving between universities and between years of study and years of work on the 'sandwich' principle. What would emerge, therefore, is something like comprehensive higher education to match comprehensive secondary education. And think of what all this would do to the cause of student participation in university affairs (Peacock and Culyer, 1969)!

I have left to the last an ever popular fallacy that is sometimes employed against the concept of a graduate tax; it is the argument that graduates are already taxed progressively in consequence of their relatively higher incomes; in short, they will eventually repay the State for the costs of their education. But this is a typical confusion of different objectives. Besides, the tax which graduates pay on their undeniably higher earnings is not an adequate *quid pro quo* for the subsidy they received: if the State regarded the tax received from graduates as the only return from higher education, the implied yield on the amount now spent per student in British higher education is, in fact, negative. However, if we were to accept this sort of reasoning – confusing the motives behind the progressive income tax with the reasons for financing higher education one way rather than another – we ought to advocate the distribution of free annuities to all eighteen-year-olds on the grounds that part of the resulting annual payments will after all be recovered eventually via income taxation.

There are many problems about a graduate tax – its effects on the salaries of graduates, for instance – which ought to be fully explored before we venture to introduce a specific scheme. This is not the place to pursue such questions further. Our basic concern has been to emphasize the gross imbalance in the present structure of public subsidies to education. Equalization of opportunity requires that students be assisted from the public purse at an age where lack of means really matters, not at eighteen but at fifteen. To do both would seem to be out of the question in the foreseeable future. Savings have to be made somewhere and it seems only reasonable to take from the later stages of education to give to the earlier. If the proportion of working-class boys and girls seeking access to higher education goes up, as it surely must with increased grants in secondary schools, the taste for education will soon overcome the reluctance to shoulder the burden of repaying a 'grant' for higher education out of enhanced earnings prospects. Once the nature of the proposed loan scheme or graduate tax is fully grasped, and particularly when it is recognized that the funds that it releases can be more effectively reapplied elsewhere within the educational system, the case against loans in favour of grants in higher education collapses.

Education Vouchers

One of the most interesting recent ideas in public finance is the concept of a 'voucher', a coupon with a prescribed purchasing power over a specified service. It was proposed for American education by Friedman (see 1962), and applied to British education by Wiseman (1959; Peacock and Wiseman, 1964) and has since been zealously advocated by West (1965, chs. 13–15; 1968). The key to the voucher scheme is the distribution to all parents of vouchers exchangeable for education in any school, whether State or private, that satisfies minimum educational standards, the value of the voucher being related to some notion of the average costs of education of children of different ages. State schools would charge cost-covering fees and would compete with private schools on equal terms. Parents could supplement the voucher out of their own pockets as much as they liked at private schools that might charge fees above the standard level. Education would still be compulsory up to a legal school-leaving age but parents would now be free, as with compulsory third-party automobile insurance, to choose among alternative suppliers of the compulsory service. And compared with a tax rebate, vouchers would have the advantage of helping even those who paid little in direct taxation; they could be scaled inversely to income, so that their value would be less, the greater the income of parents.

The voucher scheme is in some sense very similar to the existing British system of family allowances except that it can be used to buy only one service: a voucher is a cash grant, earmarked for compulsory education, that can be supplemented by ordinary cash. The idea is obviously inspired by the writing of John Stuart Mill: in fact, it is pure Mill but for the additional idea of State finance.[7] Its advocates claim that free choice between State and private schools backed up by the purchasing power of vouchers would create a wider variety of educational institutions, stimulate competition among schools, raise standards in both State and private schools, promote educational innovation, increase the responsiveness of schools to the wishes of parents, educate parents in the art of choice and, as a bonus, raise total public plus private expenditures on education.[8] In contrast, the opponents of the voucher scheme argue that the encouragement it would give to private schools would increase existing differences in the quality of schooling; private schools would admit only able students and bid for superior teachers while resorting to blatant and misleading advertising to mould the choices of parents in their favour; State schools would become a dumping ground for 'problem children' and social stratification in education would be sharply increased. They do not deny that it might offer a way of increasing total expenditures on education by stimulating voluntary additions to the funds provided out of taxation, but they argue that the extra finance would come largely from the well-to-do, buying better education for their offspring. Their basic objection to vouchers, however, appears to be directed against the very idea of distributing education in any relation whatsoever to purchasing power (see Chapter 4, p. 116).

It is perfectly clear what the advocates of the voucher scheme believe. They have candidly declared their value judgements, announced

7. In point of fact the roots of the scheme go back to Tom Paine's *Rights of Man* (West, 1967b).

8. Vouchers have been proposed not only to enable families to pay school fees, but also medical fees and medical insurance premiums, rents and mortgage payments, and premiums on life insurance with pension options (Seldon and Gray, 1967). In all cases, families would be free to add to the value of the vouchers as they wished and the State, besides setting minimum standards and perhaps minimum levels of purchase, would simply compete in the market with other producers of services. Clearly, the central thread in all these proposals is that we need, not the Welfare State, but simply more equal means to purchase welfare from whomsoever provides it. A voucher scheme can always be made as equalizing as is desired by negative progression, but the principal effect in any case must be to stimulate the growth of private schools, private hospitals, private medical insurance, private housing and private pension schemes.

the social objectives to which they subscribe and committed themselves to specific predictions about the probable consequences of the voucher scheme (see, for example, Peacock and Wiseman, 1964, pp. 33, 35, 40, 45, 53, 54; West, 1965, pp. 70–72, 227–30). It is not so clear why the opponents of the voucher scheme reject it out of hand: what little discussion there has been of educational vouchers takes the form of disagreements about fundamental values, about the short-comings of the present system of State education and about the actual effects predicted from vouchers, typically combined in such a way that it is difficult to see where one objection leaves off and another begins (Benson, 1968, pp. 52–60; Horobin and Smyth, 1960*; Miner, 1963, pp. 24–36; Vaizey, 1962, pp. 28–36). If we are to make any sense of this debate, we must begin by sorting out the wheat from the chaff.

The first problem is that of the competence of parents to choose education. The great difficulty with free choice in education is that some parents are obviously better equipped to choose than others and this advantage is handed on to their better-educated children, thus producing a cumulative advantage through time similar to the in-equalities created by the inheritance of property. The question is how best to deal with it: to restrict choice by compelling attendance in State schools, to permit a latitude of choice among institutions that come up to prescribed minimum standards or to go further and to permit choice among all 'recognized' schools while overcoming inadequate finance out of public funds? The nub of the dispute is the actual scope for choice, not the idea of choice itself. Even the proponents of the voucher scheme agree that we must compel school attendance until a certain age and that all schools must satisfy minimum educational standards, the latter presumably determined by publicly elected officials acting in consultation with teachers; in other words, their demand for free choice is far from being absolute. Likewise, the opponents of vouchers are committed to *de jure* choice within the State sector and have never been willing to prohibit private education altogether.

Since the issue is one of the degree of choice, the argument is really about the meaning of State intervention in education. One can agree with Vaizey (1962, p. 29) when he says that 'education, indeed, can in a substantial degree be regarded as an intervention to save the individual from the family', the operative phrase being 'a substantial degree', and yet applaud Peacock and Wiseman (1964, p. 39) when they declare that 'we regard education as a means of safeguarding the family from too great reliance upon the state rather than as a means for the state to take over the responsibilities of the family'. Be that as it may, parental incompetence as such cannot be advanced as a definitive reason for rejecting the voucher scheme, particularly as the obvious incompetence of most parents in educational matters is itself the result of lack of experience in the art of choice (see Chapter 4, p. 104).

We come now to another fundamental difference of opinion between the two camps, namely, whether or not education should be distributed according to purchasing power, as it would be if free State education were replaced by open-ended vouchers cashable at any school whatever. Surprisingly enough, the contention here is more a matter of facts than of values as both parties to the debate agree that attempts to equalize educational opportunities are desirable.[9] Peacock, Wiseman and West all argue that the present system of British state education imposes severe social and geographical inequalities on working-class families that could be overcome by the voucher scheme (Peacock and Wiseman, 1964, p. 54; West, 1965, pp. 63–5). But West goes further and claims the free market to be an ally rather than an enemy of egalitarianism by virtue of the fact that the average British household pays in direct plus indirect taxes a sum roughly equal to the monetary value of the benefits it receives in welfare services of all kinds, including education. He reproduces official calculations that have been made at regular intervals in Britain of the incidence of all taxes paid out and welfare benefits received (National Insurance, the National Health Service, family allowances, supplementary benefits, free State education, etc.) by households in different economic circumstances, purporting to show that all taxes and benefits combined tend to redistribute income from the extreme upper to the extreme lower income groups in the community, leaving the vast majority of families breaking more or less even. He concludes, therefore, that most families

9. Friedman's position (1962, pp. 91–2) is not self-evident and the notion of reducing the value of the voucher as income rises formed no part of his proposal. However, Peacock and Wiseman (1964, p. 15) leave no doubt about their intentions to use vouchers to achieve egalitarian ends. West hedges a little: at times he almost implies that equality of opportunity is a will-o'-the-wisp (1965, pp. 50–70, 225–9), but elsewhere (1968) he agrees that the principle of progressive taxation should apply to vouchers.

would be no worse off if the State withdrew from the field of education and rescinded taxes accordingly (West, 1965, pp. 44, 64). Unfortunately, no breakdown of taxes and benefits assignable to individual social services has ever been published, so that we cannot in fact argue from the global results to education alone. Furthermore, the official calculations themselves are really misleading, and particularly so with reference to the imputed value of health and education (Peacock and Shannon, 1968b).

In all probability, the tendency to redistribute real income in any one period, via the relationship between taxes inadvertently paid out by all to finance free State education and the benefits of free education which is only received by parents, is quantitatively of little significance. In that sense, West is probably near the mark. If indeed there is any tendency to redistribute, it applies only to the very poor with three or more children. This particular problem could probably be attacked more directly by direct financial aid in the form of bursaries, scholarships, grants, loans or means-tested vouchers.[10] We conclude, therefore, that if we are concerned with the distribution of income, if we favour equality of educational opportunity, we should be advocating more vigorous use of State finance to assist parents to buy education. To call for State provision in these circumstances is besides the point. It is very much to the point, however, if instead we are aiming at 'social cohesion' (see Chapter 4, p. 118).

The advocates of the voucher scheme make no bones of the fact that the system they propose would encourage the proliferation of profit and non-profit-making schools, owned and operated by religious organizations and similar bodies concerned with propagating a particular view of society. Peacock and Wiseman (1964, p. 55) grant that the problem of assimilating a large immigrant population and a sizeable coloured minority justifies State provision of schools in the United States to disseminate common social values. What they deny is that this consideration is applicable to a more homogeneous society like Great Britain. Friedman and West, however, do not qualify their argument in any way and they would not object to a

10. It would not be enough, however, to make the value of the voucher vary inversely with income if, as is usually proposed, the full-valued voucher covers only the direct costs of education. To be an effective redistribution device, vouchers at their maximum value would have to meet both the direct and indirect costs of education in the form of earnings forgone after the school-leaving age.

private school that, without barring Negro and immigrant children from entry, would effectively keep them out by the device of raising fees, trusting to the fact that most Negroes and immigrants are poor; if that proved insufficient, a certain atmosphere of disdain towards coloured students and foreigners would do the rest. Now it is perfectly true that even this difficulty could be overcome under a voucher scheme by giving Negro and immigrant families a larger voucher; this might well be more effective in overcoming segregation in schools than the present arrangement which prohibits segregation by law but does nothing to give Negro and immigrant parents effective power to choose schools outside the ghettoes (Levin, 1968, pp. 10–11). Both Friedman and West, however, dismiss all worries about racially segregated schools under a system of vouchers, and indeed convert this difficulty into a virtue. As Friedman (1962, p. 8) expresses it:

The appropriate solution is to eliminate government operation of the schools and permit parents to choose the kind of school they want their children to attend. In addition, of course, we should all of us, in so far as we possibly can, try by behavior and speech to foster the growth of attitudes and opinions that would lead mixed schools to become the rule and segregated schools the rare exception.

If a proposal like that of [education vouchers] were adopted it would permit a variety of schools to develop, some all white, some all Negro, some mixed. It would permit the transition from one collection of schools to another – hopefully to mixed schools – to be gradual as community attitudes changed. It would avoid the harsh political conflict that has been doing so much to raise social tensions and disrupt the community. It would in this special area, as the market does in general, permit cooperation without conformity.

But the real question, that is, whether it is possible to persuade racial bigots of the undesirability of racial prejudice when neither they nor their children come into daily contact with coloured people, is hereby avoided.

A similar question arises with respect to schools stratified on the basis of social class, as in Great Britain. West seems in places to deny the possibility of ever discovering which children are handicapped by their home background and to what extent, implying however that the handicap in any case has little to do with social class (1965, p. 53). Most readers of his book will not find it as obvious as he does that 'we are in danger of contradicting ourselves if, having allowed some people the freedom to earn more than others, we are at the same time striving for the day when the rich men's sons are forced to school with children of the not-so-rich according to some system of conscription' (1965, p. 55). There is, of course, no contradiction whatever if one values the removal of class barriers.

Peacock and Wiseman face up squarely to the possibility that more private provision of education would exacerbate class distinctions. They demur, however:

We still know very little about the *causes* of such class differences as it is possible to identify, in the sense of being able to predict how they would be affected by policy changes. In the case of education, a good deal of evidence ... has been collected on the experience and performance of students from different social classes, variously defined. But there is much less satisfactory evidence about the extent to which these phenomena are inherent or related to particular aspects of class, and even less on the way they might be affected by specified changes in access to educational resources. The most common (though often implicit) inferences, unsupported by any satisfactory evidence, seem to be that the problem will become easier the more children are made to go to the same kinds of schools, and that it will also become smaller the larger the volume of educational resources the government makes available by existing methods (Peacock and Wiseman, 1964, pp. 25–6).

Many people in Britain do indeed believe that 'the problem will become easier the more children are made to go to the same kinds of schools'. They may be wrong in thinking that the relative classlessness of the United States has something to do with its unstreamed elementary schools and comprehensive high schools. The evidence for such a relationship has certainly not been entirely convincing. Nevertheless, it is a plausible argument and at any rate a more plausible one than the contention of the advocates of the voucher scheme that vouchers would result in 'the destruction of the present "separate" character of the public schools, without at the same time destroying what is valuable in their tradition' (Peacock and Wiseman, 1964, p. 56).

We have to face the fact however, that almost any educational policy can be defended on the grounds that it will promote 'common values', a curious defence in view of the fact that these values are frequently matters of heated controversy. Which is to say that, having defended State-provided education on grounds of social cohesion, it follows that there is little to be said for allowing private schools to exist at all. To continue to permit the rich to opt out as they now can is to imply that they stand in no need of being assimilated in the community. It is not enough to say that they have paid their taxes for 'free' state education and to prevent them from paying twice by buying private education out of their own resources would be an intolerant interference with personal liberty. If that is true for them, it is true for everyone, and we are led straight to the proposal to tax everyone for education vouchers which they may then supplement if they so desire. Furthermore, by applying marginal rates of taxation to vouchers and reducing their value proportionately, we could make opting out of State education no more feasible for the rich than for the poor. If this idea is rejected because it would destroy social solidarity by producing more 'separatist' schools, the implication is that we must deny everyone choice outside the State sector. To advocate State provision of education, while tolerating private education for those who can afford it, is to add insult to injury. It appears that many of those who instinctively recoil from the voucher scheme, as well as from Draconian measures against the existing British 'public' schools, have not fully appreciated the contradictory nature of their position. The fact is that they too wish to strike a balance between parental freedom and social cohesion. But having conceded that there is conflict between these two aims, where shall we draw the lines? As Friedman says (1962, p. 86), 'a stable and democratic society is impossible without a minimum degree of literacy and knowledge on the part of most citizens and without widespread acceptance of some common set of values. Education can contribute to both'. And what if there is no consensus on 'some set of values'? Should we produce it, can we in fact produce it, by compelling attendance in State schools?

In the final analysis, the voucher scheme stands or falls on questions of fact: will it have the consequences predicted by its advocates? We may be sure that it will extend the range of choice and increase the diversity of private and State schools available to parents. Can we also be sure that it will increase total expenditures on education? Stubblebine (1965) has shown that a mixed system of finance, like the provision of open-ended but equal-valued vouchers, will always secure larger expenditure than a wholly tax-financed 'free' school system if (a) the total level of spending is determined by referendum, if (b) parents' preferences are symmetrically distributed about a mean and if (c) voters without children are assumed to be less willing to pay taxes for education than voters with children. This follows from the fact that in all such cases, the outcome is determined by the preferences of the median voter rather than the median parent. Pauly (1967) has gone a step further in attempting to demonstrate that Pareto optimality is secured only if vouchers are taxed or means-tested, thus extracting the largest possible private contribution from rich parents; by implication, it is evident that this would also maximize expenditure on education. But although the Stubblebine–Pauly argument is impeccable as far as it goes, it is far from obvious that a voucher scheme would necessarily raise total spending on education over existing levels. The classic argument for a wholly tax-financed social service is that, by penalizing the well-to-do for opting out, it induces them to stay in and to support high levels of public expenditures; unfortunately, this argument works in reverse once the rich have decided to opt out. In the Stubblebine model, such people as well as those who are professionally involved in education have no more effect on electoral choices than the average voter, despite the fact that they include the most vocal and articulate members of the community and virtually all those who have intense preferences for particular public spending policies. The more nearly the actual level of taxation approaches the preferences of these voters, the less is the weight of Stubblebine's conclusions. It is perfectly conceivable that the 'education lobby' has actually persuaded voters to spend more on education than they would have spent if they had been free to add to vouchers of predetermined value.

In general, it can be shown that if the personal benefits of education are more concentrated than the taxes raised to finance education – a result guaranteed by the fact that the number of households with children of school-going ages is much smaller than the number of households paying some kind of taxes – 'logrolling' will inevitably take place (Buchanan and Tullock, 1962, pp. 135–45). Since parents benefit greatly from the extension of 'free' State education and incur only a small proportion of the extra tax burdens which this produces, parents will have a strong incentive to form coalitions to agitate for educational expansion. Under majority rule, it is only necessary to 'bribe' 51 per cent of the voters to get approval for more expenditure on education. The result is that it is quite easy to get more investment in education through a voting mechanism than through a market mechanism in which all parents pay directly for the education that their children receive. We must be careful, therefore, not to assume as a matter of course that the adoption of a system of means-tested, open-ended vouchers would necessarily increase the level of total educational expenditures.

The other effects of a voucher scheme are even more problematical. Will schools competing for vouchers become better schools, hiring more and better-qualified staff, providing improved facilities and buildings, while experimenting with new methods of teaching and new educational media? Will this kind of 'competition for excellence' among schools, each meeting a minimum prescribed standard, prove a sufficient guarantee against misleading advertising designed to attract parents on non-educational grounds? Will educational opportunities be more equally distributed and, in particular, will the present disability of working-class parents to keep their children at school until seventeen or eighteen be mitigated? Or will a prosperous private sector grow at the expense of an impoverished state sector, producing something like educational apartheid? I do not think that any of these questions can now be answered with great confidence. We have too little experience with market provision of education to predict the precise effect of enhanced choice backed up by purchasing power, and to argue that competition will necessarily improve education as it has improved the quality of automobiles is mere dogma.

Much more discussion of these questions is needed before we try out the voucher scheme even on a trial basis in a limited area. So far the relevant issues have hardly begun to be adequately debated: indeed, the idea of education vouchers has been greeted with a conspiracy of silence. The very notion that the way education is financed is much more important than the issue of who owns and operates schools has been ruled out of court; anything that might lead to the growth of private education, however set about with rules and regulations, is regarded as anathema. The result is that, much as education is starved for funds, the door is closed to any suggestions for exploring new sources of finance. Writers like Friedman, Peacock, Wiseman and West, whatever the pros and cons of education vouchers, at least deserve credit for stimulating fresh thinking of education finance. To read them is to look afresh at questions that are, unfortunately, regarded as settled in many quarters.

Appendix:
Analogies with Health
Economics

The purpose of this Appendix is to draw attention to some of the similarities, but also to some of the differences, between the economics of education and the economics of health. What follows is more in the nature of a series of notes than a systematic discussion of the analogies between the two branches of 'the economics of human resources'.

Scope of the Subject

The economics of education is traditionally confined to formal education: despite a general awareness of the significance of informal education, empirical analysis is far richer in the area of formal schooling. Similar difficulties about the scope of the subject arise in health economics: investment in health extends far beyond curative and preventive health services to expenditure on raising environmental standards of nutrition, sanitation, housing and clothing. Just as informal education probably contributes more to economic growth in underdeveloped countries than all school enrolments put together, so public health programmes probably have a greater effect on living standards in poor countries than personal medical care and hospital services. Nevertheless, health economics as such is largely about health services furnished by doctors and hospitals. Thus, at the present time at any rate, both subjects tend to slight much of what is relevant to their disciplines. The reasons for the respective emphases are, no doubt, obvious.

Investment and Consumption

Health expenditures are just as much 'investment in people' as educational expenditures and, moreover, they are frequently joint investments made in the same person. This suggests that there may well be difficulties in separating returns on investment in health from returns on investment in education: the lengthening of an individual's life expectancy through improved health raises the returns on investment in his education and, conversely, an improvement in his productivity through education raises the returns on investment in his health. This would not matter if capital markets were perfectly competitive, or if public policy were omniscient, such that both types of investments were always carried to the point where marginal rates of return are equalized; there is an obvious analogy here between investment in schooling and investment in labour training, on the one hand, and investment in education and health, on the other. But in the real world characterized by uncertainty, imperfect information and poorly organized capital markets, there is great danger that returns on investment in health will be attributed to investment in education and vice versa, particularly as use of health services is everywhere highly correlated with educational attainment.

Health is similar to education in that it is partly carried out for investment and partly for consumption motives. As with education, however, this means, not that health expenditures are either investment or consumption, but rather that they are both. Health expenditures can be regarded from either point of view, depending on the nature of the problem that is being investigated: if the question is one assessing the contribution of health services to economic growth, the relevant framework is the investment view; if the question is instead that of measuring the private demand for health, the relevant framework is either the consumption or the investment view, the question being which view explains more. The identical argument holds with respect to transport and indeed all consumer durables.

Measuring the Returns

In one sense, the returns from health programmes are easier to measure than the returns from educational programmes: health services not only improve the *quality* of labour in employment – a perfect analogy to the effects of education – but also increase the *quantity* of labour available for work, either by reducing the amount of working time lost or by reducing the incidence of death among workers. The latter effect of health services on the size of the labour force provides a direct measure of the returns from health programmes – the present value of the future earnings of additional man hours – not available in the case of education. But this advantage is offset by the greater difficulties of assessing the indirect labour-augmenting effects of health services. In the case of education, the inputs are clearly defined as number of years of schooling of standard length, the problems of measurement being largely confined to the benefit side. In the case of health, however, not only are the benefits in the sense of improved labour quality difficult to measure, but the inputs into health can only be inadequately represented by such proxies as number of hospital beds or numbers of physicians per 1000 of population in the case of formal medical care, and hardly at all in the case of public health programmes.

Furthermore, the familiar problems of disentangling the effects of education from the influence of other factors on labour quality, such as better capital, superior organization, favourable home background etc., are even more formidable in the field of health economics, where better nutrition, better working conditions, higher incomes and better medical care are all highly correlated. In the case of education, age–specific earnings differentials associated with various amounts of education provide a basis for assessing the benefits of education. In health economics, however, no evidence on differences in earnings associated with different personal states of health is available in any country. There is some American and British data on sickness rates and associated days-lost-from-work by size of family income – revealing a negative relationship between the two – but it is not clear which is cause and which is effect. The central difficulty in measuring the effects of health services is a function of the distinction between preventive and curative medicine: it is much easier to measure the economic benefits of curative than of preventive treatment. This explains why most of the work in America on the benefits of health services has dealt with the cure of specific diseases, such as cancer, polio and tuberculosis, leaving aside the much larger area of general preventive medicine.

For health services directed at specific diseases, it is frequently possible to estimate the man hours added by reductions in (a) 'mortality', that is, the absolute loss of man hours, (b) 'disability', that is, the relative loss of man hours and (c) 'debility', that is, the loss of productive capacity per man hour, although the last two *morbidity factors* are always more difficult to estimate than the effects of changing *mortality rates*. These man hours are then valued by introducing age–

specific hourly earnings (occasionally real output per man hour has been used instead), yielding a money estimate of the resources gained from curing or preventing a particular disease. Although no rate-of-return calculations are available for investment in treatment of specific diseases, the present values at various discount rates of the output added by improved life expectancy – ignoring the morbidity aspects of the problem – via the eradication of particular diseases have been calculated (see Mushkin, 1962, pp. 143, 149). Measures of the capital value of particular cohorts of human beings, given the costs of rearing children and prevailing life expectancies, go back to the nineteenth century and even the eighteenth century (Mushkin, 1962, pp. 149–53). Once again, however, these studies have ignored morbidity rates and concentrated on mortality. Attempts to apply cost–benefit analysis to occupational health programmes and to vocational rehabilitation services have not so far yielded reliable numbers.

Contribution of Health Expenditures to Economic Growth

Denison provides a well-known example of the effort to measure the contributions of improved health to the growth rate of the United States, allowing both for reduced mortality and reduced morbidity. He shows that a further reduction of the death rate by 10 per cent would increase the growth rate in the 1960s and 1970s by 0·02 per cent, while a further reduction of work days lost through injury and illness by a quarter (or 1·1 per cent of work time now lost) would raise the growth rate in the next two decades by 0·05 per cent. These numbers are, of course, a function of his basic assumption that the present share of labour in national income measures both the present and the future contributions of labour to total output.

Mushkin (1962, pp. 144–8) has carried the Denison estimates backwards to 1900, concluding that the decline in the death rate in the United States between 1900 and 1960 contributed 10 per cent to the long-term 3 per cent growth rate of the economy. This is, incidentally, much less than Denison's estimate of the effect of improvement in the education embodied in the labour force over the same historical period (32 to 38 per cent).

An interesting attempt to apply cost–benefit analysis of the more casual type to the British National Health Service suggests that, when benefits are defined as reduced absenteeism from work and increased output from increased longevity, the rate of return on health expenditures, including expenditures on medical research, is probably negative (Jewkes and Jewkes, 1963). In short, expenditure on medical care in Britain cannot be regarded as making any contribution to economic growth.

Man-Power Forecasting

The man-power requirements approach has as firm a grip on health economics as on the economics of education. The obvious analogy to forecasts of the 'need' for doctors and dentists is forecasts of the 'need' for teachers, with the doctor–patient ratio playing the same role as the pupil–teacher ratio in defining a standard-of-service coefficient, or a staffing norm, for translating a relevant population projection into a forecast of personnel requirements. As Klarman shows (1965, pp. 88–101, 150–63), almost as little is known about the productivity of physicians and the determinants of particular standards of medical service as about the effectiveness of teachers and the consequences of various class sizes. It is interesting to note, however, that the ratio of physicians per 100,000 population in the United States has fluctuated around 133 since 1930, and has actually fallen from 150 in 1900; over this period of time, both absolute and relative expenditures on health and medical care have increased substantially. The answer lies only partly in the improved quality of American doctors and much more in the dramatic rise of nurses per doctors and, indeed, all paramedical personnel per qualified physician over the last thirty years. Clearly, there has been a great deal of substitution between labour with various medical qualifications in the United States.

Virtually every medical man-power forecast that has ever been made has gone wrong, not because of the difficulties of predicting progress in medical knowledge, but because of (a) incorrect population projections, (b) incorrect forecasts of the net migration of medical personnel and (c) incorrect predictions of the doctor–patient ratio (Fein, 1967, pp. 6–13; W. Lee Hansen, 1965a, pp. 75–9; and a superb survey by Klarman, 1969). In Britain, the 1957 Willink Committee went wildly wrong in only three years largely because of the first two factors (Seale, 1965). The 1966 forecasts of the National Institute for Economic and Social Research, on the other hand, are very likely to go wrong because of a failure to achieve the targeted doctor–patient ratio (Peacock and Shannon, 1968a). This ratio which stood at 1:2000 in

1962, is predicted to fall to 1:1775 by 1980, and the forecast of a 'shortage' in Britain of about 9000 doctors by 1980 is simply a by-product of the assertion that the ratio *should* fall by 11 per cent over the years 1962–80: more doctors per patient are said to mean healthier patients, just as more teachers per pupil are said to mean better-educated children. Nothing is said about the earnings of doctors influencing their supply, the effects of new drugs and new capital equipment, the improved division of medical labour, new ways of organizing general practice, and so forth. In short, what we have here is the man-power requirements approach *par excellence*.

Welfare Economics

Mental illness, traffic accidents and the treatment of contagious diseases have long served as classic examples of externalities. Similarly, fluoridation of water supplies and mosquito control by spraying malarial swamps furnish favourite examples of 'public goods' that cannot be priced by a market process. Clearly, consumer preferences are frequently an unreliable guide to optimum use of health resources. Indeed, it is much easier to attack allocation by a market mechanism in the field of health than in the field of education: not only is con-sumer ignorance greater in health than in education but illness impairs the ability to pay while being educated does not, at least if education is confined to the young and if parents accept responsibility for financing them. Thus, cost–benefit analysis is *the* technique for evaluating health programmes and the strengths and weaknesses of this approach are better demonstrated in health economics than in the economics of education (for a quick review of accomplishments to date, see Klarman, 1965, pp. 162–73; Mushkin, 1962, pp. 154–7).

Curiously enough, however, at least one British economist has denied the view that health is in principle different from any other service rendered to consumers (Lees, 1961, pp. 19–21). He agrees that the clearing of central sources of infection, like a polluted water supply or a malarial swamp, or the treatment of communicable diseases like polio and whooping cough, constitute clear examples of 'public goods'. But he notes that the bulk of health expenditures in an advanced economy is concerned with such illnesses as cancer and coronary diseases where the benefits of treatment accrue almost wholly to the individual patients. Furthermore, he sees no reason to believe that consumers are less well-informed about medical care than about cars, television sets and washing machines. In his view, it is education, and particularly primary education, rather than health that confers externalities and partakes of a significant degree of 'publicness' (Lees, 1961, pp. 18–9).

Lees's reasoning has been vigorously criticized by Titmuss (1968) on the basis of traditional welfare economics and on other grounds. The interesting point, however, is that Lees concedes that 'equality of consumption' of medical care seems to have been a chief motive in nationalizing health services in this country, in which case traditional welfare economics is neither here nor there: the issue is the value judgement that inequality of consumption of medical care is worse than the restriction on consumers' choices implied by a 'free' tax-financed health service. Equality of consumption of medical care or, better put, medical care in strict accordance with need, can be secured only by divorcing the distribution of medical care from the distribution of income. Given this objective, it may be argued that direct cash payments to the poor, or subsidized private medical insurance, a means-tested State insurance system (essentially, a system of health vouchers), all succeed in securing this objective, as well as that of giving wider scope to consumer preferences. Thus, ultimately, the argument turns into a trade-off ratio between two objectives: clearly Lees attaches little weight to the objective of equity and a heavy weight to the objective of free choice: Titmuss's preference function reverses these weights. All this has virtually nothing to do with traditional welfare economics, relying as it does on the concepts of externalities and public goods.

A striking omission in Lees's discussion of the economic characteristics of health is that of the uncertain and uneven incidence of illness (see Arrow, 1965; Lees, 1965). It is true, of course, that this can be insured against and no doubt Lees draws comfort from the fact that three-quarters of the population in the United States carry some form of voluntary health insurance. Nevertheless, despite government subsidies to voluntary insurance, the participation rate in America is 75 and not 100 per cent, and the remaining 25 per cent are likely to be the poorest and the least informed members of the population. In other words, the importance of the factor of uncertainty as a cause of suboptimal spending on health emerges only in conjunction with ignorance, externalities of contagious diseases and poverty, leading to a high discount rate in comparing the certainty of premiums paid in the present with the uncertainty of expensive treatment in the future. In any case, the Lees–Titmuss discussion is an instructive example of the failure of most participants in debates on the social services to clarify their objectives. Whether we like it or not, the British National Health Service effectively replaced individual choice in the distribution of health services by collective choice. Thus, arguments about 'market failure' in justifying either government ownership or government finance are totally irrelevant in Britain, unless of course the thesis is that they ought to be made relevant by returning health to the market mechanism.

It would seem that there is now a consensus among all segments of British society and among all shades of political opinion that health should be distributed in accordance with need rather than ability-to-pay, in other words, 'communism in health'. But the provision of health at zero or nominal prices tends to generate a much larger aggregate demand for health services than provision at cost-covering prices (not an infinite demand, because zero prices do not compensate the individual for the opportunity costs of illness). At the same time, the revenues on which the supply of public health depends tend to rise less than the willingness of individuals to spend on their medical care because of 'the free rider' problem, that is, the knowledge that the supply is forthcoming whether or not one pays more taxes (Buchanan, 1965). In consequence, there arises an acutely felt 'shortage' of medical provision. This suggests the need to reduce the public burden of finance by selective charges within the National Health Services. The introduction of user charges would have the further advantage of generating information about consumer preferences, without which response to need becomes arbitrary. But the more charges there are, the greater is the tendency to revert to ability-to-pay as the principle of distribution. What we have is a typical Scylla-and-Charybdis problem: either maximum consumers' satisfaction and, hence, reliance on purchasing power, or maximum voters' satisfaction, and, hence, reliance on administrative decisions by so-called experts. Lees and Titmuss write as if we must choose either Scylla or Charybdis. But perhaps we can have both. Putting aside the Great Debate between market pricing and free State provision, there is still much to argue over in terms of the effects of specific charges and concrete pricing arrangements, not to mention the weights attached to different and frequently conflicting goals.

True or False?
Dogmas, Shibboleths and
Paradoxes for Discussion

1. To talk about human capital in a society that does not allow the purchase and sale of human beings is either wrong, misleading or immoral.
2. Education is too precious a thing to be compared in crass financial terms with ordinary goods and services.
3. It is easier to measure physical capital than to measure human capital.
4. Rate-of-return calculations of educational investment are useless to policy makers because they merely tell us what has happened in the past.
5. If the social rate of return on investment in medical education exceeds that on investment in teacher training, we should invest more in medical education.
6. State subsidies to education always lead to overinvestment in education.
7. The education of women is almost certainly an unprofitable investment for society as a whole.
8. Everyone enjoys learning; therefore, education is demanded as a consumer good.
9. The dispersion in private rates of return to different occupations is proof of differences in the non-pecuniary advantages attached to various lines of work.
10. Education costs much more than we think.
11. Earnings forgone by students should not be counted in the costs of education; otherwise, the costs will be lower in a depression than in a boom.
12. No one should have to pay for his own education.
13. The externalities of education are so great, it is misleading to worry about the magnitude of the direct benefits.
14. If all income were perfectly equally distributed, education would have no economic value.
15. Students in higher education should be paid a 'living wage'.
16. Confucius said: 'No nation goes bankrupt educating its people'.
17. The reason that the State owns and operates schools in most countries is that parents do not want to be responsible for making decisions about their children's education.
18. Education must be provided by the State because it represents the formation of 'social overhead capital'.

19. It is not desirable that students should be educated in accordance with the wishes of their parents; education involves technical issues that should be judged by experts, which parents are not.

20. Parents who do not keep their children at school until sixteen or seventeen should be forced to do so by the raising of the school-leaving age.

21. We should have statutory requirements for training in industry in the same way that we have a statutory leaving age in formal education.

22. The expansion of higher education will lower the future income of graduates.

23. The best way to deal with educated unemployment in poor countries is to expand education even faster.

24. Since all decisions to expand education have man-power implications, we must make forecasts of the demand for man power, whatever the difficulties of forecasting.

25. Man-power planning is alien to a free society and simply one more example of 'creeping socialism'.

26. So long as we let students choose their own fields of study, man-power planning is impossible.

27. Automation tends to raise the demand for highly educated man power.

28. Business firms now hire more and more educated people, not because they need them but because more of them are available as a result of educational expansion.

29. The more rapid the pace of technical change, the greater the role of on-the-job training in human capital formation.

30. Monopsony encourages business firms to invest in labour training.

31. An engineer is someone who holds an engineering degree.

32. There is no shortage of teachers, only an unwillingness to pay for them.

33. Teachers should be paid on uniform scales throughout the country; to reward teachers according to individual merit or the relative scarcity of their particular skills will destroy the morale of the teaching force.

34. Educational 'vouchers' represent ear-marked currency; in a free society, it would be preferable to supply parents with ordinary currency, leaving them free to decide how they want to spend it.

35. The economist who pronounces on the true aims of education exceeds his proper function.

Glossary of British Educational Terms

Tripartite Secondary Education – division of secondary education into grammar, technical and secondary modern schools for which children are selected at the age of eleven by the 'eleven-plus' examination which is now an amalgam of reports from primary-school head teachers, intelligence tests, tests in English and arithmetic, and interviews.

Public School – an independent secondary school outside the state system, controlled by a governing body created by some statute, scheme or trust deed and belonging to the Headmasters' Conference.

Fifth Form – the age-group fifteen to sixteen and the first year of voluntary education.

Sixth Form – upper part of a grammar, technical or comprehensive school usually entered after taking GCE O-levels.

Technical College – a college, maintained by Local Education Authorities, offering mainly vocational courses for industrial occupations on either a part-time or full-time basis. Some of these colleges offer degree-level courses.

Polytechnic – a technical college with a proportion of advanced work. Current policy is to designate about thirty such colleges for special development.

RSA (Royal Society of Arts) – the Society runs examinations, mainly in commercial and technical subjects, taken by pupils at secondary modern schools and, more commonly, by students at technical colleges.

CGL (City and Guilds of London Institute) – school leavers aged fifteen to sixteen follow three-year part-time or evening courses, leading to the Intermediate Crafts Certificate. Two years of further study leads to the Final Crafts Certificate. If the school leavers have passed certain O-levels, or if they complete a one- to two-year part-time general course, they may proceed to the Final Technicians Certificate (usually a four-year course) and then to the Full Technological Certificate (two more years).

GCE O- and A-levels – subject examinations assessed by certain examination boards and the nearest British equivalent to an American high school diploma. Taken at 'ordinary' level and at 'advanced' level, and usually attempted at age sixteen and seventeen or eighteen respectively. Passes in two or three A-level subjects are required for admission to universities.

ONC (Ordinary National Certificate) – a technical qualification awarded after a two- to three-year part-time or evening study and concurrent employment at, say, the age of nineteen. Roughly equivalent to one A-level.

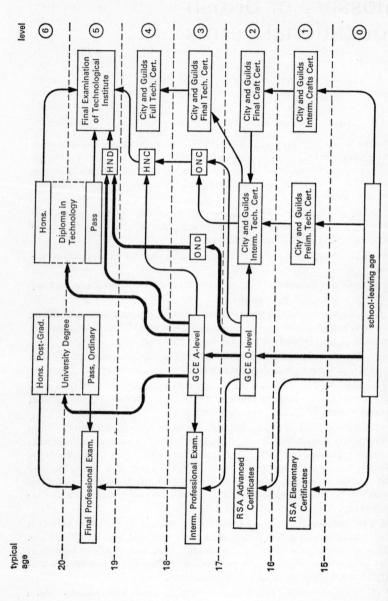

Glossary chart: types and levels of British educational qualifications. *Note*: arrows show alternative routes through the system. Thick arrows indicate full time study; fine arrows indicate part-time study

OND (*Ordinary National Diploma*) – broadly similar to ONC but covering a wider range of subjects and obtained by full-time study, usually alternating with periods of employment.

HNC (*Higher National Certificate*) – awarded to students with A-levels or an ONC after a further two-year part-time or evening course.

HND (*Higher National Diploma*) – broadly similar to HNC but obtained by full-time study, usually alternating with periods of employment. Roughly equivalent to a Pass Degree.

University Degrees – the more advanced undergraduate courses lead to an 'Honours Degree' which is usually subdivided into three to four classes of merit. Other degree courses are termed 'Ordinary' or 'Pass'. The typical degree course lasts three years and is entered at age eighteen.

Dip. Tech. (*Diploma in Technology*) – four- to five-year 'sandwich course' (full-time study alternating with periods of employment), the equivalent of a university honours degree; it is now abolished.

Professional Examinations – membership in non-scientific professional institutions (such as the Institute of Chartered Accountants) follows a number of years' employment in a particular profession combined with evening study by correspondence course for the examination of the chosen professional institution. There are no alternative full-time formal courses of study leading to these professional qualifications.

Youth Employment Service – the service usually locally organized by the local Education Authority but directed and controlled (and in some areas locally organized) by the Department of Employment and Productivity, dealing with the employment and careers of young people from fifteen to eighteen.

University Grants Committee (*UGC*) – a body which allocates and distributes grants of money from the Department of Education and Science to individual universities.

Suggestions for Further Reading

The title of this book begs no questions: it *is* an introduction to the subject. Advanced topics, such as the role of human capital formation in life-cycle theories of saving, in theories of income distribution, in the pure theory of international trade, and in aggregate growth models are ignored; in these areas the time for discerning the main lines of advance has not yet come. But students can get an inkling of some of these topics from three volumes of readings which together contain 100 outstanding articles in the economics of education: *Economics of Education*, vols. 1 and 2, edited by M. Blaug (Penguin, 1968 and 1969), and *Readings in the Economics of Education*, edited by M.J. Bowman *et al.* (UNESCO, 1968). Further references, cross-classified by countries and tendentiously annotated, will be found in *Economics of Education: A Selected Annotated Bibliography*, edited by M. Blaug (Pergamon, 2nd edn, 1970).

Other textbooks in the field, which should be consulted to sharpen one's critical faculties, are:

C. Benson, *The Economics of Public Education*, Houghton Mifflin, 2nd edn, 1968.
H. Correa, *The Economics of Human Resources*, North Holland Publishing Co., 1963.
Lê Thành Khôi, *L'industrie de l'enseignement*, Les éditions de minuit, 1967.
T. W. Schultz, *The Economic Value of Education*, Columbia University Press, 1963.
J. Vaizey, *The Economics of Education*, Faber, 1962.

References

Any mention of page references in the main text of this volume refers to the latest edition or reprint given in this reference list.

Abramovitz, M. (1962), 'Economic growth in the United States', *Amer. econ. Rev.*, September.

Adelman, I. (1966), 'A linear programming model of educational planning: a case study of Argentina', in I. Adelman and E. Thorbecke (eds.), *The Theory and Design of Economic Development*, Johns Hopkins Press.

Adelman, I., and **Morris, C. T.** (1967), *Society, Politics and Economic Development*, Johns Hopkins Press.

Adelman, I., and **Morris, C. T.** (1968), 'An econometric model of socio-economic and political changes in underdeveloped countries', *Amer. econ. Rev.*, December.

Alchian, A. A., and **Allen, W. R.** (1967), *University Economics*, Wadsworth Publishing Co., 2nd edn.

Almond, G. A., and **Coleman, J. A.** (1960), *The Politics of the Developing Areas*, Princeton University Press.

Anderson Report (1960) *Grants to Students*, Reports of the Committee Appointed by the Minister of Education and the Secretary of State for Scotland, in June 1958, H.M.S.O., Cmnd. 1051.

Anderson, C. A. (1965a), 'Literacy and schooling on the development threshold: some historical cases', in C. A. Anderson and M. J. Bowman (eds.), *Education and Economic Development*, Aldine.

Anderson, C. A. (1965b), 'Patterns and variability in the distribution and diffusion of schooling', in C. A. Anderson and M. J. Bowman (eds.), *Education and Economic Development*, Aldine.

Anderson, C. A. (1967a), 'Sociological factors in the demand for education', in *Social Objectives in Educational Planning*, OECD, Paris.

Anderson, C. A. (1967b), *The Social Context of Educational Planning*, Fundamentals of Educational Planning no. 5, International Institute for Educational Planning, UNESCO, Paris.

Anderson, C. A., and **Bowman, M. J.** (1967), 'Theoretical considerations in educational planning', in G. Z. Bereday, J. A. Lauwerys and M. Blaug (eds.), *World Yearbook of Education 1967. Educational Planning*, Evans. (Reprinted in M. Blaug (ed.), *Economics of Education 1*, Penguin, 1968.)

Argentina (1967), *Education, Human Resources and Development in Argentina*, OECD, Paris.

Armitage, P., and **Smith, C.** (1967), 'The development of computable models of the British educational system', in *Mathematical Models of Educational Planning*, OECD, Paris. (Reprinted in M. Blaug (ed.), *Economics of Education 2*, Penguin, 1969.)

Armitage, P., Smith, C., and **Alper, P.** (1969), *Decision Models for Educational Planning*, Allen Lane The Penguin Press.

Arrow, K. J. (1963), 'Uncertainty and the welfare economics of medical care', *Amer. econ. Rev.*, December; also 'Uncertainty and the welfare economics of medical care: reply', *Amer. econ. Rev.*, March, 1965.

Arrow, K. J., and **Capron, W. M.** (1959), 'Dynamic shortages and price rises: the engineering–scientist case', *Quart. J. Econ.*, May. (Reprinted in M. Blaug (ed.), *Economics of Education 1*, Penguin, 1968.)

Ashby Report (1960), *Investment in Education. The Report of the Commission on Post-School Certificate and Higher Education in Nigeria, under the Chairmanship of Sir Eric Ashby*, Federal Ministry of Education, Lagos.

Ashenfelter, O., and **Mooney, J. D.** (1968), 'Graduate education, ability, and earnings', *Rev. Econ. Stat.*, February.

Ashenfelter, O., and **Mooney, J. D.** (1969), 'Some evidence on the private returns to graduate education', *South. econ. J.*, January.

Austria (1968), *Educational Policy and Planning*, OECD, Paris.

Baldwin, G. B. (1965), 'Iran's experience with manpower planning: concepts, techniques and lessons', in F. Harbison and C. A. Myers (eds.), *Manpower and Education. Country Studies in Economic Development*, McGraw-Hill.

Baldwin, R. E. (1966), *Economic Development and Export Growth: A Study of Northern Rhodesia, 1920–1960*, University of California Press.

Balogh, T. (1962), 'Misconceived educational programmes in Africa', *Univ. Quart.*, June.

Balogh, T. (1967), 'The economics of educational planning: sense and nonsense', in K. Martin and J. Knapp (eds.), *The Teaching of Development Economics*, Cass.

Balogh, T., and **Streeten, P. P.** (1963), 'The coefficient of ignorance', *Bull. Oxf. Univ. Inst. Econ. Stat.*, May. (Reprinted in M. Blaug (ed.), *Economics of Education 1*, Penguin, 1968.)

Baumol, W. J. (1965), *Welfare Economics and the Theory of the State*, Harvard University Press.

Baumol, W. J. (1967), 'Macroeconomics of unbalanced growth', *Amer. econ. Rev.*, June; also 'Comment', *Amer. econ. Rev.*, September, 1968.

Becker, G. S. (1964), *Human Capital. A Theoretical and Empirical Analysis, With Special Reference to Education*, Princeton University Press. (Pages 7–29 reprinted in M. Blaug (ed.), *Economics of Education*, Penguin, 1968.)

Beckerman, W. (1965), 'Britain's comparative growth record', in W. Beckerman *et al.* (eds.), *The British Economy in 1975*, Cambridge University Press.

Bennett, W. S., Jr (1967), 'Educational change and economic development', *Sociol. Educ.*, spring.

Benson, C.S. (1968), *The Economics of Public Education*, Houghton Mifflin, 2nd edn.

Berg, E. (1965), 'Education and manpower in Senegal, Guinea and the Ivory Coast', in F. Harbison and C.A. Myers (eds.), *Manpower and Education. Country Studies in Economic Development*, McGraw-Hill.

Bergson, A. (1968), *Planning and Productivity under Soviet Socialism*, Columbia University Press.

Bernstein, B. (1958), 'Social class and linguistic development: a theory of social learning', *Brit. J. Sociol.*, June. (Reprinted in A.H. Halsey, J. Floud and C.A. Anderson (eds.), *Education, Economy, and Society. A Reader in the Sociology of Education*, Free Press of Glencoe, 1961.)

Bertelsen, P. (1965), 'Problems of priorities in adult education', in C.G. Witstand (ed.), *Development and Adult Education in Africa*, Scandinavian Institute of African Studies, Uppsala.

Bertram, G.W. (1966), *The Contribution of Education to Economic Growth*, Staff Study no. 12, Economic Council of Canada, Ottawa.

Bhagwati, J. (1966), *The Economics of Underdeveloped Countries*, Weidenfeld & Nicolson.

Blandy, R. (1967), 'Marshall on human capital: a note', *J. polit. Econ.*, December.

Blank, D.M., and **Stigler, G.J.** (1957), *Demand and Supply of Scientific Personnel*, National Bureau of Economic Research.

Blaug, M. (1967), 'The private and the social returns on investment in education: some results for Great Britain', *J. hum. Resources*, summer.

Blaug, M. (1968a), *Economic Theory in Retrospect*, Richard D. Irwin and Heinemann Educational.

Blaug, M. (1968b), 'The productivity of universities', in M. Blaug (ed.), *Economics of Education 2*, Penguin, 1969.

Blaug, M., Layard, R., and **Woodhall, M.** (1969), *Causes of Graduate Unemployment in India*, Allen Lane The Penguin Press.

Blaug, M., Peston, M.H., and **Ziderman, A.** (1967), *The Utilization of Educated Manpower in Industry*, Oliver & Boyd.

Blot, D., and **Debeauvais, M.** (1966), 'Educational expenditure in developing areas: some statistical aspects', in *Financing of Education for Economic Growth*, OECD, Paris.

Bombach, G. (1964), 'Comments on the paper by Messrs Tinbergen and Bos', in J. Vaizey (ed.), *The Residual Factor and Economic Growth*, OECD, Paris.

Bombach, G. (1965), 'Manpower forecasting and educational policy', *Soc. Educ.*, fall.

Bonner, J., and **Lees, D.S.** (1963), 'Consumption and investment', *J. polit. Econ.*, February.

Bowen, W.G. (1963), 'Assessing the economic contribution of education: an appraisal of alternative approaches', in *Higher Education. Report of the Committee under the Chairmanship of Lord Robbins, 1961–63*, Cmnd. 2154, H.M.S.O., 1963, App. 4. (Reprinted in M. Blaug (ed.), *Economics of Education 1*, Penguin, 1968.)

Bowen, W.G. (1964), 'University finance in Britain and the United States: implications of financing arrangements for educational issues', in *Economic*

Aspects of Education. Three Essays, Princeton University Press.

Bowen, W. G. (1968), *The Economics of the Major Private Universities*, Carnegie Commission on Higher Education, Berkeley, California.

Bowles, S. (1967), 'The efficient allocation of resources in education', *Quart. J. Econ.*, May. (Reprinted in M. Blaug (ed.), *Economics of Education 2*, Penguin, 1969.)

Bowles, S. (1969), *Planning Educational Systems for Economic Growth*, Harvard University Press.

Bowles, S. (1970), 'Towards an educational production function', in W. Lee Hansen (ed.), *Education and Income*, Conference on Research on Income and Wealth, Princeton University Press, forthcoming, 1970.

Bowman, M. J. (1962), 'The social returns to education', *Intern. soc. Sci. J.*, vol. 14, no. 4.

Bowman, M. J. (1964), 'Schultz, Denison and the contribution of "eds" to national income growth', *J. polit. Econ.*, October.

Bowman, M. J. (1966a), 'Review of F. Harbison and C. A. Myers, *Education, Manpower and Economic Growth*', *J. polit. Econ.*, October. (Reprinted in M. Blaug (ed.), *Economics of Education 2*, Penguin, 1969.)

Bowman, M. J. (1966b), 'The costing of human resource development', in E. A. G. Robinson and J. E. Vaizey (eds.), *The Economics of Education*, Macmillan.

Bowman, M. J., and **Anderson, C. A.** (1963), 'Concerning the role of education in development', in C. Geertz (ed.), *Old Societies and New States*, Free Press of Glencoe. (Reprinted in M. J. Bowman et al. (eds.), *Readings in the Economics of Education*, UNESCO, Paris, 1968.)

Brazer, H. E., and **David, M.** (1962), 'Social and economic determinants of the demand for education', in S. J. Mushkin (ed.), *Economics of Higher Education*, Washington, Government Printing Office.

British General Register Office (1960), *Classification of Occupations*.

Brown, A., Leicester, C., and **Pyatt, G.** (1964), 'Output, manpower and industrial skills in the United Kingdom', in J. Vaizey (ed.), *The Residual Factor and Economic Growth*, OECD, Paris.

Buchanan, J. M. (1965), *The Inconsistencies of the National Health Service*, Institute of Economic Affairs.

Buchanan, J. M., and **Tullock, G.** (1962), *Calculus of Consent: Logical Foundations of Constitutional Democracy*, University of Michigan Press.

Bumas, L. O. (1968), 'The economics of engineering and scientific manpower: a comment', *J. hum. Resources*, spring.

Bureau of Labor Statistics, U.S. Department of Labor (1961), *The Long-Range Demand for Scientific and Technical Personnel*, National Science Foundation, Washington.

Bureau of Labor Statistics, U.S. Department of Labor (1963) *Scientists, Engineers, and Technicians in the 1960s. Requirements and Supply*, National Science Foundation, Washington.

Burgess, T., Layard, R., and **Pant, P.** (1968), *Manpower and Educational Development in India 1961–1986*, Oliver & Boyd.

Burkhead, J., Fox, T.G., and Holland, J.W. (1967), *Input and Output in Large-City High Schools*, Syracuse University Press.
Burt, C. (1955), 'The evidence for the concept of intelligence', *Brit. J. educ. Psychol.*, vol. 25. (Reprinted in S.Wiseman (ed.), *Intelligence and Ability*, Penguin, 1967.)
Butter, I.H. (1966), *Economics of Graduate Education: An Exploratory Study*, U.S. Office of Education, Project no. 2852, University of Michigan.

Cain, G.G.Hansen, W.Lee, and Weisbrod, B.A. (1967), 'Occupational classification: an economic approach', *Month. lab. Rev.*, February.
Callaway, A. (1963), 'Unemployment among African school leavers', *J. mod. Afr. Stud.*, vol. 1, no. 3.
Callaway, A. (1965), 'Adult education and problems of youth unemployment', in C.G.Widstrand (ed.), *Development and Adult Education in Africa*, Scandinavian Institute of African Studies, Uppsala.
Callaway, A. (1967), 'Unemployment among school-leavers in an African city', in G.Z.Bereday, J.A.Lauwerys and M.Blaug (eds.), *World Yearbook of Education 1967. Educational Planning*, Evans.
Campbell, R., and Siegel, B.N. (1967), 'The demand for higher education in the United States, 1919–1964', *Amer. econ. Rev.*, June.
Carnoy, M. (1967a), 'Earnings and schooling in Mexico', *Econ. Devel. cult. Change*, July.
Carnoy, M. (1967b), 'Rates of return to schooling in Latin America', *J. hum. Resources*, summer.
Carroll, A.B., and Ihnen, L.A. (1967), 'Costs and returns for two years of post-secondary technical schooling: a pilot study', *J. polit. Econ.*, December.
Carter, C.F. (1965), 'Can we get higher education cheaper?', *Manch. stat. Soc.*, December. (Reprinted in M. Blaug (ed.), *Economics of Education 2*, Penguin, 1969.)
Cash, W.C. (1965), 'A critique of manpower planning and educational change in Africa', *Econ. Devel. cult. Change*, October. (Reprinted in M.Blaug (ed.), *Economics of Education 2*, Penguin, 1969.)
Cipolla, C.M. (1969), *Literacy and Development in the West*, Penguin
Clark, H.F. (1963), *Cost and Quality in Public Education*, Syracuse University Press.
Clignet, R., and Foster, P.J. (1966), *The Fortunate Few. A Study of Secondary Schools and Students in the Ivory Coast*, Northwestern University Press.
Cole, C.C., Jr (1956), *Encouraging Scientific Talent*, College Entrance Examination Board, Princeton, New Jersey.
Collard, D. (1968), *The New Right: A Critique*, Fabian Tract 387, Fabian Society.
Conrad, A.H., and Myer, J.R. (1964), *The Economics of Slavery*, Aldine.
Correa, H. (1963), *The Economics of Human Resources*, North Holland Publishing Co.
Correa, H., and Tinbergen, J. (1962), 'Quantitative adaptation of education to accelerated growth', *Kyklos*, vol. 15, no. 4.
Craig, C. (1963), *The Employment of Cambridge Graduates*, Cambridge University Press.

Crowther Report (1959), *15 to 18. A Report of the Central Advisory Council for Education under the Chairmanship of G. Crowther*, H.M.S.O.

Curle, A. (1964a), 'Education, politics and development', *Comp. educ. Rev.*, February.

Curle, A. (1964b), *World Campaign for Universal Literacy: Comment and Proposal*, Center for Studies in Education and Development, Harvard University.

Dainton Report (1968), *Enquiry into the Flow of Candidates in Science and Technology into Higher Education. Report of the Committee under the Chairmanship of F. S. Dainton*, H.M.S.O., Cmnd. 3541.

Danière, A. (1964), *Higher Education in the American Economy*, Random House.

Danière, A. (1965), 'Planning education for economic productivity', in S. E. Harris (ed.), *Challenge and Change in American Education*, McCutchan Publishing Corporation, Berkeley, California.

Davies, B., and **Williamson, V.** (1968), 'School meals – short fall and poverty', *Soc. econ. Admin.*, January.

Debeauvais, M. (1963), 'Methods of forecasting long-term manpower needs', in *Planning Education for Economic and Social Development*, OECD, Paris.

Denison, E. F. (1962), *The Sources of Economic Growth in the United States and the Alternatives Before Us*, Committee for Economic Development, New York.

Denison, E. F. (1964), 'Proportion of income differentials among education groups due to additional education: the evidence of the Wolfle–Smith survey', in J. Vaizey (ed.), *The Residual Factor and Economic Growth*, OECD, Paris.

Denison, E. F. (1967), *Why Growth Rates Differ. Postwar Experience in Nine Western Countries*, Brookings Institution.

Denison, E. F. (1969), 'The contribution of education to the quality of labor: comment', *Amer. econ. Rev.*, December.

DeWitt, N. (1961), *Education and Professional Employment in the U.S.S.R.*, U.S. Government Printing Office.

DeWitt, N. (1967), 'Educational and manpower planning in the Soviet Union', in G. Z. Bereday, J. A. Lauwerys and M. Blaug (eds.), *World Yearbook of Education 1967. Educational Planning*, Evans.

De Wolff, P. (1963), 'Employment forecasting techniques in the Netherlands', *Employment Forecasting*, OECD, Paris.

De Wolff, P., and **Ruiter, R.** (1968), 'De Economie van het Onderwijs', in L. Emmerij *et al.* (eds.), *De Economie van het Onderwijs*, Martinus Nijhoff, The Hague.

Doob, L. W. (1961), *Communication in Africa: A Search for Boundaries*, Yale University Press.

Döös, S.-O. (1963), 'Long-term employment forecasting: some problems with special reference to current organisation and methods in Sweden', *Employment Forecasting*, OECD, Paris.

Douglas, J. W. B. (1964), *The Home and the School. A Study of Ability and Attainment in the Primary School*, MacGibbon & Kee.

Douglas, J.W.B., Ross, J.M., and Simpson, H.R. (1968) *All Our Future. A Longitudinal Study of Secondary Education*, Peter Davies.

Dumont, R. (1964), 'Agricultural development and education', *Tiers Monde*, January. (Reprinted in M.J.Bowman *et al.* (eds.), *Readings in the Economics of Education*, UNESCO, Paris, 1968).

Dumont, R. (1966), *False Start in Africa*, André Deutsch.

Dumont, R. (1968), 'African agriculture and its educational requirements', in *Manpower Aspects of Educational Planning*, International Institute for Educational Planning, UNESCO, Paris.

Duncan, O.D., and Blau, P.M. (1967), *The American Occupational Structure*, Wiley.

Eckaus, R.S. (1963), 'Investment in human beings: a comment', *J. polit. Econ.*, October, 1968. (Reprinted in M.Blaug (ed.), *Economics of Education 1*, Penguin, 1968.)

Eckaus, R.S. (1964), 'Economic Criteria for Education and Training', *Rev. Econ. Stat.*, May.

Edding, F. (1958) *Internationale Tendenzen in der Entwicklung der Ausgabe für Schulen und Hochschulen*, Kiel, Bundesrepublik, Instituts für Weltwirtschaft an der Universität Kiel. (Reprinted in English in M.J.Bowman *et al.* (eds.), *Readings in the Economics of Education*, UNESCO, Paris, 1968.)

Edding, F. (1966), 'Expenditure on education: statistics and comments', in E.A.G.Robinson and J.E.Vaizey (eds.), *The Economics of Education*, Macmillan.

Edding, F. (1967), 'Educational planning in Western Germany', in G.Z. Bereday, J.A.Lauwerys and M.Blaug (eds.), *World Yearbook of Education 1967. Educational Planning*, Evans.

Education and World Affairs (1967), *Nigerian Human Resource Development and Utilization*, Education and World Affairs, New York.

Evans, P.C.C. (1962), 'Western education and agricultural productivity', *Africa*, October.

Fein, R. (1967), *The Doctor Shortage. An Economic Diagnosis*, Brookings Institution.

Fine, S.A. (1968), 'The use of the *Dictionary of Occupational Titles* as a source of estimates of educational and training requirements', *J. hum. Resources*, summer.

Fischlow, A. (1966), 'The American common school revival: fact or fancy?', in H.Rosovsky (ed.), *Industrialization in Two Systems*, Wiley.

Fisher, I. (1906), *The Nature of Capital and Income*, Macmillan.

Flores, G. (1950), 'A study on functional literacy for citizenship in the Philippines', *Quart. Bull. fund. Educ.*, July.

Folger, J.K. (1967a), 'Scientific manpower planning in the United States', in G.Z.Bereday, J.A.Lauwerys and M.Blaug (eds.), *World Yearbook of Education 1967. Educational Planning*, Evans.

Folger J.K. (1967b), *Education of the American Population. A Census Monograph*, U.S. Government Printing Office.

Folger, J.K., and **Nam, C.B.** (1964), 'Trends in education in relation to occupational structure', *Soc. Educ.*, fall.

Folk, H. (1967), 'The response of higher education to economic needs', in *Policy Conference on Highly Qualified Manpower*, OECD, Paris.

Foster, P.J. (1965), 'The vocational school fallacy in development planning', in C.A. Anderson and M.J. Bowman (eds.), *Education and Economic Development*, Aldine. (Reprinted in M. Blaug (ed.), *Economics of Education 1*, Penguin, 1968.)

Foster, P.J. (1966) *Education and Social Change in Ghana*, Routledge & Kegan Paul.

Fourastié, J. (1963), 'Employment forecasting in France', in *Employment Forecasting*, OECD, Paris.

Friedman, M. (1953), *Essays in Positive Economics*, University of Chicago Press.

Friedman, M. (1962), *Capitalism and Freedom*, University of Chicago Press.

Friedman, M., and **Kuznets, S.** (1946), *Incomes from Independent Professional Practice*, National Bureau of Economic Research.

Furneaux, W.D. (1961), *The Chosen Few. An Examination of Some Aspects of University Selection in Britain*, Oxford University Press.

Gannicott, K., and **Blaug, M.** (1969), 'Manpower forecasting in the U.K. since Robbins: a case study of a science lobby', *High. educ. Rev.*, September.

Genovese, E.D. (1965), *The Political Economy of Slavery. Studies in the Economy and Society of the Slave South*, Pantheon Books.

Glennerster, H., Merrett, S., and **Wilson, G.** (1968), 'A graduate tax', *High. educ. Rev.*, autumn.

Goldstein, H., and **Swerdloff, S.** (1967), *Methods of Long-Term Projection of Requirements for and Supply of Qualified Manpower*, UNESCO Statistical Reports and Studies, Paris.

Gordon, M.S. (1965), *Retraining and Labor Market Adjustment in Western Europe*, U.S. Government Printing Office.

Gorseline, D.E. (1932), *The Effect of Schooling Upon Income*, Graduate Council of Indiana University.

Griffiths, V.L. (1968), *The Problems of Rural Education*, Fundamentals of Educational Planning 7, International Institute for Educational Planning, UNESCO, Paris.

Griliches, Z. (1970), 'Notes on the role of education in production functions and growth accounting', in W. Lee Hansen (ed.), *Education and Income*, Conference on Research, Income and Wealth, 1968, Princeton University Press, forthcoming.

Gurney-Dixon Report (1954), *Early Leaving. A Report of the Central Advisory Council for Education (England) under the Chairmanship of Sir S. Gurney-Dixon*, H.M.S.O.

Hanoch, G. (1967), 'An economic analysis of earnings and schooling', *J. hum. Resources*, summer.

Hansen, N.B. (1966), 'Uddannelsesinvesteringens rentabilitet', *National-Økonomisk Tidsskrift*, vol. 104, nos. 5–6.

Hansen, W. Lee (1961), 'The "shortage" of engineers', *Rev. Econ. Stat.*, August.

Hansen, W. Lee (1963), 'Total and private rates of return to investment in schooling', *J. polit. Econ.*, April. (Reprinted in M. Blaug (ed.), *Economics of Education 1*, Penguin, 1968.)

Hansen, W. Lee (1965a), ' "Shortages" and investment in health manpower', in S. J. Axelbrod (ed.), *The Economics of Health and Medical Care*, University of Michigan.

Hansen, W. Lee (1965b), 'Human capital requirements for educational expansion: teacher shortages and teacher supply', in C. A. Anderson and M. J. Bowman (eds.), *Education and Economic Development*, Aldine.

Hansen, W. Lee (1967), 'The economics of scientific and engineering manpower', *J. hum. Resources*, spring.

Harbison, F. H., and Myers, C. A. (1964), *Education, Manpower and Economic Growth*, McGraw-Hill. (Pages 23–48 and 173–87 reprinted in M. Blaug (ed.), *Economics of Education 2*, Penguin, 1969.)

Harris, S. E. (1962), *Higher Education: Resources and Finance*, McGraw-Hill.

Hartley, H. J. (1968), 'Program budgeting and cost–effectiveness in local schools', in *Budgeting, Programme Analysis and Cost–Effectiveness in Educational Planning*, OECD, Paris.

Heijnen, J. D. (1968), *Development and Education in the Mwanza District (Tanzania). A Case Study of Migration and Peasant Farming*, Brouder-Offset, Rotterdam.

Hemphill, J. K. (1959), 'Job descriptions for executives', *Harv. bus. Rev.*, fall.

Henderson, P. D. (1965), 'Notes on public investment criteria in the United Kingdom', *Bull. Oxf. Univ. Inst. Econ. Stat.*, February. (Reprinted in R. Turvey (ed.), *Public Enterprise*, Penguin, 1968.)

Henderson-Stewart, D. (1965), 'Appendix: estimate of the rate of return to education in Great Britain', *Manchester School*, September.

Hirsch, W. Z., and Marcus, M. J. (1966), 'Some benefit–cost considerations of universal junior college education', *Nat. Tax J.*, March.

Hirsch, W. Z., and Segelhorst, E. W. (1965), 'Incremental income benefits of public education', *Rev. Econ. Stat.*, November.

Holinshead, B. S. (1952), *Who Should Go to College?*, Columbia University Press.

Hollister, R. G. (1965), 'The economics of manpower forecasting', in M. R. Sinha (ed.), *The Economics of Manpower Planning*, Asian Studies Press, Bombay.

Hollister, R. G. (1966), *A Technical Evaluation of the First Stage of the Mediterranean Regional Project*, OECD, Paris.

Hollister, R. G. (1967), 'A technical evaluation of the OECD's Mediterranean Regional Project: methods and conclusions', in G. Z. Bereday, J. A. Lauwerys and M. Blaug (eds.), *World Yearbook of Education 1967. Educational Planning*, Evans. (Reprinted in M. Blaug (ed.), *Economics of Education 1*, Penguin, 1968).

Horobin, G. W., and Smyth, R. L. (1960), 'The economics of education: a comment', *Scot. J. polit. Econ.*, February. (Reprinted in M. Blaug (ed.), *Economics of Education 2*, Penguin, 1969.)

Horobin, G. W., Oldman, D., and Bytheway, B. (1967), 'The social differentiation of ability', *Soc. J. Brit. Soc. Assn*, May.

Horowitz, M.A., and **Herrnstadt, I.L.** (1967), 'More doubts about average training times computed from GED and SVP levels', *Rev. Econ. Stat.,* November.

Horowitz, M.A., Zymelman, M., and **Herrnstadt, I.L.** (1966), *Manpower Requirements for Planning. An International Comparisons Approach,* Northeastern University, 2 vols.

Houghton, D. (1967), *Paying for the Social Services,* Institute of Economic Affairs.

Hudson, L. (1968), *Contrary Imaginations. A Psychological Study of the English Schoolboy,* Penguin.

Hunt, S.J. (1963), 'Income determinants for college graduates and the returns to educational investment', *Yale econ. Ess.,* fall.

Hunter, G. (1963), *Education for a Developing Region. A Study in East Africa,* Allen & Unwin.

Hunter, G. (1965), 'Issues in manpower policy: some contrasts from East Africa and Southeast Asia', in F.H.Harbison and C.A.Myers (eds.), *Manpower and Education. Country Studies in Economic Development,* McGraw-Hill.

Hunter, G. (1966), *Manpower, Employment and Education in the Rural Economy of Tanzania,* African Research Monographs 9, International Institute for Educational Planning, UNESCO, Paris.

Hunter, G. (1967), *Higher Education and Development in South-East Asia, Vol. III, Part 1, High-Level Manpower,* International Association of Universities, UNESCO, Paris.

Hunter, G. (1968), 'Manpower and educational needs in the traditional sector, with special reference to East Africa', in *Manpower Aspects of Educational Planning,* International Institute for Educational Planning, UNESCO, Paris.

Huntsberger, J.R. (1968), *The Efficient Allocation of Resources in Canadian Education,* Economic Development Report, Center for International Affairs, Harvard University.

Husèn, T. (1968), 'Ability, opportunity and career', *Educ. Res.,* June.

Hutchison, T.W. (1964), '*Positive' Economics and Policy Objectives,* Allen & Unwin.

International Labour Office (1958), *International Classification of Occupations,* ILO, Geneva.

Ireland, Ministry of Education (1965), *Investment in Education,* Stationery Office, Dublin.

Jackson Report (1966), *Report on the 1965 Triennial Manpower Survey of Engineers, Technologists, Scientists and Technical Supporting Staff. Committee on Manpower Resources for Science and Technology under the Chairmanship of Sir Willis Jackson,* H.M.S.O.

Jaffe, A.J., and **Froomkin, J.** (1968), *Technology and Jobs. Automation in Perspective,* Praeger.

Jamin, V. (1966), 'The economic effects of popular education in the U.S.S.R.', in E.A.G.Robinson and J.E.Vaizey (eds.), *The Economics of Education,* Macmillan.

Jencks, C., and Riesman, D. (1968), *The Academic Revolution*, Doubleday.
Jensen, A.R. (1969), 'How much can we boost I.Q. and scholastic achievement?', *Harv. educ. Rev.*, winter.
Jewkes, J., and Jewkes, S. (1963), *Value for Money in Medicine*, Blackwell.
Johnston, B.F. (1964), 'Changes in agricultural productivity', in M.Herskovits and M.Harwitz (eds.), *Economic Transition in Africa*, Routledge & Kegan Paul.
Johnston, J. (1963), *Econometric Methods*, McGraw-Hill.
Jolly, A.R. (1964), 'Education', in D.Seers (ed.), *Cuba. The Economic and Social Revolution*, North Carolina University Press.
Jones, G. (1964), 'The needs of industry', *J. Car. Res. Advis. Cent.*, autumn.
Jorgensen, D.W., and Griliches, Z. (1967), 'The explanation of productivity change', *Rev. econ. Stud.*, July.

Kahan, A. (1965a), 'Russian scholars and statesmen on education as an investment', in C.A.Anderson and M.J.Bowman (eds.), *Education and Economic Development*, Aldine.
Kahan, A. (1965b), 'Determinants of the incidence of literacy in rural nineteenth century Russia', in C.A.Anderson and M.J.Bowman (eds.), *Education and Economic Development*, Aldine.
Kaldor, N. (1955), *The Expenditure Tax*, Allen & Unwin.
Kaser, M. (1966), 'Education and economic progress: experience in industrialized market economies', in E.A.G.Robinson and J.Vaizey (eds.), *The Economics of Education*, Macmillan.
Katzman, M.T. (1968), 'Distribution and production in a big city elementary school system', *Yale econ. Ess.*, spring.
Kershaw, J.A. (1965), 'Productivity in schools and colleges', in S.E.Harris and A.Levensohn (eds.), *Education and Public Policy*, McCutchan Publishing Corporation, Berkeley, California. (Reprinted in M. Blaug (ed.), *Economics of Education 2*, Penguin, 1969.)
Kershaw, J. A., and McKean, R. N. (1962), *Teacher Shortage and Salary Schedules*, McGraw-Hill.
Kiesling, H. J. (1968), *High School Size and Cost Factors*, Office of Education, U.S. Department of Health, Education and Welfare, Project no. 6–1590.
Kiker, B. F. (1966), 'The historical roots of the concept of human capital', *J. polit. Econ.*, October.
Kiker, B. F. (1968), 'Marshall on human capital: comment', *J. polit. Econ.*, September/October.
King, J. (1967), *Planning Non-Formal Education in Tanzania*, African Research Monographs 16, International Institute for Educational Planning, UNESCO, Paris.
Klarman, H. E. (1965), *The Economics of Health*, Columbia University Press.
Klarman, H. E. (1969), 'Economic aspects of projecting requirements for health manpower', *J. hum. Resources*, summer.
Klinov-Malul, R. (1966), *Profitability of Investment in Education in Israel*, Maurice Falk Institute for Economic Research in Israel, Jerusalem.
Knight, J. B. (1968), 'Earnings, employment, education and income distribution in Uganda', *Bull. Oxf. Inst. Econ. Stat.*, November.

Knowles, W.H. (1965), 'Manpower and education in Puerto Rico', in F.H. Harbison and C.A.Myers (eds.), *Manpower and Education. Country Studies in Economic Development*, McGraw-Hill.

Kothari Report (1966), *Report of the Education Commission 1964–66, under the Chairmanship of D.S. Kothari*, Ministry of Education, Government of India, Delhi.

Lansing, J. B., Lorimer, T., and **Moriguchi, C.** (1960), *How People Pay for College*, Survey Research Center, University of Michigan.

Lassiter, R.L., Jr (1966), *The Association of Income and Educational Achievement*, University of Florida Monographs in the Social Sciences.

Layard, R., and **Saigal, J.** (1966), 'Educational and occupational characteristics of manpower: an international comparison', *Brit. J. industr. Rel.*, July.

Layard, R., King, J., and **Moser, C.** (1969), *The Impact of Robbins*, Penguin.

Lees, D.S. (1961), *Health Through Choice*, Institute of Economic Affairs.

Lees, D. S. (1965), 'Uncertainty and the welfare economics of medical care: comment', *Amer. econ. Rev.*, March.

Lees, D.S. (1967), 'Poor families and fiscal reform', *Lloyds Bank Rev.*, October.

Leibenstein, H. (1965), 'Shortages and surpluses in education in under-developed countries', in C.A.Anderson and M.J.Bowman (eds.), *Education and Economic Development*, Aldine. (Reprinted in M.J.Bowman *et al.* (eds.), *Readings in the Economics of Education*, UNESCO, Paris, 1968.)

Leibenstein, H. (1967), *Rates of Return to Education in Greece*, Economic Development Report, Center for International Affairs, Harvard University.

Leicester, C. (1964), 'Economic growth and the school leaver', *J. Car. Res. Advis. Cent.*, summer.

Lester, R. A. (1966), *Manpower Planning in a Free Society*, Princeton University Press.

Levin, H.M. (1968), 'The failure of the public schools and the free market remedy', *Urb. Rev.*, June.

Lewis, H.G. (1963), *Unionism and Relative Wages in the United States: An Empirical Inquiry*, Chicago University Press.

Lewis, L. J. (1962), *Phelps–Stokes Reports on Education in Africa*, Oxford University Press.

Lewis, W. A. (1962), 'Priorities for educational expansion', in *Policy Conference on Economic Growth and Investment in Education, vol. 3, The Challenge of Aid to New Developing Countries*, OECD, Paris. (Reprinted in M.J.Bowman *et al.* (eds.), *Readings in the Economics of Education*, UNESCO, Paris, 1968.)

Lithwick, N.H., Post, G., and **Rymes, T.K.** (1967), 'Postwar production relationships in Canada', in M.Brown (ed.), *The Theory and Empirical Analysis of Production*, Columbia University Press.

Lyall, H. (1968), *The Structure of Earnings*, Oxford University Press.

Machlup, F. (1962), *The Production and Distribution of Knowledge in the United States*, Princeton University Press.

Machlup, F. (1963), *Essays on Economic Semantics*, Prentice-Hall.

Marglin, S. A. (1967), *Public Investment Criteria*, Allen & Unwin.
Marshall, A. (1890), *Principles of Economics*, various editions.
Martinoli, G. (1960), *Trained Manpower Requirements for the Economic Development of Italy – Targets for 1975*, SVIMEZ, Rome.
McCarthy, M. C. (1968), *The Employment of Highly Specialised Graduates: A Comparative Study in the United Kingdom and the United States of America*, Department of Education and Science, H.M.S.O.
McClelland, D. C. (1961), *The Achieving Society*, Van Nostrand.
McClelland, D. C. (1966), 'Does education accelerate economic growth?', *Econ. Devel. cult. Change*, April.
Mehmet, O. (1965), *Methods of Forecasting Manpower Requirements, With Special Reference to the Province of Ontario*, University of Toronto.
Meltz, N. M. (1965), *Changes in the Occupational Composition of the Canadian Labour Force, 1931–1961*, Department of Labour, Ottawa.
Merrett, A. J., and **Sykes, A.** (1963), *The Finance and Analysis of Capital Projects*, Methuen.
Merrett, S. (1966), 'The rate of return to education: a critique', *Oxf. econ. Pap.*, November.
Merrett, S. (1967), 'Student finance in higher education', *Econ. J.*, June.
Mill, J. S. (1909), in W. J. Ashley (ed.), *Principles of Political Economy*, Longman.
Miller, H. P. (1960), 'Annual and lifetime income in relation to education', *Amer. econ. Rev.*, December.
Mincer, J. (1962), 'On-the-job training: costs, returns and some implications', *J. polit. Econ. Suppl.*, October. (Reprinted in M. J. Bowman *et al.* (eds.), *Readings in the Economics of Education*, UNESCO, Paris, 1968.)
Miner, J. (1963), *Social and Economic Factors in Spending for Public Education*, Syracuse University Press.
Ministry of Labour, U.K. (1965), *The Metal Industries. A Study of Occupational Trends in the Metal Manufacturing and Metal Using Industries*, Manpower Studies no. 2, Ministry of Labour.
Mishan, E. J. (1969), 'Some heretical thoughts on university reform', *Encounter*, March.
Moberg, S. (1960), 'Methods and techniques for forecasting specialised manpower requirements', in *Forecasting Manpower Needs for the Age of Science*, OECD, Paris.
Montgomery, G. (1967), 'Education and training for agricultural development', in H. M. Southworth and B. F. Johnston (eds.), *Agricultural Development and Economic Growth*, Cornell University Press.
Morgan, J. N., and **David, M. H.** (1963), 'Education and income', *Quart. J. Econ.*, August.
Morgan, J. N., and **Lininger, C.** (1964), 'Education and income: comment', *Quart. J. Econ.*, May.
Morgan, J. N., and **Sirageldin, I.** (1968), 'A note on the quality dimension in education', *J. polit. Econ.*, September/October.
Morgan, J. N., David, M. H., Cohen, W. J., and **Brazer, H. F.** (1962), *Income and Welfare in the United States*, McGraw-Hill.

Moser, C., and **Layard, R.** (1964), 'Planning the scale of higher education in Britain: some statistical problems', *J. Roy. Stat. Soc.*, series A, vol. 127, part 4. (Reprinted in M. Blaug (ed.), *Economics of Education 1*, Penguin, 1968.)
Musgrave, R. A. (1959), *The Theory of Public Finance*, McGraw-Hill.
Mushkin, S. (1962), 'Health as investment', *J. polit. Econ., Suppl.*, October.
Myint, H. (1964), *The Economics of the Developing Countries*, Hutchinson.
Myrdal, G. (1968), *Asian Drama. An Inquiry into the Poverty of Nations*, Pantheon Books, 3 vols. Penguin edn, 1968; Allan Lane The Penguin Press edn. 1968.)

National Board for Prices and Incomes (1968), *Job Evaluation*, H.M.S.O.
National Institute of Industrial Psychology (1951), *Studying Work*, National Institute of Industrial Psychology, London.
Nelson, R. R. (1967), 'Aggregate production functions and economic growth policy', in M.Brown (ed.), *The Theory and Empirical Analysis of Production*, Columbia University Press.
Netherlands (1967), *Educational Policy and Planning*, OECD, Paris.
Netherlands Economic Institute (1966a), 'Financial aspects of educational expansion in developing regions: some quantitative estimates', in *Financing of Education for Economic Growth*, OECD, Paris.
Netherlands Economic Institute (1966b), *The Educational Structure of the Labour Force. A Statistical Analysis*, Netherlands Economic Institute. Rotterdam.
Netherlands Economic Institute (1966c), *Mathematical Models of Educational Planning*, Netherlands Economic Institute, Rotterdam.
Nottingham University (1962), *1962 Graduate Employment Survey*, Careers and Appointments Board.
Nozhko, K. G. (1964), *Methods of Estimating the Demand for Specialists Within the U.S.S.R.*, UNESCO Statistical Reports and Studies, Paris.

Oatey, M. (1970), 'The economics of training with notes on the Industrial Training Act', *Brit. J. industr. Rel.*, March.
OECD (1965), *Econometric Models of Education*, Paris.
OECD (1968), *Financing of Education for Economic Growth*, Paris.
OECD (1970), *Occupational and Educational Structures of the Labour Force and Levels of Economic Development. Possibilities and Limitations of an International Comparison Approach*, Paris.

Pacheco, O. R. (1963), *Some Aspects of Educational Planning in Puerto Rico*, Department of Education, Hato Rey, Puerto Rico.
Palm, G. (1968), 'International comparisons of educational outlay: problems and approaches', *Intern. soc. Sci. J.*, vol. 20, no. 1.
Parnes, H.S. (1962), *Forecasting Educational Needs for Economic and Social Development*, OECD, Paris.
Parnes, H.S. (1963), 'Manpower analysis in educational planning', in *Planning Education for Economic and Social Development*, OECD, Paris. (Reprinted in M.Blaug (ed.), *Economics of Education 1*, Penguin, 1968.)
Pauly, M.V. (1967), 'Mixed public and private financing of education: efficiency and feasibility', *Amer. econ. Rev.*, March.

Payne, G. L. (1960), *Britain's Scientific and Technological Manpower*, Stanford University Press.

Peacock, A. T. (1964), 'Economic growth and the demand for qualified manpower', *Distr. Bank Rev.*, June.

Peacock, A. T., and Culyer, A. J. (1969), *Economic Aspects of Student Unrest*, London Institute of Economic Affairs.

Peacock, A. T., and Shannon, J. R. (1968a), 'The new doctors' dilemma', *Lloyds Bank Rev.*, January.

Peacock, A. T., and Shannon, J. R. (1968b), 'The Welfare state and the redistribution of income', *West. Bank Rev.*, August.

Peacock, A. T., and Wiseman, J. (1964), *Education for Democrats*, Institute of Economic Affairs.

Peacock, A. T., and Wiseman, J. (1968), 'Economic growth and the principles of educational finance in developed countries', in *Financing of Education for Economic Growth*, OECD, Paris. (Reprinted in M. Blaug (ed.), *Economics of Education 2*, Penguin, 1969.)

Peacock, A. T., Glennerster, H., and Lavers, R. (1968), *Educational Finance. Its Sources and Uses in the United Kingdom*, Oliver & Boyd.

Peaslee, A. L. (1967), 'Primary school enrolments and economic growth', *Comp. educ. Rev.*, February.

Peck, M. J. (1968), 'Science and technology', in R. E. Caves *et al.* (eds.), *Britain's Economic Prospects*, Brookings Institution.

Platt, W. J. (1964), 'Manpower planning in Thailand', in D. Adams (ed.), *Educational Planning*, Syracuse University Press.

Plowden Report (1967), *Children and Their Primary Schools. A Report of the Central Advisory Council for Education (England)*, H.M.S.O., 2 vols.

Podoluk, J. R. (1965), *Earnings and Education*, Dominion Bureau of Statistics, Queen's Printer, Ottawa.

Political and Economic Planning (1956), *Graduate Employment. A Sample Survey.*

Pons, V. G., Xydias, N., and Clement, P. (1956) *Social Implications of Industrialisation and Urbanisation in Africa South of the Sahara*, UNESCO, Paris.

Prest, A. R. (1966), *Financing University Education*, Institute of Economic Affairs.

Prest, A. R., and Turvey, R. (1965), 'Cost–benefit analysis: a survey', *Econ. J.*, December. (Reprinted in Royal Economic Society, *Surveys of Economic Theory, vol. 3, Resource Allocation*, Macmillan, 1966.)

Pryor, F. (1968), *Public Expenditure in Communist and Capitalist Countries*, Allen & Unwin.

Psacharopoulos, G. (1969a), *The Anatomy of a Rate of Growth: The Case of Hawaii, 1950–1960*, Economic Research Center, University of Hawaii.

Public Schools Commission (1968), *First Report*, H.M.S.O.

Psacharopoulos, G. (1969b), *The Rate of Return on Investment in Education at the Regional Level. Estimates for the State of Hawaii*, Economic Research Center, University of Hawaii.

Psacharopoulos, G. (1970), 'Estimating shadow rates of return to investment in education', *J. hum. Resources*, winter.

Public Schools Commission (1968), *First Report*, H.M.S.O.

Puerto Rico, Committee on Human Resources (1959), *Puerto Rico's Manpower Needs and Supply*, San Juan, Puerto Rico.

Rado, E.R. (1966), 'Manpower, education, and economic growth', *J. mod. Afr. Stud.*, vol. 4, no. 1.

Rado, E.R. (1967), 'Manpower planning in East Africa', in G.Z.Bereday, J.A.Lauwerys and M.Blaug (eds.), *World Yearbook of Education 1967. Educational Planning*, Evans.

Rado, E.R., and Jolly, A.R. (1965), 'The demand for manpower: an East African case study', *J. devel. Stud.*, April. (Reprinted in M.Blaug (ed.), *Economics of Education 2*, Penguin, 1969.)

Reder, M.W. (1955), 'The theory of occupation wage differentials', *Amer. econ. Rev.*, December. (Reprinted in B.J.McCormick and E.O.Smith (eds.), *The Labour Market*, Penguin, 1968.)

Redfern, P. (1967), *Input–Output Analysis and its Application to Education and Manpower Planning*, H.M.S.O.

Ribich, T.I. (1968), *Education and Poverty*, Brookings Institution.

Richardson, V.A. (1969), 'A measurement of demand for professional engineers', *Brit. J. industr. Rel.*, March.

Riese, H. (1966), *Die Entwicklung des Bedarfs an Hochschulabsolventen in der Bundesrepublik Deutschland*, Steiner Verlag, Wiesbaden.

Riew, J. (1966), 'Economies of scale in high school operation', *Rev. Econ. Stat.*, August.

Robbins, L. (1935), *An Essay on the Nature and Significance of Economic Science*, 2nd edn, Macmillan.

Robbins Report (1963), *Higher Education. Report of the Committee under the Chairmanship of Lord Robbins*, H.M.S.O., Cmnd. 2154.

Rogers, D. C. (1969), 'Private rates of return to education in the United States: a case study', *Yale econ. Ess.*, spring.

Rogers, E.M., and Herzog, W. (1966), 'Functional literacy among Colombian peasants', *Econ. Devel. cult. Change*, January.

Roper, E. (1949), *Factors Affecting the Admission of High School Seniors to College*, American Council on Education, Washington.

Rosenberg, M. (1957), *Occupations and Values*, Free Press of Glencoe.

Ross, D.A. (1966), 'Economic criteria for education and training: a comment', *Rev. Econ. Stat.*, February.

Rottenberg, S. (1956), 'On choice in labor markets', *Industrial Labor Relations Review*, October. (Reprinted in B.J.McCormick and E.O.Smith (eds.), *The Labour Market*, Penguin, 1968.)

Rourke, F.E., and Brooks, G.E. (1966), *The Managerial Revolution in Higher Education*, Johns Hopkins Press.

Routh, G. (1965), *Occupation and Pay in Great Britain 1906–60*, Cambridge University Press.

Sacks, S. (1967), 'Historical trends and present patterns in educational expenditure: constraints on planning for education in developed nations', in

G.Z.Bereday, J.A.Lauwerys and M.Blaug (eds.), *World Yearbook of Education 1967. Educational Planning*, Evans.

Schatz, S.P. (1965), '*n* achievement and economic growth: a critique', *Quart. J. Econ.*, May.

Schools Council (1968), *Young School Leavers. Report of an Enquiry Carried Out for the Schools Council by the Government Social Survey*, H.M.S.O.

Schramm, W., Coombs, P.H., Kahnert, F., and Lyle, J. (1967), *The New Media: Memo to Educational Planners; New Educational Media in Action. Case Studies for Planners 1, 2, 3*, International Institute for Educational Planning, UNESCO, Paris.

Schultz, T.W. (1963), *The Economic Value of Education*, Columbia University Press.

Schultz, T.W. (1964), *Transforming Traditional Agriculture*, Yale University Press.

Schultz, T.W. (1967), 'The rate of return in allocating investment resources to education', *J. hum. Resources*, summer.

Schuman, H., Inkeles, A., and Smith, D.H. (1967), 'Some social psychological effects and non-effects of literacy in a new nation', *Econ. Devel. cult. Change*, October.

Schwartz, B. (1968), 'Introduction to programme budgeting and cost–effectiveness', in *Budgeting Programme Analysis and Cost–Effectiveness in Educational Planning*, OECD, Paris.

Schwartzman, D. (1968), 'Education and the quality of labor 1929–1963', *Amer. econ. Rev.*, June.

Scoville, J.G. (1965), 'The development and relevance of U.S. occupational data', *Industr. lab. Rel. Rev.*, October.

Scoville, J.G. (1966), 'Education and training requirements for occupations', *Rev. Econ. Stat.*, November.

Scoville, J.G. (1967), *The Job Content of the Canadian Economy, 1941–61*, Dominion Bureau of Statistics, Queen's Printer, Ottawa.

Seale, J. (1965), 'Medical emigration: a study in the inadequacy of official statistics', in D.Burn, J.R.Seale and A.R.N.Ratcliff (eds.), *Lessons from Central Forecasting*, Institute of Economic Affairs.

Seldon, A., and Gray, H. (1967), *Universal or Selective Social Benefits?*, Institute of Economic Affairs.

Selowsky, M. (1967), *Education and Economic Growth: Some International Comparisons*, Economic Development Report, Center for International Affairs, Harvard University.

Selowsky, M. (1968), *The Effect of Unemployment and Growth on the Rate of Return to Education: The Case of Colombia*, Economic Development Report, Center for International Affairs, Harvard University.

Seltzer, G. (1965), 'High-level manpower in Nyasaland's development', in F.Harbison and C.A.Myers (eds.), *Manpower and Education. Country Studies in Economic Development*, McGraw-Hill.

Sen, A.K. (1964), 'Comments on the paper by Messrs Tinbergen and Bos', in J.Vaizey (ed.), *The Residual Factor and Economic Growth*, OECD, Paris. (Reprinted in M.Blaug (ed.), *Economics of Education 2*, Penguin, 1969.)

Sen, A.K. (1966), 'Economic approaches to education and manpower planning', *Ind. econ. Rev.*, April. (Reprinted in M.Blaug (ed.), *Economics of Education 2*, Penguin, 1969.)

Shaffer, H.G. (1961), 'Investment in human capital: comment', *Amer. econ. Rev.*, December. (Reprinted in M.Blaug (ed.), *Economics of Education 1*, Penguin, 1968.)

Skorov, G. (1964), 'Manpower approach to educational planning: methods used in the centrally planned economies', in *Economic and Social Aspects of Educational Planning*, UNESCO, Paris.

Skorov, G. (1966), *Integration of Educational and Economic Planning in Tanzania*, African Research Monographs 6, International Institute for Educational Planning, UNESCO, Paris.

Skorov, G. (1968), 'Highlights of the symposium', in *Manpower Aspects of Educational Planning*, International Institute for Educational Planning, UNESCO, Paris.

Smith, A. (1776), *The Wealth of Nations*, various editions.

Smout, T. C. (1969), *A History of the Scottish People 1560–1830*, Collins.

Smyth, J.A., and **Bennet, N.L.** (1967), 'Rates of return on investment in education: a tool for short-term educational planning, illustrated with Ugandan data', in G.Z.Bereday, J.A.Lauwerys and M.Blaug (eds.), *World Yearbook of Education 1967. Educational Planning*, Evans.

Sofer, C., and **Sofer, R.** (1955), *Jinja Transformed: A Social Survey of a Multi-Racial Town*, East African Institute of Social Research, Kampala.

Somers, G.S. (1965), 'Retraining: an evaluation of gains and costs', in A.M.Ross (ed.), *Employment Policy and the Labor Market*, California University Press.

Somers, G.S. (ed.) (1968), *Retraining the Unemployed*, University of Wisconsin Press.

Strumilin, S.G. (1925), 'The economic significance of national education', *Ekonomiki Truda*. (Reprinted in E.A.G.Robinson and J.Vaizey (eds.), *The Economics of Education*, Macmillan, 1966.

Stubblebine, W.C. (1965), 'Institutional elements in the financing of education', *South. econ. J.*, *Suppl.*, July.

Svennilson, I., Edding, F., and **Elvin, L.** (1962), *Policy Conference on Economic Growth and Investment in Education, Volume II, Targets for Education in Europe in 1970*, OECD, Paris.

Terborgh, G. (1965), *The Automation Hysteria*, Norton.

Thias, H. H., and **Carnoy, M.** (1969), *Cost–Benefit Analysis in Education. A Case Study on Kenya*, International Bank for Reconstruction and Development.

Thomas, B., Moxham, J., and **Jones, J.A.G.** (1969), 'A cost–benefit analysis of industrial training', *Brit. J. industr. Rel.*, July.

Thomas, R.L. (1965), 'High-level manpower in the economic development of Uganda', in F.Harbison and C.A.Myers (eds.), *Manpower and Education. Country Studies in Economic Development*, McGraw-Hill.

Tinbergen, J., and **Bos, H.C.** (1965), 'A planning model for the educational requirements of economic development', in *Econometric Models of Education*,

OECD, Paris. (Reprinted in M.Blaug (ed.), *Economics of Education 2*, Penguin, 1969.)

Titmuss, R. (1967), 'The practical case against the means test state', *New Statesman*, 15 September.

Titmuss, R. (1968), 'Choice and "The Welfare State"', in *Commitment to Welfare*, Allen & Unwin.

Townsend, P. (1968), 'The difficulties of negative income tax', in *Social Services For All? Eleven Fabian Essays*, Fabian Society.

UNESCO (1961), *Manual of Educational Statistics*, Paris.

UNESCO (1962) *World Campaign for Universal Literacy*, Paris.

UNESCO (1964), *World Literacy Campaign*, Paris.

UNESCO (1966), *An Asian Model of Educational Development. Perspectives for 1965–80*, Paris.

UNESCO (1968), *Educational Planning. A Survey of Problems and Prospects. International Conference on Educational Planning*, Paris.

University Grants Committee (1953), *University Development. Report of the Years 1947 to 1952*, H.M.S.O.

University Grants Committee (1958), *University Development 1952–57*, H.M.S.O.

University Grants Committee (1968), *Annual Survey, 1966–1967*, H.M.S.O.

U.S. Department of Labor (1955), *Estimates of Worker Trait Requirements for 4000 Jobs.*

Vaizey, J. (1958), *Costs of Education*, Allen & Unwin.

Vaizey, J. (1962), *The Economics of Education*, Faber.

Vaizey, J. (ed.) (1964), *The Residual Factor and Economic Growth*, OECD, Paris.

Vaizey, J., and Sheehan, J. (1968), *Resources for Education. An Economic Study of Education in the United Kingdom, 1920–1965*, Allen & Unwin.

Vickerey, W. (1962), 'A proposal for student loans', in S.Mushkin (ed.), *Economics of Higher Education*, U.S. Government Printing Office.

Villard, H. (1960), 'Underinvestment in college education?: a comment', *Amer. econ. Rev.*, May.

Vimont, C. (1964), 'Methods of forecasting employment in France and use of those forecasts to work out official educational programmes', in S.E.Harris (ed.), *Economic Aspects of Higher Education*, OECD, Paris.

Walters, A.A. (1968), *An Introduction to Econometrics*, Macmillan.

Weisbrod, B.A. (1964), *External Benefits of Public Education: An Economic Analysis*, Princeton University Press.

Weisbrod, B.A. (1966), 'Conceptual issues in evaluating training programs', *Month. lab. Rev.*, October.

Weisbrod, B.A., and Karpoff, P. (1968), 'Monetary returns to college education, student ability, and college quality', *Rev. Econ. Stat.*, November.

Welch, F. (1966), 'Measurement of the quality of schooling', *Amer. econ. Rev.*, May.

Welch, F. (1970), 'Education in production', *J. polit. Econ.*, January/February.

West, E.G. (1964), 'Private versus public education: a classical economic dispute', *J. polit. Econ.*, October.

West, E. G. (1965), *Education and the State*, Institute of Economic Affairs.

West, E. G. (1967a), 'The political economy of American public school legislation', *J. Law Econ.*, October.

West, E. G. (1967b), 'Tom Paine's voucher scheme for education', *South. econ. J.*, January.

West, E. G. (1968), *Economics, Education and the Politician*, Institute of Economic Affairs.

Westergaard, J., and **Little, A.** (1967), 'Educational opportunity and social selection in England and Wales: trends and policy implications', *Social Objectives in Educational Planning*, OECD, Paris.

Wharton, C. R. (1965), 'Education and Agricultural Growth', in C. A. Anderson and M. J. Bowman (eds.), *Education and Economic Development*, Aldine.

Widmaier, H. P. (1967), 'A case of educational planning: Western Germany', in G. Z. Bereday, J. A. Lauwerys and M. Blaug (eds.), *World Yearbook of Education 1967. Educational Planning*, Evans.

Wiles, P. (1969), 'Die Bauchschmerzen eines Fachidioten', in *Anarchy and Culture*, Routledge & Kegan Paul.

Wilkinson, B. W. (1965), *Studies in the Economics of Education*, Department of Labour, Ottawa.

Wilkinson, B. W. (1966), 'Present values of lifetime earnings in different occupations', *J. polit. Econ.*, December.

Williams, B. (1963), 'Capacity and output of universities', *Manchester School*, May.

Williamson, J. G. (1969), 'Dimensions of post-war Philippine economic progress', *Quart. J. Econ.*, February.

Wiseman, J. (1959), 'The economics of education', *Scot. J. polit. Econ.*, February. (Reprinted in M. Blaug (ed.), *Economics of Education 2*, Penguin, 1969.)

Wiseman, S. (1964), *Education and Environment*, Manchester University Press.

Wolfle, D., and **Smith, J.** (1956), 'The occupational value of education for superior high-school graduates', *J. high. Educ.*, April.

Woodhall, M., and **Blaug, M.** (1965), 'Productivity trends in British university education 1938–1962', *Minerva*, summer.

Woodhall, M., and **Blaug, M.** (1968), 'Productivity trends in British secondary education 1950–1963', *Sociol. Educ.*, winter.

Youngson, A. J. (1967), *Overhead Capital*, Edinburgh University Press.

Yudelman, M. (1964a), *Africans on the Land*, Harvard University Press.

Yudelman, M. (1964b), 'Some aspects of African agricultural development', in E. A. G. Robinson (ed.), *Economic Development for Africa South of the Sahara*, Macmillan.

Zambia Cabinet Office (1966), *Manpower Report. A Report on Manpower, Education, Training and Zambianisation 1965–6*, Government Printer, Lusaka.

Zarnowitz, V. (1968), 'Prediction and forecasting, economic', in D. L. Sills (ed.), *International Encyclopaedia of the Social Sciences*, vol. 12, Macmillan.

Zschock, D. K. (1967), *Manpower Perspectives of Colombia*, Princeton University Press.

Author Index

Subject Index